SINAN

IN THE NAME OF GOD, THE MERCIFUL, THE COMPASSIONATE

SINAN

BY ARTHUR STRATTON

CHARLES SCRIBNER'S SONS ⚸ NEW YORK

PICTURE CREDITS

Courtesy of Djambatan The Hague: Map

Photographs from the Artomonov Collection, Courtesy of the Freer Gallery of Art, Smithsonian Institution, Washington, D. C.: 3, 4, 20, 34, 36, 42, 43, 44, 45, 46

Courtesy of the Department of Construction, Office of the Mayor, Istanbul: 5

Office du Livre Fribourg, Photos: Eduard Widmer, Zürich: 9-11, 17, 29, 31, 33, 39

Ara Güler: 26

Arthur Stratton: 1, 2, 6-8, 12-16, 18, 19, 21-25, 27, 28, 30, 32, 35, 37, 38, 40, 41

⤞ CHIEFLY TO THE TURKS ⤝

⤙ ACKNOWLEDGMENTS ⤚

There is no end to them. I take pleasure in recalling conversations and excursions in search of Sinan and his buildings with Aptullah Kuran, Robert Van Nice, Hilary Sumner-Boyd, Godfrey Goodwin, Keith Greenwood, Lee Fonger, and Geoffrey Lewis; with Jarl Dyrud; with Florence Codman; with Alfonso and Robert Ossorio, Edward Dragon, and Donald Gurney; with Ina Jaquinet; with Bahadir Alkim, Fahir Iz, Ezel Kural, and Cem Alptekin; with Sükrü Ezer and Yilmaz Özcan, who translated for me; with Nuri Arlasez; with Saul and Gladys Weinberg; with Kadri Bey and Mme. Cenani and James and Arlette Mellaart; with Bob and Sue Bowling; with Dorcy Stevens; with Rebecca West and Henry Andrews; with David Oswell; with Herbert Ross Brown; with my sister Barbara; with my editors Burroughs Mitchell and Alan Maclean; and my agent Diarmuid Russell; with Charles and Connie O'Neill; with Pen and Courtney Nelson; and with a great many more companions whose names, if I ever knew them, escape me.

But especially I am grateful to Sven Larsen, who first took me, in the good and the bad seasons of 1943 and 1944, walking through the streets of the walled city of Byzantium-Constantinople-Istanbul, and who is dead. All the others will recognize their contributions to my biography of Mimar Sinan.

Particularly, I thank all the Turks of the museums and of the Vakiflar, among them Messers. Mehmet Önder, Hayrullah Örs, Nusret Danisman, Sayin Ali Orhon, Hasan Ergezen, Erdem Ücel, and Mesdames Mürvet Hazerli and Cahide Tamer. I thank the librarians of Dumbarton Oaks, Robert College, the Gennadeon, the Topkapi Museum, the Süleymaniyé, Bowdoin College, and the Library of Congress.

I thank the American Academy of Arts and Letters for two grants of $1,000, and P.E.N., a World Association of Writers, for the gift of $435.

Most of the final manuscript was written at the MacDowell Colony. Many thanks, once again, to all at Peterborough and in the Edward Mac-Dowell Association.

◂ LIST OF ILLUSTRATIONS ▸

⤙ ORTHOGRAPHY ⤚

Orthography: Modern Turkish is written and printed in a phonetic alphabet of Roman letters; but, in English, some of them are unrecognizable and difficult to pronounce. I have abandoned the undotted *i;* left the circumflex on the Turkish *â* as it occurs; replaced *c* with *j, ç* with *ch, ş* with *sh, ğ* with *gh* (it is silent as in through); left the umlaut on the *ö* and the *ü* as in German; and added a confusing French acute accent to the final *e* as in Edirné, which gets me into trouble on the bridge of Büyükchekmejé with the sounds of English, French, and German in what ought to be a Turkish word. I do so for convenience; and I fail to make sense.

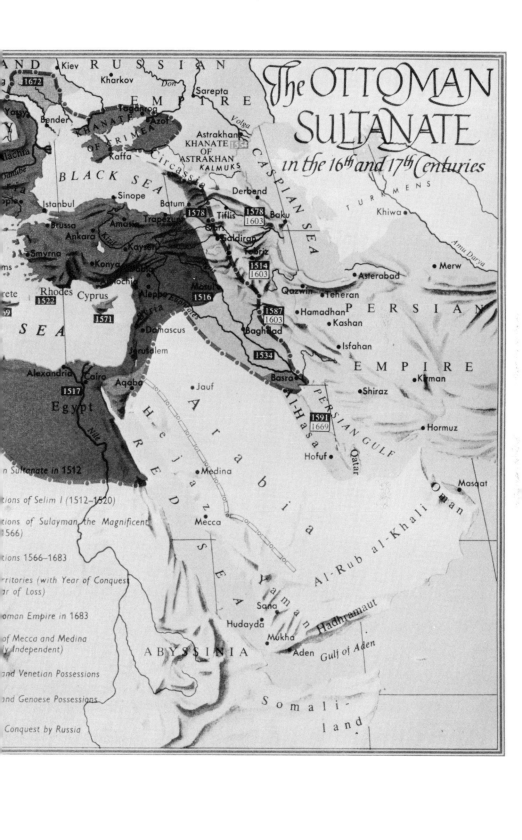

SINAN

⫷ C H A P T E R ⫸

1

As the seasons change from late winter to early spring, when all the meteorological conditions are right for it, a thick white mist forms by night and fills the trough of the Bosphorus strait. On such a still day, early in the morning, I felt my way down the slippery cobblestone path from the top tower of Rumeli Hisar to the wharf. The Sultan's European Castle took ninety days to build in the summer of 1452; it gives its name to a fishing village halfway up the Bosphorus between the Golden Horn and the Black Sea. In the thick white mist, I slid and slipped down the path to catch the ferry into the city. That was the only way to get to town from Rumeli Hisar in 1943. In my childhood it had delighted me to ask the riddle: "Constantinople is a hard word to spell. How do you spell it? " I had only recently learned to pronounce it Istanbul. And that is supposed to be a Turkish mispronunciation of the phrase in Greek meaning "to the city."

Before I could see the boat coming in to dock, I heard the clang of the bell and smelled the soft coal smoke. I made it! Smiling at my triumph over the elements and my own shaky legs, I bought a return ticket to the bridge and crossed the gangplank. It was a pleasure to smell the familiar smells of salt water, wet hawsers, fresh fish, and tar; and of human beings doing the work they knew well how to do. I climbed up to the second class saloon, forward, and sat down on the comfortable hard bench by the window on the starboard side.

Again I grinned, for I had counted on looking out at the view as the ferry zigzagged from Europe to Asia on its scheduled course down the strait. Through the window I could see no further than I could reach. *"Bismillah!"* I said aloud with, it may have been, some pride and a certain self-mockery. For I had just learned that, in Islam, when a man sets out upon a journey, he invokes his Maker, and indeed, as in this white mist, he then steps into the hand of God.

My fellow voyagers were, for the most part, working men, none of them very young. One or two, having heard my prayer, glanced my way, perhaps to see what I was feeling good about. Turks look like all the rest of us; but, sober and courteous men, they do not often smile. They saw that I was a stranger, and they turned their heads away so as not to appear to be either curious or critical. The Turks are kindly people.

Facing me on the bench opposite sat a young soldier. He looked like a countryman, fresh-faced, quiet, and compact with good health. In the days of the Ottoman Empire, to call such a man a Turk was to slight him. The word meant yokel. A civilized and a cultivated man called himself not a Turk but a Son of Osman, an Osmanli, or as we say, an Ottoman. The young soldier — it was another fact that I had learned in my six months in the Republic of Turkey — had been called up for the duration to defend the neutrality of his country, then wholly encircled by warfare. All the young men of Turkey do their military service; even the halt and the blind serve a token month or more. The young man sitting opposite me might have been an Anatolian shepherd. He wore a uniform that could have been homespun woven of undyed sheep's wool; he wore it comfortably.

In his fists he gripped the single sheet of a newspaper, and he read every word of it. Eyes fixed upon the page, his head moved slowly from left to right along the line of print. He got to the end of the column, and then he turned back and began again with the first word of the next line down. His lips shaped each letter and his teeth bit into every syllable. He had, apparently, just acquired the taste for reading. I said to myself, it is an acquired taste. In the army he had been taught how to read at the age of manhood. Black and white and read all over. Now and again the rhythm faltered as he stopped to puzzle out such words as El Alamein and Stalingrad, turning points then in the news.

I cannot remember what it is like not to be able to read and write; but only ten months earlier, I had learned, in the Libyan desert, in retreat, what it is like having my legs shot full of holes. Astonished by my emotion, I looked away from the reading soldier to peer out into the thick white mist. A bell rang. The rhythm of the engines changed. The captain brought the ferry in to tie up at the wharf — he could have done it blindfold — at Beshiktash. It is the last stop in Europe before the end of the line at the bridge across the Golden Horn in the city.

I had not learned enough Turkish to read the newspaper, but I knew that Beshiktash means "cradle stone." And that means the manger where the little Lord Jesus. . . . When the Roman Catholic Frankish knights of the Fourth Crusade, in 1204, conquered the City of God, then called Constantinople, from the Greek Orthodox Byzantine Christian emperors, the cradle stone disappeared from Beshiktash. Later on, in Rome or perhaps in the mercantile Republic of Venice, apparently the manger was transmogrified into wood. Broken up, splinters of it were sold in the brisk trade in relics.

Saint Helena, who as a girl in Britain had been captured and sold as a slave, was the mother of the Emperor Constantine the Great, the first of the Caesars to . . . to see the light, which took the shape of a cross. His mother brought the cradle stone back with her from Bethlehem, along with the crown of thorns, the true cross, and the nails from Jerusalem. In Constantinople, her son's new capital of the Roman Empire, the manger came into the possession of Byzantine monks, who built a shrine for it in this small bay in the European shore of the Bosphorus, outside the walls.

Constantine, A.D. 328, the actual emperor and the future saint, had the nails . . . how many of them are there? Three or four . . . set as rays in the gilt-bronze crown which he then had fixed to the marble head of what had been a classic statue of Phoebus Apollo. The late Roman emperor had his imperial sculptor recarve the features of the Greek sun god in his own imperial likeness. Constantine then had his nail-rayed image placed on top of a porphyry column on top of the Second Hill. It stood one hundred twenty-five feet above the mosaic pavement of his new circular Forum of Constantine.

In 1105, struck by lightning – well, no, not by a thunderbolt loosed by Jove – the marble statue fell and smashed. Some pious hand picked up the nails. If I am not mistaken, one, at least, of them is now to be seen, for a fixed price, in the treasury of the cathedral of Nôtre-Dame de Paris.

The Turks of the Republic, in Istanbul, call the still standing porphyry pillar Chemberlitash, which means "burnt column." In the one thousand six hundred and forty-odd years that have passed since Constantine the Great set it up, history, which is to say human detritus, has piled up around the base of the burnt column to raise the ground level of the city by sixteen and a half feet. And that is the combined height of three men, if they were gymnasts but otherwise average, standing on one another's shoulders, their backs to the base of Constantine's porphyry pillar.

But the water level of the Bosphorus has not changed in that millenium and a half and more. It has not risen, or not much, since the glaciers of the last Ice Age melted twenty thousand years or so ago, at which time civilization, as we know it, began to take shape. Geologists, geographers, and meteorologists now inform us that, all things being equal, we are in for another ice age sixty thousand years hence. And anthropologists, biologists, and psychologists tell us that the patterns and the shapes of human nature have not changed since, strictly speaking, before the beginning of time, which is man's invention.

The captain of the ferryboat clanged the bell. The engineers got to work. The sailors cast off the hawsers. Along the wharf and along the sides of the ferry, even by 1943, old truck tires had replaced the knotted Turk's heads. Down below, the firemen stoked the furnaces with soft coal from Zonguldak on the Black Sea. In the white mist, I could not see the plume of black smoke pour from the stack, but I could smell it. Once out of the bay and into the current, we picked up speed.

Into the forward second class saloon came another young peasant soldier in his natural-color sheep's-wool uniform. He carried his hands clasped in front of him. I saw that he did so because he was manacled, not in handcuffs but in thumb locks. Two sergeants, older men, accompanied him, their rifles slung by the straps over their shoulders, pointing up, bayonets fixed. They seemed to be on matter-of-fact good terms with their prisoner.

The three of them made as though to sit down on the bench alongside me, but having looked at me, they changed their minds. History belongs in books. I turned my head away, eyes front. I saw the other young soldier reading away at his newspaper, his lips shaping his new information. The reading soldier, it may have been, sensing that he was under scrutiny, glanced up from his newspaper. He looked at me. His eyes were black and white, and his hands were red. It is indecorous to stare. Again I turned my head, this time thinking to look out through the window. But the glass was clouded by the exhalations of our bodies. With my gloved hand I wiped the pane, and through the window I saw, hanging in the white mist, a city of gold, shining squares and rectangles of gold piled up in terraces of light, a sight as glorious as the New Jerusalem.

Yes, yes, I know and I knew then that what I saw was not a revelation. It was but an illusion, a phenomenon of the morning passage down the Bosphorus through the thick white mist. The sun had risen high enough out of Asia into the dome of heaven — no, it had not. The planet Earth, spinning in space on its own tilted axis in its place within the solar system, had reached the hour — the hell with it. Hours o'clock are man-made; such time is nowise universal. The Islamic calendar is lunar; the Christian, solar. Language cannot keep up with man's discoveries and inventions; times change. Therefore, the many windows of the Turkish houses on the hillside, invisible through the mist rising from the Bosphorus, had caught the rising sun's rays and, in coincidence, had reflected the muted golden light into my eyes. So much for the evidence of the senses. I saw what I chose to see, and I saw, hanging in a thick white mist, a shining city of gold.

In truth, if not in fact, this city for a thousand years to the Christians, and then for five more centuries in Islam, was the golden City of God when such words and phrases, and such beliefs, were meaningful. This city, rising within its triangle of sea walls and land walls upon its seven hills above the Sea of Marmara, the Bosphorus, and the Golden Horn, bridged the east and the west, joined the north to the south, and marked the geopolitical center of the world. From this city, aureoled in light, rippled the expanding universe. . . .

Again the captain rang the bell, a real bell. He brought the ferry in to tie up alongside the wharf attached to the Galata bridge. It is a floating bridge, a steel bridge rising from steel pontoons floating across the mouth of the Golden Horn. Because of my uncertain legs, I was the last to leave the ferry. From the dock at water level, I watched the reading soldier and the soldier in thumb locks under escort disappear in the mist. Then I climbed the staircase to the sidewalk of the floating bridge.

The harbor of the Golden Horn takes its name from its shape, a horn golden in the wealth that it brought into the city. A backwater today, the narrow harbor is golden only in the reflected light of the setting sun. But on that morning, nothing of all this was to be seen.

The mist at the bridge, stained and thickened by the black smoke from the ships, closed in around me as I got to the top of the staircase. Out of the gray smog materialized three young Turkish army officers walking abreast and in step. Each man wore cavalry boots of polished black leather, flared breeches, and a belted tunic tailored to fit and buttoned tight. From his shoulders a cape fell to his spurred heels. The three capes swung out as the three solid young men strode forward in the swirling mist.

I am not old enough to remember the redcoats nor even the armies of horizon blue. But I have known the protective coloring of field green, of khaki, of desert sand and suntans, and of spotted jungle camouflage. The three young Turkish army officers wore lilac. They were booted, belted, and visored in shining black, and they wore lilac capes in the mist.

It is probable that I stared at them. I know that I missed the top step, wrenched my bad leg, and, clinging to the parapet of the floating steel bridge, began to swear out loud, to call upon God, to blaspheme in English. As the caped soldiers strode along by, one said to the other two, loud enough for me to hear, "It stinks of giaour hereabouts." And then all the military virtues embodied in these three soldierly young men passed me by, their lilac capes vanishing in the gray mist. I think that, despite the trembling of my legs, I must have smiled; for I sniffed the air and all I smelled was soft coal smoke, salt water, fresh fish, and a faint trace of rose water.

It is a fine Byronic term of opprobrium, giaour – *gâvur* in modern Turkish. The *g* is hard; the circumflex flattens the *a* as in New England; the *v* is silent; the *u* is long. It is a bad word, almost never heard today. It means "non-Muslim, infidel, atheist," but in the emotional minatory pejorative, it translates roughly as "uncircumcised dog of a Christian." In actual fact, although I have been called a son of a bitch, I do not exactly qualify as a giaour. And long since 1943 the army of the Republic of Turkey has retired those lilac-colored uniforms and capes so to assume the universal khaki. As those of us who knew them in Korea know, the Turks are whole and perfect soldiers. No, giaour was not the right word for them to call me in Istanbul. I was a *yabanji*, a "stranger, foreigner," literally a dweller in the wilderness, a man come from the desert into civilization.

I had arrived from Libya in the evening of a clear day six months earlier, in late September. At sunset, I got off the train from the east, and, carefully putting one foot down after the other, I watched my step as I made my way from the railroad station on the Bosphorus shore across the dock and onto the waiting ferry. It took all my attention to get me there. The light was in my eyes. I sat down. The ship pulled out into the Bosphorus. I looked up to see where I was going.

Against the blazing sky and the blazing water, I saw a black horizon like a staff of music, notes in an unknown scale. I had seen burning cities before, but never one like this, a skyline of minarets and domes rising above high walls as flat against the flaming light as a page of history. Istanbul rises from the water on seven hills enclosed by sea walls and land walls. The thrusting minarets clamp together the jagged edges of the earth and heaven.

The city, then called Constantinople, burned like this in the evening of May 29, 1453, when the Janissaries of Sultan Mehmet the Conqueror poured through a breach opened in the land walls, and firing the houses, ran slaughtering through the streets of the hills and valleys. They shouted their full-throated battle cry, *"Allahuekber!* 'God is Most Great!' " and took the Byzantine Christian City of God for Islam

After the fires died down, the Sultan, a prince of the Renaissance, a young man of twenty-one, put an end to the killing and the looting, buried the dead, ruled the living, and set the Janissary engineers and the defeated Greek laborers to work to restore the walls. The new Emperor of the East began to rebuild the City of God as the new capital of the Ottoman Empire.

The fall of Constantinople shook the Western world. The Sultan's victory over the last of the Byzantine emperors, Constantine XI, changed the course of history, to use an old-fashioned phrase. As, after Hiroshima, some men proposed to drop the bomb upon the Kremlin, so Pope Pius II, having failed in his attempt to convert Mehmet the Conqueror by means of an epistle, so to abjure the winning side of the Prophet and to accept Christ, declared Holy War against the Turk on January 14, 1460. He lacked the backing of the Venetian merchantmen, and when he died in August of that year, the last, most foolish crusade ended before it had begun. By then, to defend the city, the Sultan's Janissary engineers had built Yedi Kulé, the Castle of the Seven Towers, to close the Byzantine Golden Gate.

From the floating bridge I crossed the city to the far corner where the sea walls join the land walls on the shore of the Marmara. By noon the sun had burnt through the mist. It was a fine day of early spring. I slowly climbed the steps built against the inner walls of the ramparts, and on top of the Castle of the Seven Towers sat down on a lump of masonry fallen from the crenellations. The castle wall is wider than a country road. Sheep graze on the thick turf rooted in the dust blown up over the centuries. I looked down at my feet. In this hanging garden grape hyacinths bloomed like patches fallen from an evening sky starred with pink anemones. I looked up at the seven hills.

There is no other city like Istanbul. Triangular within the walls, grim and magnificent, it stretches between wind and water. Trees grow tall among the houses that are built of wood weathered gray-brown and roofed with red-brown pantiles. Above the roofs rise the minarets and domes of the mosques. No one knows how many of them there are because nobody has bothered to count them; three hundred and sixty-five is a number given. They are built of weathered limestone and sheathed in lead that has taken on the patina of the breasts of doves. Sober and disciplined, man-made, the city is as natural as the four elements, earth, air, fire, and water, and it is full of life.

On the hills and the ridges, in the valleys and on the littoral stand the mosques, the great ones and the small. From the spoils of Holy War each sultan, from the seventh Son of Osman, Mehmet the Conqueror, to the tenth, his great-grandson Süleyman the Magnificent, in the Ottoman Golden Age, paid for the building and the endowment, as his memorial, of an Imperial Friday Mosque. Each one in Islam is as a cathedral in Christendom. There are eight of them in Istanbul, and one more, the first of the great domes raised above the floor plan of the circle inscribed within the square. Haghia Sophia Ayasofya, the Church-Mosque of the Divine Wisdom, was already nine hundred and sixteen years old when, on the evening of Tuesday, May 29, 1453, Mehmet the Conqueror stopped the slaughter and the looting and claimed the building as his own.

After Sultan Süleyman's long reign of forty-six years, the later Sons of Osman went on building monuments, but sporadically throughout the long slow decline. They were great builders, but one man, the Royal Chief Architect for Sultan Süleyman the Magnificent, gave shape to the city of Istanbul.

His name was Sinan abdür-Mennan, which, in translation, is Spearhead the Son of the Slave of God the All-Giving. He was a slave. From 1512 to 1538, first as a cadet, then as a Janissary, the general of the engineers, and finally as the commanding officer of the Sultan's own chosen bodyguards-men, he was a soldier. Then Süleyman appointed him Royal Chief Architect at the age of forty-nine. For fifty years thereafter, until he died aged niney-nine, he built more buildings than any other architect who has ever lived. All the best of them still stand. Three of them are Imperial Friday Mosques, two in Istanbul, and one in Edirné, the second capital of the Ottoman Empire in Thrace. In such buildings history and the man who built them come to life.

Shot full of the history of my own times, to exercise my legs and to find out what had happened to me I got up from my seat on the fallen block of mortar in the hanging gardens, and slowly I went down the steps from the ramparts of the Castle of the Seven Towers, which time alone has ruined. I have been informed by my betters, which is not to say my elders, but by younger men, that the day of the individual human being is done. We have bred ourselves into statistics. There are so many of us now alive on earth that none of us can make a go of it alone. Mass produced, we must give ourselves over to the organizations of the various standard brands. I am told that the humanism of the Renaissance has turned in its full cycle to close the circle, alpha and omega. Perhaps so. The power of free will active in free choice, like the power of Islam, which means "submission, resignation" to the will of God, has gone out of men's lives on earth. Instead, fatalism, a resignation, a submission to historical forces (one such is called communism) has settled like a thick white mist upon the world. Again, perhaps so.

But Sinan the Royal Chief Architect, a Slave of the Gate of the Sultan's Household of Slaves, a specimen chosen for his nobility of spirit, his unsullied character, his physical perfection, his high intelligence, and his handsomeness in conformation, and enslaved in an aristocracy of merit and achievement, died a free man, honored, respected, accomplished, and very rich. Call no man happy before his death. I got down from the hanging garden on the castle walls, and I set off across the seven hills of Istanbul to see what I could see.

‑‑‑ C H A P T E R ‑‑‑

2

Sinan was born possibly on April 15, almost certainly 1489, in Aghirnas, a village of Greek Orthodox Christians in the center of the high Anatolian plateau. It was a stone-built village on a ridge above the alluvial plain and behind it loomed the extinct volcano, Mount Argeus to the Greeks and the Byzantines, Erjiyash Dagh to the Turks. Forty days after his birth his parents took their firstborn son to the parish church to be baptized and registered. They christened him Joseph, perhaps in honor of the patron saint of carpenters and builders, for his father was the carpenter and stonemason of the village. He knew all there was to know about the houses set around the village square, which lay in the shadow of the plane trees growing beside the central fountain. Built of dressed blocks of pale volcanic stone, the houses of the hill town today are flat-roofed and much the same as they were then. Small, square buildings, some of a single story, some of two, they rise according to the lie of the land and according to the law of gravity. Shaped by the four seasons, the rooms served the family; they still serve, although it is true that the ablest of the young men, Turks of Joseph's age, having finished their military service, go off to work in the factories or to study in the universities of the cities. But the tools that the stonemasons and the carpenters used in Joseph's time still fit the hands of the men who choose to do the work in 1970.

As he grew up Joseph learned from his father how to work in stone and timber. In the good weather he hauled the stone from the quarry to the building site. There he sat on the ground, as masons do today, the rough stone block between his outstretched legs. The chisel in his left hand, the mallet in his right, he dressed the stone to the required dimensions. Then he stood up and lifted the block into its place in the rising wall.

The chisel in his left hand, the mallet in his right, he shaped the stone and the stone shaped him. As a young man, he was remarkable for his strength, for his intelligence, and for the sobriety of his character.

In the summer of 1512, when Joseph was twenty-three years old, the Ottoman Sultan Selim the Grim levied for the first time the blood tax of tribute youths upon the Christian communities of Asia Minor. And so it was that the Keeper of the Cranes, the veteran Janissary officer and collector of the blood tax, marched his detachment of slave soldiers up the cobblestoned road and into the village square. The news of his approach had already reached Aghirnas. Perhaps an itinerant tinsmith brought the news of the advancing *devshirmé,* the "collection," to Aghirnas three or four days earlier in that week. Coming from the walled city of Kayseri or from the Christian villages to the west, he may have climbed the ridge road which zigzags up to Aghirnas from the plains. He walked behind his donkey in a clatter of tinned copper pots and pans for sale. He was too old and ugly to run any risks; the disciplined Janissaries would have no use for him. To them he was not worth a tinker's damn. He may have been a Christian, a Greek, an Armenian, or an Arab from Syria. On that day perhaps he did not do much business in Aghirnas, but he brought the news.

On the morning of the Janissaries' arrival all work ceased. Joseph stood waiting beside his father, with all the other young men and their fathers, in front of the village church in the square. Above them on the steps of the church, perhaps in the open door, stood the village priest, who was also the headman of the village. He may have been young, but probably he was old enough to have sons liable to the collection. Eighteen was the average age, but exceptionally good tribute youths were as young as fifteen and as old as twenty-five. The priest wore a long black robe, long-sleeved in the Turkish style, a flat-topped and brimless stovepipe hat on his head. Neither his hair nor his beard had ever been cut, in order not to desecrate God's handiwork.

He had put a lookout in the bell tower of the church. He had chosen the most responsible young men, those with good eyesight and good sense. For three or four days, in the bright summer light from dawn to dark, Joseph (if it were he) watched. To the southeast he saw the city of Kayseri. He and his father knew the stones of the towers and the high walls first built by the Greeks, then restored by the Romans, enlarged by the Byzantines, repaired by the Seljuks, and maintained by the Dulkadirli Turkish garrison. They had kept out the Frankish Crusaders. Within the walls the Christians, workmen and masons like Joseph and his father, were safe. The Janissaries did not collect sophisticated youths of the cities. Joseph turned from the houses, the caravansaries, the mosques and minarets, and the walls to look out across the plains to the north, the south, and the west.

At daybreak on the day he was enslaved, as the smoke from the chimneys rose around the bell tower, he first saw a plume of dust rising from the plain, dark in the shadow of the mountain. It caught the level rays of the sun above the horizon, a plume of pale dust rising from the dry earth where goats grazed among the steel-blue thistles and the thorn bushes. Then he heard, above the crowing of the cocks, the cackle of the hens, and braying donkeys, the drumbeat and reed woodwinds. Perhaps he struck a bell with the flat of his hand to sound the alarm. In the fields under the ridge the men and women dropped their hoes and ran home through the rows of broad beans and eggplants. The black and white storks flew up from the banks of the irrigation ditches and then settled down again.

Up in the bell tower, Joseph (or another) made out the colors of the uniforms of the column of men marching closer — white, red, and blue. In the still air of the early morning, the plume of dust rose higher, incandescent in the sun. It was the dust of Joseph's ancestors, first the nomads, then the men and women who settled down in the earliest of cities, ten thousand years ago, and then the many invaders from the east and the west. They looked like their descendants, the rest of us, these first civilized human beings now known as the Mediterranean people. Then came people known in history as Hittites, Sumerians, Assyrians, Egyptians, Scythians, Phrygians, Cappadocians, Galatians. And then all the others: the Greeks, the Romans, the legionaries, the Byzantines, the mercenaries, the Praetorians, the Varangians, the Persians, the Slavs, the Arabs, the Crusaders, the Armenians, the Mongols, the Tartars, the Circassians, the Seljuks, and the many clans and tribes of the Gazi Turks. There is no way to hit upon Joseph's ancestry.

But in 1512, when he was collected, according to the hard and fast rules of the *devshirmé,* the tribute youth could not have been a Turk or a Muslim of any sort. He was neither a Russian, nor a gypsy, nor a Negro. Nor was he an Armenian or a Christian Arab of the various Monophysite heresies which came uncomfortably close to orthodox Islam in their interpretation of the single nature of Jesus. Joseph was an Anatolian Greek and he was a Greek Christian. His father and his mother loved their son, and he loved them. Aged twenty-three, he was a stonemason and a carpenter; such was his inheritance.

Before he came down from the bell tower, Joseph felt the heat of the rising sun on his back; he felt the air begin to stir. He may have turned from the sight of the advancing column and the plume of dust rising from their marching feet to look once more at the solitary mountain behind him. Against the clear blue sky, the snow-covered cone of the extinct volcano rose high above the foothills of the high Anatolian plateau. Below the snow the forest of cedars and pines on the flanks was dark. By midday clouds would form to hide the peak. In the forests Joseph and his father cut timber. They hunted and trapped deer and stone marten. In 1512 there may still have been leopards high up under the snows. In spring and autumn ducks and geese passed by in their migrations. Father and son fished for trout in the mountain streams. Alone he could have survived.

Joseph might have run for it, after the tinsmith brought the news, to escape the Janissary collector; but he did not do so. Instead he came down from the bell tower to join his father and the others when they heard the drumbeat, the shrilling woodwinds, and the marching feet of the approaching Janissaries. All the women, the girls, and the children went inside their houses. They closed the doors and pulled the window shutters together to lock and to bolt them.

The Keeper of the Cranes, astride his Cappadocian horse, rode between the houses at the end of the ridge road and came glittering into the tree-shaded village square. He called a halt; the drums and woodwinds ceased. In the silence he called the men to attention and, with a clash of arms, put them at ease. He dismounted. For the space of a moment he stood beside his horse to give the villagers the measure of the power of the Sultan Selim the Grim.

Joseph saw a man as tall as he, but heavier in muscle, and magnificent in uniform. The Keeper of the Cranes stood in yellow leather boots, blue jodhpurs, and scarlet tunic buttoned in gold and belted. He glittered with arms; his saber, hafted and sheathed in gold and jewels, was a damascened steel blade, curved, inlaid with gold and silver. His face was uniformly handsome, the regular features marked by the extraordinary intelligence that had caused him, when he was Joseph's age, to be enslaved. Lined and sunburnt in the years of his service, his face may have been scarred, but certainly he was clean-shaven except for the wide and thick moustache. It was the sign and symbol of the Janissary's disciplined ferocity.

The veteran officer was a man about forty years old. On his head he wore a high, pointed cap of white felt, brimless, banded at the forehead with brocaded cloth of gold. From the peak arose a tall and thick panache of white egret feathers. They fluttered in the breeze from the mountain. The man stood still; under the plane trees, the sunlight, filtering through the leaves, flashed and glinted on the jewels set in his weapons and in his horse's gear, and in the splashing water of the fountain.

The Keeper of the Cranes moved. He broke the stillness of the morning with a command. Behind him the Janissaries broke ranks; each man knew exactly what he had to do in the familiar task force. A slave soldier was sent across the square to salute the parish priest and request his co-operation. Silently the men and their sons who stood on the church steps made way for the priest to cross the square.

The Janissary officer spoke courteously to the headman of the village. He spoke in Osmanlija, a Turkish enriched and adorned with Arabic and Persian words and idioms. Then he addressed the priest in Byzantine Greek, the language of the church, and asked him to present the baptismal records of the past twenty-five years. In the meantime his lieutenant had posted guards at the outskirts of the town to prevent escape.

The Janissary scribe had a table and chairs brought out and set down beside the fountain in the shade of the plane trees. He opened his register, sharpened his reed pens, and prepared his lampblack ink. Then, when the priest had given him the church records, he read aloud the names of the village youths baptized between the years 1487 and 1497: Michael, George, Emmanuel, Joseph, Christos, Peter, Demitrios, Paul, Panaghiotis, Basil, Theodore, Constantine, Alexander, Pericles, Achilles, Ulysses. . . . Fifty or so answered to their given names.

The assistant collectors got to work. As these Janissary non-commissioned officers walked among the village males of the fifteen to twenty-five age group, a glance was enough, with a tap on the shoulder, to cull the physically malformed and the obviously traumatically scarred. First to go were the dwarfish and the gawky, the halt, the lame, the hunchbacked, the one-eyed, the cross-eyed and the shifty-eyed, and of course the blind. Out went the tubercular, the acned, and the leprous; the village idiot, the self-loathing, the youths despised by their fellows – all the misfits whose faults were to be seen at a glance. After consultations with the priests and the elders, the collector read out the orphans, the only sons, the youthful heads of families, the married young men, and the enterprising early businessmen. These few were disqualified because their responsibilities had forced them into maturity. They were left behind to breed for some future *devshirmé*.

Next to be told to step aside were the young shepherds and swineherds, perhaps no more than three or four. Dogs and swine are peculiarly unclean animals in Islam. Shepherds with their sheep dogs spent months alone with their flocks in the high pastures, moving their sheep and goats according to the seasons. Marked by solitude, such youths did not easily give up their individuality. They found it hard to surrender their independence in discipline, so wholly to lose identity in the unit. From perfect unity comes the high morale essential to any military elite. Such individual young men as the shepherds, left behind, were natural rebels. They took to the hills as bandits or to the roads as highwaymen.

Pig drovers were told to step aside because some of the filth of their swine had rubbed off on them. Occupationally diseased, in contagion by association, it was believed that such a youth's ignoble work humiliated him. The Prophet listed the unclean animals in the Koran, dogs, swine, and apes among them. The Keeper of the Cranes, in 1512, had no need to scrape the bottom of the barrel

True, in the heat of victory, a swineherd or a shepherd boy of exceptional merit occasionally found his way into the *penjik* – the sultan's "fifth part" – of the spoils of war and was enrolled in the Janissary cadet schools or the palace school for pages. Choban ("Shepherd") Mustafa Pasha, a Slovene and husband of a daughter of Selim the Grim, for whom both the Royal Chief Architects Ajem Ali and Sinan built a splendid pious foundation at Gebze across the Marmara from Istanbul, demonstrated the exception to the rule. He was exemplary. But the Grand Vezir Rüstem Pasha, Süleyman the

Magnificent's only son-in-law, had been a Croatian swineherd, a prisoner of war. Sinan built several mosques, caravansaries, and colleges for him. Despite his financial genius, Rüstem Pasha proved the wisdom of the rule. An ignoble man, indeed a lousy man, he introduced corruption into the hierarchy of the Slave Household by the sale of public offices to the highest bidders, if only and always, in his day, among the Slaves of the Gate otherwise fully qualified for the position that they bought.

Joseph, aged twenty-three, may have tended sheep or even butchered swine; if so, the bestiality had not rubbed off on him. From the broken shade under the plane trees growing about the fountain in the village square of Aghirnas, there begins to emerge the handsome face and the upright figure of a well-built young man dressed in peasant homespun. "The mark of a slave suited for arms-bearing," wrote Kai Kaus out of a lifetime of experience in a book that the Janissary collector had learned by heart, "is that his hair is thick, his body tall and erect, his build powerful, his flesh hard, his bones thick, his skin coarse, and his limbs straight, his joints being firm. The tendons should be tight and the sinews and blood vessels prominent and visible on the body. Shoulders must be broad, the chest deep, the neck thick and the head round. . . . The belly must be concave, the buttocks drawn in and the legs in walking well extended. And the eyes should be black. Any slave who possesses these qualities will be a champion in single combat, brave and successful." Six feet was very tall in those days. The Janissaries, matched in height, probably varied between five feet eight and five feet ten.

For such a close inspection, Joseph and the other two or three dozen selected youths had to be stripped, but not naked; the Muslims, puritans, are given wide latitude in matters sexual, but they are specifically and scrupulously modest.

"You must take him and lay him down," said Kai Kaus. Joseph, in turn, stripped and stretched out perhaps on a long table, one that he or his father had made, or perhaps on the stone margin of the fountain basin where the women of the town on ordinary days sat to gossip when they went out to fill their copper water jugs. "It is essential to be alive to defects, both external and internal, through knowledge of the symptoms of latent or incurable disease."

"You must carefully inspect all the limbs and organs to ensure that nothing remains hidden from you," said Kai Kaus. Dry, discolored lips were the symptoms of hemorrhoids; swollen eyelids, of dropsy; redness in the eyes and engorged veins in the forehead, of epilepsy; tearing the hair, flickering of the eyelashes, chewing of the lips, of melancholia. Crookedness or irregularity in the shape of the nose were the marks of "fistula" – erysipelas? Certainly not yet syphilis, although across the Mediterranean in Italy, in 1495, a virulent strain of this new disease like a plague destroyed the French army besieging Naples. "If here and there upon the body," Kai Kaus warned, "you perceive the marks of branding where no branding should be, examine closely to ensure that there is no leprosy under it." Yellow eyeballs and yellow skin were signs of jaundice; the viral infectious sort is endemic in those regions today.

Next, the Janissary collector bent over Joseph to press and thump his belly, back, and sides, the while he watched closely for any flinching against soreness or sharp pain. Liver, spleen, gallbladder, intestines, heart, lungs, all were sound. He probed for hernia, common to lifters of great weights like blocks of stone and heavy timbers. None of Joseph's joints was swollen or stiff. He walked a straight line steadily in balance. He kicked in reflex action. His teeth were sound in his head. No noxious odors issued from his mouth or nose. He was not hard of hearing, or hesitant in utterance, or irregular in speech.

In the last phase of the physical examination, the Keeper of the Cranes, by means not of "the art and sombre craft" of today's psychologists but of an earlier sister "science," arrived at an estimation of Joseph's intelligence quotient. It had to be high. "Human beings," said Kai Kaus, "cannot be known except by the science of physiognomy and by experience, and the science of physiognomy in its entirety is a branch of prophecy that is not acquired to perfection except in the divinely directed apostle. The reason is that by physiognomy the inward goodness or wickedness of men can be ascertained." "God," said Kai Kaus, ". . . placed the beauty of the human beings in eyes and eyebrows, delicacy in the nose, sweetness in the lips and freshness in the skin." And He ". . . created the hair of the head for adornment."

Perhaps Joseph was redheaded, perhaps fair; perhaps his hair was black but highlighted, as was the wine-dark sea. His brow was high and broad — or so it can be said from what survives of the "science" of physiognomy; his eyes large, clear, and well spaced; his nose high, his nostrils sensitive. Delicacy, in Kai Kaus's opinion, was to be preferred to classic beauty; his upper lip shaped like a strung Turkish bow, his lower lip full, his mouth firm and generous; the planes of his cheeks caught the light and shadow; his jaw was firm, his chin round; his head well-placed on his muscular throat, well set on wide shoulders; he carried himself well. He may have been bearded, at the age of twenty-three, like a young Zeus; if so, after his collection, he was shaved.

Beauty is an aesthetic order, relative to time and place and to all other ideas of order, political, social, statistical, ethical, religious, military, commercial, philosophical, and scientific, a matter of functional purpose in proportion. Whatever he looked like, Joseph was a handsome young man according to the Janissary standard.

The Ottoman miniaturists, later to be his friends, colleagues, and contemporaries in the sixteenth century, in their battle scenes, give us ranks of youthful Janissaries as standard as standards. Each has the same face with the same features fixed in an identical expression of concentrated purity, a wholehearted intensity not to be confused with innocence.

Oval of face, wide-eyed, open and steadfast of regard – stylized and formalized but recognizable human beings – the Janissaries were in fact young men, soldiers, perfected as statistics. Called the handsomest and the finest body of military men in history, the appearance of these Janissaries struck terror among their Christian enemies on the European fields of battle. Joseph was chosen as one of them.

He was a man like another in character. When, four hundred and thirty years earlier, Kai Kaus summed up his experiences with the slaves of his princely household, he observed that the Byzantine Greeks made excellent artisans and craftsmen; they had the gift for creative art. Furthermore, they understood money. As thrifty managers they calculated the costs before they embarked upon any undertaking, which they then successfully brought off. All this is known to be true of Joseph-Sinan, the Slave of the Gate.

Kai Kaus goes on to say that Greeks love display; they like to accumulate valuable possessions. Ambitious men, they work best when they are rewarded. Their great merits are that they are cautious and affectionate. A happy breed of men, they take thought to establish the facts needful to achieve their ends in view.

The great defects of the Byzantine Greeks are that they can be foul-mouthed and evil-hearted, quick-tempered, and easy to take offense. Such a Greek slave is both cowardly and indolent. If the Greek passion for worldly power and great wealth gets out of hand, such a man can be covetous and greedy. If he is thwarted, to achieve his ends, all that is devious and intricate in his nature makes him liable to lose himself in hatefulness.

There is no way to know whether Joseph, later called Sinan, had any or all of these Byzantine virtues and defects, or the defects of the virtues and the virtues of the defects. It is apparent in the tragedies of Aeschylus, Sophocles, and Euripides, in the comedies of Aristophanes, in the philosophy of Plato's Socratic dialogues, and indeed in Homer's *Iliad* and *Odyssey* that such are to be called classic Greek virtues and defects – which is to say, those of the human kind.

During his lifetime as an architect Sinan used the varying proportions of the golden section of classic Greek and Renaissance humanism; the mathematical and geometric exactitude of the Ottoman system; and the systematic irregularities of the Byzantines. He understood what he was doing. He was an Ottoman and a Greek, a man like another, who honored the golden mean and the golden rule as ideals of conduct, not necessarily applicable to daily life.

In his seventy-six years as a Slave of the Sultan's Household, Joseph-

Sinan threaded his way through the labyrinthine intrigues that flourish in military barracks and in the courtyards, the corridors, and the rooms of palaces in all competitives societies. He came out whole.

In 1512 it was more than luck that brought him through the final test of the Janissary collector. In the same way that a judge of horseflesh or of other livestock calms the animals he handles, so the Keeper of the Cranes talked quietly to Joseph stripped down for physical inspection. As he tallied the points in conformation, he measured the tribute youth's specific knowledge, his powers of observation, his capacity to think, and his degree of intelligence. The collector's questions came not from the *Mirror for Princes* of Kai Kaus but from Nizam al-Mulk's pages in the *Book of Government* on how to gather secret intelligence.

In that first year of his accession, the Ottoman Sultan Selim the Grim planned to wage Holy War against his neighbors to the east, the heretical Shah of Persia and his ally, the independent Gazi Turkish Emir of Marash and Elbistan. In fact, when the Sultan's Keeper of the Cranes collected Joseph from his hill town in the county of Kayseri, he crossed the eastern frontier of the Ottoman Empire to invade the territory of the Dulkadirli emir of Marash, a vassal of the Mameluke sultan of Syria and Egypt. Therefore, Joseph of Aghirnas was collected as a tribute youth in what we call today a border incident. It was a calculated act of provocation, a test of strength.

In preparation for his campaigns against the Shah of Persia in 1514 and in 1517 against the Mameluke Sultan of Syria and Egypt, and under the cover of the *devshirmé,* Selim the Grim instructed his Janissaries to collect order of battle and all the other facts of military intelligence: the name of the Dulkadirli Turkish Bey of Kayseri, his past commands, his cast of character, his strengths and weaknesses; the conditions of the walls of the fortified city; the number of soldiers in the garrison, a description of their equipment, their arms, their supplies, and their morale.

The Janissary collector asked Joseph for the gossip of the bazaars of Kayseri, which is to say, for political and economic intelligence. More specifically, he asked about the condition of the roads, the bridges, the water points, and the fortified outposts. Was the postal service kept up? What of the bandits and highwaymen; what of the police force, the crime rate, and the justice of the lawcourts? He asked about the taxes and the Dulkadirli Emir's tax collectors, about the crops and the estimated harvest, and about the pasture lands. He got meteorological and demographic information, both general and specific.

In Joseph and his father, the stonemason, the collector found experts trained to observe the state of things, to estimate the costs and the amounts of raw materials to effect repairs or to build new walls, and then capable of carrying out specified assignments. As men who knew their business, they worked directly with administrators and executives. There is reason to believe that the father and the son had made the journey to Marash and Elbistan, the chief cities of the Dulkadirli Emir's principality (when Sinan designed and built his first Imperial Friday Mosque, in Istanbul in 1543, he used a plan known to have existed at an earlier date in Islamic architecture only in the mosques of Diyarbakir, Marash and Elbistan). If so, having supplied reliable military intelligence to the Keeper of the Cranes, Joseph may well first have been brought to the attention of the Sultan in the description of the source of the information in the report. He was chosen.

He got up and put on his clothes. He stood with his father in front of the scribe. He gave his name, the names of his father and his mother, his religion, his place and date of birth and baptism, his occupation, his height and weight, and the color of his hair and of his eyes. There were no peculiar identifying marks to record. The scribe wrote down the list of Joseph's vital statistics in the appropriate columns of the Janissary register. Probably the collected tribute youth was assigned a number or a symbol, which possibly was tattooed in blue on the back of his hand — a six-pointed star, for instance, or a raying sun disk.

All the Janissary ledgers have disappeared, almost certainly burned on June 16, 1826. That was the day when the most liberal of the later sultans, Mahmud II, unable to reform or to discipline the corrupt Janissaries, who were no longer slaves but freeborn Muslims, in mutiny, self-barricaded in their barracks in Istanbul, set fire to them and, as they ran out, turned his artillery of modern French cannons on them. No Janissary escaped alive.

Three centuries earlier, in 1512, Aghirnas was not a village of crushing poverty. Surely there was a timepiece in the Christian hill town, if not a clock with a pendulum then a horologium, or an hourglass, or a sundial. But perhaps not. Each country man is his own gnomon. Joseph was allowed a quarter of an hour, or perhaps a half, to get ready to go off. It must at that instant, as we say, have dawned on him that thenceforth he was to live out his life in the shadow of the Shadow of God on Earth, in a double darkness where nothing ever again would strike his eye in the recognizable shapes of the familiar past. He was, of course, mistaken; for he carried himself with him.

But, stunned as though blind, he walked back in silence beside his father to their house to take leave of his mother and his younger brother. No one knows their names. The brother, uncollected, married, died a Christian, young. After 1538, Joseph took his two nephews from Aghirnas into his own household in Istanbul, to convert them and to educate them, along with his own sons, to be Islamic Ottoman gentlemen. His mother and his father died equally anonymously, sometime before 1563. They died Christians. After two years of burial, the village priest dug up their bones, washed them in wine, and placed them in the village charnel house to return to dust.

In Greece, as elsewhere, men weep when their sons go off into exile. Woman lament. Neither the angel, nor the ritual, nor the release of death came to put an end to their grief. His mother did not let her tears keep her from providing for her elder son. Ahead of him he had a journey of six weeks or two months on foot. How old was she? Eighteen at her marriage, . . . not more than forty. On the shores of the Black Sea, men and women often live to be centenarians, but women in those days died more frequently in their fifties. By the age of forty, country people, having come to terms with life and with themselves, have learned how to think. To have borne and brought up such a son, she must have been an excellent woman and a realist.

In her storeroom she reached up for a sausage, some pepper-cured strips of dried beef, a hard cheese, a round of bread, some nuts, a cluster or two of raisins, some dried figs. She fetched a change of underwear and a pair or two of socks from the chest that her son, her husband, or their fathers may have made and carved for her. She had grown and retted the linen fibers, and shorn and washed the wool to card and to spin the thread and the yarn that she then wove, cut and sewed, or knit together. She packed them in a square sack, or in saddle bags to sling over his shoulder, that she had loomed and embroidered in patterns and dyes inherited from ten thousand years of women like her. Perhaps, lacking daughters, from her dowry she took a coin or two of Byzantine or Cappadocian gold to put in her son's hand. She stayed behind in the locked and barred house when Joseph and his father went back to join the levy in the square.

In ragged step, herded by the white-capped Janissaries in their red tunics and blue trousers, carried by the conditioned muscles of their legs, the dozen or so tribute youths marched down the zigzagging road. Through the soles of their feet, shod in rawhide moccasins laced on with thongs, they felt the smoothed cobblestones, and picked up the cadence of the Janissary drumbeat. Whole, perfect, complete; physically, mentally, and spiritually untouched by man or demon, the tribute youths marched off to enter into servitude for life. But unlike the gilmans of Paradise whom they resembled, Joseph and his fellows went off to be manhandled into shape as Janissaries, the demons in the service of the Sultan, the conquering hero of Islam.

Behind his delegate, the plumed and glittering Keeper of the Cranes astride his Cappadocian horse – perhaps from the imperial stables, if so more valuable than any raw slave youth – they marched out into the irrigated fields of wheat and of beans growing where they had been sown and planted, no blade, no leaf changed in the two hours of the collection. In the distance on the high plateau, Joseph turned his head to look back through the golden motes of the plume of dust rising in the noonday sunshine. He saw the stone-built village on its ridge above green fields under the snow-capped mountain.

In the Ottoman style of Islamic architecture that he made classic, Sinan gave his mosques the gravity and the shape of that extinct volcano, snow-capped and solitary, piled up in the natural growth of its own magma flowing thicker than milk, solider than blood. The mountain may be no older than the million or so years of human evolution in the age of mammals. It took a natural shape in a natural order. Sinan built his mosques into the lie of the land. He leveled the foundation and drew a circle inside a square. From the circle arises a globe standing upon a cube inside an invisible cone within a pyramid that the mind instructs the eye to see.

He remembered the birds in the forests on the mountain slopes. They are nesting birds from Europe and from Asia; northern and southern migratory birds: black and white barred woodpeckers, scarlet capped; crested and barred hoopoes, said to have aided King Solomon build his Temple. High up in the walls of his mosques, Sinan built nesting places for the doves and pigeons. In unsentimental Islam, they do not coo, but instead proclaim (in Arabic) the fact that "God is one with nature." Inside the mosque, the doves may bring along with them the mess of reality; if so they also fill the spaces of the domes with the sound of wings.

Had I been Joseph's brother in the noontime of that summer day in 1512, I would have climbed up into the topmost branches of the plane trees rooted by the fountain in the village square. Left behind, I would have wept and cried out, shouting protests against the facts of life.

But I am an American, a romantic caged in my own moment. Howling, I would have watched my brother marching off, diminishing in the sunlit distance, vanishing into the unknown, pulling a plume of luminous dust after him. I would have watched until the wind from the mountain blew the dust away; or until my mother called me down to eat. The romantic agony is silly stuff.

⊰ C H A P T E R ⊱
3

At the nearest holding area, a Seljuk caravansary like a desert fortress on the trade routes of the empty high plateau, the Keeper of the Cranes signed over the levy of tribute youths to the Janissary Drover, who received them in good condition. The levy from Aghirnas and the neighboring hill towns of Kayseri must have been the last to be collected. Mission accomplished, next morning the herd set out.

In the ravines, the fords, and the passes, brigands and highwaymen, bands of outlawed Greek Christian rebels, tried to stampede the *devshirmé,* so that the young men might get away. During the six weeks of the march a few did. Some troublemakers, trying to organize escapes by night, were weeded out. Others, young ones who broke down before they hardened up, had to be discarded. Blistered feet, legs and hands torn by sharp rocks or thorns festered. Some not immunized by hardship came down with such diseases as amoebiasis. It is unlikely that the endemic diseases of smallpox or of the black bubonic plague, carried by the diseased fleas on rats, overtook this particular collection. Some of the youths fell and broke bones. They were left behind in the hospitals of the Seljuk and Ottoman Turkish cities, perhaps to be forwarded at a later date, or to be sold to private bidders. A very few went mad, berserk, and had to be put into the insane asylums, by no means Bedlams, where they were well fed and gently treated. Others died from natural causes or, it may be, threw themselves from cliffs or into wells. These were the exceptions. Most of the blood tax youths, having already survived in their native habitat the natural selection of infant mortality and the onslaught of puberty, proved the expertise of the Keeper of the Cranes and the excellent management of the Janissary Drover.

They arrived at the end of the road, at Usküdar, the point of departure for campaigns against the eastern enemies, before the September rains. Later during the Crimean War the town, which lay round the shallow harbor on the Asian shore of the Bosphorus, was known as Scutari. The Drover had brought the three of four thousand tribute youths into rudimentary discipline along the line of march, after dividing them into manageable groups. In the military installation everything was ready to receive them.

The bathmen and the barbers of the quartermaster then took over, so as not to let the levy offend the Sultan's nose. Joseph, one of the oldest, once soaped and scrubbed, deloused, depilated, his nails cleaned and pared, his face and head shaved, his sores and scratches tended, probably showed the youngest how to take a bath for the first time in their lives. Laughing, unable to recognize themselves, they were then issued clean clothing, some sort of uniform suitable for their ultimate inspection and presentation to Selim the Grim.

Along the stages of the way, and at night in the caravansaries, those of us who choose to do so can imagine Joseph . . . getting on with it. There is a stimulus in voyages through any transition that is as exciting, for some of us, as sudden freedom. For others the change is a terror; for a few, a responsibility. Perhaps at night, after rations, lying around the fire of dung or thorns, Joseph told stories to the fifteen-year-olds who had never been away from home before. Or he tried to answer questions about what was going to happen to them. If so, they trusted him as he led the way down to the barge, not as a bellwether but as an elder brother. In the gray light of dawn, galley slaves rowed them across the Bosphorus and into the Golden Horn, to disembark in Istanbul. There was a gate in the sea walls at the landing stage near where the bridge ends at Eminönü Square.

Through it the Drover marched them up the cobblestoned streets, under the outer walls of the Sultan's Palace, past the Church-Mosque of the Divine Wisdom – Haghia Sophia or Ayasofya. At last they came out into the Hippodrome of the Byzantines, the Ak Meydan of the Ottomans.

The great rectangular public square is no longer rounded at the ends as it was then. Along the axis of the level green space still stand the Egyptian obelisk, the twisted bronze serpent column from Delphi, and the masonry Byzantine obelisk. Herded among the ancient monuments, and halted to await the Sultan's pleasure, it may be that Joseph and the other tribute youths fell out, sat down, or, lying full length on the grass, plucked a blade to chew on. They knew enough to spit it out and jump to their feet when a huge-voiced Janissary bellowed, "Attention! "

Selim the Grim, aged forty-two in 1512, was a puritan in orthodox Islam. He knew himself to be an imperfect man, a tyrant. He was tall, barrel-chested, long and muscular of arm but short in the leg; he looked his best, as he well knew, astride a horse or seated, legs folded, on the hard brocaded cushions of his jewel-studded throne. But on that day of the close inspection of his first tribute youths, probably he walked out of the palace through the Bâbi-Hümayun, the Imperial Portal of the Slaves of the Gate, accompanied only by the Grand Vezir, the Grand Mufti, the lesser vezirs, the foremost pashas, the agha of the Janissaries, and a dozen of his senior guardsmen. He knew when to take leave of ceremony. He walked among the most excellent and beautiful crowd of youths.

Over a long robe of honor, he wore a long, loose-sleeved kaftan. Cut of gorgeous stuffs, gold-threaded, heavy silk brocades and cut velvets woven in large patterns of crimson and delicate colorings, his finest robes have outlasted him by four hundred and fifty years. He designed them himself to fit his wide and massive shoulders and then to fall in straight folds to the ground. Slit at the sides, the kaftan, lined for winter with ermines or sables, gave him ample room to stride along. Under the robes he wore loose-fitting pantaloons, a collarless shirt, and drawers of fine cotton or linen.

In the hierarchy of the Sultan's Household, what a man wore on his head identified him, or rather, placed him in his position and his grade. The Sultan was supreme. Instead of gold oak leaves embroidered on the visor of a peaked cap, the Sultan, who was the supreme commander of both the Ruling Institution and the imperial forces in action, wore a turban wound in the imperial style. No other man could imitate it. The Grand Vezir, next in rank and grade as the executive of the Ruling Institution and the general of the armies, wore, instead of a constellation of stars, a turban wound in another style, his own. So the shapes of the headgear changed down through the ranks. The Grand Mufti, necessarily as a free man – the head of the Religious Institution, stood outside the aristocracy of the Slaves of the Gate. In theory, he was the equal of the Sultan. But, brought into the Divan to guarantee justice dispensed according to the sacred jurisprudence, he was assigned a uniform. The Grand Mufti wore a tall conical hat of felt, brimless, covered with fluted silk. It was white, as were his robes and kaftans of heavy silk. He wore no jewels or embroideries; he carried no weapons.

Within the scope of the customary law of the Turkish Tribe, and his own sovereign canon law, Selim the Grim found permissible flexibility granted him by the Prophet's Sacred Law to make his own imperious rules. As a man, he knew when to break them. An ordinary feudal soldier, a freeborn Muslim Turkish tribesman, happened to set the style of Selim the Grim's imperial turban known as the Selimiyé. The story illustrates the Sultan's human nature.

After a victory in the field, Selim the Grim sat his horse on a hillock, perhaps an ancient tumulus. In the evening sunlight, he watched the conquering soldiers bring in the spoils of war. The Judges of the Army, in the Grand Mufti's jurisdiction, and the Sultan's Defterdar, "Treasurer," a Slave of the Gate, evaluated the total plunder brought in for equitable redistribution according to rank and grade. The Sultan and the Grand Mufti shared the *penjik*, the "fifth part," which meant that Selim the Grim took first choice of the treasure as well as the likeliest young male prisoners of war. Like the tribute youths of the *devshirmé,* the captives of the *penjik* were enslaved as cadets for the Janissary corps, or as pages for the palace school.

According to the story of Selim the Grim's new turban, a Turkish feudal soldier walked by, carrying his loot, below the hillock on which the Sultan sat on horseback. He probably drove six or seven captives ahead of him, say, a mother with her sons and daughters. The husband and father had either been killed in battle or, too old to change his ways and thus unfit for slavery, he had been slaughtered. Certainly the Turkish raider, a descendant of the original nomadic Turkish mounted bowmen, had his arms full of armor and weapons stripped from the vanquished dead. On his head he wore an unusually tall and bulky turban.

Something on top of it, not quite covered by the folded cloth, flashed in the rays of the setting sun. It caught Selim the Grim's watchful eye. Men are born to evil as the sparks fly upward. He roared out a command. A gentleman-at-arms brought the man up the hill to stand at his stirrup. The Sultan reached out his long and muscular arm and hand to snatch the turban from the soldier's head. Thus to be uncovered is a grave dishonor to a Turk.

The dirty folds of white cotton cloth fell away to leave a golden chalice in the Sultan's hand. Instead of striking off the thieving feudal soldier's head, Selim the Grim guffawed. He handed the cup for the wine of the Eucharist back to the Turk and told him to rewind the turban. The soldier balanced the bowl on his shaven head like a hard skullcap, the stem and the round flat base upright on top. While the Sultan watched, he rewound the yards and yards of battle-stained cloth around the chalice to conceal it in a high, round ball. Having seen how it was done, Selim the Grim rewarded his fellow Turkish tribesman with the unlawful prize (which he probably sold as a historic treasure for enough to buy himself a country estate).

A gentleman-in-waiting, called the Master of the Turbans (or one of his assistants, a page in the palace school), learned the trick of winding a similar turban. The immaculate length of folded muslin – a fine white cloth of silk or equally costly cotton, originally woven in Mosul on the Tigris – went around the base not of a chalice but of a high, pointed cap of red felt fitted to Selim the Grim's head. In place of a crown or a tiara, the Keeper of the Jewels pinned on a plume of white egret or birds of paradise feathers. The massive pin of pure gold was set with gross jewels, pearls from the Persian Gulf, Golconda diamonds, emeralds from the Urals or from Jaipur, sapphires from Kashmir, rubies and spinels from Ceylon and Burma. To one side in the folds, the Keeper of the Jewels thrust a "phoenix feather" of gold and enameling, the imperial sign, the symbol of the death and resurrection of the immortal Sons of Osman.

The exalted Slaves of the Gate in attendance on the Sultan as he walked forth rayed in light among the tribute youths were only less resplendent than he. Each was a man, himself, as well as his own image in the Ottoman iconography of men placed and ranked according to God's law given the Prophet upon earth. Each man knew his rightful order; each man knew that he had earned and merited the right to walk beside the Sultan. Each man thus held himself able to dominate the splendor of his heavy robes of state, and to animate the weight of his jeweled weapons.

All contemporary observers make note of the hushed stillness surrounding the Sultan; he moved in pure silence among men standing like statues. None coughed, none cleared his throat, none belched, no stomach rumbled; no man fell to the ground in a faint, no weapon clashed on steel or stone, nothing of leather creaked.

Like all the other tribute youths, drawn up in ranks according to the heights within the prescribed range for tall men, Joseph stood erect. Feet together, joined hands hanging in front of him at arms' length, belly sucked in, chest thrown out, spine straight, shoulders back, chin in, head upright, he stood, according to the etiquette of the Sultan's Slave Household from the Grand Vezir down to the last page and cadet, with his eyelids lowered over downcast eyes as though to protect the sight from the blazing majesty of the Imperial Presence.

It may have been that Joseph glanced out of the corner of his eye or, better, that he was commanded to look up for the final judgment of his quality. He saw a face unlike any other of the first nine Sons of Osman – indeed, unlike any other man's. Selim the Grim shaved his beard, but he cultivated a thick and wide moustache that curved up at the pointed ends like the tusks or horns of certain ferocious wild animals – the buffalo of Africa at best. Such was the desired effect, a calculated image of terrible ferocity. High-nosed, beaked like a bird of prey, high-colored, choleric in humor, portrayed in fierce, open-eyed regard, he wore hanging from the lobe of either ear a great, round Oriental pearl.

In all, he chose the tenth part of the collection, three or four hundred youths, on the average eighteen years old. By doing so he guaranteed the future of the empire. He gave these slaves, his pages, as careful an education as he had given his own seventeen-year-old son, Prince Süleyman the Shehzadé. The Ottoman palace schools for pages into which they were enrolled in 1512 were at least as good as the contemporary Christian universities of Oxford and Cambridge. The graduates emerged from them better educated than the British clerks of Chaucer's day or the gentlemen of Shakespeare's.

The pages were taught to read, write, and speak Osmanlija Turkish, Persian, and Arabic. They studied the literature and the sciences of Islamic civilization, and, in translation or in the original, the Greek, the Roman, and the Byzantine classics. But they majored in the Sacred Law. If a slave youth showed a remarkable aptitude for it, he was permitted, upon graduation, to continue his studies in the Islamic universities of Ayasofya or of the mosque of Sultan Mehmet the Conqueror, or later in the university colleges that Sinan built for Sultan Süleyman. Ultimately, such a student may have been appointed Judge of the Army, or even to the Ulema, the high court of the land.

But to educate the pages marked for the Ruling Institution, the directors of the palace schools brought in specialists, such as Sinan when he was Royal Chief Architect, to lecture on higher mathematics, on engineering, and on architecture. The Sultan's artists and musicians taught their arts. Janissary officers lectured on the science of war and drilled the youths in the manual of arms. Artisans taught them how to make and to take care of weapons and armor. From the imperial stables, the Master of the Horses, a graduate of the palace school, came to teach the pages how to ride and to take care of their horses, and, it may have been, how to play a lost equestrian game similar to polo. The Sultan much enjoyed the matches.

Champion wrestlers supervised athletics. The pages were taught to swim, how to bathe, how to take care of their health, their skin, their teeth, their hair, their nails. They were taught how to carry themselves, how to think, how to act, how to defend themselves, how to dress. Above all, the pages were disciplined in comportment, how to obey and how to give commands; they were taught fine manners. It was a total education. The Circassian White Eunuchs, supervisors of the pages, saw to it that the Sultan's young slavemen were intellectually, spiritually, morally, and physically disciplined, each one to attain his full potential. So by the time the pages graduated at the age of twenty-five, they were prepared to enter the hierarchy of the Sultan's Slave Household as educated, cultivated, civilized men of action.

The finest in the graduating classes were honored by appointments as gentlemen-in-waiting upon the Sultan. There were thirty-nine of them: the Chief Falconer, the Sword Bearer, the Cup Bearer, the Royal Taster, the Chief Equerry, the Master of the Hounds, the Master of the Wardrobe, the Turban Winder, the Keeper of the Jewels, and so on. The ordinary page was given a robe of honor, a jeweled sword, a horse from the imperial stables magnificently saddled and bridled, a purse of gold, and a commission as subaltern in the Sipahi cavalry, so to begin his career as a Slave of the Gate.

There is no way of knowing whether or not the Ottoman Ruling Institution was based on Plato's *The Republic*, from the philosopher king on down through the administration and the military branch of the highly organized establishment. Now, it does not matter; the one was theoretical, the other practical. Socrates knew that the one would never work; the other produced Sinan the Royal Chief Architect and all his works. In many ways, the sultans outdid Plato and Socrates. For instance, although he was himself one of the greatest writers and biographers of all time, Plato distrusted poets and playwrights. He would have censored Homer and Sophocles, and he did not know where to place artists in his state. The Sons of Osman were educated and cultivated men; they were patrons of the arts and of artists. They were themselves poets, musicians, and artisans. Both Selim the Grim and Süleyman the Magnificent were goldsmiths, as boys in training apprenticed to a master craftsman, who had the right to beat them for their failures. A page likewise was punished, put in stocks and beaten, no more than ten strokes at a time, on the soles of his feet.

Joseph was not chosen as a page. His individual and peculiar quality of genius was not apparent on the day when he stood up for inspection and selection in the Hippodrome. No one knows what genius is, except in effect, nor how a man comes by it. Joseph was graded second rate. True, he was five years over age, a young man less intellectual and more physical in character than those selected for the page school. He was rejected for education in the highest schools of the empire and classed as Janissary material.

It may have been that he disconcerted his examiners by, in his turn, examining them. Selim the Grim was, in historical fact, a monster; his Slaves of the Gate feared him. He was, however, a general and a soldier second to none. Therefore, he may have recognized Joseph's capabilities primarily as a man of action, one who worked with his hands. Joseph was to make himself superior to all but a score or so of his contemporaries, the foremost architect and engineer of his time. It may have been that, on that summer day, his anger, barely contained, gave him a sullen aspect mistaken for peasant brutishness. Or, it might have been that the atmosphere of the cattle market struck Joseph as humorous. He may well not have been deceived by the Emperor's new clothes. Or perhaps he stood still, rigid, not catatonic, but in a state of shock which could be mistaken for stolidity or spiritless docility.

His genius was to handle stone, to give life to inanimate materials, not primarily to manipulate men. As the commanding officer of the Janissary engineers, he learned how to do so. But it took him ten years of experience in discipline in training and in active warfare to demonstrate his special and individual abilities. Only then was he nominated "to Pass Through the Gate," fully equipped as a Janissary slave soldier.

So perhaps this tall and grave young man, who proved to have the gifts of powerful invention and imagination, was frightened as he stood still confronting the unknown. If so, under the handling, he concentrated on keeping his skin from twitching, to keep his hands from trembling, and knees from shaking as his bowels writhed like snakes under his belly muscles. Perhaps the officers smelled his fear and terror. This was the end of the voyage out of the past, and the beginning of the future. Bullock-like, he held himself together in an act of faith; he had nothing else to go on. After the pages, eyes flashing, left the field, stepping high, the remaining tribute youths in the majority closed ranks.

Joseph marched off; he concentrated on keeping in step with the others in the cadence. The Janissaries led them up the Divan Yolu (Road to the Council of State), into the Yenicheri Jaddesi (Street of the Janissaries), and down the last stretch of the road from the First to the Third Hills, until they reached the sprawling Janissary barracks. There, in his turn, Joseph finished his processing. It must have taken several days.

A Bektashi chaplain of the Janissary religious confraternity had the young man parrot a sentence of the Prophet's classical Arabic, which may have been translated for him. As he uttered the words, "There is no god but God, and Mohammed is the Prophet of God," Joseph abjured and denied the Christ of Greek Orthodoxy, to convert himself to Islam. Theoretically he was free to refuse, and there is some evidence to believe that his refusal would not have mattered very much. Probably he would have forfeited his promotion and remained a private until he was killed in action. If Joseph had hesitated, unable to get the words out, the Bektashi chaplain, chosen because of his benign wisdom, may have given the troubled young man a word or two of encouragement. His mystical and secret religious confraternity, later wholly identified with the Janissary corps, was not really the equivalent of the Roman Catholic militant order, the Society of Jesus. As the Jesuits used to be, as we say, reactionaries, so the Bektashis were liberal to the point of heresy. The dervishes of Islam are not monks who swear vows of obedience, chastity, and poverty. *Dervish* translates as "simple, contented, humble" and "poor man." These followers of the Pilgrim Haji Bektash chose to accept all gods and all Gods as God; and all prophets, philosophers, messiahs, and "messengers" as the Prophet – Adam, Moses, Abraham, Zoroaster, Buddha, Confucius, and even the Zen Masters and the Alid Imams, at one with Mohammed. Therefore, Joseph may have found it easy to say the words. As a man who did what he agreed to do, he lived and died a devout Muslim.

Having made his act of faith, Joseph moved on to the next step, to be circumcised. Nowhere in the Koran or in the Traditions did the Prophet make of this minor surgery an essential of Islam. The ceremony is now the approximation of a first communion. Circumcision came into the body of the Sacred Law as part of the *urf,* the custom of the country of Mohammed's birth. No one knows the origin of this ancient hygienic operation which smegma, accumulating in the hot desert landscapes, in itself sufficiently justifies.

A doctor-surgeon, who was perhaps likewise a Bektashi dervish as well as a Janissary of the medical corps, did the surgery swiftly and efficiently. And having given the new young Muslim the emblem of his manhood, he sent him on his way to be given a suitable new name.

In those days, as in the time of the Prophet, a Muslim's identity and his family tree were rooted in his name; his own, his father's. perhaps a most distinguished ancestor's, that of his clan and that of his tribe. Because there are but a limited number of first names, some men added the name of the place of their birth to the list. As the man grew older, shaped by his peculiarities, his experiences, and his achievements, he collected nicknames, designations, cognomens, and honorifics.

But the tribute youth was to be cut loose from all family ties and freed from his past. Orphaned, he joined the Sultan's Slave Family as a convert to Islam and as an adopted Son of Osman. The ordinary Janissary cadet was given a common Muslim name such as Mehmet; then for lack of a specific Muslim father, he was given the generic patronymic Abdullah. It means (Son of) "the Slave of God," perhaps in honor of the Prophet's father of the same name, who died before his son was born, or perhaps in reference to the Sultan, who prostrated himself only before God Almighty.

When Joseph's turn came, he was given an unusual name. The Janissary scribes may have run out of common names. Or it may be that the name is descriptive. Perhaps he stood up straight throughout his trials, his spine as stiff not as a ramrod but as a spear. Or, perhaps he had volunteered to go first into conversion and circumcision to show the young boys that they had nothing to fear. His conduct may have pleased the Bektashi chaplain and the surgeon. Greek men being notably well endowed, Joseph may have been renamed in stockyard or bullpen or barracking good humor. His name rhymes. He was registered as Sinan abdür-Mennan, "Spearhead the Son of the Slave of God the All-Giving." God had, and God has still, ninety-nine beautiful names.

In the proper columns of the Janissary ledger, the scribe wrote down Joseph's new name and the date of his conversion. A week or two later, Sinan and the other tribute youths were put up for auction. A Turkish country gentleman, perhaps an Ottoman feudal nobleman or a retired Janissary veteran, one of a group of privileged and (as we say) screened landowners, then bid for him. The man who got him paid a gold piece or two into the imperial treasury for the hire of the Sultan's new slave. The name of the landowner, the location of his country estate, the price paid, and the date of the transaction were then written into the Janissary ledger.

There must have been a set form filled in to spell out the precise terms of the contract signed in duplicate or triplicate by the landlord and, in the name of the Sultan, the Janissary master of the raw recruits. Then Sinan, along with his group of fellow slaves, was sent off to labor for his new lord and master. His name may have been Ibrahim Pasha. Fifty-one years later, in 1563, when Sinan was seventy-four, he applied for and received from the *Evkaf* of the Religious Institution a charter to build and to endow a pious foundation – a charitable institution including a small mosque, a school, an orphanage, and a public fountain. In this charter, one of the few authentic documents known to have been drawn up by Sinan when he was the Royal Chief Architect, he requested that his modest foundation be administered by the chief trustee of the much larger and wealthier pious foundations built and endowed by "the late Ibrahim Pasha." Sinan identified this Ibrahim Pasha (who may indeed have been the Grand Vezir and favorite, whom, later on, he served) only as his *"efendi* and *mu'tik"* – to the confusion of his biographers.

Efendi is easily translated as "master," but *mu'tik* is troublesome. In literal translation, the Arabic word means "emancipator, manumitter;" that does not make sense. In 1512, as a Christian tribute youth, Joseph could never have been a domestic slave, and therefore could not have been freed for subsequent collection, and thus re-enslaved. As an august Slave of the Gate of the Sultan's Household, Sinan, the general of the Janissary engineers, the commanding officer of the Sultan's own Chosen Guardsmen of Honor, and the Royal Chief Architect, never was, nor did he choose to be, manumitted. In Osmanlija, without the Arabic *ain,* a glottal consonant for which there is no equivalent in Turkish, *mu'tik* means "patron." Toward the end of his long life, looking back, Sinan told his friend and first biographer Nakkash Mustafa Saï that, after his collection and conversion, he next spent "some years" (on, it may have been, his temporary master and patron Ibrahim Pasha's estate) "in Anatolia." Apparently none of the details of this stage in his training struck him as worth remembering.

Yet these two or three years in Anatolia made up part of a wise and practical system of training for the Janissary Slave of the Gate. The newly collected tribute youth, put to hard labor at the work he knew best, was given time to get his full growth, to resign himself to slavery, to accept the will of God, and, in the Islamic order, to learn his place, his function, and his purpose as a member of the Ottoman Ruling Institution. Probably Sinan, a Greek from the high Anatolian plateau, already spoke Turkish, but otherwise he knew Islam only as the conqueror's religion, a foreign way of life. On the country estate, he began his education as a Muslim in a sort of preparatory school to enter the Janissary military academy. On his return from Anatolia, in Istanbul he was selected as an apprentice engineer.

Somewhere, at some time in his life, Sinan, the future town planner, builder of ramparts, and Royal Chief Architect, studied the buildings of the past. As the son of the village stonemason, he had worked with his father to repair the Byzantine walls and the Seljuk mosques and caravansaries of Kayseri, and, it may be, the Dulkadirli Turkish buildings of Elbistan and Marash. So, once again, it is possible and highly probable that he spent his "some years" in Anatolia on an estate near the ancient Greek and Roman cities along the southwestern coast of Asia Minor, Ephesus or Priene, or inland at Pergamum, called Bergama by the Turks, the town where "Holbein" carpets were made by Greek weavers. If so, then, like Brunelleschi, he may have measured the stones and the foundations of the ruined classic orders. Or if he worked on an estate near Bursa, the ancient city under Bithynian Olympus and the first capital of the early Sons of Osman, he may well have been called in to repair the tombs and the mosques of the earliest sultans built in what is now called the Bursa style of Ottoman architecture.

In fact there are two Bursa styles; Sinan, whenever he studied them, knew them both. He saw that the rectangular Ulu Jami, the Great Mosque begun by Murad I in 1379, was in its architecture like the Janissary slave army that he perfected, an arrangement suitable and pleasing to the military mind. Like a standing army, the four-square mosque is an assembly of identical entities. The basic unit of the small dome upheld by four masonry piers is multiplied so that the prayer hall could be extended in all four directions, if need be, like a body of soldiers on parade, to cover the world for Islam. As such, the enclosed space of the place of prostration, its outer rows of arches filled in by screen walls, serves its purpose, which is to protect the assembled worshipers from the inclement weather. But the massive piers standing at attention get in the way. The space of the prayer hall lacks the effortless infinite serenity of God's universe.

The later Bursa style made clear to Sinan, who had an eye for architectonics and who saw meaning in architecture, how far and how fast the Ottomans advanced in civilization as they pushed the frontiers of their empire both to the east and to the west. The Yeshil Jami, built by Mehmet the Gentleman in 1421, is an elegant mosque. The frames of the door and the windows in the rectangular walls of white marble, carved with calligraphic inscriptions and arabesques, place the architecture in the Seljuk and Persian traditions of Islam. But the interior is arranged in a new and purely Ottoman concept of space.

Built upon a T-shaped floor plan and roofed accordingly by domes of various dimensions, the unit of the central square, enlarged, freed of pillars and piers, and centered upon a fountain, was opened on three sides by means of high arches — with the portal in the façade on the fourth side. Through the arches, the architect then extended the central space by means of three square chambers, like deep stages raised above the floor level of the original square unit. The prayer niche that points the direction of Mecca to the southeast stands in the kibla wall at the base of the T.

Sinan, who gave unity to the assembled elements of Ottoman architecture, saw that the fault of this plan in the Yeshil Jami is a lack of coherence. The space flows through the mosque, but again the various parts do not quite merge to form an indivisible whole.

The prayer niche and the interior walls of the Green Mosque, which is what Yeshil Jami means, are framed and surfaced with green enameled tiles of faience arabesqued with gold in the Persian style. And whether the tiles were fired in the kilns of Tabriz or of Iznik, they are (almost certainly) the work of Persian artisans. It may have been that Sinan spent his three years "in Anatolia" not in Bursa but on an estate near Iznik – the Nicaea of the Creed – then as now a quiet walled town on a lake in a placid landscape of dairy farms and poplar trees. If so, in 1515, after Selim the Grim's conquest of Tabriz, Sinan may have witnessed the arrival of the five hundred Persian potters and their families, part of the Sultan's plunder sent back from the northern capital of the defeated Shah of Persia and settled in Iznik.

During the next three generations, these potters produced the incomparable faience that decorates the mosques of the late sixteenth and early seventeenth centuries. In the fifty years of his life spent as Royal Chief Architect, Sinan worked with the designers, the enamelers, and the glazers who fired calligraphic and floral tiles to line the imperial tombs and to face the prayer niches and the kibla walls of his great prayer halls. The potters of Iznik brought their arts to perfection at the time that Sinan reached his fullest achievement, in 1570; they and their work survived him by only twenty-one or twenty-two years. After 1620 the tiles of Iznik declined in quality. In his three years in Anatolia, if Sinan worked on an estate near Iznik, he could have learned the principles of the craft and the art of the Persian and the Ottoman tilemakers. In 1515 he might have helped to lay the bricks to build the kilns. Three hundred and fifty worked full blast to fill his orders in 1575; not one kiln is left today. The secrets of the bolus red, the dark blue, the turquoise, and the emerald enamels, and of the glaze as clear as spring water, are now lost.

Wherever he was put to work to build walls and to plough fields, Sinan unearthed fragments of the past. Each spring in the green fields of these ancient landscapes scattered with broken marbles, stretching inland from the classic shores of the Aegean Sea, crimson anemones, cup-shaped flowers called the blood of Adonis and of Our Lord, bloom through the fingers of young hands lying in the grass. As he dug his foundations and quarried the ruins for building stone, Sinan (as young men still do, so he may have) discovered the heads and torsos of beheaded gods and heroes and perhaps a Tanagra goddess. Now and again he came upon coins of bronze, or blackened silver, and of astonishingly bright gold, some minted with the profile of Hercules or of Alexander on the obverse, and on the reverse, a palladium—a wingèd victory, an owl, Zeus with his eagle—surrounded by lettering that he could read. So he learned the feel and the shapes and the sizes of his inheritance; so he found his place inside the duties expected of him within his own lifetime.

As Royal Chief Architect for Sultan Süleyman the Magnificent and for his son Selim the Sot, the collected and converted Greek slave orchestrated all the arts of Islam and put the various craftsmen and artisans to work to build and to adorn his mosques. He knew the potters of Iznik, the carpet weavers of Bergama and Ushak, the stainers of glass for the floral windows, the carvers of marble, the workers in *opus sectile*, the inlayers of wood for the doors and window shutters, the cabinetmakers and carpenters, the blacksmiths of wrought iron, the founders and gilders of bronze hardware, the painters and the calligraphers; and they knew him. Somewhere, at some time, he began his own education and training in the Islamic, the Byzantine Christian, the pagan Roman, Hellenistic, Greek, and the prehistoric artifacts of his inheritance.

In his lifetime of ninety-nine years, he taught himself all these crafts and trades as well as gardening and town planning, the art and the science of war and engineering, and, of course, how to build.

But by the end of 1515, according to the terms of the contract, Sinan's first master and patron, the Turkish landowner, returned the Sultan's slave to the Janissary barracks in Istanbul along with an efficiency and a training report properly filled in. After a cursory examination of the slave, the Janissary registrar gave the landowner a receipt for Sinan. Master and slave did not shake hands. The Turks bow to salute their elders, and with the right hand make a gesture to touch the forehead, the chest above the heart, and then to point to the earth underfoot. Sinan then kissed the hand of his first patron, who went off to select another lot of freshly collected tribute youths.

Sinan, aged twenty-five or twenty-six then, was carefully examined. He may have been asked which branch of the service he chose to join. Certainly his preparation, his aptitude, and his preference indicated the Zemberekji regiment, the fire handlers, the miners and sappers, the engineers at that time, as we say, being beefed up in preparation for Selim the Grim's new methods of total warfare. Historians all agree that the three greatest of the Ottoman sultans were Mehmet the Conqueror, his grandson Selim I, the Grim, and his son Süleyman the Magnificent; of the three, Selim I was the greatest general, a military genius. According to Sinan's own legend, he was assigned to the Janissary training school in the Palace of Ibrahim Pasha, the favorite and the future Grand Vezir in the early years of Sultan Süleyman's long reign.

4

In the summer of 1512, at the time that Sinan was farmed out to an Ottoman landowner of Anatolia, Selim the Grim installed his eldest son, Süleyman the Shehzadé, five years younger than Sinan, in Manisa, the capital of his own principality of Sarukhan.

Sultan Murad II, the new Prince Imperial's great-great-grandfather, a mystic, a poet, and a mild voluptuary, as well as a conquering hero of Islam, built the royal palaces of Manisa on a terraced green hill outside of the town under the pine forests of the mountain and above the fertile plain. The palaces were bright pavilions set in a high walled garden planted to fruit trees and shade trees, open to the breezes from the pine woods and the Aegean Sea.

Mountain springs and streams (the Greeks called them Niobe's tears) flowed through the gardens over cascades of carved marble along flower beds of roses and carnations, and rippled into pools where water lilies bloomed. The Lady Nilufer, Water Lily, was the name of the Shehzadé's five times great-grandmother, a beautiful Greek heiress of the Castle on the Cliff, who came down to marry Orhan Khan the Golden in the earliest love story of the Sons of Osman.

Tulips, anemones, narcissus, and asphodel grow wild there. In early spring the nightingales sing in the pink and white clouds of the Judas trees. In summer sunshine the figs and the grapes ripen in the salt sea winds from the west. In the nights of velvet skies, the stars hang down almost within the reach of any tall young man of seventeen.

Süleyman at seventeen was fully grown. He was physically in as good shape as any of his blooded Cappadocian horses from the imperial stables, and as well broken to the saddle and the bridle. In his training and education, he had been thoroughly prepared to organize and administer his principality, no bigger than a toy. For the past ten years – for his entire life – he had carried his share of the weight of his father's and his mother's calculations to survive. Having survived his father Selim the Grim's violent seizure of power, suddenly at peace in Manisa, Süleyman the Heir Apparent was free to do as he saw fit.

His father the Sultan's secret agents sent in satisfactory reports upon the Shehzadé's conduct. The *lala*, his tutor, sent along as his adviser, smiled upon him. The veteran Janissaries attached to his bodyguard did not smile in his presence; but they looked upon him with benign approval, which they showed him in the way they snapped smartly to attention as he passed by and in the alacrity and deference with which they carried out the trivial routine of the miniature court. They knew and he knew that all of them might as well have been playing at war games with lead soldiers. Selim the Grim had usurped the throne in Istanbul from his ill and aging father Bayazid the Pious. The defenses of the empire were once again in good hands. God was Great.

The two ladies of the Shehzadé's model harem were Circassian slave girls even younger than he. Like him, they had been born and bred to the purpose. Their parents had brought them up on what amounted to slave ranches in the mountains of Georgia and, with the bloom of first youth on them, had taken them to the Crimea for sale. There in the famous slave market of Kaffa, Gülfem and Gülbahar, as they were called, caught the discriminating eye of Prince Süleyman's mother, the Lady Hafisa. Not a slave but an Ottoman lady, the mother of all Selim the Grim's children, the Lady Hafisa is remembered for her beauty and her intelligence.

The two Circassian girls, Rosebud Lips and Rose of Spring, were ready-made, so to speak, for their lives in the harem. Because of a crisis in his schedule to seize the throne from his father, Selim the Grim could not give the Lady Hafisa time to prepare the slave girls properly for their fifteen-year-old husband. Therefore they lacked education. But all went well. Two years later in Manisa they were fully occupied with conceiving, gestating, bringing forth, and caring for the infant son and the daughter or two that the Prince Imperial by the age of seventeen years and six or seven months had bred upon them.

They wore charming clothes. The Shehzadé gave them delightful jewels for their ears and their hair – perhaps a floral pin, a spray of rose diamonds and gold that he had made during his apprenticeship to the Greek goldsmith in Trebizond where he was born. Later, when he succeeded to the throne, Sultan Süleyman graciously was pleased to add the honorary presidency of the Goldsmiths' Guild to the titles of the Emperor of the East.

According to the poets, these two Circassians were as graceful as palm trees; according to their names, they were as lovely as roses opening in their moment of springtime. But they were very young. Full of life but empty-headed, they chattered and they giggled. Prince Süleyman smiled and left their woman's world for a little peace and quiet.

None in his man's world could find fault with his conduct, not even he himself; he was a serious young man. In May and June of 1512, Süleyman the Shehzadé in his admirably operating miniature court of Manisa did not know what to do with himself. He strolled through the gardens by the splashing fountains and stopped to pluck a rose. In his old age, gray-bearded, leaden of complexion, somber of countenance, but still lean and straight, Süleyman posed for a court painter. In the miniature he strolls alone in a garden by night, two stylized Pages of the Privy Chamber, one the young Sword Bearer, the other perhaps an Usher, silently pacing behind the solitary man. The Sultan wore a long kaftan of powder blue trimmed with ermine, an immaculate white turban wound high around a fluted cone of dark red felt, a black plume thrust into the folds (the turban apparently fascinated the miniaturist). Süleyman had plucked what appears to be a sprig of fruit blossom to carry in his left hand; in his right, he holds a long white handkerchief. In Manisa, aged seventeen, perhaps having plucked an opening rosebud, he held it to his nose, snapped the tender stalk in his fingers, and tossed it aside.

It may have been that he strode into the library to take comfort from old friends. Murad the Mystic had made a collection of the philosophers of Islam. Süleyman ran his fingers over the sumptuous bindings, and took down Nizam ul-Mulk's *Book of Government.* In his hands the illuminated manuscript, neglected by the Seljuk sultans but studied by the Sons of Osman, fell open upon the pages reading, "Paradise and sovereignty are never united. . . . The responsibilities of sovereigns are so terrible that the good life is all but unattainable to them." He flipped the pages.

"A king cannot do without suitable boon companions with whom he can enjoy complete freedom and intimacy. . . . Officers should always be in a state of fear of the king, while boon companions need to be familiar, . . . they are company for the king. . . . They are with him day and night, bodyguards. . . . If any danger (we take refuge in Allah!) should appear, they will not hesitate to shield the king from it with their own lives. . . . The king can say thousands of different things, frivolous and serious, to his boon companion," that are unsuitable to the ears of vezirs and tutors; ". . . and from his boon companions . . . all sorts of sundry tidings can be heard . . . good and bad. . . .

"A boon companion should be well bred, accomplished, and of cheerful face. He should have pure faith, be able to keep secrets, and wear good clothes. He must possess an ample fund of stories and strange tales both amusing and serious, and be able to tell them well. He must be a good talker and a pleasant partner; he should know how to play backgammon and chess, and if he can play a musical instrument and use a weapon, so much the better. He must always agree with the king, and whatever the king says or does, he must exclaim, 'Bravo!' and 'Well done!' He should not be didactic —"

Süleyman shut the book; smiling, it may be, wryly, he thought of his father and his abject, drunken boon companions. Poets they were but they behaved like buffoons. His father reduced them to pets; he teased them and he cuffed them – in truth, as he had not his son. Such boon companions were not for him; but the idea of companionship was sound. Süleyman sat back to think about it. Who among the young men of his own age . . . ? There were none.

He got up and searched the shelves for his old friend Kai Kaus, a much more practical and much more cynical adviser than the noble Nizam ul-Mulk. *A Mirror for Princes* makes cheerful reading as the austere *Book of Government* does not. Kai Kaus was a tolerant old man. A great sinner, he comfortably expected the worst of every human being. In the way of the world, he took for granted that no man was either perfect or perfectible. But on the subject of "The Function of the Boon Companion," Süleyman was glad to find that the easy going Persian Prince, dead and buried five centuries, in general agreed with the unequaled vezir Nizam ul-Mulk, dead almost as long. The Shehzadé decided that his boon companion could not very well be a man of princely family. He envied his ancestor Orhan the Golden, who had a friend in his brother Alaettin Ali, and another in Jandarli Halil "the Black." Osman, the founder of the dynasty, had made a convert and a friend of the Byzantine Greek Michael of the Forked Beard. Those days had gone by; better not look for an Ottoman, nor indeed a free man. Then a slave . . . .

Süleyman opened Kai Kaus to read over the chapter on "The Purchase of Slaves." He skipped through the general information on the science and the art of physiognomy. "The slave suited to play musical instruments is marked out by being soft-fleshed (though his flesh must not be overabundant, especially on the back), with his fingers slender, neither lean nor fat. (A slave whose face is over fleshly, incidentally, is one incapable of learning.) His hands must be soft, with the middle of his fingers lengthy. He must be bright-visaged, having the skin tight; his hair must not be too long, too short, or too black. It is better, also, for the soles of the feet to be regular. A slave of this kind will swiftly acquire a delicate art of whatever kind, particularly that of the instrumentalist."

He skipped; his eye fell on another passage. "Never buy a slave who has been treated with affection in another place. If you do not hold him dear, he will show ingratitude to you, or will flee, . . . or will nourish hatred in his heart for you. Even if you regard him with affection, he will show you no gratitude, . . ." And so on. The old man grew tedious. Süleyman flipped through to find the chapter "On Taking One's Pleasure," that always made him smile.

"Let it be clear to you, my son, that if you fall in love with a person, you should not indiscriminately and whether drunk or sober indulge in sexual congress. . . . Do not indulge each time the thought occurs to you; that is the behaviour of beasts, who know not the season for any action but act as they find occasion. A man, for his part, should select the proper season and thus preserve the distinction between himself and the beasts.

"As between women and youths, do not confine your inclinations to either sex; thus you may find enjoyment from both kinds without either of the two becoming inimical to you. . . . During the summer let your desires incline towards youths and during the winter towards women. But on this topic it is requisite that one's discourse should be brief, lest it engender appetite."

Süleyman slapped the manuscript together and fastened the flap of the leather binding. He picked up a volume of *The Arabian Nights' Entertainments.*

The full moon had risen over the walls of the garden. The young man put down the books. He got up and went out of the library. In his dressing room, he threw off his imperial robes and put on mufti. Like Harun al-Rashid, Caliph of Baghdad, he walked through his own private gate in the walls of the palace compound, shut the door, and locked it behind him. Perhaps he pocketed the key; it may be that he reached up to hide it in a crevice between the stones. For the rest of his long life, fifty-four years, Sultan Süleyman made a practice of leaving the palace to walk the streets of his capital, incognito, so to keep an eye on things and to listen to what the townspeople had to say. But he never again went out alone. After 1536, he chose a few Janissaries or a senior page or two; he had them lay aside their uniforms to dress like ordinary men, as he was dressed. By then he knew that he could never walk alone; he had no right to risk his life. And it was unwise to rouse the palace and to set rumors and alarms flying through the courtyards and the corridors.

But this first time, as he stepped into the unfamiliar reality of unremarkable existence, he may have thought that he had successfully left himself behind him. He was six feet tall, and although lean and well made, his back had not been shaped by stooping to lift blocks of stone to fit in place on top of rising walls. His shoulders and arms had not been muscled by felling trees and hewing timbers, but instead by pulling bowstrings and hurling lances into targets. His chest and legs had not filled out in high mountain snow. His hands were strong from gripping the hafts of swords. He could wrestle with the best men of his own age and weight, but he could not plough a straight furrow. This was a young man marked not by the seasons but by the habit of obedience. He carried himself like a command; but his high-arched feet stumbled on the path. In his ignorance and innocence, he looked at everything he saw as though it had just been minted for him.

Down the hillside and into the town he walked in the moonlight. The moment of spring in the ancient Mediterranean landscape is bewilderingly powerful. Whoever saw him recognized him. He was the stranger. They were used to princes, and they lay still until he passed. If he saw them, he knew better than to greet them. He spoke Demotika, the Greek of Trebizond, better than he spoke the Turkish dialect of his principality – he spoke Osmanlija, the language of the court. He spoke the Persian of the poetry and the Arabic of the Koran. He knew only whatever he had been given to know for his imperial preparation to survive, but he had no common knowledge. He was unused . . . to walking down a flowering hillside path alone.

At the edge of the town he heard a violin. All the Sons of Osman were poets; he had inherited his ear for music. Turkish music progresses geometrically. Until the last years of his life, Süleyman surrounded himself in his very few free hours with music. Then, toward the end, some busybody of a Muslim seeress bustled in upon his solitude to lecture the Sultan upon his wickedness of self-indulgence. He listened quietly to the sibylline fury, and he smashed the long-necked lutes inlaid with tortoiseshell and ivory, broke the violins and bows, and burnt them. The old woman wanted more austerity. She pointed to his ewers and basins of gold and silver inset with turquoises and corals and to the cups cut from single hollowed emeralds. She rose to smash the Chinese celadons and the cobalt-blue and white porcelains, but he restrained her. She had to be satisfied with replacements of earthenware and pewter.

In his youth in Manisa, Süleyman stopped in the shadows below the open window of a candle-lit room high up in a prosperous house on the outskirts of town. It was good music, very well played. He could not see the player in the room on the top floor, projecting on brackets over the cobblestoned street and the high walled gardens. He watched the shadows of the arm and bow and the fingered violin move across the ceiling painted in arabesques centering upon a carved and gilt multifoliate rose.

On the street, the wide front door was closed and barred in the dark, as were the few small windows, iron-grilled and wooden-shuttered. On the floor above, under the brackets, the bigger windows were dark behind carved wooden screens. The prince did not see her, but one of the privileged slave women of the house sat in an open window behind a lattice that bulged out like an aviary. She had her elbows resting comfortably on a cushion on the sill. Pots of sweet basil and carnations grew and bloomed on a shelf below her. Caged birds, silent in the night, hung from hooks in the corners. She looked down into his face as he looked up, rapt by the arabesques drawn from the bowed strings.

The invisible old slave woman knew at once that he was the young Shehzadé from the palace, come down out of his boredom to stand listening, and she knew why. She must have smiled (if it happened like this) and inched away from the window, backing into the dark room, feeling for the squeaking floorboard with her toes, to do something about it. She knew all that passed in the town of Manisa and she knew at once what to do.

This was an act of Providence. The time had come to free her mistress, the wealthy woman of Manisa, from her Greek slave. He had served to amuse her after the death of her good man. All the sons and daughters of the household had married, and married well, and had gone off about their business. The widow found herself alone with nothing to do. Now the town had begun to gossip most disagreeably about the good lady; her darling boy, her toy, had grown up to be a disturbingly handsome young man. Ibrahim was sixteen going on seventeen.

In fact, Ibrahim was exactly a year younger than Süleyman, born the same day, November 6, the one in Trebizond in 1494, the other in Parga in 1495, the one on the shores of the Black Sea, the Kara Deniz, the other on the White Sea, Ak Deniz, which is what the Turks call the Mediterranean. The widow may have come back from a visit to her married daughter or her son in Izmir, which is Smyrna, on the coast of the Aegean. The climate there can be langorous in the summer heat. Wherever and however it happened, she purchased a slave, a boy of twelve or thirteen, caught by the corsairs while he was out swimming on the beach of Parga. It is still a beautiful beach on the mainland across from Corfu; the fishing village still is there; the fishermen still have sons like Ibrahim on the beach.

To give him his due, Melek Ibrahim was at the age of twelve or thirteen as beautiful as an angel, but he had the wisdom of a limb of Satan! And no wonder. The old slave woman had been a slave girl and a virgin once, herself. She knew what everybody knows, which was that handsome boys, unlike lovely girls, have no hymens to keep intact, demonstrable for warranted virginity, to fetch the highest prices in the bargaining in the slave market.

All the town, as the old slave woman knew, watched and tittered and gossiped, waiting for the inevitable freeing of the young slave as the first step in a most unsuitable, barely legal, marriage with his benefactress. The widow lavished affection upon the Greek slave boy. She had him washed and scrubbed, and properly circumcised and converted. She brought in imams and learned men to tutor him; she gave him an education fit for a prince, in all the liberal arts and sciences. She herself corrected his manners and taught him etiquette. She dressed him like a doll in Persian silks, Chinese brocades, Milanese cut velvets, stuffs in the brightest, truest dyes from Bursa, cut and tailored in the latest styles. She brought in music teachers. Ibrahim was talented. He had the gift, it must be said. He studied hard. He played beautifully. And he had the temperament. Ah, these passionate Greeks! The old slave woman smiled, remembering in the dark her own youth. There is no comparison! As all the old women of the town knew only too well.

The other slave women, veiled and covered in black, passing in the street below this very open window on their way to market and back again, their baskets full of fruit and vegetables, stopped for a moment to pass the time of day. They chatted. They knew. She knew what was bound to happen next. All the widow's friends, the good Muslim ladies of Manisa, were up in arms. It is all very well to amuse oneself, but at her age (she may have been forty) it is scandalous. She knew no better than to do it practically in the streets. She was besotted! She might as well have danced around him in the village square. It amounted to idolatry. The young men snickered. The old men shook their heads.

However it happened, it happened. The widow either gave or sold Ibrahim, the skillful violinist, to the Shehzadé, if not that first evening, then in negotiations through the proper channels. The new favorite at sixteen and a half was short in stature but well made. Quick in all his reflexes, he was feline in character. Süleyman later called him, after the brilliant victory of Mohács in 1525, "the leopard in the forest of courage"; it was a figure of speech in Osmanlija. His curling hair was thick and dark, not on his head, which was shaved, but in his beard. He had flashing dark eyes, long and narrow rather than round, heavily lashed under arching eyebrows. His skin was as brown and as smooth as an egg. His face was oval, his chin pointed (the Austrian and Venetian ambassadors filled their reports with detailed description of this favorite with whom, later, they had to contend). He was gap-toothed, his white teeth as sharp as the lower jaw of an undomesticated animal. As prescribed by Kai Kaus, his fingers were long and slender, the soles of his feet were smooth and narrow; his flesh was firm but not soft, and he had no fat on his back.

At first sight of Ibrahim, the palace tutor must have raised his eyebrows. This was no proper boon companion for the Shehzadé. The Janissaries and the gentlemen-in-waiting must have kept their faces straight in front of their Prince Imperial, but behind his back, they surely winked at one another as the corners of their lips turned up. In the kitchens the domestic slave men must have slapped their thighs and guffawed under the covering clatter of pots and pans. The masculine merriment was designed to reach the favorite's ears. He was Greek. Greeks are flexible. They have to be in order to survive. But Greek honor can not put up with ridicule.

Beside the fountains of Manisa Ibrahim the Favorite and Süleyman the Shehzadé swore an oath of eternal fealty. The one swore to the other not to separate himself from the person of the other while he lived. The Greek slave knew what he was doing. Sultan Süleyman knew only what he had done when he transgressed, and then did his best to transcend, the Household rules of the Slaves of the Gate and the Sacred Law confining the boon companion to his idle hours.

In those first two years of his first friendship in his first freedom, Süleyman must have enjoyed himself. He and Ibrahim went down to the

Aegean Sea to swim together – or so it seems possible and wholly probable and reasonable in imagination to suppose. They both knew how to swim from their childhoods spent along the Black and White Sea shores. But the Prince Imperial had all the manual of arms to teach his boon companion: how to grip in the left hand the famous Turkish bow of laminated horn, lacquered and painted with floral patterns, and shaped when strung like the outline of the upper lip of Cupid, and like love's own bow. He taught him how to pull the silken bowstring back to his ear, to release the feathered arrow to hit a target no bigger than a hand mirror. He taught him horsemanship, the dressage of the *haute école*: how to ride, how to grip the Cappadocian stallion with his knees, the gentled high-spirited animal at one with the man, equally sensitive, equally well trained. He taught him how to get into the leather breeches tight from below the kneecap to the hipbone; and how to oil their naked torsos and arms to wrestle together on the grass of the iron ground.

In the evenings they read history in the pavilion library of Murad the Mystic, the epics of the champions and heroes of Islam, of the Bible and of Greece and Rome as well as all the philosophers and the lyricists. Together they studied astrology and the other sciences and worked out the patterns of Euclidean perfection. Best of all, the one played the violin while the other listened. Soon the Shehzadé began to read the dispatches of official business from the Imperial Court in Istanbul out loud to Ibrahim, and to talk things over. Historically, there is no question of Ibrahim's breadth and depth of understanding, nor of his brilliance as an administrator.

In the summer of 1514, the two young men, nineteen and eighteen, went together to Edirné to share the regency to which Selim the Grim appointed Süleyman for the duration of the Persian campaign. Side by side they worked in the hunting palace on the island in the Tunja River. It was here that Süleyman received and read the dispatch from his father at winter quarters in Amasya, giving him the intelligence of his three younger brothers' death by bowstring in the hands of their father's mutes. Or it may have been more horrible in that the news came from their mother, the Lady Hafisa. She was the new Validé Sultan – "the Imperial Mother;" she was the only woman whose official title was recognized and respected by the Slaves of the Gate and the freemen of the Ulema, telling her only living son that all her other sons had been put to death in the New Palace, where they had been left to complete their studies in the care of their tutors. It seems likely that, although they lay side by side by night, Süleyman and Ibrahim did not sleep; perhaps they talked. In 1515, for the summer and the next few years, they went back together to Manisa, sobered.

No one knows, and will not until the archives in Istanbul have been explored, and even then it may not be discovered, when Sinan met the other two young men whose lives shaped his. But it seems likely that by 1516 they had met. At this time Selim the Grim with all his government and his armies, and with his Grand Mufti and the Ulema, were away from Istanbul on campaign in Syria and Egypt, and the Shehzadé was called upon to act as regent. Only the inexperienced Janissary cadets, one of whom might have been Sinan, no more than at most ten thousand, were left behind to guard the walled city on the Golden Horn, and Edirné and Manisa, too.

As regent, the Shehzadé Süleyman, aged twenty-five in 1519, was kept informed of his father's plans. As an essential part of his global strategy, Selim the Grim had cleared the way for his only surviving son's immediate take-over of the total power. Once in possession of the throne, Sultan Süleyman was prepared to carry on without delay, so to fulfill the function and the purpose of the Turkish leadership in Islam. Had either Selim the Grim or Süleyman the Magnificent succeeded, he literally and legally would have entered into the possession of the world as his imperial and private estate.

The period of transition between the death of the Sultan and the arrival in Istanbul of the successful contender to the throne usually was a time of chaos. Of all the sultans, the Shehzadé Süleyman of Manisa had the least trouble. It took three days for the couriers to reach him with the news of his father's death, and another three days for him to make the journey across western Anatolia and the Sea of Marmara. An imperial barge brought him and Ibrahim to the sea walls; the sea gate to the New Palace was locked and barred to him; his own Bostanjis (the Gatekeepers) and the other Janissaries refused to let him in. He was prepared to meet their demands.

Having shouted, "Our Padishah is dead!" and mourned, the Slave Soldiers of the Gate, free in the interregnum, seized the palace at Istanbul and barricaded the gate, of which they were mementarily no longer the slave soldiers of the Sultan's household. Before they unlocked the gate to shout, "Long live our Padishah!" the Janissaries demanded key money, or bakshish; in the polite term, donative. The new Sultan had to purchase their loyalty. The slave soldiers sold themselves back into slavery either to the highest bidder among the dead Sultan's sons, or to their own chosen prince, but always for a high price. Such had been the case with Selim the Grim. As a younger son, without their active help he could not have usurped his father's throne and driven the aged Bayazid the Pious to his death in exile. Therefore his generosity taught the Janissaries their own power and worth. For his son, to whom, for lack of living brothers, the law of fratricide could not apply, they raised the price. Süleyman had no choice; he could not bargain with the Janissaries.

Because Selim the Grim's death came slowly in pain, it seems probable that the father and the son had set aside the enormous sum of money and had made all other arrangements for a peaceful succession well in advance. They had, for instance, set up a series of posts with relays of fast horses for the couriers between Istanbul and Manisa. Then, having calculated his risks, Selim the Grim refused to be hurried in his plans, which by then included his own death. He knew the future of the empire to be in safe hands. Therefore, slowly and carefully, he built up the strength of his powerful new Ottoman fleet the while the cancer fulminated in his thigh.

The smell of death is sobering. In his miniature court at Manisa within the walled gardens as beautiful as Paradise, Süleyman thought of his father. He was, as a man and as the Sultan, a monster of cruelty, but a monster of steadfast courage and resolve. He had done his best for his son and then had let him alone to lead his own life as the Shehzadé. When the matter of his son's admiration (it is the word in the Koran) for the Greek slave Ibrahim was delicately and tactfully brought to his attention, he probably guffawed and said, brushing the trivial extravagance aside, "So long as he does not allow his slave to fiddle with the privy purse strings . . ." and got on with the business in hand, which was to secure and to rule the most powerful empire on earth. The father, who had written Persian poetry to a youth, silvery-skinned in moonlight, knew that death and maturity bring young men into line.

In his apprenticeship in Manisa, Süleyman no longer played the Oriental potentate. He had enjoyed his six or seven years on the horizons of his father's absolute power. But as the cancer spreading in his father's thigh brought him closer to the throne, Süleyman began to weary of his fading roses, Gülfem and Gülbahar. His favorite was a quick and subtle man who saw the way the wind had changed. It is not certain when the Lady Hafisa put out her hand to regulate her son's private life, then in turmoil.

By 1519, the year before Selim the Grim got down from his horse and died on the road, the two Circassian Roses had borne three sons and at least two daughters to the Prince Imperial. In the harem of Manisa, while he amused himself in his man's world, he had done his sacred and dynastic duty, but with a certain lack of enthusiasm. Even so, the Lady Gülfem's sons Mahmud Sultan, born in 1512, and Murad Sultan, born in 1515, (both princes died young; so did their mother) and the Lady Gülbahar's only son Mustafa Sultan, born in 1515, gave ample proof of their sire's virility. The boys were splendid Sons of Osman. But the Greek slave favorite Ibrahim's ascendancy may well have begun to trouble his hardheaded father and his wise mother.

Therefore it may be that, soon after he had been girt with the Sword of Osman and the Sword of the Prophet, the new Validé Sultan spoke gently to her son, say, early in October of 1520. Sultan Süleyman had brought Ibrahim with him from Manisa to Istanbul. The Greek slave was not a Slave of the Gate. He had not been put through the disciplines of either the palace school for pages or the training schools for Janissary cadets. He ought not, by all the rules according to the books, have straddled the Sultan's two lives, the public and the private. Süleyman broke the rules to regularize Ibrahim's status. He appointed him Chief Falconer, first among the Sultan's thirty-nine gentlemen-in-waiting, and made him chief of the pages of the palace.

It was unwise; as things worked out, it would have been kinder to have thrown Ibrahim into the pool of Slaves of the Gate, to let him sink or swim according to his own merits. He was only twenty-five; the Ottoman system was still flexible enough to have taken in a young man of such unusual capacities. In historic fact, Ibrahim made an excellent Grand Vezir. Quick of intellect, he was broad-minded; he was a gifted administrator. But the young Sultan's unseemly behavior caused the elder Slaves of the Gate to regret the death of Selim the Grim, whom they called Selim the Just, and whose embalmed body still awaited proper burial in the unfinished mausoleum. On trial, the rash act of the new Sultan gave the wise men of the Ulema and the grandees of the Slave Household cause for alarm. There was but one person capable of remonstrance.

The young Sultan honored and respected the only human being whom wholeheartedly he could trust, his mother the Lady Hafisa. He listened to her. But not even the Validé Sultan had the power to leave her realm, the imperial harem, to enter her son's man's world, in which the favorite Ibrahim was at home. Therefore, she chose not to appeal to her son's head but instead to his heart.

There is reason to believe that she had foreseen the difficulties. Back in the Crimea when Süleyman was fifteen, his mother had chosen three slave girls for her son's harem. It was imperative that he prove himself as a potent and fertile Son of Osman. Therefore, she gave him the two Circassian Roses. But the third girl, this one no more than eleven or twelve years old, the Lady Hafisa kept by her in the Old Palace throughout the eight years of her son's freedom in Manisa and her own husband's grim and violent short reign. She got to know the girl and named her Hürrem, the Joyous One. The Venetian bailiffs and the Viennese ambassadors, not knowing her forbidden name in the imperial harem, described her at hearsay in their secret reports as *la Rossa*, the Russian Redhead, which was twisted into Roxelane in Italian and Roxane in French.

The daughter of a Russian priest, captured by Tartar raiders on the banks of the Don, Hürrem never came wholly to terms with servitude. She proved to be any man's equal in brains, in courage, and in strength of character. In high spirits she was unmatched. As a mother in the defense of her young, she was unscrupulous and she was fierce when the needs arose. Once she had understood the conditions imposed upon her as a slave and a woman in the forbidden enclosure within the man's world, she paid no attention to the rules except to break them. She was a realist. It is impossible to know whether or not she loved her husband. She made his life her life. In the imperial harem, during the seven or eight years after her purchase in the Crimean slave market of Kaffa, she was gentled, she was disciplined, she was educated, but she was not brought to heel.

The Fortunates, slave girls called Ikbals, candidates to receive the imperial sperm and to bear the Sons of Osman, were as rigorously instructed and educated as were the cadets of the Janissary corps to win Holy Wars and the pages of the palace school to command and to administer the empire. They were the female Slaves of the Gate, but they were trained to a different purpose, which was to please in private. They won (or lost) their battles alone behind the locked gates of the imperial harem.

To catch the eye of the Sultan, the Ikbals were put through courses of domestic science, but all these lovely girls were also highly educated. Only one of them, it is true, as the fortunate Validé Sultan after the death of her husband, would come into real power as the executrix of the imperial harem for her son the new Sultan. But none knew on which of the Ikbals' foreheads God had written her good fortune. Therefore, each slave girl had to be prepared in all the applicable disciplines from needlework and cookery – the Ottoman embroideries are unsurpassed, the Ottoman cuisine ranks with the Chinese and the French – to ciphering the higher mathematics.

Like Scheherazadé, she earned her rank of Haseki (which means, having borne a son, that she was "Chosen") as a royal entertainer; therefore, she had to know how to dance, how to sing, how to play the lute. She had to know Islamic literature and history as well as what we call philosophy and psychology. As a specialist, she was taught all the arts and the techniques of love. She was put through all the courses of what we call finishing schools. She was taught the values of things, the worth of sables, of musk and ambergris, of silken stuffs and jewels, how to bargain in the markets, and how to dress and to undress.

So Hürrem spent the first few years in self-analysis. Coldly she stood in front of the glass, and through wide-open eyes as clear and as hard as sapphires she saw a thoughtful and elegant young woman. She took stock of her points, both the good and the bad, and came to the conclusion that the value of the Sultan's blade lay not in its emerald haft, a single polished hexagonal crystal, nor in its sheath of gold enameled in pink roses and set with faceted Golconda diamonds, but in the temper of its pointed steel honed to a delicately lethal cutting edge. Her wit was the choice weapon in her armament, not the ephemeral fashion of the flesh. She was a career woman, a specialist; she concentrated her course of study upon a single man. Wisely she began to cultivate his mother, the serene and powerful Lady Hafisa, a woman who had learned how to keep her counsel. She survived.

In tracing Hürrem's rise out of six or seven years of obscurity inside the imperial harem, to take first place in rank after the Imperial Mother Hafisa,

1. Aghirnas in 1965; Sinan's birthplace, renamed in his honor Mimar-
sinanköy, the "Village of the Architect Sinan."

2. Sinan's first imperial commission as Royal Chief Architect for Sultan
Süleyman the Magnificent, the pious foundation built in 1538 for Haseki
Hürrem.

3. The *hamam* – Turkish bath – of Ayasofya built for Haseki Hürrem in
1556.

4. The memorial for Shehzadé Mehmet, Hürrem's and Süleyman's first son, who died a natural death, aged twenty-two, in 1543. The first of Sinan's three Imperial Friday Mosques, built between 1444 and 1448. In his old age, Sinan called the Shehzadé mosque the work of an apprentice. To me the mosque, as large as a cathedral, has the character of a Janissary slave soldier in full dress with all his decorations standing at attention on parade.

5. The urban complex of the Süleymaniyé, a sort of university city surrounding the second of Sinan's Imperial Friday Mosques, built between 1550 and 1557 (photographed in process of restoration in 1950).

6. The Süleymaniyé on the crest of the third hill from the further shore of the Golden Horn.

7. The southwestern elevation of the Süleymaniyé.

8. The exterior walls in process of restoration of the theological seminaries and schools of Sacred Law to the northwest of the Süleymaniyé.

9. The Süleymaniyé from the colleges to the southwest (now housing part of the library of the University of Istanbul).

10. Under the dome of the Süleymaniyé, lost in space, looking toward the prayer niche of the kibla wall, in the direction due southeast of Mecca.

11. Two of the university colleges to the southwest of the Süleymaniyé.

historians have had to listen to the gossip spread by the Black Eunuchs and the female domestic slaves; and apparently by one of the Circassian Roses, the Second Lady Gülbahar herself. This undisciplined woman outlived them all to die in retirement in the Old Palace on the Third Hill on February 3, 1581, aged eighty-three or eighty-four. The scene of her defeat must have taken place late in 1519 or early in 1520, soon after the removal from Manisa to Istanbul.

Under the lowering leaden skies, day after day the chill and rainy weather of that first winter on the Bosphorus, 1520, kept the ladies out of the great gardens behind the Old Palace on the Third Hill. In the high and spacious but draughty rooms of the Validé Sultan's apartments (it may have been that) the two Roses, the Joyous One, and the Imperial Mother, wrapped in fur-lined and quilted cloaks, sat about a small table spread with a heavy velvet covering. They lapped their legs in its folds and warmed their feet, shod in jeweled slippers, around the covered brazier of glowing embers placed under the table. The two Circassian matrons had just recently come up from Manisa where mimosa was in bloom. Perhaps they played parchesi. There was no love lost among the rivals. Their tempers flared up.

No one knows at what season the redheaded Russian third lady, a virgin and indeed an old maid at the age of nineteen or twenty, went forth with the Validé Sultan's blessings to break the Greek favorite's hold upon Süleyman's affections. Her first child, Prince Mehmet, was born in 1521, but it is not known at what time of year. (He died as the Shehzadé in the winter of the year 1543.) It seems likely that at the latest in the early spring of his accession, Hürrem the Joyous, with her red-gold hair and clear seawater-blue eyes, had caught the Sultan's eye. For her he set aside the two Circassian Roses. He loved her from their first encounter until her death on April 15, 1558. After Hürrem, he promoted no other Ikbal and took no other woman to bed.

Unlike the mild First Lady Gülfem, the Second Lady Gülbahar refused to be discarded. She gave way to a scene of furious jealousy and so played straight into the Third Lady's hands. As Hürrem prepared to answer the imperious call to the bedchamber in Süleyman's apartments in the Old Palace, perhaps she taunted Gülbahar with some such words as, "She who laughs last laughs best." The tall Circassian shoved back from the table and threw herself upon the Russian. She pulled the red hair, she scratched the magnolia petal skin; she screamed out that Hürrem was nothing but a piece of butcher's meat bought and sold in the open market, and flyblown at that. When the Sultan's messenger, the chief Black Eunuch, a huge and powerful slave from the Sudan, came hard on the heels of the unseemly fracas to enquire as to the causes of the delay, Hürrem, her hair disheveled, her scratched cheeks bloody, her dress torn, quietly excused herself. She said she was unworthy of entering her master's presence, being no more than a piece of bought flesh and battered to boot.

Hafisa, the Validé Sultan, put an end to the uproar. Probably henceforth the Lady Gülbahar was confined in solitude to her own apartments in the imperial harem. Hürrem retired from her first test of strength to wash the blood from her face and to comb her hair. The fingernail scratches healed; the bruises blackened, turned green, and faded from the milky skin. In bed she made her way into the Sultan's heart. When it was apparent that she had conceived, she retired to study how the Sacred Law affected her position. The Prophet liked women; he did his best to guarantee their rights.

One day in the Sultan's New Palace on the First Hill, after the nine months and the forty days of abstinence following the conception and the birth of his first son begotten and born of love, Süleyman impatiently called a halt to the official business in the late afternoon. He made ready for his visit to the Old Palace on the Third Hill. Accompanied by his egret-plumed Life Guardsmen and his escort of pages from the palace in their cloth-of-gold uniforms and golden berets, astride his prancing Cappadocian horse he rode the mile or more along the Divan Yolu and the Avenue of Janissaries to the portal of the imperial harem. All the Slaves of the Gate and all the artisans and craftsmen and wealthy merchants of the town knew where he was going and what he was going to do. The Black Eunuchs' spies kept the Validé Sultan and Haseki Hürrem informed of Süleyman's progress.

That evening in the big and little harems of the town the ladies went visiting to gossip over spoonfuls of rose-petal jam and glasses of clear cold water. They pooled their bits and pieces of gossip, and, whispering told one another that Haseki Hürrem and Hafisa the Validé Sultan had put their heads, the one red-gold, the other iron-gray, together.

There can be no doubt that the two women got on well; they had a common enemy; they had a plan worked out. To be called Joyous, the Russian must have known how to laugh and how to please. To have come through her life with Selim the Grim renowned for her beauty and intelligence, Hafisa the Validé Sultan must have had the wit and humor that goes with a sound sense of proportion. Together the two ladies loved and honored by Süleyman must have spent the hours of the morning and the early afternoon of that day of the visit selecting, trying on, discarding, and then choosing dresses until they hit upon the most fetching one. Splendor was not their aim; they looked for an effect of delicacy and fragility. Perhaps Hürrem wore white. In her long hair, a woman's glory in Islam, wine-colored and rippling, Hürrem's body servants concealed fillets of fine chains of red gold set with cabochon rubies and fine pink pearls. For fragrance, the two ladies discarded the Roses' floral perfumes; peppery spices would have been too obvious. They chose ambergris.

Probably the Validé Sultan stepped back a pace or two, gestured for Hürrem to twirl, observed the liquefaction of her clothes, kissed the Joyous One, and sent her off with a witty word to make her smile. In possession of herself she stood demure at the foot of her lord and master's bed. According to the ritual, she should have, meekly in her shift, lifted the quilted coverlet – in winter – or the fine muslin sheet in summer, and crawled up to lie beside the man ready and waiting after the long months for this moment.

Instead she stood there. Surely Süleyman sat up, puzzled and impatient. He threw back the coverlets – but these are western imaginings. The erotic sculptures of Konarak, the erotic Moghul and Persian and Arabian and Ottoman miniatures do not have bedsteads in them, nor do any of the Islamic manuals of the arts of love. The young coupling takes place among silken cushions in situations requiring considerable elasticity, specifically developed muscles, and elaborately studied expertise; and neither one is every fully naked. It does not matter much how it was to have been done; for it was not done. He called to her. She refused. He gestured. She began to talk.

Haseki Hürrem spoke as briefly to the point as any Philadelphia lawyer. Her son's birth, said she, citing chapter and verse of Abu Hanifa's interpretation of the Koranic Law, had freed her from slavery. As an orthodox Muslim lady, she refused to countenance the unthinkable act of adultery even with the Grand Turk on, or off, the Ottoman throne. Such heinous self-indulgence in each other would be a shame, a sin, and a crime – a breach of the peace totally immoral and in the worst of taste. She thanked her lord, and the Lord, for the abiding pleasures of her brief sojourn in his company. He had made life meaningful for her and had enabled her to give life to their son. Now she begged his Imperial Majesty's leave to withdraw from the august presence of the Shadow of God on Earth, her Lord of the Angelic Countenance.

Perhaps then, instead of bursting into joyous laughter, she burst into tears and fled. "Wait! Come back! I love you! I'll marry you!" the young man called after her, the deserted chamber filled with the scent of ambergris stirred up in her long-legged flight. I myself like to think that he burst out in belly laughter, and that she came back and joined in. If he had thrown her, weighted at the ankles, into the Bosphorus, no one would have lifted an eyebrow. Süleyman had very little cause for laughter in his long life.

He married her. He dowered her with estates and a private income. Independent as an Ottoman lady, she went to her marriage bed. He loved her from the time they met until he died. Mehmet the Shehzadé, her best loved son and her emancipator, was followed by other sons and a daughter. When she died in 1558, Süleyman ordered Sinan to build a mausoleum of classic simplicity lined with Iznik tiles of most beautiful enamelings, plum trees and cherry trees in bloom in spring. Those who have seen her tomb see that she was beloved. His fidelity to her, bewildering to his Slaves of the Gate and to the citizens of Istanbul, brought down upon her their fear and hatred. Hürrem was called a witch.

In 1555 or 1556 Busbecq, the Austrian ambassador, a Flemish bastard, a gentleman, and a man of Renaissance curiosity, tried to buy a hyena for his collections in the covered bazaar of Istanbul. The merchant refused. He had set aside the exotic animal for Haseki Hürrem's purchasing agents. She was said to brew love philters and black magical potions to hold her husband in thrall, using its glands – musk? – as one of the ingredients. Or so the ambassador was told and so he wrote home in his letters. The "forbidden" harem behind its high walls, the secret place housing the Sultan's private life, fomented intrigue in a miasma of gossip and slander. No one knows what took place inside the harem. He loved her. In a man's world such love is called a weakness.

The Lady Hafisa and Haseki Hürrem saw eye to eye as they looked at Süleyman's favorite, the Greek slave Ibrahim. Nothing they could do could deflect Süleyman's confidence in him as a friend and as a man valuable to the Ottoman Empire. On June 27, 1523, he named Ibrahim to the grand vezirate over the heads of Selim the Grim's tested and venerable Slaves of the Gate. On May 22, 1524, he gave his sister, the Imperial Princess Khadija, in marriage to him. It was most magnificently celebrated for sixteen days of public festivals with fireworks in the hippodrome before his own new Palace of Ibrahim. The Princess Khadija was now to be considered her husband's ally. When she entered the imperial harem at will to spy upon the imperial ladies, Ibrahim was in a sense encroaching upon their private world.

It may be that he took Gülbahar's side in the dispute with Hürrem. He certainly recognized her son Mustafa Sultan's Osmanli qualities and backed the man, the eldest of Süleyman's sons, as his choice to inherit the throne. When, as Grand Vezir, in 1534 he persuaded the Sultan to name Mustafa the Shehzadé of Manisa, their father in effect condemned all Hürrem's sons to death. No wonder she hated Ibrahim.

In the late spring of the first year in his succession, the twenty-six-year-old Sultan Süleyman took up the Sword of Osman to carry out the campaign that his father had planned for 1521. He led Selim the Grim's army of one hundred thousand men into the Balkans to capture the island fortress of Belgrade, the outpost of Christendom thrusting like a spearpoint down into Islam. The Balkans were first fragmented – balkanized if you like – by the Roman Caesars and legionaries in their policy of divide and rule. Uneasy allies, the Serbians, the Macedonians, the Croatians, the Bulgarians, and the Hungarians held Belgrade. The Hungarians, with their artillery, were the first to desert. The castle was betrayed from within by two men, François de Hederwer and Valentin Toeroek, who showed the Janissaries where to aim the Sultan's great bronze cannons to open the weak spot in the walls. In the chilly light of dawn the splintered allies in the castle of Belgrade heard the Janissary music, the double-reeded, short and flaring hautboys shrilling arabesques above the beat of the elephant drums, the camel drums, the mule drums, the man-sized drums, the clashing cymbals, and the struck steel triangle.

The waves of sound rolling across the water meadows came in to beat upon the castle from all the cardinal points. The sun rose upon the invincible Ottoman armies marching across green fields. First came the rabble of Turkish clansmen, the raiders, undisciplined and expendable. They scourged the countryside; their bodies filled the moats. Behind them marched in battle order rank after rank of Janissaries, uniform in their red tunics and blue trousers, their white felt caps on their matched heads.

Flanking them rode the companies of Sipahis, the cavalry of graduate pages and slave soldiers astride their Cappadocian horses, black, white, chestnut, bay, red roan and blue roan, dappled and piebald. In the forefront rode the "Wildmen," volunteers of the Deli Regiment, particularly ferocious men wearing the outstretched wings of black eagles on either side of their spiked steel helments and tigers' skins on their armored shoulders. They carried maces, clubs from which spiked steel balls hung to swing on chains. Then came the glittering Life Guardsmen and the *Hasekis* of the Color Guard carrying the seven imperial banners, red and green, red and gold, white, red, green, white and gold and red and green. After them came the men of the *Alem,* the Honor Guard, and the Standard Bearer carrying the golden staff of the imperial emblem, the seven horsetails hanging from its peak and the ends of the three cross bars. All their drawn and jeweled weapons flashed in the rays of the rising sun.

Among his aides and his pashas rode the Sultan, armored in burnished steel chain mail damascened in gold, embossed with diamonds. Within the flight of arrows, he stopped to put on the high spiked helmet of the Grand Turk. It was panached with black heron's feathers and a gold and enamel phoenix plume, fixed and chained to the gilt steel with diamonds and emeralds. He blazed, aureoled in shattered light.

The Sultan and his least cadet, Sinan, fought to live; but if the slave or the Son of Osman died in battle a martyr's death in Holy War, he slept but in the flickering of God's eye to awake in Paradise, a free man and an immortal hero, to live eternally in the flowering and fruiting oasis. He lay back on a divan of gold and green brocade to be served with imperishable delicacies by houris and gilmans as beautiful as pearls as yet untouched by man or jinni. But alive that summer day at dawn, Sinan looked forward on his first campaign to his share of the spoils of victory – maidens to be enslaved, and youths such as he had been ten and a dozen years earlier, good Janissary material. He was thirty-two, powerful, moustached, and in his captives' eyes, horrible.

From the battlements the defenders of Belgrade looked down at the banks of the rivers. They saw Sinan and the other engineers building rolling towers of timber to push up against the battlements, battering rams to burst the gates, and catapults to hurl fire bombs. They watched as he and the rest of the pioneers dug zigzagging trenches on the glacis, and then, burrowing like moles, lay mines against the foundations of the battlements.

Then, when all was ready, from the barges floating down the Danube and the Sava the Janissary battle cry, "God is Most Great! " soared up the castle walls. Under the arching flight of arrows, the men followed, glittering, their eyes flashing, some falling from the ladders to splash among the barges packed solid with other slave soldiers in their red and blue uniforms, waiting to scale the breached walls.

The drums and the hautboys broke off the music. In the silence of victory, the Janissaries cut the throats of the Christian defenders and plundered the fallen. On August 29, 1521, Sultan Süleyman and his Chief Falconer and aide-de-camp Ibrahim rode into the castle through a line of pickets topped by the severed heads of Serbian noblemen. He ordered the Janissary engineers to restore the walls of the castle and convert the cathedral into a mosque.

The Sultan chose to save the lives of the Bulgarian mercenaries, who had acquitted themselves honorably. He sent them and their families back to Istanbul and settled them as woodsmen in the Belgrade Forest, which he renamed in honor of his first victory. The forest still stands between the Bosphorus and the Black Sea, as do the aqueducts and dams that Sinan built for Sultan Süleyman forty years later to bring fresh water from the forest streams and pools. In spring wild cyclamen and wild peonies bloom in the open valleys of the watershed.

After Belgrade, Sinan returned to work for the royal chief builder to enlarge the arsenal on the Golden Horn in preparation for the next victory. Early in the following year, 1522, they finished the Mosque of Selim the Grim, the memorial to the dead Sultan who had planned the amphibious campaign against the Knights of Rhodes.

On June 18, in accordance with Selim the Grim's schedule, the new Ottoman fleet sailed out of the harbors in the Bosphorus and the Golden Horn, and crossed the Sea of Marmara to sail down the Dardanelles into the Aegean Sea. The fleet sailed southeast, close to shore, past Lesbos, past Izmir, past Chios, Samos, and the lesser Dodecanese to anchor opposite Rhodes in the bay of Marmaris. Three hundred galleys, triremes, and men-of-war, together with the full complement of immense cargo ships manned by the regular Janissary crews and the Christian galley slaves, transported eight thousand Janissary marines and two thousand Janissary engineers. One of these was the cadet Sinan.

Meanwhile, Süleyman and Ibrahim rode at the head of an army of a hundred thousand men from Üsküdar on the Asian shore of the Bosphorus opposite Istanbul down the coast of western Anatolia to join the fleet in the bay of Marmaris at Bodrum. This town was the ancient Greek Halicarnassus of the Mausoleum, one of the Seven Wonders of the ancient world, then replaced by as a Christian castle commanding the enemy's beachhead on the mainland. But the Knights Hospitalers had withdrawn across the bay to their fortified island of Rhodes, where another wonder, the Colossus (or so William Shakespeare, Sinan's young contemporary, erroneously believed), once bestrode the harbor entrance.

The Christian Knights of the Order of the Hospital of St. John of Jerusalem on Rhodes had made ready for the siege. There were five thousand men in the garrison, six hundred of them knights, who were also monks and noblemen. They were arrogant, they were staggeringly wealthy, and they were corrupt according to their vows of chastity, poverty, and humility. Expelled by Saladin from Jerusalem in 1291, and from Acre in that same year, the Knights Hospitalers took Rhodes in 1310 and fortified the Greek Byzantine island.

Until 1517, the Knights maintained St. John's Hospital for the poor and the ill in Jerusalem. For this privilege they had paid tribute to the Mameluke sultans of Syria and Egypt. But they had, as we say of business corporations, diversified their interests and their holdings. For instance, they were travel agents with a monopoly in the Holy Lands. They controlled the lucrative conducted tours of pilgrims to Bethlehem, Nazareth, and Jerusalem, for whom they invented the traveler's check. They were bankers and money-lenders. Some of their income came from piracy. Their fleets policed the Mediterranean and now and again raided the coastal cities of Turkey. They plundered Ottoman and, occasionally in error, Venetian, Genoese, or Spanish merchantmen. Protected by the Pope of Rome, they owned vast estates in Europe. On their remote island inside Ottoman Islamic waters, they did as they pleased.

In 1320 an English lady on an Easter pilgrimage to Bethlehem and Jerusalem stopped at Rhodes to enjoy the hospitality of the Knights. She was taken on a conducted tour of the dungeons to see the six thousand two hundred and fifty Turkish captives chained to one another and to the stone walls. There they awaited the completion of the negotiations for their ransom. If these were unsatisfactory or the ransom was not forthcoming, they were sold as galley slaves to the Christian maritime powers. The English lady must have been rich and highborn. The story goes that the grand master indulged her. She borrowed a sword and slaughtered one thousand men – the very old, the emaciated, the very young, no longer worth their rations.

On July 28 Sultan Süleyman and his high command landed on Rhodes and on August 1 they began the siege of the eight bastions – the English, the German, the Italian, the Spanish, the Portuguese, the Auvergnat, the Pro-vençal, and the French. On Christmas Day the Roman Catholic Tower of Babel fell. It was the first victory of amphibious modern warfare. The Holy Roman Emperor Charles V, the first Hapsburg King of Spain, remarked in satisfaction when he heard of the rendition of the French Grand Master Philippe de Villiers de l'Isle-Adam of Beauvais: "Nothing in the world has been so well lost as Rhodes."

Sinan and the rest of the two thousand miners, sappers, pioneers, and flamethrowers of the new Ottoman regiment of Janissary engineers won the campaign of Rhodes for the young Sultan. Many Greek and Slavic bones of the Janissaries and cadets, buried where they fell in battle, were disinterred from the dugouts and trenches in the glacis when Mussolini's archaeologists were restoring the castle as a tourist attraction. Sinan's *oda* of the engineers hurled the first incendiaries in the first saturation bombing known to history. They set fire to the town.

When at last they blew up the English bastion, there appeared on the ruined battlements, silhouetted against the flames rising from her burning house behind her, a young Rhodian Greek woman bringing up supplies to her knightly monkish English lover manning the walls. She found him lying dead in the *chemin-de-ronde*. She threw down her load, took up her two children and, straddling the body of the father, kissed and blessed first one and then the other; then she made the sign of the cross upon each of them, stabbed them, and hurled their bodies into the flames of their burning house. The Christian chroniclers quote her as shrieking, "The Turks shall not violate you dead or alive! " She then wrapped herself in her slain lover's black cloak of the bloodstained white cross, took up his sword and, wielding it, threw herself into the breach. She killed a converted Greek Janissary or two as he climbed the scaling ladder before she died.

It is to be taken for granted that Sinan, a victorious young man of thirty-three, bloody and alive, yelling for all his friends the dead cadets to get up on their feet and stand behind him, impaled a few in front of him upon his thrust; and he laid hands on his share of Greek boys and girls in the total spoils of war.

But not all the Greek Christian women had enjoyed the occupation of Rhodes by the international Roman Catholic monkish knights. The plump young women sponge divers of Symi had volunteered to work beside Sinan and the other sappers to lay underwater mines against the bases of the sea walls of Rhodes, Kos, and the other fortified islands of the southern Sporades. To reward them Süleyman left the islanders a measure of autonomy, remitted their taxes, allowed them to keep their churches, and honored the sponge divers with a special mark of favor, a turban especially designed for them.

The grand master capitulated after a siege of four months and twenty-five days. On Christmas Day he and his surviving senior knights walked silently through the gate, across the lowered drawbridge, and up the path to the Sultan's imperial tent pitched on a hill. The night before Süleyman had sent the grand master an Ottoman robe of honor, quilted and fur-lined against the winter weather. Outside the silken tents he stood waiting in the mud and slush of wet snow and sleet until the early morning meeting of the Divan adjourned. From Süleyman he got the most generous terms.

Villiers de l'Isle-Adam left the island of Rhodes for Malta with all his surviving companions and all his portable treasure except for the four golden bowls heaped with oriental pearls and rubies that he chose to present to the Grand Turk. The young Sultan, watching their departure, turned to his Chief Falconer Ibrahim and said, "It is not without regret that I force this brave man from his demesne in his old age."

The King of France and the Pope of Rome, neither of whom had chosen to send aid to the besieged grand master, blamed him because he had not defended the island to the death. In fact, had he held out until Epiphany, he might have kept Rhodes by default. The Janissaries, exhausted by the long months of heat and dust in summer and cold rains and mud of winter in constant assault across the bodies of their comrades choking the moat and blocking the glacis under the walls and the eight bastions, were ready to mutiny.

The Knights Hospitalers, unaware of the Janissaries' murmuring, chose to blame their defeat on a Sephardic physician, a man expelled by the Inquisition from Spain whom they had hired to do their Christian duties among the poor and the plague-stricken in the hospital. They said the Jewish doctor had betrayed them. Whatever the explanation of the victory and the defeat, the fact is that Süleyman is given the credit – or the blame – for bringing Rhodes and the Dodecanese into Islam.

Back in Istanbul, the time had come to celebrate in triumph his earned right, as conqueror of Belgrade and of the Knights Hospitalers, to rule the growing empire of his Osmanli inheritance. As part of the ceremonies, he may well have re-enacted the age-old ritual of Janissary investiture and benediction. On June 27, 1523, he signed an imperial edict appointing his favorite Ibrahim to preside at the Divan as Grand Vezir. It was a revolutionary act. The Sultan henceforth withdrew from the meetings of the Imperial Council of State to delegate his inherited power to a man who, raised in grace and favor, a purchased Greek slave, could in no way rightfully supplant the Son of Osman as the khan, the hereditary chieftain of the Turkish clan and tribe. At Rhodes, Ibrahim, as he stood beside Sultan Süleyman, had had great privilege but no official capacity in authority. When they returned to Istanbul, he entered the Divan as fourth and least vezir. But the Grand Vezir, the wise Piri Mehmet Pasha, whom Süleyman had inherited from his father Selim the Grim, had suffered a heart attack and was too ill to preside at the meetings of the Divan; Second Vezir Choban Mustafa Pasha was in Cairo as governor-general of Egypt. Their absence left the Third Vezir Ahmet Pasha, like the new Fourth Vezir Ibrahim a Greek slave, but unlike the favorite, a graduate of the palace school of pages and the commander in chief of the triumphant Rhodes campaign, to conduct the affairs of state in the Divan. They lost their tempers daily in altercations that disrupted the dignified proceedings of the Ottoman Divan. The two Greeks, as Greeks still do, shouted at one another and shocked the decorous Slaves of the Gate.

Süleyman acted. He officially retired the Grand Vezir Piri Mehmet Pasha with honor. From Cairo the Sultan recalled his brother-in-law Choban Mustafa Pasha, an excellent general officer but not an administrator, and sent Ahmet Pasha, the third vezir, whom he misjudged as an admirable Slave of the Gate despite his bad temper, to govern Egypt. Perhaps Süleyman, acting in haste, did so to clear the way for Ibrahim, his boon companion, whom he then appointed to the highest office in the Ruling Institution.

The young Sultan had no one to question his pleasure or his exercise of absolute power. It suited him to recall his brother-in-law Choban Mustafa Pasha, the second vezir, from Cairo not to appoint him Grand Vezir but to please his sister the Imperial Princess Hafisa – or so the story goes. Ottoman history is largely gossip written down. It is certain that the daughters and the sisters of the Sultans were powerfully privileged, but otherwise of little importance. They were no longer married in political alliances to neighboring Islamic rulers. Daughters of Osman, in their veins ran the undiluted imperial blood, which, according to the biological law revealed to the Prophet, they could not transmit; for, in the act of love, they received the child whole and miniscule in the drop of sperm. According to the rules of the House of Osman, their sons, freeborn men and nobles, could enter the Household, but, among the Slaves of the Gate, they could not rise above the rank of *Sanjak Bey,* which means governor of a minor province, such as Bosnia.

Choban Mustafa Pasha, a Slovene shepherd boy captured in war and a splendid Slave of the Gate, was recalled from Cairo when his wife, Hafisa Sultan, calling herself twice widowed, complained to Süleyman that their father Selim the Grim had executed her first husband, the then Grand Vezir Ahmet Dukaginzadé, in 1515, in punishment for one of his Janissaries' trifling breach of discipline. And now her brother the Sultan had separated her second husband, the second vezir, from her in the first year of their marriage. Perhaps Süleyman, laughing, granted his sister her wish, saying that he would not risk her imperial pleasures by raising Choban Mustafa Pasha to the grand vezirate. Or perhaps, as we say in Italian *papabile* while discussing the candidates in the College of Cardinals during a papal election, Choban Mustafa Pasha was not grand vezirable. He died in 1529 and was buried in Gebze across the Marmara in the tomb behind the mosque that Sinan helped Royal Chief Builder Ajem Ali design and build in an Egyptian style.

Ibrahim the favorite, although his unorthodox appointment disturbed the senior Slaves of the Gate in the Household, proved at once to be a great Grand Vezir.

Vezir in Arabic means "the bearer of the burden." From the time of Orhan the Golden to the fall of Constantinople to Mehmet the Conqueror, the title was hereditary in the Jandarli family of Turkish noblemen, descendants of a Companion of the Prophet, and from the once-independent Emirs of Kastamonu and Sinope, their counties on the Black Sea long since absorbed in the Ottoman Empire. But since 1453, when Mehmet the Conqueror, the new Caesar of the Eastern Roman Empire, retired into remote Byzantine majesty and reorganized his government to separate the Ruling Institution of his Slaves of the Gate from the Religious Institution of the tribal Ulema, the Jandarli grand vezirs no longer inherited the right "to bear the burden." The Sultan appointed whatever man he chose, slave or freeborn Muslim, to serve him at his pleasure. In his eight years on the throne and in the field, Selim the Grim had six or seven of his grand vezirs executed – even Ahmet Dukaginzadé, his first cousin and son-in-law.

There is reason to believe that Süleyman, feeling that the time had come once again to reorganize the Ottoman Ruling and Religious Institutions, was planning realistically and wisely to share with the Grand Vezir the intolerable burden of government that, as the Son of Osman, he alone had inherited:

I, who am Sultan of the Sultans of East and West, fortunate lord of the domains of the Romans [Byzantines], Persians, and Arabs, Hero of creation, Champion of the earth and time, Padishah and Sultan of the Mediterranean and the Black Sea, of the extolled Kaaba [in Mecca] and Medina and the illustrious and Jerusalem the noble, of the throne of Egypt and the province of Yeman, Adan, and San'a, of Baghdad and Basra and Lahsa and Ctesiphon, and of the lands of Algiers and Azerbaijan, of the regions of the Kipchaks and the lands of the Tartars, of Kurdistan and Luristan and all Rumelia [the Domain of War], Anatolia [the Domain of Peace] and Karaman, of Wallachia and Moldavia and Hungary and many kingdoms and lands beside; the Sultan Süleyman Khan, son of the Sultan Selim Khan.

Süleyman of the Angelic Countenance, the Shadow of God on Earth, did not call himself Caliph, which is to say that he did not consider himself to be the "Successor" or the "Substitute" of the Prophet Mohammed as supreme ruler of both the organized religion and the state. The Ottoman Religious Institution was ruled by the Grand Mufti Ali Jemali, a powerful freeborn Turk appointed by Sultan Bayazid the Pious. This "veritable guardian angel" (as the historian Joseph von Hammer-Purgstall described him) of justice under the Sacred Law was able, throughout the eight-year reign of Selim the Grim, to control the excesses of that terrible puritan. Selim, a bigot in all matters of religion, spent his short reign in Holy Wars to restore the power and tarnished glory of the Sword of Islam.

In all audiences of state requiring the presence in joint session of the Divan and the Ulema, Sultan Bayazid the Pious rose to receive the Grand Mufti Ali Jemali and seated him ceremoniously in his rightful place as guardian of the Sacred Law higher than the throne of the Sons of Osman. Süleyman in turn left the ruling of the Religious Institution to the Grand Mufti Ali Jemali when, in 1520, he inherited his father's and his grandfather's empire.

The Institution of the Ulema – comparable to the U.S. Supreme Court and the College of Cardinals combined – had taken shape over the years of decadence in Islam, when the last Abbasid Caliphs of Baghdad, lost in luxuries and in sophistication, debased the name and nature of the successors and substitutes to the Prophet. Selim the Grim had captured the last of these, Mutawakkil IV, who was by then the puppet of the heretical Mameluke sultans of Egypt, when he took Cairo in 1517. He had brought the abject man as a prisoner of war to Istanbul, at the same time that he brought the Prophet's standard, his sword, his mantle, a tooth, a few hairs of the beard, and a petrified footprint, all of them attributes of both Mohammed and his power. Three years later, when he was secure and supreme in Islamic power, Süleyman freed his father's captive. The valueless title of caliph died with the humiliated man.

It seems clear, although he drew up no table of organization, that Süleyman meant to divide his total power into three parts. As the Son of Osman the Lawgiver, he would govern as chief of state with the help of his left arm, the chief justice and Grand Mufti of the Religious Institution, his delegate in all matters of sacred jurisprudence, and his right arm, the prime minister and Grand Vezir of the Ruling Institution, his administrator in the legislative branch of the government. The Sultan would remain supreme in power, and at the same time he would take command of the armies, and later of the navy, but his *serasker* or commander in chief would lead the armies on campaign in the field.

The two young men, the Sultan Süleyman and the Grand Vezir Ibrahim, sworn inseparables, knew enough to conceal their revolutionary reorganization of the government from the hierarchy of the Household of Slaves and from the Grand Mufti of the Ulema. These men, aging Slaves of the Gate and freeborn Ancients of Islam, had risen to power and position under Süleyman's father and grandfather. Conservative and traditional servants of the state and the religion, they were neither good nor bad men; most of them were older in years and in experience than the young Sultan and his dubious favorite. Their established interests were vested in the Ruling and Religious Institutions. They were satisfied with the way things were — but not in fact with the way things always had been.

It was likely, therefore, that Süleyman and Ibrahim made use of age-old ceremonies, such as the hallowed ritual of the Janissaries' first benediction, in order to reassure them. The Slaves of the Gate and the Judges-Divine had been ruffled by Ibrahim's unseemly promotion, and they must be made to think that all henceforth was to be as it was in the beginning. Theirs was the only opinion that was to be heard and borne in mind. Public opinion was of small account, and nobody else, whether Turk or Christian, had any say in the government. The people, to Selim the Grim, was a great beast, only to be brought to order by the use of the whip. The Sons of Osman in their established institutions ruled for themselves — in resignation and submission to the will of God.

In the spring or summer of 1523 when he was thirty-four, Sinan, the cadet still in training as an engineer, was recommended to "Pass Through the Gate" as a full-fledged Janissary of the Sultan's Household of Slaves. He had earned this right and privilege by his admirable and meritorious conduct at Belgrade and Rhodes. As all soldiers know, a man earns his stripes, his promotions, and his medals always above and beyond the call of duty; and he is fortunate. Before Sinan could be promoted, some superior officer in the Household of Slaves had to sponsor him. It may have been Ibrahim. In his brief biography, noted down or dictated sometime after 1566 and before 1574 when he was between seventy-seven and eighty-five years old, Sinan did not recall in detail his early years as an aspirant and a Janissary. He did not see fit to name his sponsor. Those were the days of anonymity in Ottoman history, but perhaps Sinan had reason for his silent discretion. It may be purely coincidental that both Sinan and Ibrahim joined the Household of Slaves at the same time, the one at the bottom the other at the top of the hierarchy. It is possible that the new Grand Vezir chose to sponsor the aspirant cadet Sinan to "Pass Through the Gate," to share with him his growing ascendancy. All the historians agree that Ibrahim crossed Süleyman's night skies like a comet. He was a brilliant man.

On that late June day of 1523, on the occasion of Sinan's investiture in the Hippodrome, the *Agha* of the Janissaries drew up his immaculate companies of meritorious cadets who had been judged worthy to "Pass Through the Gate" in a kind of graduation exercise or tattoo. From each company a representative was told to fall out. The honored young soldiers then formed up and closed ranks to stand at attention in front of the Sultan's tribune.

It may well have been, in this imagining of times past, that Süleyman decided to take part in this ritual ceremony in the place of his six-times-great-grandfather Orhan Khan; and if so, perhaps Ibrahim, the intimate friend and the new Grand Vezir, stood beside him in the place of Kara Halil Pasha, the first of the early dynasty of hereditary Jandarli grand vezirs. These two men had organized the first Janissary slave army sometime in the years after they captured Bursa, twenty years besieged. The long, slow, disorderly siege itself had taught Orhan Khan and his general Kara Halil the need to organize a standing army of trained and disciplined soldiers, who unlike their free born clansmen were ready to answer instantaneously to command. Like Süleyman the Magnificent and like Mehmet the Conqueror, this second Khan and first Son of Osman and of the Osmanli clan was a revolutionary. He would have understood his lineal descendant's need to disguise his plans for revolutionary and progressive changes in tribal and governmental organization behind a show of satisfactory legend – to save the surface, thus to save all.

Orhan Khan was called "the Golden." Like Süleyman, he was a tall man, high-nosed and handsome. But Orhan had blue eyes and a golden beard. A smiling man, he had a black spot on his white skin under the left ear, "like a poppy seed floating on a dish of milk." In contrast, his general, Kara Halil, a tall, vigorous, commanding man, was called "the Black." Together they agreed to save the surface of the nomadic tribal institutions, as we save the outside of an ancient house; but to modernize the interior by taking power unto themselves. There emerged the Son of Osman supreme in his inherited leadership and authority as absolute chief of state, with Kara Halil, as his prime minister, likewise the inheritor of his place and power.

They were wise enough not to interfere directly in the organization of the Religious Institution, made up at first of tribal elders and later of distinguished savants in sacred jurisprudence invited from all parts of the empire to join the Ulema. The Sultan reserved the right to appoint one of his legal advisers Grand Mufti. Once in office, he served for the rest of his life – Jemali Ali served three Sultans as Grand Mufti. The title, as the word mufti in English implies, means that the man was a civilian, a Muslim, a free man, not a slave – although he could have been emancipated from the Slave Household or been born the son of a Slave of the Gate. The Sons of Osman's grand muftis in the early days were all traditional but progressive men, able to keep up with the developments of the Ruling Institution, and able when necessary to apply the brakes to such ferocious puritans as Selim the Grim.

The myths of the early Sons of Osman are as bright as miniatures in medieval manuscripts illuminated in mineral colorings: lapis lazuli, cinnabar, veridian, zinc white, vermilion, chrome yellow, and red chrome, such unfading pigments highlighted in polished gold. In the surviving paintings, the streams, the fountains, and the seas once were burnished silver; now time has oxydized the water and it is velvet black. Orhan the Golden marched his first company of tribute youths, the New Troops, in red and blue uniforms, trailing a plume of dust across the spotless distances under the dome of heaven in the sunshine of the high Anatolian plateau, to be blessed by the holy man Haji Bektash. He was a mystic and a liberal, catholic man who lived in a grotto in a mountain of green and fawn-colored onyx, perhaps fifty miles as the crow flies from Sinan's home town of Aghirnas. To him and to his followers, the Bektashi or "humble men," all gods and Gods were the one God; all prophets, messengers, philosophers, messiahs, and leaders in prayer were as the Prophet.

On the red-gold high plateau under the hill of onyx, where green, flamelike poplar trees grew on the banks of the rivulet flowing from the spring in the grotto, Orhan the Golden drew up his troops and set them at parade rest. Down to them came the white-bearded holy man dressed in a long robe of white homespun with flowing sleeves, with a white turban on his venerable head. He called the youngest youth, a *penjik* prisoner of war. The boy, bareheaded, knelt at the tall old man's feet. Haji Bektash looked down and put his hand on the bewildered young slave's bent head and said (in the English of my paraphrase of the French translation from Joseph von Hammer-Purgstall's German translation from the Osmanlija):

"May your face forever remain white and shining. May your right arm never fail in strength. May your sword keep its edge. May your bow shoot straight the arrow into the target. May you be fortunate in battle. God grant you triumph on the field of honor or the death of heroes, which is victory eternal in Paradise! "

Then Haji Bektash lifted his arms (perhaps to raise his palms upward, outstretched) to bring down God's blessings on the boy, as on a sacrifice. But apparently his long hanging sleeve caught in a buckle or a hook at the back of the tribute youth's belt, and the saint's white sleeve ripped free at the shoulder. It was a sign, an omen. Haji Bektash tore off his sleeve and fitted the armhole end of it on the New Trooper's shaved head. The empty sleeve fell down the boy's back. So goes the legend; the legend has its own story.

This myth of the sleeve and the blessing of (the ghost of) Haji Bektash (he had died a century earlier) is now accepted as a piece of propaganda as carefully worked out as an epic poem. At the end of Sinan's long life, the arrogant Janissaries had lost all respect for the Sultan, who dared not leave his harem to lead them into battle. They called Selim the Sot the Stalled Ox, and they made the little fat man tremble. This grandson of Selim the Grim and son of Haseki Hürrem and Süleyman the Magnificent had frivolously granted a Turkish acrobat the right to enroll his freeborn Muslim son among the Janissaries. Soon there were more privileged Muslim volunteers than there were slave-soldier-dervishes in the corrupt elite – many of them married men who drew their pay but hired mercenaries to replace them on the fields of honor.

The later Janissaries of the seventeenth century, no longer slaves but instead free men in a kind of Praetorian Guard, deposed Mustafa I – he was, it is true, insane; they raised and then deposed and murdered his nephew Osman II, who tried to reform them; and, in 1648, they deposed and murdered Osman's brother, another mad Sultan, who contained his thick and curly black beard in a fillet of gold and jewels, and whose folly for sables, ambergris, and a monstrously fat Armenian giantess, whom he called "Sugar Bit," exhausted the privy purse and brought the empire to the edge of bankruptcy.

The trouble began in the reign of Selim the Grim's pacific father, "the Sainted, the Pious" Bayazid II. His misunderstood policy had been to live at peace with his Christian and heretical neighbors, and to consolidate the many racial and ethnic bits and pieces of the Ottoman Empire so violently collected by his father Mehmet the Conqueror. Sultan Bayazid the Sainted's idle Janissaries helped his grim son usurp the throne, defeat the shah of Persia, and conquer Syria, Egypt, and the Prophet's Holy Cities. The Janissaries respected Selim the Grim, but in making use of them, he taught them the nature of their own enormous strength. By the time Sinan was collected as a tribute youth, the grand vezirs and the aghas, and perhaps the judges of the armies, wise men of the Ulema, had merged the Janissary slave army with the liberal order of Bektashi dervishes. Some one, perhaps a chaplain, then was inspired to invent the legend of the Janissaries' patron saint Haji Bektash and his blessing and his sleeve in an effort to restore the waning mystique of Janissary loyalty both to God and to the Shadow of God on Earth.

In historic fact, the *ketch* that Sinan put on his head was not the (modified) sleeve of the mild and pleasant Pilgrim Bektash, but instead the hooded cap that the original New Troopers of the fourteenth century had inherited from the Ahiler, another mystic and secret Islamic Brotherhood, in many ways similar to the Freemasons. The fact is better than the fiction, for the cap made an excellent inheritance.

The Ahiler Brotherhood had grown up in the times of chaos when the Mongol invaders such as Hulagu Khan had shattered the excellently patrolled roads and irrigation systems that maintained the peace and the prosperity of the Great Seljuk's Sultanate and the lesser Seljuk Sultanate of Konya. With the breakdown of law and order, highwaymen took to the roads. Islam has always been a civilization of walled market cities and capitals on crossroads and in seaports, a product of hardworking and prosperous artisans and craftsmen, and not, as in medieval Christian Europe, of feudal lords and robber barons. The craftsmen and the merchants organized themselves in guilds and trade unions.

These sensible and orderly men, unable to work in chaos, formed secret confraternities to police the streets which were threatened by robbers and marauders. They guarded the city gates; they manned the walls; they kept the peace. The Ahiler patrolled the streets throughout the night and gathered again at daybreak – perhaps inside the gates in the masons' guildhall, but more probably for their own security outside the walls in the tannery.

The tanners, because of the smelly nature of their craft, worked in strongholds outside the gates down by the river or the sea. They cured the hides of flayed animals with the excrement of dogs, beasts specifically mentioned by the Prophet in the Koran as unclean. Their guild, in the curious, spiraling pattern of mysterious and secret growth, absorbed the Ahiler, and with it some of the virtue of the disbanded chivalric society. The master of the guild came to be called the *Ahi Baba,* "Father Brother." Young outlaws, delinquents, and riffraff, youths abused by the Janissaries, young men caught in adultery, orphaned children caught stealing bread – the outcasts ran for their lives into the arms of the tanners outside the city walls. The *Ahi Baba,* having heard privately each one's story, saved those he judged worthy and capable of rehabilitation. The various tanners took them in as apprentices, gave them new clothes, fed them, gave them means of earning a livelihood. The tanners gave them, as we say, a new identity and as a result they usually turned into prosperous, law-abiding citizens.

The Ahiler as a secret and mystical brotherhood of vigilantes within Islam had served their purpose by the time Osman Khan and his son Orhan the Golden, from their emirate on the marches of the shrinking Byzantine Empire, began to enforce what might be called the *Pax Osmannica*. At the beginning of the fourteenth century, the Ahiler owned a private estate big enough to be called an independent country with Ankara as their capital.

To cement the peace with his neighbors, Osman Khan had taken as his second lady the daughter of Sheikh Edebâli of the Ahiler confraternity; and the Second Lady Bâli had borne him a son, Prince Alaettin Ali, who was, in fact, the second son of Osman. When the eponymous leader of the minor clan of Turkish nomads, late comers from the Altai Mountains of Central Asia, knew himself to be too old to sit his horse and pull the Turkish bow, he got down from the saddle and asked his father-in-law, Sheikh Edebâli of the Ahiler, to choose one of his two sons to succeed him as tribal chieftain.

In those days there was no need for the law of fratricide, promulgated as an imperial edict by Osman's four times great-grandson, Mehmet the Conqueror. The early Sons of Osman, who called themselves not sultans but khans, were given to collecting not ladies for the harem but provinces for the empire. Sheikh Edebâli decided against his own grandson; the wise old man of the Ahiler chose the better man, Osman's elder son, Orhan the Golden.

As regent for his father in retirement, and then as Khan in his own right, Orhan the Golden and his general, Jandarli Kara Halil Pasha, having conquered Bursa after twenty years of siege in 1326, called his half-brother, Sheikh Edebâli's grandson Prince Alaettin Ali, out of retirement in his library to give his wisdom to the state. The three men then organized the New Troops, the standing army of slave soldiers belonging wholly to Orhan the Golden, and answering to his and to General Jandarli Kara Halil's commands.

Whether or not Sheikh Edebâli (and not Haji Bektash of the myth) actually blessed the first company of New Troops, to take the cap of the Ahiler and to give it to the Janissaries as a sign and a symbol was an inspired stroke of genius. It gave these violently uprooted Christian youths, captured in war, later collected in the levy of the blood tax but always selected for individual perfection according to exacting standards, then enslaved, marched off, converted, and trained as Janissaries to win Holy Wars for their master, both cause and reason for self-respect and loyalty. It gave them a tradition and an inheritance to be proud of. The *ketch* comforted and united the slave youths. It gave each one of them something of his own to have and to hold on to, something none but one of them could put upon his head. They had to earn the right to wear it.

The cap that the meritorious and admirable slave-cadet Sinan put on was banded at the cuff end, now worn on the head, with the colors of the Janissary *oda* – the "regiment" – of the Zemberekjis, red, green, blue, gold brocade, or whatever it might have been. The forearm of the sleeve, stiffened with buckram or a wire frame, stood up about eight inches high. Then in a fold straight across, the rest of the sleeve fell down the young man's flat back.

In prosperous times, a socket of gold or silver gilt, jeweled with corals and turquoises, was pinned to the cuff band in front. In poor times it was of base metal set with bits of colored glass. In this socket, the Janissary wore instead of a plume a wooden or a horn spoon with which he ate his soup and his pilaf. In better times the spoon, his insignia, was made of tortoiseshell or of ivory with a handle of black coral or of ebony ending in a branch of red coral.

The spoon mixed still one more ancient Turkish ingredient in the Janissary's mystical inheritance of loyalty. In the Altaic Mountains and on the Central Asian steppes, before the nomads entered Islam, they were shamanists. To protect their families from the evil spirits of the air, as well as from the corporeal dangers of armed raids and rapines, when the able-bodied clansmen rode off in search of new pastures and a camp site besides a spring of water, they left the women, the children, and the old men, as well as the flocks and herds, in the protection of loyal slavemen. These domestics of the tribal chieftain's slave family ordinarily were cooks and watermen – they did the heavy work at camp.

Thus, by Sinan's time, in the proud tradition of the Slave Household, the emblems and the palladia of the Janissary regiments were a soup ladle six feet long and a soup and pilaf cauldron of bell-metal bronze. One of their general officers was called the Chief Soup Dispenser, another the Chief Water Pourer. In mutiny the Janissaries refused their rations, overturned the soup cauldron, and drummed upon it like a gong with the long soup ladle.

Who knows whether Sinan abdür-Rahman, on that day in June of 1523 when he proudly put on the coveted Janissary cap, knew the mixture of history and of myth that culminated in his passage through the Gate into the handsomest and finest body of military men in the world? His own myth and his evident achievements prove that he entered into the spirit of the Slaves of the Gate of the Sultan's Household with wholehearted, whole-souled, and intelligent devotion to the idea and the purpose of his sovereign lord and master Süleyman the Magnificent.

In the silence that has come down to us as part of their perfection, the company of elect Janissaries marched out of the Hippodrome on the First Hill. They turned to the right through what had been the Byzantine August-eon; they marched to the left behind the apse of Haghia Sophia. They halted before the Bâbi-Hümayun in the outer walls of the New Palace. Then silently in single file they passed through the Gate of Felicity, the Imperial Portal, to enter the outer Courtyard of the Janissaries, there to join the regular Household troops.

In his lifetime, Sinan changed the aspect of this space. As a Haseki, the commanding officer of the Guard of Honor, in 1535 and 1536, aged forty-six and forty-seven, this tremendous man strode across the familiar ground under the Janissaries' plane tree, hurrying to take his place on duty in some court ceremony. He was a tall man in a blue and red dress uniform, clean-shaven except for the Janissary guardsman's thick and wide-pointed moustache. On his head he carried the mark of his long service and high favor rising like a fountain from his turban, a crescent-shaped plume of white ostrich feathers pointing ahead of him and falling behind him down to his knees.

There was, and there has been, nothing like them, these matched and graded men, chosen for their physical perfection, their strength of character, their nobility of soul, and their great intelligence; then raised to the statistic of the highest order, to shine like stars in the pure beauty of the mathematical kind, of the order that turns the heart over in the breast to behold.

Withal, the Janissary's was a way of life like another.

6

Two years later, in 1525, when the rains of the winter and the vernal equinox came to an end and the sunshine of the fine days of May dried the green fields and the mud of the road from Istanbul to Edirné and on up into the Balkans, Sultan Süleyman went hunting for deer in the forests beyond the land walls, and falconing for waterfowl in the marshes of the Domain of War. The Janissaries, pent up in idleness inside their barracks on the Third Hill since their return in triumph from Rhodes, mutinied. Ready and willing to fight the Hungarians on land; or by sea to besiege "the Red Apple," which is what they called Rome; but unable to put up with a third year of peace, they looked for enemies at home. It having been borne in upon them that one more season of campaign was to be wasted in ceremonial display and war games, they broke open their own locked gates and poured out of the barracks into the streets of the Third Hill. Apparently they knew what they were doing.

Exactly one year earlier, on May 22, 1524, in the Hippodrome in front of the vast Palace of Ibrahim, the Janissaries had fought mock battles to celebrate the wedding of the Grand Vezir and favorite to the Imperial Princess Khadija, a daughter of Selim the Grim, a sister of Sultan Süleyman. But after the sixteen days and nights of nuptial festival marking the unprecedented splendor and power of the Ottoman Empire for all the ambassadors of all the Christian and the Muslim rulers to take note of had gone by, their aghas ordered the Janissaries back into their barracks for one more summer of routine duties. They murmured, they stood about in scowling groups, they spoke out, they began to shout; on May 22, 1525, they burst forth into the sunlit and quiet street like a flash flood, blood red and sea blue, white-capped and glittering.

In the imperial harem across the Street of the Janissaries from the rioting barracks, the Validé Sultan Hafisa and the Sultan's wife, Haseki Hürrem, heard the angry men batter down the gates and break into the palace of the imperial treasurer, Defterdar Iskender Chelebi. He was absent in Cairo on official business. A Turkish gentleman, a voluntary Slave of the Gate, the Defterdar Iskender Chelebi was the only man to rival the Grand Vezir Ibrahim Pasha in the Sultan's confidence, and the only man in Istanbul rich enough to equal the Favorite in the splendor of his life.

From behind the barricaded doors and shuttered windows of their town houses along the Divan Yolu, the well-to-do men and women of the city saw the Janissaries, their arms full of loot – gold and silver plate, jeweled swords and daggers, brocaded and embroidered robes of honor, Persian carpets and damascened armor – pour down the Third Hill into the Hippodrome. They gathered at the locked gates of the Palace of Ibrahim. The Grand Vezir, like the Defterdar, was absent in Cairo. Six months after his wedding, Süleyman had sent the *damat* and favorite, for the first time since their meeting in Manisa a dozen years earlier separated from the person of the Shehzadé and the Sultan, down to settle the affairs of the imperial province of Egypt, troubled by the aftermath of revolt.

Inside the huge Palace of Ibrahim, the absent Grand Vezir's two ladies of the harem were in residence. Each had withdrawn into her own "forbidden" apartments in the "protected" women's quarters in distant courtyards within the vastnesses of the walled enclosure. They listened to the smashing and the looting of the *selâmlik*, "the place of salutations" (now restored to house the Janissary museum). The great hall was then the largest covered space in any secular building within the Ottoman Empire, and it was splendid in its proportions and its embellishments.

Both the favorite's ladies of the harem were safe from attack because the second of them was a Daughter of Osman named for the first wife of the Prophet. The Imperial Princess Khadija had brought with her from the imperial harem her own company of retainers, powerful black eunuchs, devoted slave women, and a detachment of steadfast imperial Life Guardsmen. The mutinous Janissaries had timed their revolt to break into the Palace of Ibrahim exactly one year to the day after her magnificent wedding honored by the unprecedented presence of the Padishah himself, her brother the Sultan Süleyman Khan, son of the Sultan Selim Khan.

Her situation was extraordinary; it was unheard of for a bride of the imperial house, a daughter of a Son of Osman, to permit her chosen consort, a Slave of the Gate of Süleyman's Slave Household, the shocking privilege of keeping his first lady in his house along with the Imperial Princess of the Blood, thereby to be called his second lady of the harem. Although she could not transmit her powerful and glorious inheritance to her son by Ibrahim, she was his superior. She kept a dagger by her even in the act of love to remind them of the fact. Divorce is simple in Islam. The husband claps his hands thrice and utters the formula: "I divorce thee. I divorce thee. I divorce thee." To marry an Imperial Princess, the chosen *damat* – the slave to become the imperial son-in-law – was called upon by dynastic law to put aside his existing wives, and to take no other, so not to force the Sultan's daughter to share her husband with a lesser woman.

Ibrahim's first lady was called Muhsiné Hatun. Her name translates as Lady Beneficence. A lady bountiful, a shadowy figure, veiled, remote, no one knows why her husband the Grand Vezir chose to be loyal to her; or why Sultan Süleyman saw fit to grant his favorite, and thus through him his First Lady Muhsiné, such special dispensation; or why the Princess Khadija tolerated her.

Had she been an ordinary slave girl, purchased as Ibrahim had been in a slave market, or had she been a freeborn Turkish virgin, surely neither she nor the favorite would have been honored in the breach of the imperial dynastic house rules, which, in the Sultan's exercise of the *wilaya*, the sovereign royal will, had the effect of the Sacred Law. Nobody shall ever know more of the Lady Muhsiné, than her name and that in Ibrahim's harem she bore no recorded sons or daughters.

Fortunately for Sinan, when the veteran Janissary mutineers broke into the Palace of Ibrahim on the anniversary of the absent Grand Vezir's wedding, he was not there. Thus he neither risked his career nor endangered his life in defense or otherwise of his master and patron's ladies and household. Ten years earlier, on his return from Anatolia, Sinan had been assigned to the school of Janissary engineers in the Palace of Ibrahim, which he and the Royal Chief Builder Ajem Ali had enlarged to house the Grand Vezir and his attendant pages and guardsmen, his protégés and slaves. At the time of the wedding, like Leonardo da Vinci at the court of the duke of Milan, Sinan probably had set the stage and built the pavilions in the Hippodrome for the days of ceremonies and the nights of entertainments. As a Zemberekji, which originally meant "fireworks handler" and was the name of the regiment of engineers, Sinan may have designed and built the pyrotechnical displays, set pieces, great castles like miniatures of Belgrade and of Rhodes – complete even to toy cannons, and, upon the towers, mechanical storks in small scale that spouted rockets and sparklers, flapped their wings, and then exploded in colorful flames.

After the wedding, as part of Ibrahim's suite, Sinan accompanied the Grand Vezir to Cairo. The revolt in Egypt had come about in direct consequence of Süleyman's favoritism. By right of earned rank in the hierarchy, not Ibrahim, who entered the Divan in 1523 as the fourth and least vezir, but either Second Vezir Choban Mustafa Pasha, or Third Vezir Ahmet Pasha should have been promoted to the grand vezirate. Whatever Choban Mustafa Pasha thought about the irregular appointment of Ibrahim the favorite, he kept his peace. But Ahmet Pasha, a Greek Slave of the Gate marked for preference by his master, Selim the Grim, and in 1523 a young man in his prime, the triumphant commander in chief of the conquest of Rhodes, certainly did not.

Sent out of the way down to Cairo to govern Egypt, the ambitious and brutal man did not set about calming the imperial province, conquered but not pacified by Selim the Grim in 1517. Instead, Ahmet Pasha, known in Ottoman history as "the Traitor," revolted. He took Egypt for himself and called himself the new Mameluke Sultan. Süleyman ordered Choban Mustafa Pasha to go back to put down Ahmet Pasha's revolt. He did so. In Cairo Ahmet the Traitor, himself betrayed, fled from the citadel; he was once again betrayed, captured, and executed. Choban Mustafa Pasha returned to Istanbul with the severed head of Ahmet the Traitor pickled in brine. But he left Egypt in turmoil.

At peace, the annual revenues of the imperial province brought four hundred thousand gold ducats into the Sultan's privy purse (the equivalent of twenty million pre-World War I gold dollars, but of astronomical purchasing power). Therefore, six months after the wedding, Süleyman sent the Grand Vezir Ibrahim Pasha with the Defterdar Iskender Chelebi to Egypt. The two men, two of the four pillars of the canopy of state, the one a Greek slave, the other a Turkish nobleman, rivals in power and in wealth, bitter rivals in the confidence of the Sultan and in his Household of Slaves of the Gate, rode into Cairo most magnificently on March 24, 1525, with Sinan the Janissary in their escort.

The proconsul Ibrahim rode astride a Cappadocian horse from the imperial stables, saddled and bridled with the finest work of the tanners', the saddlers', and the goldsmiths' guilds, in all to the value of one hundred and fifty thousand Venetian gold ducats, the parting gift of the Sultan. On his departure from Istanbul by sea, Süleyman, in still another signal honor, had accompanied Ibrahim on his flagship from the Golden Horn to Büyükada, the Great Island, of the Princes' Islands in the Marmara. Alone he entered Cairo on March 24, 1525, surrounded by his pages like the Sultan's uniformed in cloth of gold, a detachment of Sipahi cavalrymen carrying his house banners in the Greek colors, blue and white, and five thousand Janissaries, one of them Sinan.

The Grand Vezir and the Defterdar Iskender Chelebi did their work well. The revenues of Egypt tripled. The income for the privy purse rose from four hundred thousand to one million two hundred thousand gold ducats a year. There can be no question of either of the two men's depth of understanding, brilliance of mind, and capacity for hard work, nor of the Grand Vezir's tact and diplomacy.

In Cairo Sinan, or his assistants in the office of the Royal Chief Architect, later built a number of mosques and pious foundations. Now, in 1525, the Janissary engineer saw to the restoration of the walls and of the fortifications of the citadel. It may have been that he restored the Divan-i-Kebir, the Great Hall, formerly the council chamber of the Mameluke sultans. Selim the

Grim had stripped from it the revetments of precious marbles and inlays when he conquered Cairo in 1517. (The panels later were used to decorate the outside walls of the pavilion of the Prophet's Mantle built by the Royal Chief Architect Ajem Ali in the innermost courtyard of the New Palace in Istanbul, it seems likely with Sinan's assistance, under the direction of Choban Mustafa Pasha in 1526.) Certainly, off duty in Cairo, Sinan crossed the Nile to visit the pyramids. In the city he studied the tombs and the mosques from Ibn Tulun's primitive spiraling ziggurat minaret to the last of the Mameluke sultans' gorgeous domes. They are higher than a hemisphere, bulbous, intricately carved to make a play of light and shadow in the desert air of the hot Egyptian sun. They lack Sinan's Ottoman discipline and sobriety.

At the end of June the Grand Vezir and the Defterdar left Cairo to begin their return journey by land. They crossed the isthmus of Suez, the desert of Sinai, and reached El-Kuds, Jerusalem. There, in 1538, in his first year as Royal Chief Architect, Sinan restored the citadel, the Dome of the Rock (and its substructure the Wailing Wall of the Temple of Solomon), on the spot where the Prophet dismounted from his fabulous steed Burak, the mare with the face of a woman and the tail of a peacock, on which, accompanied by the Angel Gabriel, he had made his nocturnal journey from Mecca, to glimpse Paradise; and Sinan built the Damascus Gate in the restored and enlarged walls of Jerusalem the noble.

The Grand Vezir and the Defterdar then went on to Damascus, the capital of the Omayyad caliphate, from which the Syrian caravan of the pilgrimage departed.

They stopped in Marash and in Kayseri, where the Grand Vezir and the Defterdar restored the properties sequestered in 1515 by Selim the Grim to their rightful owners, the heirs of the Dulkadirli emirs and beys, and regulated the system of taxation of the annexed county. Sinan once again worked to repair the Dulkadirli and the Seljuk buildings and the city walls. It seems safe to imagine that he returned to Aghirnas to visit his mother, his father, and his brother, to let them see him in his Janissary glory, and to bring them gifts – it may have been money to buy fields and houses in the town.

Then the cadet Sinan in the army of the Grand Vezir Favorite crossed southwestern Anatolia, the ancient Greek and Hellenistic and Roman and Byzantine lands where he and Ibrahim studied the ruins of their past; and, it may be, the Grand Vezir took back a marble head, a marble torso or two. He was a collector of Greek antiquities as Iskender Chelebi was a patron of the Islamic arts and artists.

From Cairo Ibrahim had written in unseemly familiarity to his pregnant wife, Khadija Sultan. He made shocking references to Süleyman as *kardashim*, "my brother, my companion," and in even greater indecorous familiarity inquired after the health of the Sultan's disgraced First Lady Gülbahar. Ibrahim even spoke lightly to his wife of Haseki Hürrem. True, although no courteous Muslim man, no matter how intimate a friend, inquires of another man after the health, or even the existence, of his wife or his ladies of the harem, Ibrahim was addressing not a man but a woman, his imperial lady-wife. Khadija Sultan seems to have been a gentle and a mild woman. Her husband never wrote her given name or spoke it in public. Indeed, this Imperial Princess, although undoubtedly Selim the Grim's daughter and Süleyman the Magnificent's sister, and the wife of the Grand Vezir-Serasker Ibrahim Pasha, *Makbûl* and *Maktûl,* the "Favorite" and the "Assassinated," his wife, may not have been Khadija Sultan, but instead one of her anonymous sisters. Resigned and submissive, she retires and vanishes from her men's history.

Ibrahim and the Defterdar arrived back in Istanbul on September 1 to find the imperial city restored to peace and quiet. It had been very different in May when Süleyman first had news of the Janissary revolt. He had interrupted his hunting and galloped up to the walls of the city to bring his disorderly Household of slave soldiers to heel. He saw the flames and smoke rising from the Customs House. At the point of the Golden Horn, he pitched camp in a meadow beside the Sweet Waters of Europe. With a handful of chosen Life Guardsmen and pashas, like him in hunting clothes, Süleyman entered the city and rode through the Gate of Felicity into the outer courtyard of the Janissaries, mutinous in his own palace.

Their ringleaders, veteran sergeants, came up to him shouting insults, demanding that their Padishah do his Islamic duty to lead them into battle against the Christian enemy. Süleyman drew his sword and struck off the heads of three men within his reach. In the sudden silence, he retreated from their fallen bodies, stepping backward like a disciplined Janissary from his own august presence, facing down the drawn bows and the notched arrows aimed at him, the Janissaries' target.

It cost him two hundred thousand gold pieces to buy back their good will. And that was the worth, in the estimation of the Venetian bailiff's mercantile eye, and in his intelligence report to the Doge, of the second Cappadocian horse from the imperial stables, saddled and bridled in trappings of leather and velvet, embroidered in gold and studded with gem stones, that Süleyman gave Ibrahim on his triumphal return from Cairo. Eighteen years later, if the Royal Chief Architect stayed within his estimate, the memorial foundation, the mausoleum, and the Imperial Friday Mosque that took Sinan five years to build in the name of Hürrem's son, the dead Shehzadé Mehmet, cost three hundred thousand gold pieces.

When Süleyman in hunting costume faced down his mutinous slave soldiers, they held their fire. They did not choose to kill him, but they taught their young Sultan that, although they lived or died at his pleasure, he could not reign or rule without them. They did not care how he used or abused his absolute power in the Divan, or out of it, so long as he did his sacred duty as the Son of Osman. It was his obligation as the wielder of the Sword of Islam to lead them on to the field of honor in battle against the heretics and the Christians. It was their purpose, their cause, and their reason for existence to win the Holy Wars begun by the Prophet, with whose sword Süleyman had been girt on his accession to the throne of Osman.

Süleyman took care not to dishonor his slave soldiers. From then on, the Janissaries lived in fear of him and he in fear of them. If they had no life without him, he could not survive without them. The Janissaries taught Süleyman that although he was the only free man in his Slave Household, he could not use his total and absolute power in freedom. He had no choice but to lead his Janissaries out into battle to conquer the world for orthodox Islam.

After the shock of their ringleaders' beheading, the Janissaries settled down. Once more in command of himself and of his slaves, Süleyman court-martialed and executed the general officers of the Janissaries and the Sipahis, and reduced in rank the field officers and company commanders – with the consequence that other men of proved loyalty and ability rose from the ranks. Sinan was one such man. For the coming campaign, he was seconded from the Zemberekjis to the Seghmens, and took the field in 1526 as a subaltern of the "Kennelmen," in the early days the handlers of the hounds of war, but in the modern army a regiment of Janissary cavalrymen.

Then in a gesture of solidarity, Süleyman volunteered to join his slave soldiers as one of them, no more than a private first class. As such he set a dangerous precedent. He was a freeborn Muslim; no man could own him. His father, Selim the Grim, plagued by a wealthy armorer to whom he owed a great deal of money, refused to enroll the man's son, otherwise excellently qualified but a Muslim and a Turk, in the Janissary corps. Instead, he paid the debt out of his privy purse and lived a spartan life until his share, the fifth part, of the spoils of war reimbursed him.

The Sultan could call no man his master. On the Janissary register, he was enrolled not as Sultan Süleyman Khan, son of Sultan Selim Khan, as it was minted on the reverse of the coin of his realm; nor as Süleyman Son of Osman; nor as Süleyman Abdullah; nor, for instance, abdür-Rahman, nor as the Son of the Slave of God or any other of the ninety-nine beautiful names; but he was inscribed as Süleyman Son of the Slave, his mother. So from then on the Janissaries addressed him as one of them; he received his soldier's pay in silver coins of his own minting.

One pay day, an unseasonably hot day in spring which had been spent on the drill field and in war games to harden the men for yet one more campaign, Süleyman dismounted at the barracks gate to walk into the courtyard among his fellow slave soldiers to draw his wages. A bold and jaunty fellow, bursting with high spirits, had spent the first of his cash to buy himself a cup of fruit-flavored sherbet. The Janissary turned from paying the vendor to see the Sultan Süleyman Khan, a tall man in his Janissary uniform, passing by.

To test his luck and to test the temper of the Son of the Slave, not in lèse majesté but as a man bites into a new coin to test its metal, the stout fellow held out his frosted cup of sherbet as he would have offered the cold drink to a thirsty comrade, man to man in turn. He knew that he risked his head, but the odds were for him in this test of strength.

Süleyman took the cup. He put it to his lips, but he did not swallow a drop of it, not for fear of contamination but in prudence to abide by the Imperial House rule set by his ancestor Mehmet the Conqueror. The Sultan dined and drank alone, served by one of his thirty-nine gentlemen-in-waiting, his Chief Taster. He drank from a cup hollowed out of a gross emerald; he ate from Chinese porcelains, celadon, the green of the jewel and of the glaze absorbing whatever poison may have been added to his fare. The Sultan took for granted that from time to time an enemy, such as the Shah of Persia or the Pope of Rome, had managed, as we say, to penetrate his kitchens. Ordinarily, he fed three thousand men and women, domestic slaves and Slaves of the Gate. On the days of the Divan, Saturday, Sunday, Monday, and Tuesday, the cooks prepared to feed as many as ten thousand, the Grand Vezir and the lesser vezirs, the Grand Mufti, the Kazasker — the Judges of the Armies of the Domains of War and of Peace; the Defterdar — the Treasurer and his staff; the Nishanji Pasha, the Lord High Keeper of the Privy Seal, and his assistant, the Reis Efendi, later to do the work of the secretary of the interior and the secretary of state, and their bureaucracies; and all the scribes and all the retinues. On certain days of audience, the cooks prepared to feed the foreign ambassadors to the Sublime Porte and their secretaries and guardsmen, and all the pleaders for justice, the petitioners, Turkish peasants come to speak to their Tribal Chieftain, and the country gentlemen come to consult their Khan.

Therefore, the Son of the Slave's gesture sufficed. His lips had kissed the cup, perhaps of silver, perhaps of tinned copper. Süleyman returned it to the Janissary, who tilted back his head, his ketch swinging out from his flat back, his adam's apple rising and falling in the muscles of his throat, his narrowed eyes smiling as he stared into the Angelic Countenance. On each subsequent pay call, a meritorious Janissary, ready for promotion, was singled out to have the honor of offering the Son of the Slave a cup of sherbet.

The next spring, after the end of the vernal rains, Sultan Süleyman and the Grand Vezir Ibrahim led an army of one hundred thousand men, a park of three hundred pieces of artillery, and a caravan of two hundred thousand pack animals, camels and donkeys, with a reserve of cavalry mounts and herds of cattle and flocks of sheep, north into Hungary to win the Battle of Mohács on August 28, 1526. The Magyars and the Huns were once taken to be cousins of the Turks, but always they are enemies. For the next century and a half, the bells in the church towers, peculiarly unpleasant to all Muslim ears, did not ring in Hungary.

Sinan rode into battle as a subaltern in the Ottoman equivalent of the hussars, his enemies sitting their horses in spectacular uniforms frogged and furred. He distinguished himself; he was mentioned in the order of the day. And, it may be, he was promoted on the battlefield as captain of a company of the Yaya division made up of Janissary cadets.

Mohács was the last of Süleyman's triumphant victories; from then on, he held his ground, but he was contained. We can see what it looked like, this high point in Islam in Europe, in a miniature illumination of the *Hüner-namé* and the *Shahinshah-namé*, the Sultan Süleyman Khan's *Book of Accomplishments* and *Book of the King of Kings*. Turkish miniature painting, in the Islamic traditions absorbed from the caliphates, the Byzantines, the Mongols, and the Seljuks, is a major art on a minor scale. Abstract in concept, a matter of pattern and color, the miniatures are peopled with the ideas of Ottoman Islam, and not the flesh. The Ottoman miniatures of the classic sixteenth century, only now being rediscovered, are epic and heroic, masculine, as the Persian miniatures are lyric and delicate, intimate – the Ottoman, small and great; the Persian, great and small. Like the Ottoman faience of Iznik, and especially the tiles enameled in floral and calligraphic arabesques, perfectly achieved in all the values of the ceramic art and craft, the perfection of the Ottoman miniatures is impersonal. The technical mastery and discipline imposed upon the painter equaled the military discipline imposed upon the Janissary and the other Slaves of the Gate. Sinan the Janissary, portrayed in the miniatures of the Battle of Mohács, was fortunate in that he survived his military career; still more fortunate in that his gift and his values enabled him not to pain, nor to write, nor to compose music, nor to carve in the round, but instead to build. Architecture is the only major Islamic art, and possibly the greatest of all the arts.

The eye can see that the sky above the plain of Mohács, on August 28, 1526, was pure gold. The Hungarian field was painted in the forms and colors of a supine woman, breasts, belly, and thighs, skin-pink with blue in the flesh and some green, trodden by a world of booted men and shod horses. The bronze cannons mounted on pairs of disc wheels shoot frothy charges, but not in love of death. The cavalry and the Janissary infantry back up the cannon balls.

As in the erotic passion, in the moment corresponding to this instant chosen by the painter to depict, the male rhythm still goes on pulsating in wave after wave of men in ranks giving themselves purely and impersonally to the military act.

It was a still day. On their golden staves, the imperial banners of heavy silk, seven in a row, crimson, red and green striped, green, white, red and green striped, crimson, red and gold striped, stand like goddesses of war. Surrounding them march rows of perfect men, white-turbaned, white felt-capped, gilt-helmeted, plumed, each man with his own weapon in hand. The Angelic Countenance, Ibrahim's pointed oval face, and all the faces of the pashas are portrayed from the life.

They rode horses, each animal a Cappadocian, Cilician, or Arabian stallion or mare, black, white, chestnut, bay, roan, dappled-blue, or piebald-pinto, matched in conformation, ears pricked on small head on arched neck, the slim legs dancing under their quarters.

The face of the Janissary is a dedicated man's face, young, smooth, bright-skinned, marked by arched eyebrows over eyes wide open, focused straight ahead. None regarded the decapitated heads of the tousled Hungarians, as round as cannon balls, bled white, eyes and tight lips closed in decorous death, but lying piled helter-skelter to await the pike to set them up at man-height again to ring the silken pavilions of the Sultan and the Grand Vezir.

Ibrahim in fact won the battle before Süleyman arrived upon the field of Mohács. The next morning at daybreak, the Sultan rode with Ibrahim, whom he called the "pearl in the ocean of power" and "the leopard in the forest of courage," through the dead warriors to the far edge of the graying pink battle field. The Sultan looked down on the resplendently armored body of King Louis II Jagiello of Hungary, the visor of his helmet pierced by a Turkish bowman's feathered arrow. At the end of the day, in defeat, the wounded king, a young man of twenty, had fallen from his saddle when his horse slipped on the grassy bank. And heavy in his golden armor, Louis had rolled down the soft slope to drown in the burnished silver water of the stream. The last of his house and his dynasty, King Louis had been betrayed in an act of treachery. The Hapsburgs claimed his throne.

Süleyman looked up from his drowned foe lying under the surface of the clear water. He turned to Ibrahim beside him and said:

"May God be merciful to him, and may God punish his bishops and magnates, who misled him to do battle with us in his inexperience. I came indeed in arms to conquer him; but it was not my wish that he be thus cut off, young, before he had tasted the sweets of life and royalty."

In June of 1528, in an *iradé*, an imperial edict signed with the great *tughra*, the Sultan's own seal and device, Süleyman raised Ibrahim to the highest dignity as well as the greatest power ever officially bestowed on any man or any slave or any Slave of the Gate in the six centuries of the history of the Sons of Osman. Henceforth, by exercise of his sovereign will granted him by the Prophet's Sacred Law, for him alone to wield, Süleyman raised Ibrahim not only to bear the burden but also to share the imperial power of the state. Henceforth, Sultan and slave, the two men cast but a single shadow if not upon the earth, then upon their own lives and time.

"I order by these present that, from this day forever, you be my Grand Vezir, installed as such by my Majesty in all my states. My vezirs, beylerbeyler, judges of the armies, muftis of the Ulema, justices, all the descendants of the Prophet, the sheikhs, the dignitaries of my court, upholders of my empire, governors, generals of the cavalry and of the infantry, colonels of my feudal troops, and all my various soldiers, great and less, all major and minor officials, all the inhabitants of my states and provinces, and of the towns and the country, rich and poor, in sum, whoever they may be, will recognize my Grand Vezir as Serasker, the Commander in Chief of the Armies, to respect him and honor him in that quality; to go before him in order to pay him homage; to consider his thoughts and words as orders emanating from my own mouth; to listen to his words with all possible attention; to accept them with submissive countenance; and to hew the line of his chosen course of action."

The Sultan ordered his treasurer, the Defterdar Iskender Chelebi, Ibrahim's only rival in the imperial confidence, to pay the new Grand Vezir-Serasker in perpetuity for life an annual salary of thirty thousand gold pieces – three million gold dollars of 1900.

Ibrahim's power and glory went to his head.

In the unparalleled document, Sultan Süleyman Khan made Ibrahim responsible for all the major decisions of the Ottoman Empire "marching along the paths of justice in the law"; and made him responsible for all appointments to high office within his Ruling Institution of the Slaves of the Gate in the imperial city, in the field, and in the two Domains of War and of Peace. Twice in the text, Süleyman defined Ibrahim's judgment and his council as "certain," and his intelligence as "penetrating," as though these qualities were not self-evident.

The Sultan brought to a close the statement of his sovereign will with a threat. "None shall have the audacity to refuse obedience to my Grand Vezir and Serasker's orders. . . . If ever – God preserve us from it! – against my sublime will and against the fundamental law of the Koran, a member whosoever of my victorious army refuses to obey the order and the word of my Grand Vezir and Serasker, . . ." (I paraphrase) no matter what his quality and rank, shall be brought to justice, tried, and punished in a way to serve as an example, so to strike "salutary terror in all others." It is a revolutionary document, a powerful attempt within the accumulated traditions of the

Ruling Institution to reorganize the government of the empire. Had Ibrahim been able to free himself from his own golden moment, had he been another Solomon, Süleyman might have carried his inheritance into a Renaissance, and brought Islam into modern times. But Ibrahim was a slave of the Sultan in whom he had his being, and Süleyman was imprisoned in his inheritance. He was the absolute and total Son of Osman.

It lay within his sovereign power to present his Grand Vezir-Serasker with three robes of honor, with eight war-horses richly equipped, and a ninth charger carrying sabers, bows, quivers of arrows sparkling with jewels. But the Sultan could not confer upon Ibrahim more than six horsetails, to his own imperial seven, *tughs*, the horsetails that were as stars to us, in the hierarchy of their military order.

To have done so would have been to risk disaster and defeat. The Turks are conservative and traditional in character, and having been shamanists in the Altai Mountains and on the steppes, in Islam they are strong mystics. In the mythos of the Sons of Osman, the sign and symbol of Süleyman's inherited and inherent power was called the *tugh*. It was a horsetail. According to the legend, Süleyman's ancestor, the nomadic Turkish chieftain of the nameless clan, Ertughrul the Right-Hearted, in a battle of mounted bowmen saw his standard and his Standard-Bearer, riding ahead of him, fall in the first charge against the enemy. It was a bad omen. Before his men could turn tail, Ertughrul leaned forward in his saddle, seized the tail of the standard-bearer's riderless horse, and with a slash of his saber, cut it off. He tied the long horsetail to his spearhead, and holding it on high, shouted, "See my standard! " The Turks won the day.

As the Ottoman Empire expanded, it grew in complexity. The Sultan-Khan multiplied his horsetails to seven — the number of the *odas*, or the divisions, in his army? At Mohács, Süleyman could not reduce himself, but he could raise the Grand Vezir-Serasker Ibrahim Pasha to the standard of six horsetails and seven banners. He could and did order his tailors to design for himself and Ibrahim identical robes of honor cut from the same bolt. The Sultan alone wore the plumed imperial turban and the imperial jewels. With the insignia on his head, Süleyman stood eight feet tall with Ibrahim beside him shorter by a foot but wearing the turban signifying his own double distinction as Süleyman's Grand Vezir and Serasker for life.

At Buda, after Mohács, who knows what Süleyman thought and left unsaid as he watched Ibrahim put his new powers to a trivial test? From the King of Hungary's hunting castle, the Grand Vezir-Serasker took, as part of his share of the loot and booty, three works of art, three ancient Greek bronzes — the larger than lifesize nude statues of Apollo, the sun god; of his sister Artemis the virgin huntress, the original patroness of Byzantium, whose crescent moon became the symbol of the Mother of God, the patroness of Constantinople and then of Islam; and of Hercules, the hero of the labors.

Back in Istanbul, Süleyman condoned Ibrahim's erection of these two naked bronze Greek deities and the naked demiurge in a triangle pointing out upon a single round plinth. The Grand Vezir, who was once a Greek slave, set up his statues in the Hippodrome beside the Delphic Oracle's tripod, the twisted serpent column in front of his Palace of Ibrahim. Sinan may have done the actual marble-cutting and stonemasonry, rigged the pulleys, hoisted the hollow cast bronzes, and fixed their feet in place.

From the King of Hungary's palace at Buda, Ibrahim had also taken for himself the magical iron crown of Saint Stephen, the symbol of Hungarian royal and divine right to independent rule. He did not display the trophy, which was of no intrinsic value, but kept it out of sight in his strong room.

The Household and the Ulema were not pleased with the bronzes, doubly and triply offensive to the Islamic eye. The Prophet forbade displays of immodest nakedness and the setting up of idols. The traditions had absorbed the Judaic puritanical customary law prohibiting the worshiping or the carving of representational works of art (as usual, artists broke the rules to paint miniatures even of the Prophet, although always his effulgent face is veiled in green against the contemplation even of the rich and the privileged). The sculptor who reproduced recognizably detailed male and female human forms of life in the round impiously set himself up as God's equal in a competitive act of sacrilege.

A poet, a witty satirist, a Turk named Figani, wrote an epigram upon the subject of the three bronzes in which he played upon the favorites's given name. Ibrahim means Abraham as Süleyman means Solomon.

Figani's joke was all about how the first Abraham had toppled the graven images, and how the second Ibrahim had set them up upon their feet again. Short, it may be, on Biblical history, Figani was long on topical allusion. Enraged, Ibrahim had his guardsmen arrest the poet. They beat him; they cut off his nose and ears; they tied him to a donkey's back so that he faced the tail; they paraded him through the back streets where the housewives obliged the Grand Vezir by emptying their chamber pots over the poet's head, and the men threw shit in his face. Then Ibrahim had Figani hanged in the public place of execution for criminals. So he avenged himself and also the Olympians. Apollo, Artemis, and Hercules remained upon their plinth until Ibrahim's downfall.

On Monday the 10th of May, 1529, the Sultan and the Grand Vezir-Serasker planted the golden staves of their standards, the one of seven, the other of six horsetails, in the high fields outside the land walls beyond the Edirné Gate. It was the declaration of war in the first German campaign to Vienna.

Sinan, the commanding officer of the Zemberekji Brigade of Janissaries, the regiments of pioneers, miners, sappers, and the handlers of high explosives, the engineers, rode ahead of the army of two hundred fifty thousand men and the artillery of three hundred bronze cannons. To span the marshy water meadows on both banks of the Drava River, a tributary of the Danube, he designed, and his engineers built, a bridge five miles long – six thousand Janissary paces. They felled a forest to cut the massive timbers. Guarded by high towers built on piles at intervals, the fortress bridge carried the Ottoman line of march into Hungary for a century and a half. In 1683, it took lesser men than Sinan's Janissary engineers six months to repair his structure to carry the Ottoman army a second time up to the gates of Vienna.

In 1529, after a summer on the march, Sülyman and Ibrahim arrived in the autumnal rains before Vienna on September 27, Saint Wenceslaus Day. Twelve thousand imperial Life Guards and Body Guards surrounded the imperial pavilions pitched on a hill to the west of Vienna. At three o'clock in the afternoon of October 14, Sinan's miners and sappers exploded two final charges to enlarge the breach in the walls by the Carinthian Gate opened by the siege guns four days earlier.

The Sultan and the Grand Vezir-Serasker sent the Janissaries into action. Three times in three waves three columns of slave soldiers charged and were repelled. Their dead in red and blue uniforms, their white Janissary caps fallen from their heads, piled up in a ramp below the breach in the walls, which the living then refused to scale. Their officers whipped them, clubbed them, and beat them with the flat of the sword. The Sultan and the Grand Vezir-Serasker walked among the slave soldiers to urge them on and to put a gold piece in the hand of each man, with a promise of a prize of still more gold to the victors.

The breach was wide enough. Eighty Janissaries marching shoulder to shoulder could have, might have, should have, but did not charge through the breach – or so one Viennese historian describes its size to give the dimensions of the Ottoman failure.

The Janissaries refused. They had taken the Ottoman Empire as far as it would go into Chistendom. Their nature as slave soldiers, the natures of the Sultan's Ruling and Religious Institutions, and nature itself in that wet European autumnal equinox worked on the side of Count von Salm, the defender of the city, a very old and a very valiant man, to save Vienna from Süleyman and Ibrahim. At that distance from Istanbul, the Ottomans could not support a winter-long siege.

Had Vienna fallen, the walled city on the Danube would have been reduced to an enemy-held fortress, an Ottoman garrison on the distant frontier, islanded in sullen Christian territory. Or if Austria were depopulated, then the Janissaries in the rebuilt city would have been isolated in a green and fertile desert. The Religious Institution had no interest in the conversion of the Roman Catholics to Islam. The Ruling Institution picked and chose only the best of the *penjik* and *devshirmé* Christian youths to convert and bring into the aristocracy of the Slaves of the Gate of the Sultan's Household. The Ottoman Empire failed to develop a national identity as a sovereign state if only because Islam takes into account no territorial limitations, such as frontiers. Therefore, Turks did not go out as pioneers to settle their own Far West.

On the night of October 14, 1529, after seventeen days of rain and mud and failure, Süleyman gave the order to raise the siege. The Hapsburg Holy Roman Emperor Ferdinand I had not chosen to defend his capital in person. But Count von Salm, the protector of Vienna, a man of eighty, led the way up to the ramparts with all the defenders who could still climb to man the city walls. They saw and they heard the flames of the burning houses in the suburbs, and they watched the pillaging of the humiliated Janissaries, the Sipahis, and the Turkish feudal raiders let loose upon the countryside and the country people.

While the defeated armies raged across the green hills and valleys and farmlands, the Sultan conferred with the Grand Vezir-Serasker in the imperial tents surrounded by their twelve thousand Janissary guardsmen, who watched and heard their plundering fellow slaves and knew that they would be allotted their fair share of the total loot and booty.

After Mohács, which had been an honorable victory won in pitched battle in an open plain, the Ottoman army of one hundred thousand men had gone on to Buda, the Hungarian capital. There the victors had taken one hundred thousand captives. They cut the throats of forty thousand useless able-bodied men, and led off sixty thousand serviceable women and girls, and the youths – save for the Sultan's share – to be offered for sale in the slave markets of Edirné and Istanbul.

After the defeat at Vienna, no one knows the comparable statistics; such was the savagery permitted the slave soldiers and the raiders. But out of his army of two hundred fifty thousand men, Süleyman lost forty thousand beneath the walls. Sinan and the general of the artillery, and their two commands of engineers and cannoneers, were the only slave soldiers to leave Vienna having done what they had come to do, their best, with honor.

To take Vienna was the military and the religious ambition of Süleyman's life. The armies had not known defeat since Mehmet the Conqueror had raised the first siege of Rhodes two generations earlier. The grandees of the Household of Slaves, the wise men of the Ulema, and the people of the imperial city of Istanbul, unable to read the writing on the wall, could not bring themselves to understand the causes and the effects of their earth-shaking failure. The greatest of Ottoman armies led by the most magnificent ruler of his epoch should have won. In history, Sultan Süleyman Khan has taken his rightful place as first among his sovereign peers, the Popes of the High Renaissance and the Reformation, the Doges of the Republic of Venice at its richest, and Charles V, Francis I, Henry VIII, and Ivan the Terrible. Against such men and such Christian states, Süleyman waged total Holy War at the head of the most efficient and best organized war machine of the sixteenth century (and relatively, it may be, of all time). At Vienna he met his own historical defeat; but he forced the Europeans into the Western World that we have inherited.

Because the defeated Janissaries and the pashas refused to take upon themselves any personal responsibility for their failure; and because to criticize the Shadow of God on Earth were heinous, the Sultan's Slaves of the Gate cast about to hit upon a scapegoat. They chose the Sultan's favorite. They whispered that Ibrahim was a sorcerer; his charms had enchanted and bemused the Sultan. Among themselves they called him a traitor. Aloud they said that the Grand Vezir-Serasker had conspired with the defenders of Vienna to save the capital for the Holy Roman Emperor. Back in Istanbul, they spread the story that he intended to preside over the dissolution of the Ottoman Empire. From the ruins, he would emerge as King of Hungary – why else had he chosen to take the iron crown of Saint Stephen from Buda? In historical fact, none of the enemy historians of the Ottoman Empire has found a suggestion, let alone a proof, of such treachery on the part of Ibrahim in the archives of Vienna or Venice. There can be no question of his perfect loyalty; but of his terror it may be that his growing megalomania gives proof.

Süleyman heard the whispered rumors. To demonstrate his faith in his appointed Grand Vezir-Serasker, and also in an attempt to disguise his momentous defeat as but a momentary setback, the Sultan appeared at the Divan on horseback on October 16, 1529, and distributed military honors and awards as though to victors. Each Janissary received twenty gold pieces. The Grand Vezir-Serasker was rewarded with great estates in Hungary, four robes of honor, five purses of gold (the equivalent of sixty thousand gold American dollars), and still one more saber, hafted and sheathed in the finest goldsmithery roughened with diamonds and emeralds. In his autobiography, Sinan did not see fit to record his own distinctions and prizes, but from Vienna he returned a wealthy man singled out for future honors.

Failure was a new experience for Süleyman. The Sultan thoughtfully took stock of himself and his favorite. In 1527, when he had returned to Istanbul after the clear victory of Mohács, Süleyman had been sure enough of himself and of Ibrahim to lose his temper with the Grand Vezir in front of the full Divan. By then the Sultan no longer presided regularly at the weekly sessions of the Council of State. Instead, he delegated his authority to the Grand Vezir.

Turkish historians call this withdrawal of the Sultan from the daily life of his people the first step in the decline of the Ottoman Empire, but in hindsight none offers any other practical solution to the problem. The Sultan could no longer move under the crushing weight of his accumulated powers; therefore, he had to delegate his authority but not entirely to relinquish control. As in all mosques, the Prophet in spirit is present seated under the canopy at the top of the stairs to the *minber*, once his throne of justice, so the Sultan was present, always in the spirit, not often in the flesh, seated behind the iron grilles and the silken curtains of the window of his observations post in the Divan. Süleyman's great-grandfather, Mehmet the Conqueror, having withdrawn into the remote majesty of the conquered Byzantine emperors, hit upon the plan.

He had a room built out behind the rear wall of the council chamber. Halfway up between the floor and the dome, behind the seated Grand Vezir, the lesser vezirs, the Grand Mufti, the two Judges of the Armies, the Defterdar (the Treasurer), and the Nishanji Pasha (the Secretary of State, Keeper of the Privy Seal), he had a window cut through the rear wall. From his place behind the curtains and the grille, the Sultan could oversee and overhear the Divan at work without being seen or heard. None knew in fact whether or not he was there. So he made his presence felt even in his absence.

Süleyman had climbed the hidden staircase late in the day of his last intervention, so that he had overhead only the final decision of the Grand Vezir. He watched the general discontent as Ibrahim revoked the ruling of the Judges of the armies of Europe and of Asia, the highest magistrates of the supreme judicial tribunal of the empire. Freeborn Muslims, members of the Religious Institution, ex-officio members of the Council of State, they had condemned to death a member of the Ulema, likewise a freeborn Muslim in the Religious Institution, a man named Kabiz, for heresy. When the Sultan's Grand Vezir of the Ruling Institution nullified their decision, the Judges of the Armies raised their voices in angry protest. Kabiz, a wise man learned in sacred jurisprudence, had strayed from the Path. He had come to the conclusion that Jesus Christ, as a Messenger of God, was greater than the Prophet Mohammed. What is more, Kabiz could not contain himself. He proclaimed his heresy from the Prophet's *minber* in the mosques of the city, to the consternation of all orthodox Muslims. The Judges of the Armies brought Kabiz to trial, found him guilty, and condemned him to death.

In a sudden hush, Sultan Süleyman appeared on the floor of the Divan. The vezirs and the judges, the Defterdar Iskender Chelebi, the Nishanji Pasha, the Grand Vezir, and the Grand Mufti ceased their indecorous uproar. They stood, hands clasped, eyes cast down in the presence, but they had seen the anger in the Angelic Countenance.

"Why," Sultan Süleyman Khan demanded of his Grand Vezir, "have you remitted the death sentence of this man who dares to place Jesus above your Prophet Mohammed? " Ibrahim was the protector of all the Greek Christians in the Ottoman Empire. It was whispered that in his heart he was a pagan.

"I did so," Ibrahim replied, "because the judges condemned the man in anger; they did not, as our Prophet advocates, first use rational arguments to persuade him to change the error of his ways."

Süleyman upheld Ibrahim's decision. The Sultan requested the Grand Mufti to use powerful persuasion in an inquisition to convince Kabiz of his faulty reasoning. He failed. The Judge of Istanbul presided at the second trial. Kabiz chose martyrdom. He was duly hanged. The Gate of Interpretation in Islam was closed and locked.

In his imperial displeasure, Selim the Grim would have called in his mutes to silence so bold a Grand Vezir. But Süleyman, in recognition of the penetrating intelligence of his Grand Vezir, issued the astonishing imperial *iradé* decreeing Ibrahim Grand Vezir and Serasker for life. Further to strengthen Ibrahim's position, he let it be known that he no longer intended to seat himself behind the silken curtains and the iron bars of his observation post to look down upon his Grand Vezir's conduct in the Divan.

Therefore, after Vienna when he heard the rumors of Ibrahim's treachery, Süleyman could take no outright action to silence them without tacitly admitting his own failure by calling attention to the inherent weaknesses of the Ottoman Ruling and Religious Institutions. Few men of destiny fully comprehend their places in history. The Sultan may have done so; the Grand Vezir-Serasker did not.

On May 27, 1533, in the hall of audience of his own palace, Ibrahim received the Austrian and Spanish ambassadors of the Holy Roman Emperor Charles V, who was also King Charles I of Spain, as well as the Italian bailiff of the Doge of Venice. Their secretaries wrote down what are to be accepted as verbatim reports, which are still filed in the archives of Vienna and Venice. These great European enemies of the Sultan had come to make a kind of non-aggression pact with Süleyman.

Their meeting with Ibrahim was, and remains, a turning point in history. In sending their ambassadors to the Sultan's Court, the Sublime Porte, the Christian sovereigns acknowledged the power and the supremacy of the Grand Turk. But in coming to terms with his European enemies, the Sultan, bargaining for time, demonstrated the vulnerability of his frontiers. The defeat before the gates of Vienna proved the limitations of the single summer campaign into Europe. In 1529 it had taken the Ottoman army of two hundred fifty thousand men and at least as many sumpter horses and pack and victual animals from May 10 to September 27 to march from Istanbul to the Austrian capital. In 1534 and 1535 it was to take a similar Ottoman army twice as long a march, broken by a stay in winter quarters at Aleppo, to reach Baghdad.

The ambassadorial audience in the Palace of Ibrahim, on May 27, 1533, marks the rise of the Sultan's enemy to the east. Shah Tahmasp of the vigorous Safavid dynasty had reoccupied Tabriz, the ancient Persian capital, and had refortified Baghdad, the city of the caliphs. As the enemy of my enemy is my friend, so the Persian Shah in the east contained the Ottoman Sultan within his European frontiers. The Sultan could not divide his army to fight on two fronts. Before Süleyman and the Grand Vezir-Serasker could march off at the head of their government and the armies, to leave the capital in the care of a handful of old men, a boy prince regent, and ten thousand Janissary cadets, they had to fix the terms of peace along the frontiers of the European Domain of War. Süleyman and Ibrahim knew, if the Western powers did not, that with such defenders, Istanbul lay open to a united Christian amphibious attack. The Pope could have mounted a last crusade to take back the imperial city and rename it, if not Constantinople then New Rome.

The ambassadors opened their negotiations with the presentation of gifts. In his palace, Ibrahim was pleased to accept a Renaissance jewel of gold and enamelings set with a ruby worth (in 1914) two hundred thousand American gold dollars, a diamond worth half as much as the ruby, and a tear-shaped Oriental pearl worth half as much as the diamond. But apparently the Spanish ambassadors, haughty men of impeccable noble birth, grandees in a court etiquette even stricter than that of the Ottoman hierarchy of Slaves of the Gate, let it be known to Ibrahim that they knew that he was a slave, the son of a Greek fisherman, and that they understood the causes for the strong preference by which he had climbed to power.

The Grand Vezir began to ask questions. Why had their Emperor allowed the cultivated gardens and orchards that made Spain bloom in the days of the glorious Spanish Caliphate to revert to wasteland? The ambassador announced that the King of Spain and all his noblemen were gentlemen born to the sword, not to the ploughshare.

"Such pride," Ibrahim commented, "is an inheritance of noble blood. So it is with the Greeks, men audacious in their probity and honor, generous men. . . . It is I who govern this vast Ottoman Empire," said he, and not the Turks. He then recommended that the Spanish ambassadors follow his example and learn how to lead their King-Emperor Charles V along by the nose.

"The lion, the proudest and most terrible of beasts, cannot be tamed by force. But the subtle lion-tamer feeds the lion food the lion likes to eat. So he accustoms the king of beasts to the presence of the lion-tamer, and so wins his confidence. Then, with the whip of truth and the club of justice, the lion-tamer tames the lion." You would do well, said the Greek slave favorite to the Spanish grandees, to tame your Emperor as I have tamed my Lion.

"I am the power in the land. I can if I choose raise a stableboy to govern a conquered kingdom. Look around you at this great hall; it was built for me by my master. These robes I wear are no less splendid than the robes he wears, cut and tailored from the identical bolt. Yet what I say is to be done is done. This seal I carry is the duplicate of the seal of the Padishah, the Emperor of the East and of the West, and of the Black Sea and the White Sea."

The ambassadors signed, and the Grand Vezir-Serasker sealed the treaty of peace. In their intelligence reports, the verbatim account of the Greek favorite's harangue covers page after page with what reads like outrageous boasting in humorless self-aggrandizement. There is no way of knowing if the Hapsburg brothers, Charles V and Ferdinand I, read and understood the troubled vainglory of the words. Perhaps they wrote it off as mere evidence of Oriental pomp and circumstance. They took no immediate action. Süleyman was kept informed. If Haseki Hürrem's spies did not report to her in the imperial harem, then certainly the Defterdar Iskender Chelebi's secret agents reported to him.

Süleyman was too wise a ruler to allow enemy action to disrupt the order of his Household on the eve of Holy War. Indeed, who knows whether or not the Spanish or the Austrian ambassadors had not distorted the Grand Vezir's words to suit their own purposes? The Sultan went ahead with his plans for the Persian campaign.

After the end of the September rains, in September 1533, he sent off the Grand Vezir-Serasker marching at the head of half the Ottoman army, and half the members of the Divan. They crossed Asia Minor to winter at Aleppo. According to the plan, after the spring rains ended in May 1534, Süleyman would leave the capital at the head of the other half of the army and the government to join Ibrahim. Together they would lead the united army on to take Baghdad.

Süleyman knew of the rivalry, which by then amounted to hatred, between Ibrahim and the Defterdar Iskender Chelebi. These two men, the Greek slave and the Turkish gentleman, were the greatest grandees of the Household. The assignment of Iskender Chelebi as quartermaster general and second-in-command to the Grand Vezir-Serasker Ibrahim demonstrates that the Padishah knew and understood the virtues and the defects of both his men. Together they counter balanced one another. The Defterdar acted as a brake upon the favorite's mounting extravagances of word and deed. The Treasurer controlled the iron-bound coffers of gold coin and bullion that accompanied the army.

As a Turkish feudal noble, the Defterdar in the Divan and the Household, Iskender Chelebi led a cavalry of one thousand two hundred mounted knights and bowmen. According to his rank, he rode forth with a mounted retinue of three hundred pages of the palace in gold berets. True, Ibrahim had the right to four hundred pages similarly uniformed in cloth of gold. Iskender Chelebi's private household included six or seven thousand slaves, his own possessions, and a private army modeled on the Sultan's own Janissaries. In his palaces and on his country estates, Iskender Chelebi had established private schools for cadets and pages, all of them converted Christian youths, either his share of the spoils of war or his choices purchased in the open market, equaling in quality those of Ibrahim's palace and rivaling the Sultan's own. One of them, taken into the Imperial Household after 1534, was the Bosnian slave Sokollu Mehmet, who replaced his master, Iskender Chelebi, as Defterdar and, as Süleyman's last Grand Vezir, ruled the empire and led the armies throughout the eight years of the reign of Selim the Sot.

Iskender Chelebi's wealth and magnificence, all of it awarded him by the Sultan for meritorious service in office, proves that the Defterdar was a man in Süleyman's confidence. His slaves, the future vezirs and grand vezirs, prove his excellence of character and judgment. He was a Turkish nobleman, an educated and cultivated Muslim, a man of honor. He was a better organizer and administrator than the Grand Vezir-Serasker.

For the Persian campaign, as quartermaster general Iskender Chelebi had to muster a baggage train of some forty thousand camels and nearly as many mules. The greater part of the pack animals carried supplies of rice, flour, dried beans and peas, the basic rations for the army of two hundred fifty thousand for the two-year campaign. The lands on both sides of the Persian frontier had been laid waste in a scorched-earth policy to discourage border raids and invasions. For three centuries Mesopotamia, the heartland of the Abbasid Caliphate, had been reduced to deserts since the Mongol Hulagu Khan had destroyed the dams, the reservoirs, and the irrigation canals between the Tigris and the Euphrates in 1258. From Istanbul to Aleppo to Tabriz to Baghdad is about one thousand five hundred miles as the crow flies. It is twice that distance on foot across the accidented topography of the rivers, the littorals, the mountains, the high plateaus, and the deserts. Ibrahim left for Aleppo in September 1533; the Grand Vezir-Serasker and Sultan Süleyman returned to enter Istanbul in triumph on January 8, 1536.

Along with staples, Iskender Chelebi's eighty thousand camels and mules carried the imperial pavilions and the Janissary tents, uniforms, gear for the cavalry, armor, tools for the blacksmiths and the saddlers, all the munitions, feed for the reserve of horses and the pack animals, the rations for the Janissary cauldrons, and the hospital. Each cavalryman led a sumpter horse carrying his own equipment, a small canvas tent, extra clothing and bedding, a leather bag or two of flour, a small pot of butter, some spices and salt, ground cereal for gruel, and a water can. Some brought along luxuries, a sack of hard-baked biscuits, a bladder of powdered dried beef. The man counted on eating the horseflesh of the war casualties. If both his horses were killed, he took up his saddle and bridle and stood alongside the Sultan's line of march to catch the eye of his Padishah, who would remount him from the reserves herded along with the packtrain.

The ordinary Turkish soldier of the raiders was better clad than he was armed — the Sultan protected the man's health. The soldier defended himself against the enemy and armed himself with the weapons of the men he killed. Before he left on campaign, he stood in line in the dark and slowly filed past the bundles of cloth piled up in a mountain in the barracks courtyard. A sergeant handed out the uniform-lengths to each man in turn. Luck only was to blame if some cloth was of better quality than the stuff in other bundles. The man saw to the tailoring himself.

The Janissaries, however, were well provided with the best. Each man wore three garments; his underwear woven of coarse cotton or linen thread for warmth; the red and the blue woolen cloth for the Janissary uniform came from Salonika, where it was woven for hard wear; over the regulation uniform, made to his measure, he wore a great coat of thick wool against the cold weather in the mountains. His boots, his shawl wrapped like a bellyband, and his wide leather girdle, studded with silver ornaments, depended on his own means for their quality, as did his spoon and his cutlass. The weapons assigned to them were the finest of their time; the improved harquebus of the Janissary was taken over by the Spanish and Austrian armies for their riflemen.

Iskender Chelebi did his work admirably well, but between him and his superior officer Ibrahim, things began badly. According to the traditional requirements incumbent upon his office in the hierarchy, the Defterdar was called upon, in time of war, to furnish thirty fully armed and equipped cavalrymen; it was his feudal obligation to his liege lord, the Sultan. In a test of strength, the Grand Vezir-Serasker, addressing his second-in-command the Defterdar in tones of calculated benevolence, begged Iskender Chelebi to contribute, above and beyond this outdated regular contingent of thirty horsemen, one hundred and ten more. The Defterdar, wholly occupied as quartermaster general, may have misunderstood. But probably he knew what he was doing when he sent in one hundred and ten of his horsemen, including among them the requisite Defterdar's thirty. Ibrahim took umbrage — the fight was on.

In that summer of 1533, the Sultan assigned another Slave of the Gate in whom he had full confidence, a tried and proved Janissary officer, to Ibrahim's command. Sinan, the General of the Engineers, went ahead to build the timber and pontoon bridges across the rivers of southern Anatolia and the Taurus Mountains, swollen in the autumn rains. At Aleppo, he planned and built the winter quarters in the dry and windy steppes outside the walled market town.

The Ottoman camps were notable for their order and hygiene. Busbecq, the Austrian ambassador to the Sublime Porte, particularly remarked the sanitary arrangements of slit trenches and garbage pits, the first that he had seen. In Austria and France, the army posts and bivouacs stank with the piled-up refuse and dunghills of both the men and the horses. The Janissaries policed the orderly grid of streets laid out between the rows of tents, each sheltering the pallets of twenty-five to thirty slave soldiers. Perhaps, through the Byzantines, the Ottomans had inherited Julius Caesar's Roman Legionaries' castrametation.

The Janissaries kept themselves clean with weekly baths in the famous *hamams* of Aleppo where, in the days of the Crusaders, the Christian European knights and ladies, immodestly and barbarously stripped, first learned to bathe and to keep down the lice. The Turkish soldiers guarded the citadel where Tamerlane had filled the moat with the bodies, and piled up a pyramid of heads of the slaughtered Assyrians, Syrians, Arabs, Cilicians, and Turks of the mixed blood of the international market town.

In camp the Janissaries neither gambled nor brawled, nor did they complain of their simple rations of rice, bread, a turnip or an onion eaten raw with salt and olive oil, with now and again a bit of meat or the fruit in season. They drank water, not wine or beer. Their health astonished Busbecq.

To keep his engineers busy while the rest of the Janissaries drilled, Sinan, it is reasonable to imagine, put his men to work to repair the walls and the citadel, and to restore or to enlarge the famous covered markets of Aleppo, the last stage on the caravan routes from Persia, India, and China. In winter quarters, Sinan found his first patron, Hüsrev Pasha, then the Beylerbey of Damascus, the Governor General of the Syrian Province. This very wealthy Ottoman nobleman commissioned Sinan to design and build his first pious foundation around a small mosque (it was finished two years later, in 1536). The buildings still stand today, much and badly restored under the cliffs and walls of the citadel. In architecture, the mosque and its dependencies, although recognizably Ottoman, and thus neither Syrian, nor Seljuk, nor Persian, is undistinguished. But it is well built upon the plan of the circle in the square, its construction of dressed stone solidly engineered. It must have pleased the Gazi Hüsrev Pasha. Seven years later, the new Royal Chief Architect built his first patron a classic mausoleum in Istanbul. The tomb makes a romantic ruin today, with curtains of green ivy hanging from its arabesqued cornice, and a wild fig tree rooted in the drum of the dome. Snapdragons and valerian bloom from the crevices.

In winter quarters at Aleppo, Iskender Chelebi and Sinan found plenty of work to do. Ibrahim the supreme commander devoted his idle energies to snaring the Defterdar. In a council of war, Iskender Chelebi, backed by the Beylerbey Hüsrev Pasha, and, it may be, by Sinan, the general of the engineers, had prevailed in the planning and the mapping of the strategy for the spring campaign. The Grand Vezir-Serasker Ibrahim had proposed to march through Diyarbakir to take Mosul on the Tigris. From that city he planned to lead the armies down through Mesopotamia to Baghdad. Iskender Chelebi had better military intelligence. His agents had reported to him the shah's strategic withdrawal from Tabriz, the northern capital of Persia. On the march to his southern capital of Isfahan, Shah Tahmasp sent out what we call commandos and guerrillas to harass the Ottoman enemy in their homeland of mountains and deserts. Iskender Chelebi proposed marching not upon Mosul, a town not worth the cost of a siege or a battle, but to Diyarbakir. This fortified strongpoint of the turbulent Kurds, nominal subjects of the Ottoman Sultan, in any case had to be pacified.

From Diyarbakir, Iskender Chelebi proposed to march his slow baggage train to the east while Ibrahim went north around Lake Van and down to recapture Tabriz. From the regained Persian capital, he would head south to rejoin the baggage train and to meet Sultan Süleyman with the rest of the Ottoman forces. Then on to Baghdad according to the original plan. Ibrahim recognized the superior logic of his lieutenant general's reasoning; he concurred, and he hated the man.

Perhaps, having prevailed, Iskender Chelebi scornfully smiled. Greeks cannot put up with ridicule. The favorite, long-separated from his master, may well have been badly frightened by his own lapse of judgment. Perhaps he intercepted a secret or a critical dispatch, or a personal letter that the Defterdar had written to Istanbul. Army posts in winter quarters are hotbeds of gossip. It is the nature of such men as Ibrahim to give way to anxieties that are now classified as paranoid. The Grand Vezir-Serasker decided to rid himself of his rival, if not his tormentor, Iskender Chelebi.

Apparently the favorite's emotions got in the way of his intelligence. He made a mess of his plan. Ibrahim foolishly conspired with a man named Nakkash Ali, a scribe employed as bursar in the government of the Beylerbey of Damascus, Hüsrev Pasha, the Sultan's first cousin, Sinan's first patron, who was an honorable man. Nakkash Ali talked too much in camp. To make himself important, he spread rumors that he soon was to replace the Defter-dar Iskender Chelebi as minister of finance to the Sultan in Istanbul. Known to the Janissaries in winter quarters as a notorious liar and a petty crook, this much despised man was believed by no one.

When the army broke camp, Nakkash Ali arranged with a claque of rowdies to cry "Stop thief!" as the Treasurer at the head of his camel caravan packing the iron-bound chests of gold bullion and the soldiers' pay marched past the Grand Vezir-Serasker taking the salute astride his war-horse. Ibrahim had Iskender Chelebi arrested for questioning. But in total disbelief, the Janissaries, along with Hüsrev Pasha, the Beylerbey of Damascus, and Sinan the general of the Janissary engineers, and (it may have been) a court-martial of the lesser vezirs and the Judges of the Armies in the Divan, refused to give credence to the transparent ruse. Iskender Chelebi was exonerated. However, nothing could stop the gossip of Ibrahim's lethal and petty jealousy from spreading; it made too good a story.

Sinan and the engineers, assigned with the artillery to a detachment of Janissary marines commanded by Hüsrev Pasha, brought the victory that restored the unity and the spirit to the Grand Vezir-Serasker's army. Lake Van, the greatest of the Turkish lakes, 1,454 square miles of salt water, 5,260 feet above sea level, surrounded by desert mountains and steep rocky shores, had stopped Tamerlane and all the invading forces of antiquity. The fortified towns and castles on the islands and along the shores were impregnable by land. Held by heretical Shiites, Christian Armenians, and independent Gazi Turks, they withstood years of siege. The excellent Armenian and Persian architects had built solid defenses in depth from the approaches through the trackless mountains down to the cliffs and beaches. In the mountain passes and narrow defiles, a handful of defenders could stop an army.

An act of treachery gave Hüsrev Pasha a foothold. The keeper of the castle of Van, on the southeast shore, surrendered his keys. To reduce the other fortresses along the waterfront, Sinan built gunboats, barges of heavy timber strong enought to float the light siege guns of the Ottoman artillery. He built a landing craft to take the Janissary marines onto beachheads and into harbors defenseless from waterborne attack. Sinan's fire-bomb hurlers reduced the towns. His gunboats collected the islands and shore castles, one by one. From then on, the Ottomans controlled Lake Van.

According to the list of his works, Sinan the Royal Chief Architect built one of his eighty-three mosques and a pious foundation in the town of Van. The buildings stand in ruins. The Czarist Russians destroyed the place in 1917.

The Grand Vezir-Serasker entered the open city of Tabriz on July 13, 1534, and he began to govern it intelligently and thoughtfully. The most beautiful of Persian cities, as it was in those days, was intact; all the splendid buildings were unspoiled in their gardens and orchards. Ibrahim had put the city out of bounds to all but the engineers and the Janissary military police. Sinan built a fortress outside the walls on the main highway, in which a thousand Janissary musketeers were garrisoned to keep the Persians and the Ottomans in check. None looted; none raped; there were no uprisings and no reprisals. Before he left on the march for Baghdad, Ibrahim set up a court of law with a judge from the Ulema to dispense orthodox Sunnite justice among the Shiite Persians; but he had not forced conversion upon the inhabitants of Tabriz. All was well. He sent the keys of the city to the Sultan. Süleyman was pleased.

He marched south to join Ibrahim. The only casualties of the Grand Vezir-Serasker's army came as a result of Iskender Chelebi's logical but mistaken decision, based on faulty military intelligence. The Defterdar, without consulting Ibrahim, had detached a small task force of ten thousand men to take and hold a defile in the Green Mountains of Azerbaijan. They were waylaid and wiped out by the Shah's Kurdish and Persian guerrillas. Ibrahim made the most of it when, on September 27, 1534, the two halves of the Ottoman army rejoined, and the favorite moved in to share the Sultan's tent. Even so, the next day, in the Divan, the Sultan presided to decorate his Grand Vezir-Serasker, his Defterdar Iskender Chelebi, his cousin Hüsrev Pasha, the Beylerbey of Damascus, Sinan, and all the other generals with kaftans and robes of honor. Each Janissary and Sipahi cavalryman received one thousand gold dollars — two hundred gold pieces.

The Sultan then honored Sinan, the General of the Janissary Engineers, with a most personal and individual promotion, to command his Color Guard in the Sultan's Own Life Guard, the Hasekis — the Chosen. There was no greater military honor within the Padishah's gift. From then on, except for two years during which he chose to leave the center of power, Sinan worked man to man with his master.

At the age of forty-five, Sinan, the commanding officer of the imperial Life Guard, chosen for individual merit, must have been a powerfully handsome and intelligent man, wholly trustworthy, courageous, able to take and to give orders, meticulously courteous, and excellent at counting costs. I can think of no other architect with all these distinctions, as well as genius of the inventive and imaginative kind.

In the autumn of 1536 things began to go wrong. In the mountains near Hamadan between Tabriz and Baghdad, the autumnal rains and snows washed out the rough roads in the high passes. The overladen camels fell and rolled down the cliffs. Others, mired, froze to death at night. The wheels of the carriages of the heavy bronze cannons sank into the mud. The greatest of them had to be dismantled and buried, left behind in caches to be dug up again in spring.

In the Divan, the shouting and recriminations between Ibrahim and Iskender Chelebi brought on explosions of imperial bad temper. Ibrahim prevailed. The Sultan disgraced and demoted the Defterdar, and stripped him of his offices, his titles, and his command. However, he did not strip him, or his father who had joined his son as an officer in his suite, of their personal properties and wealth. Nor were their lives put in jeopardy. Reduced in rank, the two Turkish gentlemen continued to serve their Sultan as voluntary Slaves of the Gate. The favorite had to be content with what appeared to be a temporary eclipse of a valuable member of the Household.

The Grand Vezir-Serasker, unrivaled in grandeur, his confidence restored, displayed all his executive and administrative brilliance in the taking of Baghdad. The city of the Tigris, no longer the gorgeous capital of Harun Al-Rashid's caliphate, had been rebuilt as a market town after the sacking and destruction by Hulagu Khan in 1258. But the Shah of Persia's governor did not defend Baghdad. He opened the gates in the solid and massive walls of baked brick, the portals adorned with winged bulls and dragons of green and yellow glazed faience.

Ibrahim, with Sinan the general of the engineers, rode ahead into the open city, bringing with him a police force of Janissaries to patrol the streets. He put Baghdad in order and sent the keys to the Sultan in his imperial tent pitched on the banks of the Tigris.

Then came the triumphal entry. Sultan Süleyman Khan, Gazi of Baghdad, and his Grand Vezir-Serasker rode, as on a cloud, surrounded by Sinan's Color Guardsmen and the Sultan's Own Life Guards, white-capped, high-plumed, red and blue uniformed, glittering and blazing in the dun-colored landscape under the sun. They marched through the gates of the heraldic animals to take up residence in the palace throughout the four winter months of the occupation.

While the Grand Vezir-Serasker worked out the new administration, the Sultan rode out among the ruined mausoleums of the ancient caliphs. Particularly, he searched for the tomb of Abu Hanifa, whose gospel in liberal interpretation of the *Shar* and the *urf* was the Sacred Law of the Sultan and of the Ottoman Empire. The martyred saint lay buried in a forgotten grave, his shrine demolished in spite and terror by the Shah of Persia's Shiite henchmen when they fled before the Ottoman armies. They had unearthed the desecrated bones of the wise old man, who had died A.D. 767, and who had lain in an honored grave for seven hundred and sixty-seven years, and scattered the ancient dust.

It seems probable that Süleyman told Ibrahim, as they lay down in the palace to sleep at night, of his devout wish for God's help in the finding of the lost grave and the scattered bits of bone of the sainted Abu Hanifa. As Süleyman grew older, his piety increased. He knew ultimately that no decision can be made by means of logic and reason unaided. None but God has all the data at his fingertips.

Next morning, or shortly thereafter, Ibrahim called in his agents and informants among the Arabs and the merchants of Baghdad. According to instructions, they found the former guardian of Abu Hanifa's shrine, idle and at a loss since the retreating heretics' baneful destruction of the mausoleum. Once satisfied with the man's identity and character, Ibrahim chose one of his own men, an usher in the Divan. The young man, as though by chance, came upon the old guardian, perhaps sitting in the sun on the terrace of what today would be a teahouse or a café. It took the usher several days to gain the old man's confidence.

It seems that on the night before the Shiite vandals went out to wreck Abu Hanifa's shrine, the saint appeared in a vision to the guardian asleep on the floor of the tomb. Abu Hanifa explained to the guardian what was to take place. He asked the old man to save his mortal remains from a desecration that would offend God, and incidentally put the guardian out of work.

The old man fetched his tools, a crowbar, a pick and shovel, and unearthed the coffin to find a miraculously incorrupt body, in itself proof of God's intervention. He transferred Abu Hanifa's mummy to the carved stone sarcophagus of an early Christian Arab, whose bones he put back in the Muslim saint's grave. These the vandals dug up again and threw onto dung-hills.

The guardian then sealed the cavelike tomb containing the body of Abu Hanifa in the borrowed Byzantine sarcophagus; he bricked it up and piled rubble and fragments of Hellenistic marbles to hide the entrance to what might have been a catacomb. He then went back to Baghdad to sit out the Ottoman invasion and occupation.

Ibrahim acted upon his secret information with extraordinary circumspection. He reported the bare facts to Süleyman. Then he appointed a grave commission, headed by a Baghdadi professor of theology named Tashkunt ("Solid Stone"), famous for his piety and orthodoxy. The committee of impartial intellectuals and dignitaries examined the guardian of the demolished shrine. The old man's story did not waver in veracity.

Professor Tashkunt then formed a search party, to which Sinan assigned a squad of Janissary engineers. The guardian led them to the pile of detritus covering the entrance to the underground tomb. The engineers cleared away the broken stones and rubble of bricks and mortar to disclose the rough new masonry blocking the passage.

The professor called a halt. He got down on his hands and knees to examine the wall. Through the interstices a strong odor of musk came into Tashkunt's nostrils. He got to his feet, ordered the guardsmen to protect the holy place, and went back to Baghdad to report to the Grand Vezir-Serasker.

The professor had orders to interrupt any official business of the Divan in session. He brought the Grand Vezir-Serasker back with him to sniff the musky wall. With his own hands, Ibrahim broke the new-laid bricks free of the soft mortar. In the barrel-vaulted underground chamber he found the ancient Christian sarcophagus, its sealed lid intact, but even so, giving off an even stronger fragrance of musk.

Ibrahim brought Süleyman to do the final work. The Sultan borrowed a lever. He pried up the lid. So it had been given to his ancestor, Sultan Mehmet the Conqueror, to discover for himself, in the days after the fall of Constantinople, the long lost grave of Job, the disciple, the Companion, and the Standard-Bearer of the Prophet. Eyüp, or Job, then an old man, had fallen in the first attempt of Islam to take Constantinople in A.D. 670. His shrine on the Golden Horn beyond the walls is now, after Mecca, Medina, and Jerusalem, the most holy ground in orthodox Islam.

While Sultan Süleyman watched Sinan and his engineers raise a new dome in the shrine over the old grave and the reburied body of Abu Hanifa, the Grand Vezir-Serasker made plans to rid himself of his rival, Iskender Chelebi. Ibrahim arranged his court calendar of the day's work in the Divan so that the case of the demoted and disgraced, but still enormously wealthy and potentially dangerous, former Defterdar came up at dawn as the first business of the day. On that day, the Grand Vezir-Serasker saw to it that he presided alone in extraordinary session of the Council of State. The lesser vezirs, having been delayed, came late. By then Ibrahim had summarily decreed that Iskender Chelebi be hanged at once in the public marketplace of

Baghdad like a common criminal; to make a clean sweep, he ordered that his old enemy's father, Hüseyn Chelebi, be beheaded.

Furthermore, he ordered that their bodies be displayed to strike salutary terror among all potential evildoers, and then to be buried in a potter's field. All their wealth of property, of gold and of jewels, of armor and of works of art, of slaves and other valuables, and their many estates and town houses reverted to the throne.

That night in the palace while the Defterdar's body still hung in chains in the marketplace, Süleyman and Ibrahim lay down as usual side by side to sleep. To the Sultan alone, Iskender Chelebi appeared in a vision aureoled in celestial glory. The Defterdar appeared to stride to the foot of the prostrate Sultan's pallet. He covered his master with reproaches. He said that, captivated and enchanted by his Greek slave favorite, the Padishah of the Ottoman Empire, the living Son of Osman, had lent himself to the perversion of all divine and human justice. He said that the perfidious Grand Vezir-Serasker had immolated, for spite, a loyal servant of the Household innocent of all and any wrongdoing.

The raging ghost illuminated in radiant light then threw himself upon Süleyman and seized him by the throat. He awoke shouting for help. Sinan's guardsmen came running to find – what? Süleyman on his feet warding off Ibrahim, beside himself with horror. Süleyman was forty years old; Ibrahim a year younger; they had just celebrated their shared birthday. Joined inseparably by an oath, the two men had known one another for more than half their lifetime.

It took them and their armies a year to get back to Istanbul. They shared the bedchamber in the Shah of Persia's palace in Tabriz for the last two weeks of June. They shared the imperial tent, a huge pavilion of canvas lined and curtained with embroidered silk, throughout the six months of the march across the length of Asia Minor. Süleyman saw that he had destroyed Ibrahim.

Or he saw that Ibrahim had made use of his favor to destroy himself. He realized that the Sultan cannot share the power of his inheritance. "Paradise and sovereignty are never united. . . . The responsibilities of sovereigns are so terrible that the good life is all but unattainable to them. . . . Men must learn to endure the evils arising from sovereignty; it is like rain, which may bring loss and destruction to caravans, towns, and ships, but it is withal the life of the earth and its inhabitants. . . . Alas, kingship in being is but a poor compromise between the ideal and human imperfection, and tolerable only because the sole alternative is anarchy." So, in his youth in Trebizond, his father Selim the Grim had seen to it that he had learned by heart the wisdom of the ancient masters of Islam.

When they arrived back in the imperial city, the two men separated, each to enter his own palace. In the evening Süleyman rode into the courtyard of the Old Palace of the imperial harem. Hürrem was not at the gate to welcome him, nor was his only daughter, Mihrimah Sultan, a young lady of fourteen. She and her mother waited the Sultan's pleasure, to be called in his apartments. But (it may have been) his youngest son, five years old, his father's favorite, was privileged to come running out of the palace. There was no need to discipline the hunch backed, pigeon-breasted boy for the succession. Laughing – he grew up to be a witty young man, in a way his father's boon companion – Prince Jehangir ran out to be taken up onto his father's saddle, to sit astride in front of the man.

Süleyman rode a horse gentled to the bit and bridle, A Cappadocian mare, careful where she put down her small shod hooves so as not to crush the child underfoot. The tall Black Eunuch picked up the boy, bundled in quilted silks lined in squirrel skins, and put the deformed "Holder of the World" into his father's hands. Old-fashioned historians blame the "bad blood" that the Russian slave girl Hürrem brought into the House of Osman for the weaknesses of the succeeding Sons of Osman.

Süleyman and Jehangir ambled along the paths under the bare trees and among the cypresses of the great park on the Third Hill. In January snow falls in Istanbul. The father had a present in his pocket (if indeed he had a pocket in his silken robes), and, it may have been, Persian jewels for Hürrem, who joined him in a cabinet small enough to warm by means of glowing charcoals in silver braziers. Perhaps she served him sweet pastries and glasses of cold water from his favorite spring. Turks value the various waters of Europe and Asia as the French know wines and vintages. She gave him her humorous accounts of the goings-on, the stories accumulated and refined for the telling during his absence of eighteen months and a fortnight. She gave him the gossip of the bazaars and of the corridors in the palaces, and of the harems in the city.

Their daughter came in; Mihrimah Sultan, Moon of the Suns, was a little person, never to be a beauty. She was wholly feminine, plain of face, and a bit twisted although not deformed like her youngest brother. The father had seen his other sons, Mehmet, Selim, and Bayazid, with their tutors in the New Palace. Süleyman and Hürrem probably talked together about Ibrahim, for she had now come into her years of power. Süleyman's mother, the wise and beautiful Lady Hafisa, had died in March 1534, and was buried near her husband in a mausoleum behind the kibla wall of the Mosque of Selim the Grim. Süleyman had grieved like any man bereft of the source and origin of his life. Her death had cut the last tie with his father, whose plans, up to Vienna, he had triumphantly carried out. It had left her son a man alone wholly responsible for his own choice of action. Alive she had kept the peace in the imperial harem throughout his fourteen years on the throne.

Whatever she thought of his favorite, Ibrahim, she had given her son his wife. Helplessly Hürrem had watched her rival, the Lady Gülbahar's son Prince Mustafa, the Grand Vezir-Serasker's choice, installed at Manisa as the heir apparent. It was part of her husband's and his favorite's strategic planning of their Persian campaign. At the investiture, after Prince Mustafa had kissed his father's imperial hand, Ibrahim had held the new robe of office for the Shehzadé to put on. Now, as they talked together, she must have been glad to tell Süleyman what he had to hear about his favorite.

In his last official act, the Grand Vezir-Serasker Ibrahim Pasha, in the great hall of the Palace of Ibrahim, sealed and signed the treaty of the capitulations with Laforêt, the ambassador of King Francis I of France, the Sultan's first Christian ally. By the terms of the capitulations, drawn up in the winter of 1536, the Sultan granted the King of France the privilege of calling himself protector of all the Christians living within the borders of the Ottoman Empire. More specifically, the commercial treaty gave the French Levantine merchants special privileges and protections. Henceforth, they had the right to trade in factories in Galata across the Golden Horn, in Trebizond, in Smyrna, and in Aleppo. Any French merchant accused of a crime was to be tried not before the Ottoman judges in Islamic courts of law but before the French ambassador in the embassy according to French Christian law.

Ramazan, the month of fasting, began on Shrove Tuesday in 1536. On that day at sunset, when a man no longer can distinguish between a white thread and a black thread held in the fingers of his hands, he goes into his house to eat and to drink, according to the Sacred Law, and to lie with his wife, seeking what God has prescribed for him. At daybreak he bathes and goes about his business, fasting, if he is an old man. If he is young or strong in sexual temperament, he finds it wise, as the Prophet did, to cleave to the company of sedate men in the mosque. By day he can take into his mouth neither food nor drink, neither solid nor liquid; nor can he smoke; nor can he allow himself to be excited until, once again after dark, he can no longer distinguish between the black thread and the white thread. Ramazan is a time of trial, a test of faith, in Islam.

In the Divan, Ibrahim was short-tempered with the ambassadors of Shah Tahmasp of Persia, come to negotiate the treaty of peace. He rejected the Shah's gift of a Koran illuminated, illustrated, bound in fine leathers, clasped with gold and jewels. "I have Korans enough of greater value in my own library! " It was whispered that the Grand Vezir-Serasker fasted not in Ramazan but in Christian Lent.

In the course of business he issued an edict in the Sultan's name to settle a question of customary law in the newly conquered Kurdish territories surrounding Lake Van. He affixed the imperial seal and signed the document "Sultan Ibrahim." It was the usage in Kurdistan, but not in Istanbul. Finally, the Grand Vezir-Serasker received a petition from a man named Meliki Abdullah, of Bokhara, who addressed him as "Sultan Ibrahim."

Süleyman, son of Selim, son of Bayazid, son of Mehmet, son of Murad, son of Mehmet, son of Bayazid, son of Murad, son of Orhan, son of Osman, was the Sultan, alone in imperial power. Sometime between the first and the twenty-second night of Ramazan, Süleyman went privately to consult a simple dervish renowned for his piety. He asked how an honorable man could break an oath binding him to another man sworn before God, and reinforced by imperial decree.

"As sleep is the image of death," the wise old man replied, "so a sleeping man differs not from a man dead." (A Zen master might have laughed and said, "So a man asleep is dead to the world," but all the chroniclers agree on what the dervish told the Sultan.)

On the Ides of March Ibrahim left his own palace on the Hippodrome to make his familiar way to the postern under its pointed arch that Süleyman had had opened for him in the outer walls of the New Palace. He stepped through into the garden. The familiar Janissary gatekeeper saluted him as usual. Alone Ibrahim walked his usual path in the gathering darkness and entered the inner courtyard. Again the Janissary guardsman on duty recognized the Grand Vezir-Serasker and let him pass.

The Sultan must have told Sinan, the commanding officer of the Guard of Honor, enough to silence him and the men he had chosen to stand guard on that night, Tuesday, March 15, 1536. They had to be given orders not to leave their posts and not to raise the alarm – not to respond to whatever cries for help or sounds of struggle might break the silence of the twenty-second night of Ramazan, A.H. 942.

They knew that Süleyman, the Son of the Slave, was not asleep in his imperial bedchamber in the New Palace. Forbidden to visit the imperial harem in daylight, as soon as he could no longer distinguish between the white thread and the black thread, Süleyman had gone to spend the night in sleep beside Hürrem in the Old Palace. Perhaps she had given her husband a sleeping draught, and perhaps she lay awake to listen to his uninterrupted breathing.

In the other bedchamber, Ibrahim fought off the waiting mutes. He was a short man, but powerful. There must have been a number of the Sultan's silenced executioners. He drew a knife and cut one of his arteries. Or the mutes botched it. His blood spurted high enough to splatter the white plaster of the walls above the flower-patterned tiles. In the morning, his body in torn robes of honor lay sprawled outside the Gate of Felicity.

A man in authority knew what to do. The body was thrown across the back of a black horse and covered with a black pall. Before sunrise, a man led the horse through the streets down to the shore of the Golden Horn and lifted the body into a rowboat. On the farther shore, the man recognized as authorized buried the body of the Greek favorite in the garden of a monastery of Bektashi dervishes in Galata. Nothing of it remains in the crowded streets and blocks of Karaköy, the modern Turkish section of the present-day city.

All of Ibrahim's wealth reverted to the Sultan. His widows, the shadowy First Lady Muhsiné and his Second Lady the Imperial Princess Khadija (or, if that was not her name – there is reason for doubt – then one of her anonymous sisters, the lesser daughters of Selim the Grim) vanish from history and gossip. Her son, Mehmet Shah, who would have been nine years old at the time of his father's sudden death, died young. The boy's two younger sisters grew up to be adequately married; they lived, gave birth, and died out of the way, inside one harem or another.

Haseki Hürrem reached out from the imperial harem to obliterate the most visible evidence of Ibrahim's long hold upon her husband's imagination. She had the three Greek bronzes thrown down from their pedestal in front of the Palace of Ibrahim (as it is still called) in the Hippodrome. Apollo, Artemis, and Hercules were broken up; their metal was hauled off to be melted down at the cannon foundry across the Golden Horn in Tophané.

9

Whether or not Ibrahim walked past Sinan, the commanding officer of the Sultan's chosen Guard of Honor, standing at attention on duty in the Sultan's palace on the night in which the favorite went to his death; indeed, whether or not it was Sinan, the man in the Sultan's confidence, who buried the dishonored body of his fellow Greek slave and Slave of the Gate, no one knows. Some man did. It is known that Sinan had shared Ibrahim's rise. The avalanche brought on by the favorite's downfall swept away the power structure built up by the Grand Vezir-Serasker in the Ruling Institution and the court. Sinan chose to get free of the ruins.

He petitioned the Sultan for permission to volunteer for active duty in the field. In the scheduled military operations of that campaign season, there was no call for the abilities of the general of the Janissary engineers. But Süleyman granted Sinan's request and assigned him as inspector general to account to the Sultan on the action of the expeditionary force commanded by Lütfi Pasha, one more *damat*, the quiet husband of the Imperial Princess Shahhuban. Both men were glad to go when they sailed out of the Golden Horn on the way to Corfu. Sinan was pleased to get away from the turbulence and the jockeying for place in the hierarchy at the center of power; Lütfi Pasha was relieved to leave his lady wife, who was as much a termagant as her father, Selim the Grim, had been a tartar.

With the small army, the two men left Istanbul in the spring of 1536. They failed to take Corfu from the Venetians. They then sailed across the Adriatic to land on the heel of Italy where they scourged and raided Apulia. They returned perhaps through the port of Ragusa (now called Dubrovnik), then an Ottoman protectorate and vassal state of merchants, rivals of the Venetians. Perhaps they wintered in Greece. In the spring, they marched across the Balkans into Moldavia, now part of Romania, then a tributary Christian principality in need of a show of Ottoman force.

These minor operations occupied Sinan and Lütfi Pasha pleasantly for two years while, in Istanbul, the Sultan reorganized his government. Sometime in 1538, Süleyman recalled Sinan to fill the empty post of Royal Chief

Architect. Ajem Ali, the Persian chief builder whom Selim the Grim had brought to Istanbul from Tabriz in 1515, had died of old age in the year that Ibrahim met death at the hands of the mutes. The Sultan, once again in command of the situation, had made ambitious plans to adorn his imperial city of Istanbul. He knew Sinan, and he knew the man's work.

I cannot believe that his appointment came to Sinan as a surprise. He knew that he had risen as high as he could go in the ranks of the Janissary engineers and in the Court. It seems probable that, when he got news of Ajem Ali's death, perhaps even before he set off with Lütfi Pasha for Corfu and Apulia, he had let his friends and patrons in the Divan and in the hierarchy know that he was willing to take his old master Ajem Ali's place. But at first sight, Sinan's fellow officers and Slaves of the Gate may have seen his new appointment as a comedown and a setback.

In fact, before Sinan took office, Mimar Bashi was a title to be translated not as Royal Chief Architect but merely as Chief Builder. Ajem Ali, whose work makes clear that he was a competent man, had been a minor official in the Slave Household, a servant of the Sultan rather than a grandee in the hierarchy of the Slaves of the Gate. Perhaps Sinan's fellow slaves thought that the Sultan had sent him off with Lütfi Pasha as a sign of displeasure, and, in consequence of his association with Ibrahim, had removed him from the military high command and banished him from the imperial presence at Court.

However, Sinan's first commissions as Royal Chief Architect prove that he stood high in the Sultan's confidence. In 1538, Süleyman had the Janissary engineers restore the walls, build the Damascus Gate, and rebuild the citadel of Jerusalem, the third of the most holy cities of Islam. Then Süleyman recalled Sinan to Istanbul and set him to work on the first of his imperial urban complexes, the small mosque and college and the large hospital and charitable institution endowed in the name of his belovèd wife Haseki Hürrem.

She chose the site. Her restored pious foundation now stands in a poor but delightful section of the city, out of the way on a low hill in the wide plain between the Sea of Marmara and the Second, Fourth, and Seventh Hills. But in 1538, Hürrem chose to build her hospital near the busy Avrat Pazar, the female slave market.

As architects do, and must when they build to order for their patrons, and especially for women, Sinan first listened while Hürrem told him exactly what she wanted in the way of buildings. Perhaps later, with Süleyman, she visited him – he could not have taken the drawing boards to her in the imperial harem – in the workshops on the Vefa. It would have been for her a reason to get out of the Old Palace, if only to go around the corner. There over cups of tea or dishes of rose-petal jam and glasses of clear water, she talked, as women will, about the proper sort of wife for him now that he was free to marry, and she offered to find him the right one.

He built for her a mosque that was both modest and simple, and in fact too small. It had to be doubled (clumsily) in size within a century. The mosque, standing alone on one side of a narrow road, is a square building with a dome held up on squinch arches thrown across the corners, their conchs ridged and fluted like scallop shells. On the other side of the street, a lane in a residential section of artisans and tradesmen, he built a college. It is a rectangular courtyard, arcaded, with rows of cubicle domical cells opening from it, a lecture hall in one side of it, and a fountain in the center of the paved rectangle. Like all the rest built over fifty years, Sinan's first college is functional, practical, and beautiful. Here no two of the white marble capitals are exactly alike. The pillars are smooth monoliths of various colored marbles recovered from Byzantine and more ancient buildings and ruins. The capitals, cut in both Islamic patterns of stalactites and lozenges, are "signed:" Sinan cut mandalas on the flat surfaces in a variety of shapes: discs, swirls, rosettes, stars in circles, and snowflakes.

Next to the college stands the narrow courtyard, planted to shade trees, of the L-shaped refectory and soup kitchen for the students and the poor of the quarter. It is a pleasant place for the old and the infirm, and it was restored in 1965 to serve its original purpose. Back to the *imaret*, as the charitable soup kitchen is called, and below the college on the hill stands the large *darüshshifa*, the hospital of several courtyards, an excellent group of buildings still functioning as a clinic.

In one of the waiting rooms, a cube of space covered by a dome, Sinan put up pendentives that are, in terms of strictest functional and architectural design, disproportionately large. Furthermore, they are not smooth. Sinan covered the surfaces of the spherical triangles with intricate and exact stalactites carved boldly in high relief. It looks as though he sacrificed unity and balance to give the patients waiting to be examined something to look at as comforting as puzzles are to do. The room is like a matrix; it is alive and absorbingly interesting.

Hürrem was pleased. In Sinan's legend a story goes that Hürrem and Süleyman visited Sinan's work in progress. They came with the minimum of fanfare, perhaps sitting together in a screened carriage. She was veiled, but not heavily, with a transparent silk scarf across the lower part of her face. She wore a hooded mantle – it must have been spring – of silk in a color suitable to the season and to her red-gold hair. At that, it was darkening to auburn for she was thirty-eight; she may have worn leaf green or lilac. Süleyman, always a spare man, dark of skin, at the age of forty-four probably already was iron gray. But surely on that sunny day with white clouds in the blue sky, he was smiling to see his wife in delight. When he laid aside his gorgeous robes of state, he chose to dress in tailored costumes of mohair, the soft wool from the bellies of Angora goats especially woven for him and dyed in the sage green color that the Prophet preferred.

She was delighted with what she saw, and especially pleased with the cheerful young Janissary cadets working as masons on the walls and as carpenters in the scaffolding. Her eldest son was not much younger than they, and he was as hard at work as these young engineers in his education and training for the succession. She asked her husband for money to tip them well.

It is to me a charming scene to imagine, the handsome youths in all their colorings of hair and eyes, but all of them equal in age and size, up in the falsework or standing high on the platforms of the walls, eagerly peering down, fresh-faced and excited by their sudden glimpse of the august Sultan and his enchantress wife. She was rumored to be a sorceress. Hürrem looked up to find the young slaves, the pick of the engineering cadets, looking down at her. And pretending not to know that she was observed – it was forbidden, for the youths to look at her – she laughed, her teeth and her pearls glowing through the gossamer veil, her sapphire-blue eyes, outlined in kohl, flashing. She might have winked, she probably did, and flirted, and bent her head on her white throat. Oriental women know how to be outrageous in the flickering of an eyelid, in the curl of a finger, and in a fluttering of veils. She knew that within her husband's love for her she was safe. Sinan, a privileged man, looked on, smiling, missing nothing.

In 1538, that summer, she chose to marry her daughter, not yet seventeen, to Rüstem Pasha, the Lousy Ikbal, as he was called. At thirty-five or thirty-six, he was a singularly unattractive man, twice the age of the imperial princess, the Lady as Beautiful as the Face of the Full Moon (her name is variously spelled and translated). She was a short and a twisted girl, but vivacious like her spirited mother. She died in her mid-fifties, in old age for women of her day. Rüstem and his brother Sinan Pasha, who was to be named lord high admiral, were the sons of a Croatian peasant. Captured in war and enslaved as *penjik* youths, both the brothers in their boyhood were sufficiently handsome and intelligent to be entered in the palace school for pages. Rüstem's life had put lines in his face; he had the miser's hardbitten look of total lack of confidence in his fellow man. As Grand Vezir, Rüstem allowed his uncle and first cousins, Christians, to beg for bread in the streets of Edirné.

Sinan the architect built each brother a mausoleum and a memorial mosque in a pious foundation. The Admiral Sinan Pasha's, which is heavy, is the earliest of the Royal Chief Architect's experiments in the hexagonal plan. He built it in the year of the donor's death, 1555. For the Grand Vezir, Sinan built a great many other colleges, mosques, and caravansaries in both Domains; and in the end he built Rüstem's tomb. It is classic, octagonal, domical, and lined with Iznik tiles of the second period, which is to say that they are mediocre. In architecture, the mausoleum is irreproachable, but, I think, noncommittal. Any other sufficiently wealthy pasha might have commissioned the tomb, a standard work, as its occupant was not.

As Grand Vezir, Rüstem proved to be one of the three great administrators of Süleyman's long reign. He was less brilliant and less perceptive than Ibrahim, the favorite, the assassinated, and in all but his one great characteristic, Rüstem was less able than the greatest and last of the three, the Grand Vezir Sokollu Mehmet Pasha. But Rüstem had the gift for money; he understood money; he made money. He was a financier and a collector of whatever had intrinsic value.

Both Ibrahim and Rüstem, as exceptional men irregularly admitted to the Sultan's Slave Household, prove the excellence of Süleyman's judgment based on their individual merits, and also the wisdom of the rules governing the selection of *penjik* and *devshirmé* youths, which if applied to them should have excluded them from the Sultan's Household of Slaves.

Ibrahim, purchased in the slave market, acquired irregardlessly, was promoted from boon companion without the benefit of the decorum and the discipline ingrained in pages and cadets. He lost his head. Rüstem, as a boy, had been a pig drover on his father's farm in Croatia (now northern Yugoslavia). The regulations of the *devshirmé* disqualified youths filthy by association with swine, beasts proscribed by the Prophet. Nicknamed Mekri, the Abominable, Rüstem was mean-spirited all his life. As Grand Vezir and *damat* of the Ottoman Empire, the prime minister in a golden age, he sold the seconds from the imperial fruit, vegetable, and flower gardens in the city marketplaces, and he pocketed the profits.

At the time of Ibrahim's downfall, Rüstem was beylerbey of the province of Karaman, to which administrative district Sinan's home country of Kayseri has been attached in 1515. Rüstem moved up to govern the province of Anatolia, the Sons of Osman's first estate, with the capital at Bursa. When the Sultan informed him of his wife's and daughter's choice of him as the imperial son-in-law-elect, Rüstem was unencumbered by a harem of ladies, or concubines, of his own choice.

Hürrem then was displeased to hear the rumor spread that the Abominable skinflint had a hidden sore on his thigh – that Rüstem was leprous. But she understood the reason for such gossip; she had grown up in it. Hürrem took thought. She sent a faithful slave woman, perhaps Mihrimah Sultan's wet nurse, to prepare the bridegroom-elect's wardrobe, to wash and iron his linen, and to spy out the fact, if it were so, of the leprous spot. A slave man, say a bath attendant or a masseur, could not have done a thorough job of inspection. Perhaps Rüstem did not frequent the *haman*. If he did, he wrapped a striped towel about what are imprecisely called the loins. Did the gossip explain Rüstem's celibacy by putting the sore on his genitals?

The slave woman had her work cut out for her. Rüstem lived in a womanless palace jam-packed with his acquisitions and accumulations of remarkable material worth. When he died, the inventory of his valuables listed five thousand fur-lined kaftans, robes of honor, and embroidered uniforms of state.

In one of the ceremonial garments, say a winter cloak lined with stone marten, or better, in his dirty body linen given her to launder, Hürrem's slave woman came upon a louse.

"God be praised! " she exclaimed in the hortatory, unable to contain herself when Rüstem came in. "God be praised for this louse that proves thy purity and thus renders thee worthy of joining the imperial family as the Sultan's son-in-law." Then she hurried off to bear the glad tidings to her imperial mistress. She seems to have been a comfortable body, if not a particularly discreet spy. The point of the louse is that, according to Ottoman old wives, lice stay clear of lepers.

The story got around. A poet wrote a distich called "The Lousy Ikbal." It goes: "He whom fortune favors will find a louse at the propitious hour" – so to imply that Rüstem had planted the louse for his future mother-in-law's good woman to find.

So Rüstem and Mihrimah were married in 1538. On May 9, 1541, he entered the Divan as his wife's and his mother-in-law's tool. Come to think of it, Rüstem's reputation for sagacity – Evliya Chelebi a century later called him an Aristotle in wisdom – may well be due to Hürrem's telling him what to do, where to do it, when to act, and also how and why.

In 1544, when Sultan Süleyman brought the *Damat* Grand Vezir Rüstem into the Divan, he introduced the corrupt practices that, after three centuries had passed, finally brought down the House of Osman. The costs of government were mounting now that the diminishing spoils of war no longer sufficed to finance the expanding empire in the shrinking Holy Wars. To raise money the Grand Vezir inaugurated the sale of offices to the highest bidders among, it is true, only the qualified and meritorious Slaves of the Gate.

In the hierarchy of the eighty thousand Slaves of the Gate, the competition had risen to fierce intensity. The Sultan tacitly permitted his son-in-law's perversion of the Slave Family's integrity. He looked the other way. He controlled Rüstem by means of fear. The Grand Vezir lived in terror of his father-in-law and, indeed, in even greater terror of his mother-in-law, on whose approbation his life depended. The Lousy Ikbal lived the life of a parasite upon his wife, the Imperial Princess, and her mother, the only wife of the Sultan. Both ladies despised him and made use of him. But Rüstem Pasha was an able administrator, and he amassed, not necessarily honestly, the greatest of grand-veziral fortunes. Süleyman, after the long years with Ibrahim, never again permitted himself to work on terms of intimacy with any other of his grand vezirs. All the historians agree that the *Damat* Rüstem Pasha, although a disgusting man, the Lousy Ikbal, was an excellent Grand Vezir.

Therefore, it can be said that in 1538, when Haseki Hürrem chose him as a convenience to marry to Mihrimah Sultan, although she denied her daughter love, and, it may have been, passion, she knew what she was doing. Hürrem herself was an excellent manager of her own and all other, but her sons', affairs. She was pleased with the mosque and hospital that Sinan built for her; she was pleased with him. He married as soon as he was freed from Janissary celibacy. Perhaps she arranged things for him. Certainly from then on until she died twenty years later, in no way did she come between her husband and his Royal Chief Architect in the work of their growing partnership.

Sinan was a man of forty-nine when he married in 1538. He took his bride to live in a town house that he had built for himself and for her. He chose a parcel of land in Yeni Baché, the New Garden, a quarter of the city that lies inland below the Fourth Hill, which as a town planner he had just redesigned following a fire. If his house (it has long since burnt down) was like the houses surviving from that time, it was generous in size, set in high walled gardens but built flush with the edge of the cobblestoned and narrow street in which it stood. The walls of the ground floor and second story were built of stone or brick plastered over and painted. The few windows opening on to the street were small, iron-barred, glazed, and heavily shuttered on the inside. Above the ground floor the windows in the service rooms – the kitchens, pantries, the quarters and living rooms of the domestics, perhaps the nursery – were bigger and wider, screened with carved wooden lattices. The top story was built out on brackets above the street and the gardens. This top floor, half-timbered and plastered under its low-pitched roof of pantiles and overhanging eaves, was high enough for two levels of great windows in the walls. The upper windows were filled in with screens of elephant's-eyes; the lower windows of small panes opened wide to let in the light and the air.

In their proportions, the rooms of this sixteenth century Ottoman house are equaled only by the eighteenth century rooms in the houses built in the Age of Reason. The rooms are beautiful, the high ceilings carved and decorated, the walls paneled and painted usually in floral patterns sometimes upon a background of gold leaf. Fine rugs and carpets covered the raised floor – there is a sunken passage from the door opening upon the hall and the staircase. It runs along an inner wall. Sinan, his lady, their children, and the domestic slaves kicked off their shoes and slippers when they stepped onto the carpets, which were Persian, Caucasian, and Anatolian.

Against the outer walls ran a low "divan," a wide bench, hard-cushioned, with other such cushions on the floor. But not much other furniture cluttered the space: a low table or two; a hinged reading stand shaped like a wide X when open, but flat when folded to put away; a chest or two, with tall and short candlesticks of brass or silver. Sinan built cupboards and closets behind the closed doors along the inner windowless walls, the partitions between rooms. In them were stored the pallets and quilts that were unrolled by night. Others held the wardrobes, the books, the chessmen, and the backgammon boards and counters. The living rooms were full of light and air, and quiet tranquility.

Or perhaps for his establishment, Sinan built two separate houses, or a single rambing house of several courtyards; one for the *selâmlik*, his reception rooms, a great dining room, his library and study; the other for the harem. Certainly he had no need to economize.

His bride's name was Gülruh, and he was old enough to be her father. She was perhaps fifteen, at the most eighteen. Little is known of her origins, and such was the courteous anonymity of her lifetime that no one knows much more than her name, and the names of her two sons, Mehmet and Mustafa; and her three daughters, Ummi, Hüma, and Khadija. He gave his sons and daughters the names of princes and princesses of the Imperial House of Osman. Mehmet and Mustafa are also the names of the Prophet, as Khadija (Hadice in the modern Turkish phonetic spelling) was the name of Mohammed's first and best loved wife. Ummi means Hope; Hüma, Phoenix, Fabulous Bird of Good Omen, Good Fortune.

It is within possibility to imagine that Haseki Hürrem chose a slave girl, or, indeed, a Turkish girl of good Osmanli family, say, the daughter of another Slave of the Gate, for Sinan. Perhaps she did so as a reward for the pious foundation built and endowed in Haseki Hürrem's name and dated 1538, the year of his marriage. He had no other woman to negotiate the marriage settlement with the Lady Gülruh's parents. If he bought her in the female slave market, of course, he could have done so by himself.

Yet, it is more than possible that Sinan sent a message to his mother in Aghirnas, or that he went there himself, perhaps on his way to Jerusalem to rebuild the walls in 1538. He then could have chosen a bride from among the Greek girls of his home town. It is again possible that she made the journey to Istanbul with Sinan's nephews, young men of her age or a bit older, all of them to be converted at the same time. The two nephews, his adopted sons, were given Islamic names, but only one has come down, and it is imperial: Süleyman.

Sinan was a good provider; as a father, husband, uncle, brother, son, cousin, and ancestor, he looked after his own. It is easy to imagine for him a happy household with his wife the Lady Gülruh. She held his love and until 1563 he chose to be monogamous.

What's in a name? Hers means the spirit, the essence and the attar of a rose. In her house in the Chief Architect's Quarter of the New Garden, she blossomed. In her lifetime she had reason to be a happy woman; it was her nature. Orientals make no mistake of marrying in search of ideal, which is to say, romantic love. The Lady Gülruh was brought up to enter some man's harem, there to work to make her life a success. She had the luck, or it may be, the destiny to marry Sinan.

So Sinan began his own private life as a man alive. At home the Lady Gülruh welcomed him; he was himself with her and their children, a man who knew himself to be fortunate, interested, and fully occupied in the years of his long life.

By 1563 Sinan had accumulated a great deal of money from his share of the Janissary loot and booty, from his awards, and from his salary and commissions as Royal Chief Architect. He was healthy and strong, but he was seventy-four, four years beyond his Biblical three score years and ten; he had survived the then average age of death by at least fourteen and perhaps even twenty years. He made his first will in this year, and he obtained the charter for his first pious foundation. He endowed and built this and another one as a sort of life insurance, an annuity, a marriage settlement in case of her enforced retirement at separate maintenance. The Lady Gülruh and her daughters may have been threatened by powers outside his own control. Or he may have made his first will as the first step in planning a major change in his way of life. Shortly thereafter he took a second wife, the Lady Mihri. Her name does not appear in the charter of 1563. It does, after her death, in the second charter of 1585-86. Sinan earmarked a sum of money to pay for prayers to speed her soul's journey to Paradise. He also provided for their two living daughters and their issue female.

The Lady Gülruh probably selected the bride. She knew the Lady Mihri and she knew the Lady Mihrimah Sultan, of echoing similarity of name, coincidental in time and in space and in Sinan's life. He was working on the mosque of Mihrimah Sultan in 1563, and the Lady Gülruh, surely, was wise enough to follow her husband's career as the Royal Chief Architect. She kept herself informed so as to share his life much in the way that Haseki Hürrem had shared Süleyman's. Surely man and wife talked things over at the end of the days and nights for twenty-five years of singular monogamous marriage. Sinan liked women as women, not as things. Besides, according to the religious law of the Prophet, he had to consult her before he took a second wife. Nobody knows why any man takes a second, a third, or a fourth wife – except in the deserts and the warfare of the Prophet's early days in Islam. Then polygamy made sense in social security. The active young men died; their new-born sons died; the girls and women did not.

In the years that decided Sinan to make his will, he was wholly engaged in building an extravagant mosque for the newly widowed Imperial Princess Mihrimah, the Sultan's favorite daughter, the only daughter of his dead wife Haseki Hürrem. Freed of her servitude, she was very rich, wholly feminine, and in all other ways, except brains, the most powerful woman alive in the Ottoman Empire.

The Lady Gülruh had a great deal to lose; she had a remarkable man. She watched him and she watched the mosque of Mihrimah Sultan go up in those years 1563 and 1564. She could believe the evidence of her own acute senses. What wife does not?

In those years, in the architecture of his only spectacular mosque, Sinan released his creative energies, which are inextricable from sexual energies, in an outburst of virtuosity. His mosque for her startles and delights the eye. This is erotic architecture. It has the witty perfection of the palindrome. "Madam, I'm Adam" – the old Adam. Had Mihrimah Sultan, the wealthiest widow woman in the world, imperiously spoken to her father Sultan Süleyman Khan the Magnificent in his bad-tempered, legalistic old age to ask for the hand of his Royal Chief Architect, his Admirable Slave of the Gate and his old friend, not the Lady Mihri, an innocent child, but the Lady Mihrimah Sultan would have become Sinan's one and only second wife and first lady of the harem.

Better for Lady Gülruh to be mistress of her own household, if in sexual competition to share her husband, than to be renounced, rejected, retired, set aside, dismissed, disallowed, and divorced to make way for the Sultan's only daughter, the Imperial Princess Mihrimah, the Moon the Love of the Sun, the Lady as Beautiful as the Face of the Full Moon. However her name is translated (from the Persian), it were lunacy. Oriental women are realists. The Lady Gülruh knew that in the Ottoman Empire only the imperial Daughters of Osman were to be called free – at the end of the empire, some of them were very free indeed, as the handsome early travelers could, and did, tell.

The Lady Gülruh looked about. She found the docile virgin from among the daughters of her neighbors, a sweet child whose tender flesh could armor her husband's body in his green old age. And who knows? – bring him down safely from his perch on high in the minaret among the Mihrimah Jami's many many twinned domes.

Of the second lady, Mihri, only her name and the names of her two daughters are known. She was born sixteen or seventeen years before 1563 or at the latest 1564. She lived and had her being in Sinan's harem. She died, it may have been in childbirth, before 1585 or 1586. Her daughters of grand and glorious imperial family names, Ümmihan, Sovereign Hope, and Neslihan, Of the Sovereign Family, Of the Generations, or Of Sovereign Descent, were written into the clauses of their father's second will and charter. In Islam, a man's private life is private.

The Lady Gülruh survived Sinan, but neither she nor he could know that he would live to be ninety-nine and that she would follow him to the grave sometime after 1585, which is the date of the charter for the second pious foundation. Probably she was buried beside her husband in his tomb; her gravestone, if she had one, has vanishing along with her name, her dates, and the inscribed praise of her virtues. Sinan died in 1588.

All that is to be known of his private life as a man comes from the inscription on his tomb and a dozen existing documents, half of them suspect. Two are the so-called biographies and autobiography attributed to his friend Nakkash Mustafa Saï; two are imperial edicts issued from the Divan by the Grand Vezir Sokollu Mehmet Pasha, in the Sultan's name; two are the charters for Sinan's own pious foundations.

The tomb inscription confuses the date of his death. The biographies list the major events in Sinan's life. They do not name but list three of the four sultans whom Sinan served as a Janissary and the Royal Chief Architect (Murad III, 1574-1595, is omitted); and they list some but not all of the buildings erected in his fifty years in office. The two imperial edicts, although dated and detailed, confused the governor of the province of Karaman to whom they were directed; and their unpunctuated language still confuses the reader. The provisions of the two charters, which amount to Sinan's first and last will and testament, are explicit, but his beneficiaries, mentioned by name, are hard to identify. For instance, he lists the names of his daughters, granddaughters, grandnieces, and his two wives; but he does not include all his grandsons or grandnephews, whom he had already established independently with gifts of money and property. The young men were then on their own.

After 1563, and before 1585, Sinan's two adopted nephews and their families shared his great days. One remains anonymous. He was a professional soldier, an officer in Sinan's old regiment, the "Kennelmen" in the cavalry. Therefore, it is possible that, like his uncle before him, he was collected as a tribute youth, enslaved, and trained as a Janissary; but because the company of Seghmen was half slave, half freeborn Muslim, he may have volunteered – brought to the attention of his general or field officers by the former commander of the Janissary engineers, his uncle. This man may have had sons; if so Sinan educated them and gave them money to make their own way. He had two daughters, the Lady Raziyé, who must have been a happy baby or a cheerful virgin, for she was named Possessed of Contentment; and the Lady Kerimé, Noble, Generous, Honored, Illustrious in Descent, which was collateral from her granduncle and guardian. Sinan took care of his grandnieces as though they were his own granddaughters.

To the other nephew, perhaps younger and closer to Sinan, he gave the imperial name of Süleyman, which is the Biblical Solomon. He married. Sinan mentions his daughter the Lady Aysha, named for the Prophet's political widow, in his second will and charter.

Sinan may well have built himself a summer house, a *yali*, on the Bosphorus, a comfortable wooden building rising from the stone quay of the Asian shore. There his ladies and their children went to spend the hot dry summer months of July and August. They lived in matchlessly comfortable rooms, high, spacious, full of light and air, flawless in the proportions of cultivated and civilized life – with a great many domestic slaves to serve them. From the upstairs rooms, sparingly furnished, built out on brackets to overhang the level water, they looked out through the open windows to see the imperial city taking shape in Sinan's hands.

As they sat looking into the west, the sunset colorings flooding the skies and, reflected from the surface of the Bosphorus, rippling in watery patterns on the carved and gilt ceilings, they took their ease. They enjoyed themselves. If they saw the crescent moon come up, the ladies quickly touched pure gold, a ring, a chain, a bracelet. It seems imaginable that at the end of his years, Sinan took a day off now and again, a long weekend from time to time in summer or in spring, from his labors to enjoy his family.

Perhaps he sat among his ladies, his daughters, his sons and adopted nephews and their ladies, their daughters, and their young sons, and talked about his early days. None of them, except, it may have been, the nephews and the Lady Gülruh could imagine him as a boy, a youth, a young Christian man living in his hill town under the cone of the extinct volcano high up on the Anatolian pleateau in central Asia Minor, far away and long ago. He told them how he was collected by Sultan Selim the Grim's Keeper of the Cranes as a splendid tribute youth.

He told them of his first glimpse of the Bosphorus. In the morning, they all went for a ride in the barge shaded by canopies and awnings and parasols, and veiled from curious eyes. But the girls rolled up their sleeves and trailed their hands in the clear cool water. Sinan told them what he knew of the water course, then the only road for all the traffic, which was waterborne, between the north and the south, and between Europe and Asia.

The Bosphorus looks like a river and smells of the sea. Two currents flow in the strait, one above the other, diametrically opposed. The colder and lighter stream on the surface flows down out of the Black Sea to the north. The warm and heavier salt water from the White Sea, the Mediterranean, flows out of sight from south to north, apparently against all logic and all reason, but in fact not so. Fishermen living in the towns along the Bosphorus have known how to use the lower current since, it may be, Byzas of Megara in Attica sailed in to settle on the Golden Horn and found his colony called Byzantium in 685 B.C.

The Bosphorus fishermen of Sinan's lifetime (and still they do today) brought their catches of swordfish, red mullet, turbot, sole, tunny, and all the rest of the fresh fish down on the surface current to market in the morning in small craft shaped by two thousand years of use in the north and south winds and the two streams. In the evenings, empty and tired, the fishermen had to row home against both the prevailing summer wind from Russia and the Balkans and the surface current from the Black Sea. Long ago some one of them learned to drop not a sea anchor, but instead a sea sail weighted to catch the submerged current running from the south.

The warm, heavy salt Mediterranean stream flows down the sloping floor of the strait up to the mouth of the Bosphorus; and then it curls up and goes over the rock ledge, a kind of sill that might have been designed and built by marine engineers and architects to keep out the poisonous depths of the Black Sea water. This natural formation is too subtle for geopolitics. The Mediterranean water then flows across the Black Sea to warm the Crimea. It brings southern warmth to the peninsula sheltering under the mountains to the north. Palm trees grow there, roses bloom in winter. The Bosphorus is a landscape and a seaway bewildering to the mind and the emotions.

As Sinan knew, when winter storms blow up high waves to disturb the waters of the shallow Black Sea, the lightly saline, cold and poisonous stream pours over the rock sill to pollute the strait. At such times, once or twice a year, tunnies as long as a man's arm rise intoxicated to the surface. Then the men and the women and the children of the villages run down grinning to the shores. Armed with hooks of any kind – bent forks wired to beanpoles will do – they line up to gaff the steel-blue, streamlined fish, two and three feet long, and to bring them in to land. In hard winters, once in twenty years or so, when the Danube, the Dniester, the Dnieper, and the Don thaw, blocks of river ice as big as houses float down to choke the Bosphorus. Then Sinan, as young men still do today, walked across from Europe to Asia and back again, dry-shod and laughing.

There is no tide in the strait. The water level does not vary except in times of storm, or, since the last world war, when fast-moving tankers, cargoes, cruise ships, and battleships throw off waves in their wake. The Bosphorus shores have been corrected by dressed stone embankments from the city two thirds of the ten-mile passage to the Black Sea. Until the 1914-1918 war, the hills and valleys rising from the water were forested or planted to orchards and walnut groves; in the terraced, high walled gardens behind the summer palaces, shade trees, Cedars of Lebanon, parasol pines, magnolias, plane trees, and even sequoias were planted.

Bare now, the high pastures, green in winter and tawny in summer, are covered by the diagonal rising and descending paths worn by cloven-hooved animals, like gigantic fishermen's nets spread out to dry. Storks nest in the highest of the trees. In spring when the waterside thickets of Judas tree come into bloom and the curtains of wisteria fall from the ancient vines that are as thick as a man's — a Janissary's — thighs, blossoming in what we know to be Matisse colors, blue-pink and pink-blue, the nightingales sing; and they sing loud and clear.

In 1917, a burning cargo ship broke free from the wharf halfway up the Bosphorus at Beykoz and drifted down in flames to touch the Asian shore, slowly to turn in the stream, to get free and to drift upon the surface current, again and again firing the weathered wooden summer palaces and the smaller houses of the fishermen's villages, which were as dry as tinder and as beautiful as any human habitation can be. Today in a heavy fog, now and again, a fast-moving motor vessel ploughs into a villa or a village. One such sharp prow killed a bride asleep in bed in her many-windowed room overhanging the water on the night before her wedding. The Lady Gülruh and Sinan had similar tales to tell their children.

When the Judas trees and wisteria bloomed, on a moonlit night the family got into the barge and rowed up the strait to picnic by the fountain under the gigantic plane tree in the meadows between the two little rivers called the Sweet Waters of Asia. They looked across the glittering dark waters of the strait at this narrowest point, and in the black and white night saw the crenellated silhouette of the European Castle rising from the farther shore. Sultan Mehmet the Conqueror's Janissary engineers had built the curtain walls and cone-topped round towers on the hills and in the valley in ninety days of the summer before the fall of Constantinople.

Perhaps they saw the "lost souls" fly by. Water birds skim the surface of the Bosphorus at a mile a minute in flights of a dozen or a hundred; these are lesser shearwaters of a subspecies peculiar to the Bosphorus. They flash by on bladelike wings, tilting to either side of the boat, those to the starboard vanishing, their dark back plumage merging with the marine-gray water, those to port streaking by like silver stars until they right themselves and fly on out of sight.

Sinan and the Lady Gülruh may have called them "lost souls," but they told their children an earlier and gentler story of how the water birds got their name. It is a love story. According to the legend, a domestic slave crossed the Bosphorus carrying a secret love letter from a girl to her chosen lover, begging him to come quickly to rescue her from her unkind father's house; her marriage had been arranged, but she was to be forced into the harem of some other man. The wind blew the love letter out of the slave's hand; the old woman watched it sink below the swift and cold surface current and vanish to be carried north to another destination by the low and dense stream flowing north. Joined by the spirits of many a generation of lovers' slaves, the lost souls silently and swiftly fly up and down, back and forth, searching the two currents of the Bosphorus for the lost love letter.

Today the legend gives the water birds the souls of the unwanted harem women who, fallen on evil days, came to be sewn into canvas sacks, weighted at the ankles, and thrown by night into the strait to drown. Such was the fate of the young slave girls, any and all of whom might have been pregnant, of Murad III's harem in the days after the Sultan's death on January 16, 1595. A sailor diving to recover an anchor snagged on the bottom opened his eyes in the clear cold green water and saw a crowd of girls and women nodding and dancing in the two currents. Surfacing, he saw the lost souls flying by as fast and as silently as specters haunting the waterway.

But in 1563, in the golden age of Süleyman the Lawgiver, before the empire of the Sons of Osman tilted into its decline and fall, Sinan took all his family with him to inspect the pious foundation of the first charter and testament that he had built for the future comfort of his ladies, both the living and the unborn. The mosque stood in the corner of the walled garden surrounding his first town house, which he had given over to the pious foundation along with the new school and orphanage and a public fountain. To it, with the properties of his own tomb and the great house near the Süleymaniyé, Sinan later added thirty-five houses and business premises in the city, as specified in the charter of 1585-1586.

Sinan's oratory stood in the part of Istanbul that is no longer called the Chief Architect's Quarter of the New Garden. In the earthquake and fire of 1917, his pious foundation in his urban landscape, designed in 1538 or 1539 in the aftermath of an earlier earthquake and fire, was reduced to ashes. It was a modest set of buildings. The Lady Gülruh, surely, as patroness saw to the comfort of the orphans among whom, were she widowed, she would have retired to live.

From the ruins, the Turkish architects of the Vakiflar, that department of the government now charged with the upkeep of all religious edifices, have rebuilt the minaret, and, when funds are provided, they plan to restore the rest of Sinan's pious foundation. For himself, Sinan designed and built a minaret like a lighthouse. It has no equal in Istanbul. Blunt, sturdy, tapering, the masonry tower is octagonal in section. From a square base it rises well within the scope of a standing man. The pharos ends in an open chamber under a cupola topped by a finial and lighted by an unglazed window cut into each of the eight sides.

Sinan then carved a stone slab to fit into the top of each upright rectangular opening. He curtained the right-angular space with a ripple-draped arch of stone cut in an Islamic pattern that seems to the Western eye to be Baroque. His minaret is phallic. Sexual abstinence plays no part in Islamic puritanical morality. This is no tower for an anchorite. There is no such thing as negative virtue. Sinan loved his neighbors, his sister, his wife, as himself.

CHAPTER

10

Sultan Mehmet the Conqueror took Constantinople. Sultan Bayazid the Pious worked to consolidate the empire. Sultan Selim the Grim conquered Persia, Syria, and Egypt, Tabriz, Damascus, and Cairo; and he took under the protection of the Sons of Osman the Prophet's holy cities of Mecca, Medina, and Jerusalem. Sultan Süleyman the Magnificent set himself three goals to mark his reign: for Islam, to conquer Vienna; for his people, to bring a constant flow of fresh water into Istanbul; and for his monument, to build the Süleymaniyé above the Golden Horn.

In 1529 Sinan the general of the Janissary engineers breached the walls of Vienna, but the Emperor of the East failed to take the Austrian capital from the Emperor of the West. In 1550 Sinan the Royal Chief Architect began to build the Sultan's Imperial Friday Mosque and mausoleum surrounded by a *küllîyé*, that is, a sort of university city.

The pious foundation is imperial in size. Besides the mosque and tomb, it includes a *türbé*, tomb, for Haseki Hürrem, who died unexpectedly on April 15, 1558, the year after Sinan had completed the Süleymaniyé. He had already built a lodge for the guardian of the cemetery garden behind the kibla wall.

The four university colleges, one each for the study of the four gospels or orthodox interpretations of the Sacred Law, stand in pairs to the northeast and the southwest of the mosque enclosure. They are classic medresés, square courtyards arcaded around a garden. To prepare the students for the colleges, Sinan built a grammar school, a higher school, a school to teach aspiring muezzins the several ways to chant the verses of the Koran, and a medical school. He built a combined hospital and insane asylum; a charitable kitchen for the poor and a refectory for the students and other members of the university city; and a guest house for distinguished visitors, in size and beauty worthy of the savants, the justices, and, it may have been, saints come to talk to the students.

Sinan and Süleyman included a public fountain (today famous for its spring water), a splendid bathhouse, and public water closets. He built a library and a playing field, the "iron ground" for wrestling matches. Finally, in the foundations of the terraced mosque enclosure and the basements of the buildings raised on the steep slopes of the hill, Sinan put rows of vaulted shops for the goldsmiths of the Sultan's own guild of craftsmen. There must have been a caravansary attached to the Süleymaniyé; perhaps it was a building already in existence.

Süleyman and Sinan chose a magnificent terrain to build upon high up above the slopes of the Third Hill. The ground had been part of the walled gardens of the burnt-out Old Palace. Haseki Hürrem's fire in the imperial harem cleared the way for her husband's memorial, for her new quarters in the Sultan's Palace, and for her own grave. Sinan restored what remained of the burnt buildings as a place of retirement, much reduced, for widowed or banished imperial ladies. Gülbahar, the mother of the strangled Prince Mustafa, went to live alone there in or after 1553, for the next twenty-eight years. No one knows where she was buried.

Under the Süleymaniyé, on the slope of the hill, Sinan, who was by 1550 the custodian of all the imperial properties, bought for himself an odd parcel of the old harem's gardens, a wedge-shaped plot on which he built the great house where he died in 1588. By then he had prepared his own modest tomb of white marble. It stands in the sharp corner across the street from the terraced foundations of the mosque. His house long since has been destroyed, but in time the grounds are to be bought back and restored.

In the fine weather, probably of May, certainly in 1550, Sinan began work by laying the foundations of the walled enclosure. It is called the *sahn* and it is a rectangular "stage" that sets the mosque, its courtyard, and its cemetery garden apart from the surrounding urban complex. Sinan dug into the top of the Third Hill and built up from the steep slope terraced foundations of solid masonry for the platform.

According to the Royal Chief Architect's own legend, because the headstrong Sultan was impatient to see the work go on, Sinan then vanished from Istanbul for several years to give the excavations and the fill time to settle, and the mortar cementing the great blocks of limestone time to harden. It seems unlikely that he left the work in progress, although the routine duties of his office may have taken him to Edirné in Thrace or to the nearby provincial capitals in Asia Minor. If, indeed, Sinan himself built the famous *tekké* of Süleyman in Damascus, which was completed in 1555 as the gathering place for pilgrims at the start of the desert caravan to Mecca, he took about a year to go to Syria, do the work, and return. But that does not seem reasonable; surely an assistant architect did the work. Sinan had his hands full in Istanbul.

In 1551, he finished the mosque and pious foundation for Hadim Ibrahim Pasha, the *Damat* Chief of the White Eunuchs. In 1555, he finished the mosque of the abruptly executed Grand Vezir Kara Ahmet Pasha, whose widow Fatma Sultan then married the castrated Circassian; and in that year Sinan also built another hexagonal mosque for the Grand Vezir Rüstem Pasha's brother, the Lord High Admiral Sinan Pasha in Beshiktash across the Golden Horn on the Bosphorus.

While the mortar of the foundations hardened, Sinan assembled the mountains of limestone blocks from the quarries at Bakirköy on the Sea of Marmara. The stone was pale yellow; it has weathered light gray. He chose the columns. He got the roughed-out capitals of white Proconessus marble from the quarries in the islands of the Marble Sea. He saw to the baking of the light-weight bricks for the domes, the semidomes, and the cupolas. And he put his assistant architects and the foremen of his teams of skilled workmen and laborers, most of them Armenians and Greeks, as well as the detachment of Janissary cadets to work on the dependencies.

In the workshops of the Royal Chief Architect, which were in the Vefa, the curving street that connects the Süleymaniyé with the Shehzadé's mosque, the Sultan and Sinan pored over the drawing boards to work out all the details of the monumental plan. Süleyman was fifty-six in 1550. He allowed himself few, if any other, distractions. He had ruled for thirty years, since 1536 alone – save for Haseki Hürrem's private but increasingly open helping hand. Sinan was sixty-one; after his decade as general of the engineers, he had held office as Royal Chief Architect for twelve years.

In his old age, sometime after he had completed the Selimiyé in Edirné, the third and last of his Imperial Friday Mosques, Sinan summed up the work of his career. He described the Süleymaniyé as the work of a journeyman, which is to say, of a laborer and craftsman, in this instance an architect, new to his trade. With the Shehzadé's mosque, completed two years earlier, in 1548, he had finished his ten years as an apprentice.

But surely neither for incompetence nor for failure of imagination did the Royal Chief Architect and the Sultan choose to build the Süleymaniyé on the floor plan of the Church of the Divine Wisdom. Both the Imperial Friday Mosque and Haghia Sophia rise from the circle inscribed in the square, extended on all four sides but roofed by a single great dome "shouldered" by two semidomes in the main axis. The two side aisles, which rise only to the height of the four piers, are covered with cupolas and vaults. In both church and mosque, the high arches on either side are filled by fenestrated screen walls.

Turkish historians of art and architecture deny that these Ottoman European mosques are copies of the Byzantine church of Haghia Sophia. It is a fact that the first of the great Ottoman domes was built not in Istanbul but in Edirné, two generations before the fall of Constantinople in 1453, by Murad the Mystic. Its floor plan is hexagonal; its minarets take the form of the Seljuk Turkish style. Whatever the disputed origin of the single great dome set upon square walls, the climate of the high Anatolian plateau, of Thrace, and of the Bosphorus gives reason enough to protect the faithful at prayer under a celestial dome. In dry lands, the first countries of Islam, in Arabia, Egypt, Persia, and Moghul India, even today the mosques are open courtyards, such as those in front of the Ottoman mosques, with the kibla wall sheltered by a covered arcade.

A church is not a mosque; the one, until the Age of Reason, was with few exceptions dark; the other has always been full of light. The early Christians worshiped secretly in caverns and catacombs, underground in secret. The Prophet led his followers in prayer upon the floor of the desert under the canopy of heaven, sunlit by day, starlit by night in the dark of the moon, of which the crescent is the symbol of Islam.

The men who built Haghia Sophia, Anthemius of Tralles and Isidoros of Miletus were, like Sinan, Greeks from Asia Minor. They invented the Church of the Divine Wisdom as they went along, and they made mistakes. For instance, they did not give the mortar in the four high arches time enough to dry. The weight of the semidomes bulged the circle of the joined pendentives out of shape.

Haghia Sophia, which was dedicated on December 26, 537, is classified as a domical basilica; it was the first of its kind. The two architects and builders had no existing models, except possibly small round temples, of which the Pantheon in Rome is the great example, and probably small Christian chapels in Egypt, Palestine, and Mesopotamia. The dome, as in domicile, originally meant house. The Byzantine and Ottoman domes are hemispherical and they are set not on round but on square walls. The plan is Eastern in origin. But for the Byzantine caesaropapist Emperor Justinian and his wife and co-ruler, the Empress Theodora, Anthemius and Isidoros designed and built a prototype which, by Süleyman's and Sinan's day, a thousand and thirteen years later, had become an archetype. The church and the mosque stand about a mile apart, the one on the First Hill, the other on the Third Hill, in the imperial city of Constantinople-Istanbul.

Neither the Sultan nor the Royal Chief Architect intended to copy slavishly Haghia Sophia, nor to surpass the church – by 1550, a most hallowed imperial mosque. Instead, it becomes apparent that they planned to measure themselves, their faith, their domains, and their achievements against the Emperor Justinian the Great, the architect Anthemius of Tralles, the Christianity of the Eastern Orthodox Church, the Byzantine Empire, and the Divine Wisdom of God the One.

The dome of Haghia Sophia is larger and higher. Roughly its broken circumference measures in diameter 34 meters – (112 feet 3 inches) as against the Süleymaniyé's 26 meters (87 feet 6 inches). From floor to crown, the second, higher dome of Haghia Sophia measures 56 meters (184 feet 10 inches) against 53 meters (175 feet) for the Süleymaniyé. Anthemius built Haghia Sophia in no exact system of proportions, although the second dome's increased height brings it close to the golden section of 1:1.6+. Sinan designed the Süleymaniyé in the exact mathematical proportions of 1:2.

The two architects were comparably supreme. The Byzantine and the Ottoman emperors are both known as lawgivers and each is called "the Great." The two empires, ruled from the same imperial city, were roughly equivalent in size and in power, in grandeur and in glory; and although one lasted twice as long as the other, the dynasty of the Sons of Osman, in unbroken descent in the male line for six centuries, has yet to be equaled. Oddly, the two women, the Byzantine Empress Theodora and the "Veiled Empress" Hürrem, the one in her gynaeceum, the other in her harem, were equally powerful in their influence over their husbands. Yet the two domical buildings, the church and the mosque, each rising from the identical floor plan, are not at all the same. The one is Byzantine; the other is Ottoman.

Today it is impossible to know what the exterior of Haghia Sophia looked like when Anthemius and Isidoros finished the church for Justinian and Theodora. The exterior walls of brick masonry, now covered with hard cement plaster painted orange, were concealed by parasite buildings and dependencies. Only the dome soared above them as a landmark for all travelers arriving from Europe or Asia or by sea. The architects let the external appearances go. They built a shell to house the interior spaces of the church.

Christianity is a mystery religion. The Byzantines entered Haghia Sophia ready to welcome, in ecstasy and in enthusiasm, a purely spiritual experience. In the streets and houses and palaces and business premises of the walled city, they either accepted the rule of Justinian and Theodora or they intrigued and connived to take the worldly power into their own hands. But never did they trust any other man or woman, least of all themselves. Dynasty after Byzantine dynasty rose and fell in the course of one thousand one hundred twenty nine years, but the church and the city did not change.

In their millenium, Haghia Sophia satisfied the Byzantines as a church in which to worship not gentle Jesus but Christ Pantokrator, the All-Ruling, whose stern face looked down upon them from the mosaic in the dome, born of a tragic mother and an incomprehensible Father. In the years before Constantinople fell to Mehmet the Conqueror, when the enemy was outside the walls, a Byzantine Greek Constantinopolitan who went to the bakery to buy a loaf of bread discussed the nature of the Trinity passionately with the baker as he counted his debased change. In Haghia Sophia Anthemius and Isidoros built the unending dialogue between man and his Maker upon the realities and the spheres of divine and human power.

The discussion went on from December 26, 537, to the night of May 29, 1453, when it was silenced in submission to the Will of God. On that Tuesday evening Mehmet the Conqueror went into Haghia Sophia and drove out the marauding Janissaries and their victims, the Byzantines seeking sanctuary. He took the Church of the Divine Wisdom as his own to rededicate as the mosque of Ayasofya. In Islam God is singular despite His ninety-nine beautiful names.

Not Anthemius's first golden dome, which, being too flat, fell in the earthquake of 558, but the hemispherical golden dome of Isodoros the Younger (many times restored) covers the church and mosque today. If it does not, as the early chroniclers put it, hang on a golden chain hooked into the floor of Heaven, the dome still appears to soar in the air, to float mysteriously on golden light. Sinan, who buttressed and repaired the fabric in 1572, must have smiled when he figured out Anthemius's architectonic trickery. Sinan knew that the dome was built of lightweight bricks (especially baked in Rhodes) and held together by crystallized mortar, it is true, mixed with the crumbled bones of Christian saints and martyrs.

He saw that the dome rises from four joined pendentives which take the weight and contain the dynamics of the vertical and the lateral thrusts. Four massive piers of masonry rise up to take the weight and thrusts from the pendentives. The piers stand upon the Devonian rock of the First Hill. By training, Anthemius and Isidoros were not architects and engineers but mathematicians. In their lifetime they knew of no way to calculate the enormous weight of their building. It crushed the Devonian rock beneath the dome; in settling, the piers split open in fissures wide enough for the fingers to explore. The walls and the pillars slanted out of the true. Then the dome came down. But another, even weightier, went up again on the distorted ring of the joined pendentives.

The dome of Haghia Sophia still appears to soar — and thus it does soar — floating on golden light, which is to say, indirect illumination. Daylight enters through a few windows that Anthemius opened round the base of the dome. They are out of sight and screened behind pierced railings. The man who stands on the floor under the crown looks up and sees the gentle light of heaven diffused and refracted on the myriad surfaces of the gold tessera set in the curving mosaic. The dome acts as a great reflector. It is a celestial dome, even to the man who, like Sinan, understands the trick.

It takes imagination for any man today to realize what the church looked like in the great days of the Byzantine Empire. Then the man, himself gorgeously arrayed, stood surrounded by space adorned. Adorned with an iconostasis hung with icons of gold and jeweled enamelings to screen the altar in the apse. The altar and its canopy were made of gold and silver and precious stones, and furnished with chalices and ciboria of crystal and chalcedony. Beeswax candles stood in gold and silver candlesticks, their flames shining on the curtains of cloth of gold and figured silken brocades that hung from the arches of the exedras and the arcades.

The pillars were – and still are – smooth monoliths of porphyry and verd antique, their capitals of white marble intricately undercut. Four doves perched on the rim of a basket carry the weight, or so it seems, of one corner. Above the arcades, the spandrels are inlaid with patterns like embroideries or filigree. All the walls behind and above the polished columns are surfaced with golden mosaics, figured with crosses and mandalas, and with the hierarchies of heaven and of the imperial court. The walls below are paneled with revetments of many-colored marbles split open to make patterns like birds' and butterfly wings – or to modern eyes, like Rorschach tests.

Anthemius knew what he was doing when he ordered from the Greek quarries his monoliths of verd antique, a variegated green conglomerate marble. They are the pillars in the arcades and the galleries along either side of the central aisle – the nave or transept in cruciform plans. So he knew what he wanted when he collected the even greater monoliths of porphyry, surely the most costly pillars in existence, that he set in the curved exedras at the corners of his central rectangular space. These porphyry monoliths all come from the same quarry; but they wre old when Anthemius built them into Haghia Sophia. Perhaps some of them came from the Artemesion in Ephesus. Today they stand braced with rings of gilt bronze because these shafts of dense but brittle purple stone have fractured under the tremendous weight put upon them.

Anthemius used the monoliths of verd antique and porphyry in arcades to screen the central space under the dome and semidomes from the aisles and the outer walls. He did so to create a space within a space. From the apse at the far end, out of a gold mosaic in the shell of the small semidome, the Virgin Mary, flanked by angels, looks out with open eyes into this space enclosed in space. She carries her Son. Whatever the Mother of God sees she recognizes as inevitable.

What does it mean, this space within a space? Does it have to do with the circle inscribed within the square, each of them magical, together set in tension to form that most ancient irreducible equation, the mandala? Is this the duality at the heart of any mortal Christian, or for that matter, all men of two minds? Or is this consubstantial space the wisdom of the Son of God, who was the Son of Man? Enthroned in somber robes, the Mother of God looks out into space within space. Neither she nor her Son, the Pantokrator, when He looked down from the golden dome, smile. Byzantine architecture, Byzantine art are formal, intellectual, intricate, elaborate, and abstract, concerned less with the substance and more with the idea. Anthemius put a skin of flickering thought upon the hulking body of his faulty building.

Shabby as it is today, dirty, dusty, stripped of its furnishings and its treasure, holding the chill of winter into midsummer, and echoing emptily – Ayasofya is now a museum – the interior of Haghia Sophia is still what it has always been, sublime. To surpass this building was not Sinan's and Süleyman's intention. The Sultan and his Royal Chief Architect built to celebrate a crystal-clear religion.

By 1550, the Sacred Law was fixed as a pure science. The dome of the Süleymaniyé rises and soars. It is celestial, but it certainly does not float upon mysteriously illuminated golden air. It is held up by the law of gravity. In his building Sinan stripped bare all the technical forces at work. He revealed the structural engineering, the masonry walls, the buttresses, the solid stone piers, the granite pillars, the voussoirs of the springing arches, the thrusts and the counterbalancing resistances of the dome and its supporting members. In the Imperial Friday Mosque there is no dialogue between man and God, no space within a space. But there is perfect, and thus infinite, unity. Through tiers and rows and banks of windows, daylight fills the space flowing through the defining masses.

In this building, Sinan first worked out his principle that engineering and architecture are inseparable; the one is the other. Therefore, in all his buildings the exterior is the outside of the interior, and the inside is the interior of the outside. As with crystalline forms, the eye looks clear through Sinan's architecture. In Islam, God gives each man his life whole at the moment of his conception.

When Sinan got to work at his drawing board, he began with the circle inscribed within the square. He extended the space on all four sides. He then cubed the square and upon it set the globe in the diameter of the circle. He hollowed them out, drew in the four pendentives, and saw his dome upheld by four freestanding corner piers. Within the space there stands an invisible cone rising from the circle to the key of the dome. The mosque's walls rise within an invisible pyramid.

Inside his prayer hall, built on the floor plan of Haghia Sophia, Sinan suppressed the Christian axis. To break down the compartmentation of the space within a space, he did away with Anthemius's verd antique and prophyry colonnades, the arcades, and the galleries of the gynaeceum (in Islam women pray at home; there is no need to segregate the men from the women in a mosque). Thus Sinan opened the Süleymaniyé for Islamic liturgy. At worship Muslims stand shoulder to shoulder in ranks to face the long kibla wall, in which the prayer niche points due southeast from Istanbul to Mecca.

However, to support the fenestrated curtain walls that fill the two high arches of the northeastern and southwestern sides – the two semidomes fill the corresponding arches formed by the pendentives of the other two sides of the square – Sinan used four smooth monoliths of gray Egyptian granite. The first pillars were tree trunks. These columns are as thick and as tall as the peeled boles of Douglas firs and ponderosa pines cut down to thirty-two feet four inches in height. Sinan spaced them on the line between the piers to carry one high and wide arch and a smaller at each side. When he had set them upright, he placed their roughed-out capitals, huge truncated pyramids of white marble, upside down on top of them.

His legend, as recorded by Evliya Chelebi, gives us a story, and this one rings true. About 1556, it must have been in the last year of construction, Süleyman, as apparently was his habit, found a free moment to pay an unannounced visit to the work in progress. He had a handful of guardsmen with him, but the Sultan did not come incognito. He arrived at the side gate in the southwestern wall of the enclosure. Sinan's workmen sprang to their feet and stood at attention. Perhaps a foreman or a senior Janissary apprentice stepped up to salute the Sultan. He looked about searching for Sinan. Süleyman put the men at ease and told them to get on with their work. Although he may not have frowned, he did not smile as he walked into the finished courtyard and through the portal into the covered prayer hall. It was full of scaffolding for the plasterers, the marble-cutters, and the painters of the semidomes and the high dome. If the scaffolding of those days looked like the timbers, the crisscrossing planks, and the platforms in use during the work of restoration of 1950, Süleyman walked into a geometrical forest, a kind of very modern abstract sculpture, that cost the equivalent of fifty thousand dollars to erect. It filled the space. Silence ran ahead of Sultan Süleyman.

Then he heard his Royal Chief Architect's impatient voice cry out from the top of the scaffolding surrounding one of the gigantic granite monoliths, to say something like this: "No! No! That's not the way to cut stalactites. Here, give me that mallet and chisel. I'll show you how to carve the capital."

Then, standing at the base of the pillar, the Sultan had to put up his hand to shield his eyes as the chips flew and the marble dust rained down. He may then have smiled. I doubt that he interrupted Sinan as he cut the geometrical crystalline stalactites in the round to come out right.

Sinan finished the Süleymaniyé in 1557. It is an enormous space, full of light by day, once lit by twenty-two thousand flames by night. In the seventeenth century, when the mosque was not a century old, Evliya Chelebi saw ten "Frankish infidels skillful in geometry and architecture" take off their shoes and put on slippers to enter the southwestern portal. He followed them to watch the great spaces of the Süleymaniyé take their effect. Heads back, the ten men shuffled along in their babouches; they walked on thick carpets woven to Sinan's patterns at Ushak instead of on the rush matting and scatter rugs of today. Even so, the same space flows from the portal through an arch and then higher into the semidome and on up into the high dome.

The head goes back, the mouth falls open. Evliya Chelebi reports that each of the ten Frankish infidels raised his right hand and laid his forefinger across his open mouth. "They tossed up their hats and cried out ... 'Mother of God! ' "

These Franks seem to have been Italians. Evliya Chelebi records their cry as "Maryah! " To call upon Mary is not impious in a mosque. The prayer niche, the *mihrab*, may signify Aysha's pavilion in the Prophet's walled garden in Medina – he died in her bed and he was buried beneath the floor. But the verse from the Koran that is always inscribed above the prayer niche refers to Mary's "sanctuary" in her uncle Zachariah's house. Mary, the Mother of Jesus, is one of the four perfect women in Islam.

Open-mouthed, the men cried out as they looked up into the dome where Sinan had Kara Hisari, the illuminator, paint in a calligraphic wheel another text from the Koran (verse 35, Sura XXIV, called "Light"). Süleyman had chosen it.

> God is the light of the heavens and the earth;
> the likeness of His light is as a niche
> wherein is a lamp
> (the lamp in a glass,
> the glass as it were a glittering star)
> kindled from a Blessed Tree,
> an olive that is neither of the East nor of the West
> whose oil wellnigh would shine, even if no fire touched it;
> Light upon Light;
> (God guides to his Light whom he Will.)

"The ten Franks went around the mosque bareheaded [wrote Evliya Chelebi], and each of the ten bit his finger in astonishment, that being their manner of testifying the greatest amazement." Evliya Chelebi could not help asking them how they liked what they saw. "And one of them who was able to give an answer said, ... 'Nowhere is there so much beauty, external and internal, to be found united; and ... that in the whole of Frangistan there was not a single edifice which could be compared to this.' "

Then Evliya Chelebi asked the ten Frankish tourists what they thought of this mosque compared with Haghia Sophia. "They answered, that Aya Sófiyah was a fine old building, larger than this, and very strong and solid for the age in which it was erected, but that it could not in any manner vie with the elegance, the beauty, and perfection of this mosque, upon which, moreover, a much larger sum of money had been expended than on Aya Sófiyah."

In fact, nobody knows how much Haghia Sophia cost Justinian to build – more than Versailles cost Louis XIV – an astronomical sum. Neither the Byzantines nor the Ottomans understood or practiced what we now call the science of economics, but Justinian and Süleyman both knew the value of money. Evliya Chelebi estimated that the entire sum expended on the Süleymaniyé amounted to seventy-four million two-hundred-forty-two thousand five-hundred [silver] *piastres* – something like the equivalent of thirty-eight million gold American dollars, before the First World War.

A Muslim will not enter a mosque unless he is ritually clean. During the visit of the ten Frankish architects, whom Evliya Chelebi took to be unclean, he tells us that the air that flowed through the Süleymaniyé three hundred years ago "by the will of God" was "perfumed by an excellent odor, which gives fragrance to the brain of man but has no resemblance to the fragrance of earthly flowers." Today the air is thickened and blackened, not with the smoke and soot of the twenty-two thousand flames burning the wicks floating in the olive oil in the glass lamps, but from the stacks of soft-coal-burning cargo ships and ferryboats on the Golden Horn below. Even so, fragrant or smoky, the air and the flow of space still carry the visitor into the vastnesses under the dome. Then the man does not know where to look.

To help him and to catch his eye, Sinan cut pointed niches in the sides of the four freestanding piers built of solid limestone masonry. These elephants' feet are irregular in section but roughly square. Sinan broke their surfaces with many angles and ascending lines. The man's eye follows the vertical cuts in the mass and he looks up into the dome. Having bitten his finger in astonishment, he gets a crick in his neck.

Lost in space, he finds himself standing on a desert floor. The Süley-maniyé is too big. The volume is tremendous; the void is overwhelming. Such is not the purpose of a mosque. In it, like Sultan Süleyman Khan in his Ruling and Religious Institutions, one stands alone enclosed in Ottoman magnificence. A man answering the call to prayer does not enter to be overpowered. Today only a handful pray there.

Sinan did his best to overcome the formidable distances between the portal and the prayer niche. He called in Drunken Ibrahim to fill the windows of the kibla wall with stained glass of brilliant coloring set in screens patterned in formal arabesques, some of them floral, some geometrical, others calligraphic. Sinan called upon the potters of Iznik for tiles; he set the painter Kara Hisari to work on beautifully written texts from the Koran; he hung the wheeling mobiles of lights in place and he put gigantic beeswax candles on either side of the *mihrab*.

The prayer niche he carved himself with stalactites of marble to fill the peak in the alcove, which he framed in a rectangle of marble ending in a cornice carved in the formal pattern of mountaintops. He called upon his workers in *opus sectile* to inlay the white marble floors of the window embrasures with designs of red and green marble, purple porphyry, and black basalt. All the detail is exemplary, but the kibla wall is known to be "dry." So are the deserts surrounding total power. There is no welcome in it. It is a somber wall.

I turn my back and walk out into the courtyard through the high portal. It has been described as "pinched" and so it seems to me to be. To clear the façade of the mosque, the northwest wall, Sinan had to bring the buttresses inside the building. They are uncompromising vertical masses of rectilinear masonry. Two protrude into the prayer hall, one on either side of the portal. Sinan, working to make assets of these liabilities, built up between them a system of boxes, galleries, and loges piled one on top of the other. They are elegantly spaced and pillared in a series of horizontals, verticals, and arches, and all the volumes are harmonious. Sinan had a flawless sense of proportion.

He then reduced the actual passageway through the thicknesses at the base of the outside wall and between the buttresses. Sinan brought down this imperial portal almost to man height, a very tall man but still a human being. So he forced an almost violent descent from the high dome of heaven to the earth below — upon the man leaving the House of God to re-enter his own daily life. Islam does not make of Friday a day of rest. It is impious to believe that the work of the first six days in the Creation wearied God, Who is not human. The Muslim leaves the mosque to go about his business.

The way out is as deep as a tunnel. I step on to the porch under the high arcade roofed by nine domes in a row upheld by six tall monoliths of pink Egyptian granite, and by two more columns, one at either end, oddities that at first do not catch the eye. The courtyard is rectangular, with seven domes to a side, arcaded, paved, centered upon a fountain. It is open to the sky, low and gray in winter, high and blue in summer. The peace and quiet of the courtyard aids the man crossing the serene space in his transition into the ordinary and the everyday commerce of the bazaars.

On the far side of the courtyard, opposite the portal, stands the monumental gate, the equivalent of an arch of triumph. The gateway opens at the back of a deep niche cut in an upright limestone block of masonry (perhaps the rooms of its three stories once housed gate keepers). The cornice makes reference to the Altai Mountains of the Turks' homeland. The geometrical stalactities of the peaked niche call attention to the cave, man's first domicile; or perhaps to his tomb; or to the womb. The portal is a way of life.

For the Süleymaniyé, Sinan erected four minarets. He placed one at each corner of the courtyard. The two that stand beside the mosque are taller; the two at the far corners, north and west, of the courtyard are lower. They are classic Ottoman minarets, more like gigantic candles of limestone, topped by candle-snuffer cones of lead and set upright in their holders, than they are like church steeples, bell towers, or lighthouses which are said to be the originals of the minaret. The muezzin climbs up the tower to call the faithful to prayer: "There is no god but God, and Mohammed is the Messenger of God. Come to prayer! Come to prayer! Come to prayer! " (Today a rasping public address system does the work.)

In Süleyman's lifetime a choir of muezzins as many as two hundred and fifty strong climbed the spiraling, tapering staircases inside the towers to chant the call to prayer from the ten galleries of the four minarets. They are not round but polygonal in section; each has sixteen sides.

Sinan put three galleries on each of the two taller minarets, one above the other. The galleries are built on corbels of carved stalactites and are set about with geometrically pierced marble screens. On either of the lower pair he put two galleries. So the Royal Chief Architect worked the Sultan's biographical statistics into the Süleymaniyé.

Süleyman was the fourth Sultan to rule in Istanbul, and the tenth Son of Osman to take the throne in unbroken descent from father to son. He was born on November 6, 1494 in the first month of the first year of the Islamic millenium. Therefore, he was destined, like the Prophet at the time of the Hegira (A.D. 622), to carry the one true Faith into the darkest regions of the earth. "It was written on his forehead." It is built into his memorial.

Ten is the perfect number in Islam, a one and a zero (in our version of the Arabic, or Sanskrit, numerals, but not Sinan's, the one is the side of the square and the diameter of the circle – if it is not a goose egg). Not three, not seven, but four is the fortunate number in Islam, perhaps because of the first four "successors" to the Prophet, his "substitutes," the caliphs of the mono-lithic religion. Whatever else the numbers and the minarets may mean, they inform us that Sinan took his master Sultan Süleyman Khan, the Lawgiver, the Great, the Magnificent into account when he designed and built this mosque which is his memorial.

This man, the tenth Son of Osman, the fourth sultan to rule from Istanbul, was not perfect; nor is Sinan's mosque, the Süleymaniyé. God the One alone is perfect; only He creates perfection. To compete with God in an attempt to create perfection on earth is to question the nature of divinity in an act of impiety that is an arrogant sin. It is the worst of crimes. Therefore, Sinan built a flaw into the fabric of the Süleymaniyé, a flaw of design, not of engineering.

To make it obvious, Sinan placed this essential human failing in the corners of the courtyard where the high porch joins the lower arcades along the sides. In the colonnade of the porch six of the eight pillars are smooth monoliths of pink Egyptian granite. From each of their capitals spring three arches, two to make the arcade, the third at the back, to connect the pillar with the corbel built into the wall of the façade of the mosque.

Sinan gave each of the other two pillars, those at the ends of the colonnade at the corners where high porch joins the lower side arcades of the courtyard, a double load to bear. The corner pillars, like the six monoliths, stand on the edge of the porch floor (a platform of solid limestone masonry) that is raised a meter above the pavement of the courtyard. The pillar at the corner must carry the springers of five arches at two levels. These are, first, the springer that ends the high arcade of the porch; second, another, equally high, that joins the arcade with the wall at the end of the porch; the third, coming at right angles, a springer in the arch that joins the pillar to the façade of the mosque; the fourth, at a lower level, the springer, this one, too, coming in at right angles, to end the side arcade of the courtyard; and fifth and last, the springer of the arch at the lower level that connects the pillar with the courtyard's outside wall.

Hard to describe, harder to visualize (see illustration), these corner pillars and their work load take on powerful significance. They are as distorted, in the abstract, as the stony musculature of the baroque Atlas standing on either side of a palace door to carry the weight of an imperial balcony, but the corner pillars of the mosque courtyard are not at all humorously decorative.

To get the work done, Sinan took two more immense monoliths of smooth pink Egyptian granite, in girth as big as the other six in the row. He then cut them down to the height of the slim pillars standing below in the colonnade of the courtyard arcades (they are smooth monoliths of various marbles, some colored, some white, and of porphyry). Around the top of each truncated granite monolith, he set a band of bronze (so all the other pillars in the row are girt at top and bottom to prevent the round edges from flaking). But the thick bronze ring emphasizes the mutilation of the monolith.

Upon the disproportionate, squat column of pink granite, he set a carved stone of white marble, and it is as difficult to visualize as it is multiple in function. Half of it is a smooth drum, the size of the truncated granite monolith which it builds up in height; but half of it is carved as a triangular bracket which is, in fact, the half of a stalactite capital cut catercornered. The peculiarity in shape and function of this stone is enhanced by its color, white streaked with gray; and its substance, Proconessus marble, which contrasts with the dense, hard, pink Egyptian granite on which it stands. The half-capital, as a corbel, receives the springer of the last arch in the courtyard arcade.

On this bastard utility stone, Sinan piled up another almost as ugly; it is part drum and part voussoir. On top of it, he put one more oddity; this is a drum with a fragment of a haunch protruding from it. And so on, he piled functional oddity upon technical necessity until he had built up the truncated monolith to the height of the other whole pillars in the porch arcade. He then carved one more monstrosity out of white marble. The stone is three parts stalactite capital (to receive the three high arches of the porch), and one part haunch in the half-spandrel above the last arch of the courtyard arcade. So he contrived an emphatic solution to an engineering problem. This puzzling, and to my mind ugly, composite corner pillar works; it works hard. It is a most elaborate flaw.

What is more, Sinan could have avoided this technically perfect but unsightly job of work. He did so in other, lesser courtyards. In one he used a square pillar cut from a single block of stone. In another he separated the porch from the courtyard arcades by means of a gate on which he built a gatehouse roofed by a cupola. His pupil Mehmet the Inlayer, a lesser man who succeeded him as Royal Chief Architect, got around the bothersome problem in the courtyard of the Blue Mosque by raising the side arcades to the height of the porch. For the Süleymaniyé, Sinan might have sent his stone-cutters down to Egypt to quarry an unobtrusive monolith of pink granite cut to specifications, so to carry all five arches in the corner. He chose not to do so. Sinan had both the time and the money.

For seven years, Süleyman opened his privy purse to his Royal Chief Architect. Sinan spent the fifth part, the Sultan's share, of the total loot from the conquest of the Knights Hospitalers of Rhodes, with, in addition, the thirty-four years of accumulated annual revenues from the Dodecanese between 1523 and 1557. He had the income from the Sultan's imperial province of Egypt to spend during the seven years it took him to build the Süleymaniyé. These corner pillars, designed as conscious flaws or not, begin to take on significance as symbols.

I wonder if Sinan made of them monuments to the Son of Osman carrying the weight of his Ruling and Religious Institutions? Or perhaps the mosque itself represents Süleyman; and the corner pillars on his establishment stand for the Grand Vezir as the chief Slave of the Gate, and the Grand Mufti as a sort of chief justice and Pope of the Ulema. Even in democracies and republics, men since Socrates have lived their lives half-free, half-enslaved, or died. All these men were distorted by the weight of their power and their functions. Paranoia, to use a word, appears to be the crippling malady of all enclosures and establishments. Sinan, a Slave of the Gate, in his architecture and his engineering, was a sane man.

I walk out of the courtyard and around to the rear of the mosque. There a row of masonry buttresses, like Janissary slave-soldier-dervishes, put their shoulders to the kibla wall, and like abstract atlantes, put their backs into the work to uphold the Sultan's and the Prophet's House of God.

I pass them and walk to the edge of the walled enclosure on top of the massive foundations of the *sahn*. From there on sunny afternoons opens a wide view to the north and to the east across the Golden Horn, down to the high walls, the tree tops, and the domes and towers of the Sultan's palace on the First Hill, and across the Bosphorus to Asia. Below the mosque, on the slopes of the Third Hill the two remaining college courtyards and the lower school step down in terraces of cupolas and arcades.

How Sinan must have enjoyed himself as he worked out the placing of these buildings in the lie of the land. In these terraced courtyards, roses bloom and trees and vines grow in the gardens surrounding the centering wellheads. The sun makes a play of light and shadow in endless variations upon Sinan's themes.

I turn my back on the view to look up at the great mosque. Once again I marvel at the way the architect and engineer set the volumes and the voids, the horizontals and the verticals, the masses and the lines in tension, the one to define and distinguish the other. The buttressed walls rise in stages to the great masonry arch springing between the piers at the side. Sinan strongly emphasized the upper edge of this arch by means of serrated stepped horizontals and rising verticals. He put them there to contrast with the inner line of the arch, which is not round but slightly pointed where the two springing arcs join.

Above the arch the drum stands up like a crown. From it rises the pure bland shape of the dome, the lead sheathing ridged at the joins like the lines of latitude and longitude on a globe. On top like a pole stands the *alem,* the gilt-bronze finial of Islam. It must be taller than a man.

In architectonics, the dome can be perilously soft in bulk and in outline, and as the culmination of a building, dangerously heavy. For all the dome's structural dynamics of multiple vertical and lateral thrusts, its surface appears to be inert. Softly it rises, gently it falls. On the Süleymaniyé Sinan's dome is powerful.

He was a robust man of sixty-eight when he climbed up onto the dome to put the burnished finial in place. According to his legend, when he got down again, he said to the Sultan, "I have built thee, O Padishah, a mosque which will remain on the face of the earth till the day of judgment, and when Hallaj Mansur comes and rends Mount Demavend from its foundations, he will play tennis with it and the dome of this mosque! "

Mount Demavend, 18,600 feet in altitude, is a Persian mountain famous for its beauty. Hallaj Mansur, alive, was a mystic and a martyr, but apparently he is a sportive and a joyous saint. Perhaps Süleyman and Sinan will join him in that game of tennis at the harrowing of Hell.

Their mosque has the Renaissance quality of vitality. This is a building built in classic Ottoman Islamic sobriety and discipline. As a whole greater than the sum total of its parts, the urban complex of the Süleymaniyé, in the disposition of its components and in their proportions, has, it may be, equals in other lands. If so they are rivals – in the ruins of Greece and Rome and Egypt; at Angkor Vat; in the Gothic and the Renaissance cities; in the Moghuls' India; in the Age of Reason and in Versailles.

The Süleymaniyé gives shape to the Ottoman Golden Age, within the triangular space of the walled city on seven hills, Istanbul above the Golden Horn, the Bosphorus, and the Sea of Marmara, and the lands beyond. And this mosque, according to its builder, the Royal Chief Architect Sinan, was the work of a journeyman, the Sultan's slave.

In 1548 Sinan built new apartments for Haseki Hürrem in the New Palace, after a fire had broken out in her rooms in the Old Palace which gutted the imperial harem. Perhaps she set it alight herself. She persuaded her husband to let Sinan build new quarters for her in the inner courtyard of the *Saray* (the Topkapi Palace Museum), – and so she gave the world the new meaning of the Turkish word for "lockup," spelled by the Venetian bailiff *seraglio*. Before the fire, women had been excluded from the man's world of the Sultan's administrative offices and residence. In the courtyard inside the Gate of Felicity there was little room for the new harem, and her new apartments were not spacious. But Hürrem, a practical woman and a realist, was content. She had got what she wanted, a place at the heart of power. In this position the army of celibate slave soldiers, the power arm of the eighty thousand Slaves of the Gate, feared and distrusted Hürrem even more. They called her a witch. She was a small woman, fifty years old in 1550. The folds of loosened skin above her eyelids may have reduced the size of her eyes, but they were still clear sapphire blue. Her fair skin, it may have been, in the humid climate of the First Hill on the hook of land above the Marmara, the Bosphorus, and the Golden Horn was still smooth. Oriental ladies have understood makeup for twenty centuries. The Byzantine empresses and the Ottoman imperial ladies may or may not have wrinkled, but they kept their concentrated power as women over the years. They took to intrigue like ducks to water. The Bosphorus is the passage of migratory birds from Russia to Africa and back again. The birds of Turkey are plentiful and beautiful; so are the women. Intrigue thrives in the air enclosed within the walled city.

After the demotion of Prince Mustafa and then the natural death of Hürrem's firstborn son, Prince Mehmet, the Sultan put their next son, Prince Selim, in the Shehzadé's place. Selim resembled his mother in the flesh. He was fair of skin with light blue eyes, less sapphire, more aquamarine. They saw as clearly as his mother's; but for all his coloring, which was hers, his red-gold beard as bright as her hair had been at his age, Hürrem saw that he lacked her character. She did not like him. She backed her next son, Prince

Bayazid, very much a man at the age of twenty-five. He had her temper and her temperament, although otherwise he took after his father and the Sons of Osman. He was tall, broad, and lean; he carried himself well. But in regard to Selim, Süleyman was permissive. Who knows a father's reasoning on the score of his son's worth?

It is true that later, when it was too late, in the winter of 1561-62, the father wrote the son, in Manisa, then the only one of the brothers left alive, exhorting him to change his ways, to abstain from Cyprian wine, and at least to be more serious in observing the precepts of the Koran. Selim the Prince Imperial, having read the letter from the Sultan, lost his temper and took it out on the imperial messenger. He had the young man, a graduate page of the palace school, one of the rising Slaves of the Gate, degraded, stripped of office, and whipped.

Süleyman then ordered Selim to appear before him in an audience at court, to kiss the hand. Selim arrived in Istanbul with his boon companion in wine, a freeborn Ottoman Turk named Murad and addressed as Chelebi. Süleyman had the "Gentleman" handed over to the mutes with their bowstrings. He ordered two of his Chief White Eunuchs, gatekeepers of the Slaves of the Gate, to see to it that Selim Sultan watched his boon companion, his surrogate, put to death in punishment for the Shehzadé's sins, which are in Islam also crimes. He then separated Prince Murad, the firstborn son and heir of Selim and Haseki Nûrûbanû, the future Validé Sultan, from the noxious influences of his father's debauched and drunken court in Manisa. The boy was sixteen – he went off to govern a minor province on his own; Selim was a man of thirty-eight. He swallowed his fury and went on drinking.

Busbecq, the Austrian ambassador, describes Selim as lazy and calls him a sluggard. The people called him a drunkard and a sot. The courtiers called him Selim the Fair. The Janissaries called him the Stalled Ox. They called his younger brother Bayazid the Student Prince. But they had no fault to find with Süleyman, their Padishah, other than his age and his infirmity. He had done his best to educate his sons, and had encouraged the endowment of colleges and universities for the education of the worthy young men of his realm.

When the Grand Vezir Rüstem Pasha was at the height of his power in 1550, Sinan built for him a *medresé*, a college for scholarship students in sacred jurisprudence, in Istanbul. Sometime later, at Edirné, Sinan built a caravansary for him. Both buildings demonstrate Sinan's inventive genius and his ability to use his imagination freely within the prescribed limits.

The site of the *medresé*, a jagged irregular plot on the side of the First Hill above the Golden Horn, was clearly unsuitable for a house or for business premises. The Grand Vezir therefore surrendered it to God and Islamic youth.

It had something like sixteen uneven sides and acute and obtuse angles pitched on a steep descent and fronting on a twisted lane ill-paved with cobblestones.

Having surveyed it and plotted it, Sinan took up his pair of compasses. Where he put down the fixed leg there is now the wellhead of a cistern in the center of a level, open courtyard. It is octagonal, each of its eight equal sides arcaded. Behind the rows of pillars and cupolas, he built cells, most irregular in plan, most ingeniously disposed, and all of them convenient to live in. One or two kite-shaped rooms in sharp corners are kitchens or larders, properly covered with cupolas. Other oddly shaped chambers are water closets, store-rooms, the refectory, and a bathhouse. The outer walls are pentagonal.

Sinan placed the large *dershané,* which is to say, lecture hall, class room, and at night study hall, on the downhill northeast side. Opening from the covered arcade, the square and domical building juts out behind into the steep garden inside the irregular outer walls of the college. The professor in residence, a tutor, a don, had his apartments next to the lecture hall.

Each cell has its own hooded fireplace, its niches for lamps, and built-in shelves for papers and manuscript books. Today (in other restored *medresés*) the rooms are furnished with three double-decked bunks roughly put together of deal, a softwood table or two, a rush-bottomed chair or two. In Sinan's spacious days, one or two, or at most three, students shared each cell, with ample elbow room and plenty of fresh air to breathe under the serene dome set on pendentives in each corner – a well-lighted space. Rüstem Pasha's *medresé,* long a municipal warehouse, has just been beautifully restored for the use of university students; they live in history made visible. One is aware of Sinan's unfailing sense of proportion, and – call it the dimension of delight (elsewhere in other circumstances called the shock of recognition), as the eye follows his good-humored solution to the problems given him to work out. Sinan enjoyed himself. He took pleasure from his profession as architect and engineer. He gave – it is a kind of signature – each of his buildings his integrity and authority.

Sinan landscaped the octagonal courtyard. Today cypresses, walnuts, a terebinth, some plums and peaches grow around the octagonal wellhead. Old grapevines make screens and arbors for the arcades. Old rosebushes still bloom. Before the restoration was complete, white and the common pink valerian grew up and bloomed, rooted in the crumbling mortar where the lead-sheathed domes join the masonry arches and spandrels.

The second building, Rüstem Pasha's caravansary at Edirné, is two great courtyards built of brick. Again the skinflint Grand Vezir gave Sinan a most irregular but valuable property, a long, thin piece west of the Old Mosque. Sinan made the building self-supporting by putting a row of vaulted shops along the ground floor of the long and bent façade. The portal near the northwest end, handsome in proportions, topped by a swirled and fluted dome, opens upon the first great courtyard. The lesser, to the southwest, was the stableyard for the camels, the donkeys, and the horses, with quarters on the upper level for the cameleers and hostlers. (Now I expect it will be a garage, for the building is being restored for the Club Méditerranée.)

An earthquake has brought down a portion of the higher arcade of this courtyard (in process of repair in 1965). The destruction allowed me to find out something of Sinan's methods of construction. For instance, here I saw the need for the iron tiebars that span the arches, how they worked, and how Sinan's blacksmiths forged them.

At first the tiebeams of carved wood in Haghia Sophia and the wrought iron tiebars of the classic Ottoman buildings bothered me. It seemed to me that they stressed the essential fault in all such arcaded and domical constructions. In my ignorance and innocence, I arrogantly dismissed these rows of arches upheld by colonnades, and the domes, semidomes, pendentives, squinches, and conchs, each one spanned at the springing line by a beam or a bar, as being structurally unsound. Therefore I concluded that Byzantine and Ottoman architecture was unworthy of comparison with the Greek and the Roman orders, and not as "good" as Gothic. I left out the Renaissance, and called the Baroque decadent. Now I do not see the tiebars unless I look for them, and then I like what I see.

Something, after all, in Byzantine and in Ottoman architecture does not "occur in nature," as the foolish old criterion for architectural worth has it. The Byzantines were the first to spring arches in a row from the capitals of colonnades, the pillars almost always monoliths. Before then, the Greeks had set heavy blocks of horizontal single stones upon their Doric, Ionic, or Corinthian orders, the columns usually fluted and almost always rising in a piling up of tapered drums. Sheer weight, inert mass, acting within the law of gravity, held their matchless temples upright. The Romans, better engineers, used solid masonry arches to build their aqueducts that stride across their classic landscapes. Even the gods and goddesses of Mount Olympus and the Pantheon were earthbound.

From the Orient came the mystery religions, the barrel and the cradle vaults, the squinches and the pendentives, and the celestial dome. The tiebar, essential to such aspirations built into brick and stone, marks the difference between, as well as the union of, God and man (before he discovered reinforced concrete and the steel cage, neither of which occur in nature, either). I find it good to be reminded of human fallibility, another way of saying human continuity. A man is bound to fail, in space and time, to achieve any of his goals. The tiebar reminds us, or it reminds me, anyhow, that to reach the goal is beside the point.

On the upper level in the courtyard of the camels in Sinan's caravansary a cupola and two arches have fallen. A square column, built of cubes of limestone, still stands. At the top of it Sinan sprung three arches of brick and mortar (fallen). Two continued the row of the arcade; the third, at right angles, comes down to rest upon a corbel of stone built into the masonry wall (of the domical chamber behind the arcade). At the springing line, each arch is spanned by an iron tiebar. The ends of the three join on top of the square column.

Each bar is an exact length of squared wrought iron, bent in a right angle to make a short hook at either end. The three joined hooks fit into a trefoil of wrought iron set in masonry at the exact center of the pillar, and so on; the third tiebar fits into an iron socket cemented to the corbel in the wall. Similar tiebars span the various arches of the great and small mosques and their arcaded courtyards. Their function is two-fold: first, the tiebars hold the pillars upright and the arches in the true while the mortar of their construction dries and hardens, and in so doing they let the architect get on with the raising of the semidomes and the dome.

The second purpose of the tiebar is to counteract the shock of earthquakes, and of high explosives, both of which occur in nature: to withstand, it may be, the wrath of God aimed against the arcades of the caravansaries and colleges and the celestial domes of the Places of Prostration. It seems to me, then, that the tiebar does no more than organize man's faith in God.

The greater courtyard of Rüstem Pasha's caravansary has the quiet serenity of orderly process achieved within the given facts, which are, in this irregular piece of property, chaotic. It is a human place centered upon a fountain. The overflow waters the roots of plane trees, one of them big enough to have been planted by Sinan. Two stone staircases under the arcades on either long side of the rectangle are works of what we choose to see as abstract sculpture.

On the upper level, the square pillars of the arcade, like the walls and the voussoirs of the arches, are built of alternating courses of limestone blocks and brick (thought better able to withstand earthquakes, to give but not to fissure – a Byzantine discovery). The arches at ground level are round; above, they are pointed. Between the pillars of the upper arcade, Sinan put a solid parapet of limestone, not a balustrade, which would have been finicking in the heavy brick and stone masonry, and not a decorative pierced and carved screen. Limestone is too soft for such fine work. Marble would have been unsuitable in these business premises – and anyhow Rüstem Pasha was a tightfisted man. Sinan carved a shallow disc in the center of each parapet between the paired columns. Each is a large mandala, no two are identical: eight-pointed stars, wheels, six-pointed stars, interacting lines cut in geometrical patterns, clear and precise – witty comments on businesslike transactions. The plumbing of the water closets, each in its own booth in a row, was as good as our American equivalents today. But the motel will be equipped with bathrooms of the modern European kind. The plumbers will have to use pneumatic drills to get holes through Sinan's cement floors, harder now than stone.

He encouraged the masons to enjoy themselves. In the demilunes above the windows opening out of the rooms under the arcades of the courtyard, the men laid their thin bricks upended and slanting to make patterns like cypress trees. Apparently a handsome tree, now gone, was growing beside the road on the edge of Rüstem Pasha's precisely surveyed, irregular parcel of commercial real estate. Sinan did not cut it down. He angled the long façade around it, so to vary the monotony of round vaulted shop fronts. They brought in high rentals; Edirné was a rich city. To do him justice, Rüstem Pasha did not pocket the cash. He used the income to maintain the caravansary.

According to the Austrian Ambassador Ogier Ghiselin de Busbecq, who stopped off in this caravansary on his journey to the Sublime Porte in 1555:

"These hostels are fine convenient buildings with separate bedrooms, and no one is refused admittance, whether he be Christian or Jew, whether he be rich or a beggar. The doors are open to all alike. They are made use of by the pashas and the sanjakbeys when they travel. The hospitality which I met with in these places appeared to me worthy of a royal palace. It is the custom to furnish food to each individual who lodges there, and so, when supper time came, an attendant made his appearance with a huge wooden platter as big as a table, in the middle of which was a dish of barley porridge and a bit of meat. Around the dish were loaves, and sometimes a little honey in the comb.

"At first I had some delicacy in accepting it. . . . The attendant, however, would take no denial. [He] told me that even pashas received their dole, it was the custom of the place. . . . It was not at all bad. I can assure you that barley porridge is a very palatable food. . . . [Probably it was *bulgur pilaf,* which is cracked wheat and very good indeed.]

"Travelers are allowed to enjoy this hospitality for three full days; when they have expired, they must change their hostel."

Busbecq did not like Rüstem Pasha, but the two men got along. The Grand Vezir intercepted Busbecq's diplomatic pouch with no attempt to conceal the fact. He read the ambassador's and the Holy Roman Emperor's privileged correspondence before he sent it on. Openly he tried to bribe the Flemish gentleman with the promise of favorable diplomatic treaties if he would abandon Roman Catholicism and convert himself to Islam. But the unsuccessful conversation ended with Rüstem Pasha's remark that all faiths were equally good roads to heaven or hell.

Busbecq lodged a complaint against the Janissaries' high-handed manhandling of one of his Christian Austrian servants on his way to or from market. The Grand Vezir then warned Busbecq ". . . to remove every cause of offense which might occasion a quarrel with these atrocious scoundrels. Was I not aware that it was wartime, when they were masters, so that not even Solyman himself had control over them, and was actually himself afraid of receiving violence at their hands? " As Busbecq realized, ". . . the soldiers have it in their power to depose their sovereign and place another on the throne."

In 1552 the former Shehzadé Prince Mustafa governed Amasya as Chelebi Sultan. That year, the Grand Vezir sent off a punitive expeditionary force to warn Shah Tahmasp of Persia not to cross the Ottoman borders. Rüstem Pasha gave the command to Shemsi Ahmet Pasha, a sophisticated, witty, and joyously immoral man. He passed through Amasya and stayed to visit the princely court of the Sultan's oldest son, now aged thirty-seven.

Shemsi Pasha, who was privately working to overthrow the House of Osman, brought back to Rüstem Pasha on his return a piece of intelligence clearly designed to reach the ears of Haseki Hürrem, but phrased for Süleyman's attention. According to him the Janissaries of his own command, as well as those attached to Prince Mustafa's court, were showing dangerous enthusiasm for the young prince. Shemsi Pasha, no great soldier, reported the Janissary complaint that their Padishah had grown too old to lead the march in person against the Persian enemy; that there was only the Grand Vezir to oppose their elevation of Prince Mustafa to the throne; and that it would be an easy matter to cut off Rüstem Pasha's head and then to send the old Sultan into retirement on the country estate of Demotika.

When the Grand Vezir reported Shemsi Ahmet Pasha's intelligence to Süleyman, he added what seems to have been not a comment of his own but one of Haseki Hürrem's interpolations, to the effect that Prince Mustafa lent an ear to these words of sedition. To cover himself, Rüstem Pasha then begged his father-in-law the Sultan henceforth to take over the active command of the Ottoman forces.

"God forbid! " cried Süleyman, "that Mustafa show such impudence while I still live. If so, I shall indeed find the right punishment for him."

The Sultan took over the command of the combined armies. On August 28, 1553, he set off on one more campaign against the Persian shah. He left Selim the Sot as the Shehzadé in Manisa but sent his next younger son, Prince Bayazid, to Edirné, not to act as regent but to govern the Domain of War and to guard the European approaches to Istanbul. As usual, the Grand Vezir and the Divan accompanied the Sultan. Hürrem and Mihrimah Sultan remained in the imperial city guarded by the Janissary cadets. Sinan supplied the engineers with an architect and a team of skilled workmen, but he himself stayed in Istanbul to get on with the building of the Süleymaniyé. The army marched along the southern route across Anatolia. Prince Selim left Manisa to kiss his father's hand and beg permission to join the campaign. The show of military ardor, not in character, pleased the Sultan, who granted his son's request.

The army passed through Konya and pitched camp on the road to Ereghli, one of the several Hellenistic Greek Heraclions in Asia Minor. There, from Amasya to the north, Prince Mustafa appeared, unsummoned, likewise to kiss the hand of the Padishah and to ask his father's permission to join the Persian campaign. He arrived in the evening of October 5; he pitched his tents next to the Sultan's imperial pavilions. At daybreak of October 6, 1553, the lesser vezirs of the Divan went to kiss the hand of the Imperial Prince; Mustafa distributed magnificent robes of honor among them. He then mounted his richly caparisoned Cappadocian war-horse to ride in proper ceremonial approach to the Sultan his father's vast silken tent, a place of many compartments. The vezirs and the Janissaries cheered at the sight of the admirable young man, twelve years older than Süleyman had been when called to the throne.

Inside the tent, in the imperial pavilion of audience, otherwise deserted, seven mutes awaited Prince Mustafa. He threw them off to cry out to his father to come to his assistance. Süleyman, out of his son's sight behind a silken curtain, watched from an antechamber, and sent in Zal Mahmut Pasha, a young champion wrestler, a recent graduate of the palace school for pages, a gentleman-in-waiting, the *Silâhtar,* the Sword-Bearer of the Sultan. The champion Zal Mahmut took Prince Mustafa in a wrestler's hold, threw him, and strangled him with his bare hands. He later married Shah Sultan, a daughter of Sultan Selim the Sot. She was nine years old in 1553. He had to wait until 1577 for his reward. Sinan built Zal Mahmut Pasha a mosque in Eyüp. It is a simple, muscular prayer hall, clear in light, uncomplicated in space, housed in a hulking body.

After the failure of the seven mutes and immediately after the success of the wrestling champion Zal Mahmut Pasha, the Sultan and the Grand Vezir had the dead Prince Mustafa's chief equerry beheaded outside the tent, and had a mourning *agha* of the Janissaries decapitated in front of his army of slave-soldier-dervishes. The men then overturned their bronze soup cauldrons and beat upon them with their spoons and their fists. They howled. They shouted menaces. They demanded that the Grand Vezir Rüstem Pasha be stripped and whipped.

Süleyman refused to do so; but then, following Rüstem Pasha's own advice, he deposed his son-in-law and named the second vezir, Kara Ahmet Pasha, to the grand vezirate. The dark and powerfully handsome man was an Albanian, a cousin of the former Christian ducal family, the renegade Duka-ginzadés, many times intermarried with the Daughters and the Sons of Osman. As a freeborn Ottoman youth, Kara Ahmet had volunteered to join the Sultan's Slave Household. Judged on his individual merits, he was selected as a page and educated in the palace school. As a young Janissary officer, better known for his valor than his judgment, the high-spirited and handsome man had caught the eye of Selim the Grim's eldest daughter, Fatma Sultan. Süleyman had known his *Damat* brother-in-law all his life.

Kara Ahmet Pasha, the second vezir of the Divan, thought he knew the Sultan well enough to talk with him as man to man. In so doing, he may have shown poor judgment but he made good sense. He knew that his cousin, another Ahmet Dukaginzadé, likewise a *damat* married to the Sultan's daughter, the Imperial Princess Hafisa, had served Selim the Grim as Grand Vezir on the Persian Campaign of 1514, and had been arbitrarily and summarily demoted and executed by his father-in-law for one of the Janissary trooper's crimes, a mere detail – the slave soldier had liberated, as we say, a sheep from a Turkish peasant. Kara Ahmet Pasha asked his brother-in-law Sultan Süleyman for a guarantee of tenure before he accepted the office of Grand Vezir.

He was popular with the Janissaries. But there in Ereghli while the mourning Janissaries shouted out in grief for their strangled Prince Mustafa, and sullenly murmured together of mutiny against the focus of their hatred, the Grand Vezir Rüstem Pasha, the Second Vezir Kara Ahmet Pasha felt strong enough to make demands. He would accept the highest office in the empire on condition that the Padishah, his wife's brother, agreed not to deprive him of the seal of office so long as he lived. Süleyman, in no mood for, and in no position for bargaining, curtly agreed. Like Ibrahim the favorite, the new *Damat* Grand Vezir Kara Ahmet Pasha was thereby appointed to office for life.

Two years later, in Istanbul, on the early morning of September 28, 1555 (a Thursday), the Grand Vezir Kara Ahmet Pasha was presiding at an ordinary meeting of the Divan. Into the domical open chamber of the Council of State in the middle courtyard of the Sultan's Palace came, unannounced, one of Süleyman's ushers, a recent graduate of the school of pages, accompanied by the senior mute. He brought the Grand Vezir his own death warrant, signed and sealed by Sultan Süleyman Khan, son of Sultan Selim Khan.

"Ahmet, being a man of marvellous courage," wrote Busbecq from hearsay, at best reported to the ambassador by an eyewitness, "received the announcement with almost as much composure as if it were no concern of his. All he did was to repulse the hangman, who was preparing to perform his office, deeming it unfitting that one who had but lately held so exalted a position should be touched by his polluted hands. Glancing round on the bystanders, he begged as a favor of a gentlemen, with whom he was on friendly terms, to act as his executioner, telling him that it was a kindness he should greatly value, and the last he would ever be able to do him; after many entreaties, his friend accorded to his request. When this was settled, Ahmet enjoined him, after putting the bowstring round his neck, not to strangle him at the first pull, but to slacken it and allow him to draw one breath, after which he was to tighten the string until he was dead; this fantasy of his was duly complied with. A strange wish, methinks, to pry at such a time into the mystery of death, and pay one visit to the threshold of the king of terror before passing his portals forever! "

Such was the Grand Vezir Kara Ahmet Pasha's cadenza upon the Ottoman themes. He was deprived not of his office but of his life. Süleyman did no more than issue his imperial edict. Complete in itself, it was an act of sovereign law.

Busbecq, at a loss, wrote down the bewildered gossipers' speculations; none suffices. One is that Kara Ahmet Pasha was a secret supporter of Prince Mustafa, whose death is explicable. Rightly, even though innocent, Prince Mustafa had had to be removed. In truth, his perfect qualities as a potential ruler of the Ottoman Empire, recognized and immoderately proclaimed by the Janissaries, had thrown up a mirage that threatened not only the life of his father, the aging Sultan, but also the inherited system of the Sons of Osman.

Hürrem (not Süleyman) got the blame for the deaths of both good men. Her son-in-law, quiet in the interim, could now be brought back into power. Rüstem Pasha was restored as Grand Vezir.

The defects of the virtues of the handsome and virile man, Kara Ahmet Pasha, brought about his death. A man of action, upright and blunt of military reasoning, he was inflexible and he was right. Just, direct, outspoken, wholly masculine, he was proud of his integrity, and he was hard to deal with. He lacked give and take in discussions of right and wrong. Any other man's ideal father, brother, son, and friend, he was an excellent Ottoman gentleman but a poor Slave of the Gate. He met defeat with perfect courage. He chose a death for himself as becoming to the handsome man as the Grand Vezir's own robe of honor. Such men as Kara Ahmet Pasha deserve monuments; but few memorials can equal the mosque that Sinan built for the executed Grand Vezir.

For Kara Ahmet Pasha, a stalwart man whose masculine inflexibility destroyed him, Sinan designed a mosque on the hexagonal floor plan. He began with the prescribed unit of the circle in the square. Next, instead of erecting four piers at the corners, he put six columns on the circle. He then extended the square on either side to enclose the prayer hall in rectangular walls. Six small pendentives rise above the columns to carry the dome. Twinned semidomes roof the spaces of the lateral extensions.

Perhaps the six matched pillars, smooth monoliths of gray granite salvaged from a Byzantine ruin, suggested the hexagonal plan to Sinan. Kara

12. The facade and main entrance of the caravansary of Rüstem Pasha in Edirné, built in the decade of 1550-1560.

13. The main courtyard of Rüstem Pasha's caravansary at Edirné (in process of restoration for the Club Mediterranée in 1965).

14. The staircase, like sculpture, of the caravansary of Rüstem Pasha, Edirné.

15. The east corner of the medresé and courtyard of the Mosque of Mihrimah Sultan, Istanbul.

16. The Mosque of the Imperial Princess Mihrimah, the perhaps merry widow of "the lousy Ikbal," the Grand Vezir Rüstem Pasha, who left her the richest woman in history. Built between 1562 and 1565, it is Sinan's most architectonic mosque, and, I think, clearly erotic.

17. Interior of the Mosque of Mihrimah from southwest to northwest.

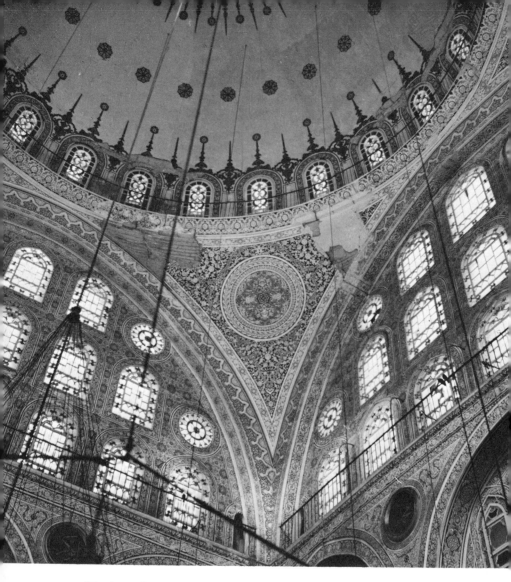

18. A pendentive of the Mosque of Mihrimah fissured in the earthquake of 1894 under the heavy weight of deep wet snow.

19. The Mosque of the strangled
Grand Vezir Kara Ahmet Pasha,
1555.

20. Interior of Kara Ahmet Pasha Jami.

21. Courtyard of the Mosque of Zal Mahmut Pasha on the hillside at Eyüp (undated, but built in Sinan's experimental period, probably between 1560 and 1566).

22. A pendentive and part of the dome in the muscular champion wrestler
Zal Mahmut Pasha's mosque.

23. LEFT: The *minber* or pulpit of Zal Mahmut Pasha's mosque.

24. The restored minaret of the oratory in Sinan's own modest pious foundation, built *circa* 1563, totally destroyed in the fire of 1917 – and photographed on a gray day in 1965.

25. Sinan's bridge at Büyükchekmejé, finished in 1567, signed "Joseph Abdullah."

26. PRECEDING PAGE: The Imperial Friday Mosque and memorial of Sultan Selim II, "The Sot," at Edirné. Built between 1566 and 1574, Sinan finished it when he was eighty-five years old. He was pleased to call it the work of a master builder — the third of the "cathedrals" that he saw completed in his lifetime.

27. LEFT: The overburdened pillar at the corner of the
porch and the arcade of the courtyard of the Selimiyé,
Edirné.

28. ABOVE: The courtyard of the Selimiyé, Edirné.

29. The interior of the Selimiyé, at Edirné, with the centering loge for the *muezzin* to chant the verses of the Koran.

30. One of the eight pillars upholding the dome of the Selimiyé, Edirné.

31. NEXT PAGE, TOP: The crystalline stalactites in the peak of the prayer niche of the Selimiyé, Edirné.

32. NEXT PAGE, BOTTOM: The *minber* of the Selimiyé, Edirné. In the Prophet's lifetime, he climbed to sit under the canopy of such a pulpit not only to preach but also to dispense justice.

Ahmet may have prized them as his share of the booty in some victory. Sinan found that the hexagonal plan suited his own ideas. In nature, snowflakes, infinite in variety, always are hexagonal in pattern. The crystal takes the shape of six isosceles triangles joined at the apices, in the molecular system of frozen water, H_2O, and in the proportions of the golden section. The human body is largely composed of water. It has been suggested that because the mind perceives the shapes and the meanings of things through the vitreous humor of the eyeball, these triangles in the hexagon appeal to mankind as beautiful and meaningful. Certainly the snowflake is a basic pattern; it is to be called pure and clear. And like each man, each snowflake is unique.

Kara Ahmet Pasha was a handsome man. In the Orient, the male is prized in principle, and in fact, as such. Valued in his masculinity, he adorns himself. The mosque of Kara Ahmet Pasha is Sinan's most gorgeous Ottoman mosque. The six monoliths of smooth granite stand up in virile strength and beauty. But they are not tall enough. In diameter, the dome measures 13.5 meters (44.5 feet) – as usual, these figures are but approximate – and in height 20 meters (66 feet) from floor to crown. Thus Sinan built the mosque in the proportions of 1:1.5, a regular mathematical figure, against the golden section's 1:1.6+. Each granite monolith is but (about) a third as tall as the dome is high, and (again about) half the length of the side of the square (say), twenty-two feet in height.

With great ingenuity and invention, Sinan put a carved impost block and then a massive capital of white marble, carved in crystalline patterns of geometrical stalactites, on top of each pillar. Perfectly functional, no two of the capitals are exactly alike, but roughly they are paired. Because their individual function is to receive the varying thrusts from above, from behind, and from either side, they are most irregular in shape. On the capitals, Sinan built up piers, irregularly polygonal in section, to carry the ring of six joined pendentives which support the dome.

Thus Sinan demonstrates that in his architecture and engineering, he knew how to adapt his given conditons to the over-all purpose. In this mosque, the six handsome, valuable, but structurally inadquate monoliths emphasize Sinan's design, which – because of these same pillars – took the most natural form of the water crystal. Sinan (I say) thus saw the shape of the ideal not only in the Sultan's Household of Slaves of the Gate, despite the imperfections, but also in the increasingly inadequate but frozen Sacred Law of orthodox Islam – as the Grand Vezir Kara Ahmet Pasha did not. These monoliths of granite, then, stand up for the handsome man, who was inadequate, and yet, in his crystalline male human nature, who was valuable.

Four of these pillars stand backed against the walls in which, above them, their extending piers are engaged, two on either side of the prayer niche in the kibla wall, the two opposite joined to the buttresses that flank the portal in the façade. The two freestanding pillars, one on either side, carry the twinned semidomes that spring from them to roof the lateral extensions.

Sinan supported these fluted and ridged semidomes against the walls on cornices and corbels of carved stalactites. The freestanding pillars, their impost blocks and capitals, and their springing semidomes, stand like winged victories, abstract angels, their curving wings half unfurled, to carry the soaring dome, which is celestial. In the disc of the crown, Sinan had painted in the shape of a calligraphic wheel, one of the shortest and most powerful suras of the Koran, CXII. It is one of the earliest that God's messenger, the Angel Gabriel, revealed to the Prophet when he was a man alone by night in the desert hills surrounding Mecca.

Say: "He is God, One,
God, the Everlasting Refuge,
who has not begotten, and has not been begotten,
and equal to Him is not any one."

To bring a maximum of light into this interior, as splendid as the Grand Vezir dressed in his robe of honor to preside in the Divan and (to me) as moving as his victory in death, Sinan opened many windows in all the walls. The two that flank the portal in the façade are unusually high and wide. Rectangular, topped by low round arches, they rise from floor level to the roof of the arcaded porch. Sinan filled these huge windows with clear glass in many lights, and, outside, in the deep embrasures, he set iron grilles.

These grids of wrought iron bars are as absolute as the intersecting lines of graph paper. They seem to me to illustrate the conditions of slavery imposed upon even the exalted and admirable Slaves of the Gate in the aristocracy of merit of the Sultan's Household of Slaves. Each vertical and each horizontal bar, round, perhaps an inch, or less, in diameter, is set at either end into its own sockets cut to fit in the stonemasonry of the window frame. Sinan's blacksmiths, who were Janissary cadets, made the grilles to fit the window before the mason had begun to raise the walls to the height of the window sill. The masons, likewise Janissary cadets chosen by Sinan and trained as apprentice engineers, had to slide each socketed stone, carved in the particular shape of the molding of the frame, into its prescribed place to receive the ends of the existing iron bars. Here everything had to be known, understood, calculated, and made to fit the requirements before construction could begin.

The round bars meet at right angles in the grilles to form precise, hard-edged, and outlined squares of space. At their point of intersection, the vertical and horizontal bars lock together in another socket, this one of iron. It takes the shape of a cube with all its corners cut and smoothed away to make a polyhedron of fourteen planes, six squares, and eight equilateral triangles. Into an exact hole drilled at the center of each square, one to a side, north, east, south, west, of this hard and solid shape, which is no more unnaturally regimented than the man who made it, fits the end of the right bar in the right place.

This wrought iron grille is Ottoman in design; the Ottomans found it good for centuries. Sinan did not invent its pattern, nor did he modify it; he accepted it. The effect is strong, it is handsome, it is reliable, it is masculine, it serves; and it is almost intolerably controlled, a tense, abstract, and arbitrary rectification, worked in the most concrete substance of iron, a pattern imposed upon space. The space thus ordered does not hold still. It flows through the squares defined by the iron bars and cornered by the socketed polyhedrons; it goes its own way, as does the soul. All this is most powerfully comforting. Such must be the nature of life lived within the Islamic law.

But the Grand Vezir Kara Ahmet Pasha, at the very end of his life, was presented with both cause and reason to examine the source of the Sacred Law of both God and of the Shadow of God on Earth. On the point of death, he had the curiosity and the courage to satisfy himself on the point of law. But with the slackening of the bowstring, breathless from his discovery, he found no need to speak out.

The mosque that Sinan built for him stands just inside the Cannon Gate in the land walls. Here, on Tuesday, May 29, 1453, the Janissaries led by Mehmet the Conqueror stormed the breach opened for them by the great bronze cannons. Sinan repaired and maintained the walls of the imperial city. Today the traffic bypasses the Cannon Gate and the man-sized mosque of Kara Ahmet to flow along an artery and out of the city through an unarched but neatly rectified opening cut across the ruinous *enceintes*, the cracked periboloi, the scarp, the waterless moat, the counter-scarp, and the green glacis. In its backwater out of the way in a remote quarter, the mosque lies under the Sixth Hill. The story goes that Rüstem Pasha, the skinflint, back in office as Grand Vezir, gave Sinan a great amount of money to finish the building, incomplete at the time of Kara Ahmet's death on the morning of September 28, 1555. His mausoleum now serves a neighboring householder on the edge of town to store his mattock, his spade, and his hoe. Perhaps he cultivates a kitchen garden in the enriched earth on the floor of the dry moat outside the land walls. In the late summer, the melons brought through the Cannon Gate in wagon loads and offered for sale piled up outside the mosque are very good to eat.

The Grand Vezir Kara Ahmet Pasha, having served his purpose for the time it took the mutinous Janissaries to cool down, went to his death according to his destiny, which suited Haseki Hürrem's plans. He came to power as a sop to the Janissaries, rebellious in the aftermath of Prince Mustafa's death. Whether or not this eldest of the Sultan's sons had planned sedition, his virtues as a Son of Osman in his prime of life had threatened to unseat the aging Süleyman the Magnificent from his throne. Had the Janissaries prevailed, the new Sultan Mustafa Khan, son of Sultan Süleyman Khan, sone of Selim the Grim, according to the dynastic law of fratricide laid down by Mehmet the Conqueror, would have had his hands tied. The empire, like a bride, could not be shared among his half brothers. Mustafa would have had to send his mutes to tighten the bowstrings around the necks of Hürrem's living sons: the Shehzadé Selim the Sot, the Student Prince Bayazid, and the hunchbacked and pigeon-breasted "Holder of the World," Jehangir Sultan, the youngest, a witty fellow of twenty-two, who loved his splendid half brother, who loved him.

According to this inexorable dynastic law, once the mutes and Zal Mahmut had put an end to Prince Mustafa's life, his father had to put an end to his strangled son's line. Prince Mustafa had but one son. In Ereghli, the Sultan called upon Hâdim Ibrahim Pasha, the chief White Eunuch, to do the work. He was a Circassian who had been born in the Caucasus and bred by his parents in the mountains to be sold to be not necessarily "clean cut," not necessarily before the onslaught of puberty; for such untimely castration would have upset the glandular balance requisite for normal masculine full growth. In 1553, he was as old as the century; as the Chief of the White Eunuchs, he was one of Süleyman's reliable Slaves of the Gate. Evliya Chelebi, the son of a Circassian slave mother, but not castrated, describes him as "a man of a brave and generous disposition."

In 1551, Sinan built Hâdim Ibrahim Pasha a mosque complex near the Silivri Gate within the land walls under the Seventh Hill. It is a simple and a straightforward mosque, a square chamber covered by a single dome upheld on squinch arches, their conchs fluted like scallop shells. The dome is about 10 meters (33.3 feet) in diameter. The aisles of the square extended to right and left are roofed, each in three sections, by cradle vaults. The cornices and the corbels of the squinches and their conchs are carved with geometrical stalactites. The mosque is unexceptional, excellent, just, and even elegant in its simplicity. The küllîvé was a modest foundation: courtyard, school, bath, and fountain, all of which have disappeared. Hâdim Ibrahim Pasha died in 1563. He is a contender, one of three, to be identified as "the late Ibrahim Pasha," described by Sinan in his charter of that year, 1563, as his "efendi" and "mu'tik" — "lord" and "patron." (I think not, but even so the eunuch may have been the man in question.)

After the strangulation of Prince Mustafa, Sultan Süleyman sent Hâdim Ibrahim Pasha back to Bursa on a secret mission. It would have been reasonable to account for his departure from Ereghli and the Persian campaign by putting him in charge of the cortege accompanying the embalmed body of the executed, but still imperial, Son of Osman for burial in the holy city of his ancestors. Having seen to the interment and arranged for the construction of the mausoleum in the garden of the mosque of his great-great-great-grandfather Murad the Mystic, the chief White Eunuch set about his other, necessarily covert business.

It may have been that the widow, an anonymous lady of the Chelebi Sultan's imperial harem, having been notified in Amasya, brought her adolescent only son, Prince Mehmet, a boy of thirteen or fourteen, the only grandson of Prince Mustafa's household, to Bursa for the burial. However it happened, she was living there in October of 1553 with her three children; her two daughters survived to be married at the proper age as imperial princesses, generously dowered. They lived in a modest wooden house in a walled garden, their handsome living rooms upstairs above the service and store rooms, the stables and the carriage house on the far side of the courtyard.

Hâdim Ibrahim Pasha had to separate the boy from his mother. As the Chief of the White Enunchs and the Sultan's messenger, properly he was able to enter an imperial harem to speak to Prince Mustafa's lady; but he could do her no violence to outrage the dignity of majesty and grief. He may have called upon her after dark to offer her condolence and to hold her attention while, downstairs and across the courtyard, his mechanics sawed in half the axletree of her screened and curtained vehicle. It was solidly built to withstand the rutted and potholed dirt roads of the countryside drenched in the autumn rains, a kind of elegantly covered wagon.

The next morning, the eunuch sent the lady a note. However it was worded, the message implied that an imperial personage, too august to be identified, had unexpectedly arrived. He or she awaited the bereft lady and her son in a country house outside Bursa. There was no time to lose. In historic fact, from the moment of Prince Mustafa's death, a legend grew up, the myth spread, that he had escaped the bowstrings of the seven mutes and also the muscular hands of the wrestler Zal Mahmut Pasha. A "false Mustafa" appeared to haunt Hürrem and Süleyman and their two surviving sons.

The lady had her coachman hitch the horses to her carriage. She put on her veils and got in; they set out. Her son rode his horse beside Hâdim Ibrahim Pasha, who, along with his guardsmen, had come mounted to escort the widow in her screened and curtained carriage. The axletree broke in half at the designated pothole. The eunuch cried out that they could not delay; he galloped ahead with Prince Mehmet; she was to follow as soon as the coachmen had patched up the axletree. She took one look at the damage, turned, and ran along the muddy road in the wet, green landscape under the snowcapped High Mountain, Bithynian Olympus. She reached the country house to find the body of her strangled son. He was buried beside his father. Perhaps the lady had the tomb adorned with its most beautiful panels of Iznik tiles enameled in patterns of red tulips and carnations and blue hyacinths among green leaves upon a snow-white background, and bordered with the ninety-nine beautiful names of God written in a band of calligraphic arabesques.

The Sultan's army, having reached Aleppo, went into winter quarters. There the Chelebi Sultan, Prince Jehangir, kissed his father's hand and listened to the story of how Prince Mustafa, greeted by the seven mutes, cried out to their father, who did not come forward from behind the silken curtains of the imperial pavilion, who said nothing, but who sent in the champion wrestler Zal Mahut. On November 27, 1553, Prince Jehangir, his father's favorite son, the baby who was close to the eldest brother, died of shock, of terror, and of grief. The father sent his hunchbacked and pigeon-breasted dead body, packed in snow and ice brought down from the peaks of the Taurus Mountains, back to Istanbul for burial in the *türbé* of his eldest full brother, the Shehzadé Mehmet.

After Hâdim Ibrahim Pasha had reported on the success of his secret mission, Sultan Süleyman promoted him, and in April of 1554 sent him back to Istanbul as *kaymakam*, which is to say, governor of the imperial city. There the Grand Vezir Kara Ahmet Pasha's widow, the Imperial Princess Fatma, chose to marry as her second husband Ibrahim Pasha, called Hâdim, Hadim, and Tavashi, the destroyed man, the eunuch. She called him *Ahret Arkadashi*, which usually is translated as her Adopted Friend. But although *arkadashi* translates as "friend" or "companion," *ahret* can also be translated as "the next world, the future life." Angels apparently always are male; see Milton's *Paradise Lost*. There must have been a beating of great wings, whatever their coupling. Fatma Sultan had a bellyfull of men: her father, Selim the Terrible, the Grim; her brother; her nephews and grandnephew (she seems to have had no sons); and her first husband Ahmet, the Grand Vezir called Kara because of his notably virile and dark handsomeness. No one knows when she died, but it was soon after her second marriage. Fatma Sultan was buried in a simple grave nearby the Mosque of Kara Ahmet Pasha. Perhaps Sinan cut her tombstone, a tablet of white marble carved with poetry and texts in beautiful writing set in a border of flowers and fruit. The graveyard has been obliterated, perhaps in the widening of a thoroughfare.

Through Ogier Ghiselin de Busbecq, the Ottoman Empire of Süleyman the Magnificent has given the Western World tulips from Anatolia, lilacs from Persia, and the oriental horsechestnut tree. The Austrian ambassador, a Flemish gentleman and a man of the High Renaissance, took back from his tour of duty at the Sublime Porte some bulbs, some rootstock and some cuttings, and a bag of buckeyes, along with several cartloads of Byzantine and Ottoman illuminated and illustrated manuscript books. He also wrote letters home in Latin.

He wrote, in the year 1557, in which Sinan completed the great Süley-maniyé, the finest urban complex in Europe as it still may be, that "the Sultan makes a practice of repairing to Adrianople at the beginning of winter, and of not returning to Constantinople till the frogs drive him away with their croaking." For Constantinople read Istanbul; for Adrianople, Edirné. In Thrace, in the near Domain of War, the old capital lies in a rolling green landscape, at the fork of the two rivers, Merich and Tunja. The palace, an enclosure of high walled courtyards and stone-built pavilions (a few ruins remain), covered a flat island among groves of trees on the edge of town. In what Busbecq called a bracing winter climate, Süleyman went hunting on horseback, hawking for wild duck, geese, herons, eagles, cranes, and buzzards in the marshes and the water meadows flooded by the rivers' overflowing in the winter rains.

Falconry is a central Asian sport. If the unhooded hawk, plummeting out of the low gray sky, did not in one fell swoop break the flying crane's wing, the crane pierced the falcon with its beak "like an arrow," Busbecq observed. Then the jessed hawk tumbled "lifeless to the ground."

When do frogs begin to croak in Edirné? Busbecq describes the Thracian fields of spring as fragrant with wild hyacinths and narcissus, and bright with anemones and tulips. I add the earlier snowflakes and cyclamen of February and March. Edirné is famous for its apples, both the red fruit of October and the pink blossom of April and May. If the frogs begin to croak no earlier than then, when the rolling green winter wheatfields are shaded with purple larkspur and the roadsides with bright blue borage, and the river banks are crimson with gold-filled wild peony cups, when the blue and chestnut rollers wheel and roll in the sunlit air, Hürrem the Joyous died alone in Istanbul, for she died on April 15, 1558. Only the dead bodies of the Sons of Osman were permitted posthumous journeys longer than the hours of the day of death to their graves.

She was about fifty-eight — old age even for a cherished imperial lady in those days. Süleyman buried her in the mausoleum that may have been ready, waiting for her in the garden behind the kibla wall of his own Imperial Friday Mosque, on the crest of the Third Hill above the Golden Horn. The East has no use for sentimentality, but a Westerner can say that Süleyman buried his heart in Hürrem's tomb.

For him Sinan had built an august mausoleum. It seems to me not to be one of his finest works. The tomb stands alone, properly oriented behind the prayer niche of the enormous memorial. Its magnificence is official. The classical octagonal and domical building, twice as tall as its cross section, and bigger than the ordinary, is worked inside and out majestically with all the Ottoman and Islamic signs and symbols. An arcaded porch, half as high as the walls, surrounds the mausoleum; it is unique. Süleyman approved Sinan's floor plan and elevation. If the Sultan did not, no man can mourn his death. The rich and sombre building was designed and built not to receive the dead body of a man, but to contain a living tradition, an idea, a principle, and an ideal. It smelled of history already while it stood empty from 1557 to 1566, and it still does. The dark blue-purple irises that bloom in May around the tomb cannot be said to make lament; they thrive in the well-drained limestone soil.

It is to be taken for granted that Sinan built Hürrem's tomb; but perhaps not until after she had died. It is not listed as one of his works. It stands apart from her husband's, but facing to the northwest, toward his.

In 1558, Sinan, twenty years a married man, the father of two sons and three daughters, clearly understood whatever love may mean. The Sultan and the architect designed and built Hürrem's last pavilion. It, too, is classic, octagonal, and domical, but plain on the exterior and simple in the interior. Inside it is a walled garden of blossoming fruit trees, with tulips and hyacinths, peonies and roses blooming in the panels of Iznik tiles. Their colors do not fade. Spring, then, was in full bloom on the day of her death? Hürrem's tomb is lyrical; Süleyman's is an epic monument. His mausoleum, ringed by its arcaded portico, is cut off from hers as by a wall of rigid Janissaries of the Honor Guard, of the Color Guard, of the Life Guard and the Sultan's Own Bodyguard. He was entombed in solitary majesty.

Two years before Hürrem died, she did her best to save the life of her favorite son, Bayazid, the younger of the two surviving imperial princes of their generation. There appears to be no such thing as an "unnatural mother." In 1556, Prince Bayazid was a tall young man of thirty-one with seven sons and four daughters. The system called upon each Sultan and every Imperial Prince to breed a reserve stock of potential heirs in case disaster struck the House of Osman. One hundred and fourteen years afterward, in *Bajazet,* a classic French tragedy acted out in Ottoman court dress, Racine called Hürrem Roxane, and (so it is written in *Le Petit Larousse*) made of her the *"type de femme passionñee et jalouse."* The French love and venerate their mothers more like the Oedipus of Sophocles and less like the Oedipus of Freud. In Busbecq's day, the French claimed Hürrem as one of them, a French girl stolen by corsairs and sold into slavery, so to make her way as the queen of the harem. It is an absurd but recurrent fantasy, peculiarly French. But Hürrem was a *femme magistrale,* a boss-woman. Having done her part to get rid of the favorite Ibrahim Pasha and the son of her rival the Lady Gülbahar and having gained control of the government through her son-in-law, the Grand Vezir Rüstem Pasha, she turned her attention to rearranging the order of the succession of the Sons of Osman. The Slaves of the Gate and the people of the imperial city feared and hated her.

After the strangulation of Prince Mustafa, as though by magic, popular opinion rose against her in the phenomenon of the "false Mustafa." This impostor, claiming to be the miraculously revived prince, was the image of popular discontent. In 1554, before Sultan Süleyman Khan had returned from the Persian campaign of that winter, the false Mustafa had raised a Danubian following of ten thousand countrymen in the Domain of War. He set himself up in a shadow sultanate. He named a poulterer Grand Vezir of the Divan, and a "burning" student (he was not burnt, but he was executed) as the Grand Mufti of the Ulema. At the head of his armies, the false Mustafa marched down through the Balkans to take the imperial city, and to break the spell of the enchantress Hürrem, a witch who, by means of charms and potions boiled down from the secretions of the hyena, was said to hold the aged Sultan in her thrall. Busbecq, who had tried to buy the hyena in the covered market reserved for Hürrem, sent off the secret intelligence to the Holy Roman Emperor in Vienna. Süleyman sent off his grandson-in-law at the head of a force of cavalrymen and Janissaries.

The Grand Vezir-poulterer sold out the false Mustafa and was rewarded with a country estate in the Balkans. Put to the torture, the man, who resembled the real Prince Mustafa only in the flesh, named his backers. Prince Bayazid headed the list. From his post as governor-viceroy in Edirné, he had financed the uprising. Back from Persia, Süleyman had all the others strangled, their bodies thrown quiety in the dead of night into the Sea of Marmara, "deeming it," as Busbecq reported, "inexpedient that any of these transactions be noised abroad." The Sultan did not want "his family misfortunes" to delight his neighbors, the Ottoman heretical and Christian enemies to the east and to the west.

"The Sultan," Busbecq continues, "who was grievously displeased with Bajazet for his audacious attempt, was debating in his mind how he should punish him; but his wife being a clever woman, his intentions were not long a secret to her." According to Busbecq, Hürrem waited a few days to allow her husband's imperious temper to cool. Then she staged her scene. She entreated, she cajoled, she wept. She called upon the aid of God the Merciful, the Compassionate. " 'It was only fair,' " said she, " 'to pardon a first fault.' " No young man wants to die. Think of your own father, Selim the Grim, who cleared the way to the throne for his own chosen son. Think of the most dread and most horrible law of fratricide. " 'Natural instinct teaches everyone to protect himself and his family. . . . Death is welcome to none.' "

She smiled through her tears, this aging woman, the backs of her narrow hands wrinkling and blotched, but her fingers gripped powerfully upon the heart strings. Cleopatra was redheaded, too. Perhaps Hürrem had her infinite variety. "She caressed the Sultan. . . ."

In the hunting palace at Edirné Prince Bayazid waited, trembling, for his father's mutes with their bowstrings to appear. "She begged for the life of the son she had borne and entreated him . . . to spare their common child. . . . She pledged her word, and undertook that he should henceforth be a good and dutiful son. . . ."

That accomplished, she wrote off secretly to Bayazid but in insufficient secrecy, to tell him not to be afraid to come when called for, but to come on bended knee to kiss his father's hand. He would be perfectly safe; she told him that "she had obtained his restoration to his father's favor." Busbecq appears to have taken Hürrem to have been one of those women who can, or who believe they can, wrap a man around her little finger. Rüstem Pasha advised her, through his wife Mihrimah Sultan, when Prince Bayazid, riding post haste from Edirné, was within a day's journey of the land walls of Istanbul.

Hürrem disguised herself. Few but the Sultan, her sons, the Black and the White Eunuchs, and her female domestic slaves had seen her face or her famous red hair, nor had they heard her voice. Sinan spoke to her when she came to visit his work in progress through the thinnest of veils, one such, it may have been, as those worn by the ladies of the last days of the empire, fine and colorless, wrapped to cover the hair and the face below the eyes. And over this, she wore a long and hooded cloak of silk dyed in the color of a flower blooming in the season, lilac, rose, forget-me-not, carnation, saffron, and the autumn leaves. But, for this trip, Hürrem put on a coarser veil and a dark brown or gray, probably a black covering cloak of heavier stuff. She took off the jeweled and embroidered velvet slippers and shod herself in serviceable and sensible grandmotherly shoes, probably borrowed from one of her old serving women.

She stole out of the harem, and out of the inner courtyard, but not through the Gate of Felicity. It would have served her purpose best to follow the almost obliterated path through the lower gardens, worn by the Greek favorite Ibrahim's feet at nightfall and at daybreak in and out of the palace, and so to have gone through the man-sized gate, the Needle's Eye, that Süleyman had had opened in the outer walls, onto the street. She traversed the city from the First to the Sixth Hills, the highest point in the land walls, and went out through the Edirné Gate. I wonder if, earlier, as the phrase goes, she had cased the joint, and had reserved the room near the front door, on the highway, of what Busbecq describes as a prosperous country inn; perhaps it was a stage for the post horses on the run into the Domain of War along the ancient Roman and Byzantine Via Egnatia. Busbecq makes it sound like a stage direction: the scene changed to the forecourt of a simple country inn in another part of the forest. If so, it was the Forest of Courage.

Prince Bayazid came riding by. He slowed down his horse to a walk; or perhaps he reined in, and sat his horse while a servant went in to fetch a cup of clear spring water — both the young man and the animal nervous, sweating. Through a small window, latticed, barred, canvas-curtained, he heard his mother's voice speak out: "*Corcoma, oghlan, corcoma!*" Busbecq's transliteration of the Osmanlija is still translatable. He rendered it, "Do not fear, my son, do not fear!" And he comments, "These words from his mother gave Bajazet no little comfort."

In the throne room of the palace, Süleyman was seated on the gold throne, jeweled and enameled, a kind of kidney-shaped bench railed part way round, upholstered with fat, hard, silken cushions, all under arching bars from which, overhead, hung down the emblem of sovereignty, an emerald as big as a man's fist. His unruly son kissed his hand. Then Süleyman "... had him take a seat by his side and proceeded to lecture him most seriously." They sat with their feet under them, or perhaps with one knee drawn up. There was room for both of them to sit facing one another. So, in miniatures, the later Sultans sat, plumed, bearded, a corslet of rows and rows of gross diamonds worn outside their sable-lined robes.

The prince had committed a most outrageous crime. First, he had tried to unseat his father. By so doing, he not only had attempted an unnatural act but also had proved himself to be unfilial, treacherous, and impious: "... an unpardonable offense, for which no possible punishment could ever atone." The younger man "... had done what he could toward destroying the very foundations of the Muslim faith, by bringing to the verge of ruin through family feuds that which was nowadays its only support — the imperial power of the house of Othman; this consideration alone ought to prevent a true believer from entertaining such a design." Busbecq continues, " 'On the wrong and insult to himself,' continued the Sultan, 'he would not dwell. . . .' "

So Süleyman went on reasoning as though pure reason could bridge the difference between a man of sixty and a man of thirty, father and son of their generations, the one thirty-four years in total power, the other wholly out of it. Henceforth, Sultan Süleyman Khan concluded, Prince Bayazid was to ". . .leave the care of the future in the hands of God; none of these matters depend on man's pleasure; it was by God's decree that kingdoms went and kingdoms come. . . . It was mere madness to toil and strive against His Will, and, as it were, to fight against God. . . . There should be no pardon for a second offense. . . . 'Go in peace.' " Prince Bayazid took the cup of sherbet offered him. It might have been one of those in the Treasury of the Topkapi Museum, hollowed out of single stone, a lump of turquoise, or of jade, or of rock crystal. It held a fruit juice iced with the snows brought down from Bithynian Olympus. His hand trembled, says Busbecq; he was afraid to drink until his father had taken a "draught from the same cup."

After Hürrem's death trouble began to flare up between the two Imperial Princes, Selim and Bayazid. There was no question in any man's mind, including their own, which was the better man, the fitter to survive to rule the empire. Outside the system, into which he was born and bred, neither man had any virtue – or, of course, defect – save in those of the animal kingdom. The Islamic standards and values were organized by God in his other kingdom for mankind; and the greatest of the Muslim sins is misbelief. Not even angels and saints appear to be able to rule themselves. Animals go on in the laws of the jungle or of the ocean or of the desert, environments inimical to *Homo sapiens*. Without God, even with the uprooted help of His two latest Hebrew prophets, Marx and Freud, mankind has not yet seen fit to survive in his own self-creations. One such was the Ottoman Empire. Another is the walled city of Byzantium-Constantinople-Istanbul. God must have many more than the ninety-nine beautiful names. Such must be a truth; it is a re-observable fact.

Mihrimah Sultan tried to take her mother's place in their other system. But born to the purple, the Imperial Princess lacked her Russian slave-girl mother's unscrupulous profundity. Her daughter, the Lady as Beautiful as the Face of the Full Moon, having lost her reflected light, waned when her mother died. In fact, it was thought, erroneously, that mother and daughter died in the same year. Mihrimah Sultan lived on until 1578.

The crescent of Islam shone bright in Süleyman's dark night. He put his faith in God. Selim the Sot chose wine. He was a generous patron of the arts, a man of excellent good taste, a connoisseur, a poet in a court of boon-companion poets. The liberal man was being manipulated, as the Grand Vezir, himself a crooked financier, well knew, by an unscrupulous Sephardic Jew. This man, Don Juan Miguez, had been a temporary convert to inquisitorial Christianity in Portugal. Conversion having failed at home, he left the realm of the Most Catholic King of Spain, Philip II, of the Armada. He broke his flight at the Italian court of the Duke of Ferrara. From there he wrote off and got permission from the Divan to settle in Istanbul. There he returned to his original religion in order to marry a wealthy Jewish heiress, one of Mihrimah Sultan's close friends; and he also took back his name and his nature as Joseph Nassy. After Selim the Sot's accession, Don Juan-Joseph got the monopoly in the wine trade and the title and estates of Duke of Naxos and the Cyclades. In anticipation of still greater things, he had had carved on the stone escutcheon above the portal to the court of honor of his great house in the imperial city, the fanciful armorial bearings of the King of Cyprus.

In 1559, Joseph Nassy spent the greater part of his time watching his investments in Selim the Sot's princely court of Manisa. He literally showered the rubicund plump man of thirty-five with Venetian ducats of fine gold and with fine pearls poured out of chalices of rock crystal over the red-golden-bearded heir apparent's head. The shallow sea-blue eyes were often red. The new favorite also lent the Prince Imperial a great deal of money at an excellent rate of interest calculated on Selim's survival to inherit the treasure of the empire. The more than two million ducats of his annual subsidy was not enough to pay for the diversions and distractions of the terrified prince.

To control all these excesses, Rüstem Pasha made bad miscalculations. He assigned Lala Mustafa Pasha to govern Prince Selim's household, first in Manisa and later in Konya. It was the sort of gambit to appeal to the Lousy Ikbal's intricate and tormented mind. The Grand Vezir figured that, economically, he had hit two birds with one stone. There are numerous portraits in miniature of Lala Mustafa Pasha. He appears in them as one of the handsomest men in history. His intrigues fomenting the fratricidal hatred between the Princes Selim the Sot and the desperate Bayazid show him to have been a most evil man.

According to Hammer-Purgstall, Lala Mustafa Pasha was the younger brother of the suicide Hüsrev Pasha, Sinan's patron for whom he built the earliest of his mosques in Aleppo and the tomb in the Chief Architect's Quarter of Istanbul. On their father's side, the brothers were descended from those blond and blue-eyed Slavs, the Bogomils, a puritanical sect, part Christian, part Manichaean, whose members chose as an heretical ethnic group to join Islam early in the fifteenth century. Thus they survived the murderous cruelty of both the popes of Rome and the caesaropapist Byzantine emperors of Constantinople. The Bogomils were powerful enough to obtain, perhaps as a condition to their voluntary submission to the Will of God, a special dispensation from the Sons of Osman. As freeborn Bosnian

Muslims, they were allowed the unique privilege of enrolling their otherwise acceptable sons as volunteers in the Janissary elite among the Slaves of the Gate. So they maintained a private identity in the empire and inside the Sultan's Slave Household.

Even more important, on the distaff side, Lala Mustafa Pasha was the son of Selchuk Sultan, a daughter of Sultan Bayazid the Pious; and thus he was a first cousin once removed of, and from, his charges, the Princes Selim and Bayazid. As their *lala* or "tutor," he governed their education when the boys left their mother Haseki Hürrem in the imperial harem of the Old Palace to enter the man's world of their father the Sultan in the New Palace. Lala Mustafa Pasha, himself, inherited, or cultivated, the imperious bad temper of the Sons of Osman and also a great deal of their ability.

After his term as *lala* to the Princes, he proved himself to have been a winning general officer, but a cruel autocrat. In and out of favor over the years, he had helplessly stood by, in 1540, to watch his elder brother Hüsrev Pasha go into a suicidal decline following their cousin the Sultan's dismissal of both brothers from the Divan. Lala Mustafa Pasha came back to power in 1553 as a member of the Grand Vezir Kara Ahmet Pasha's inner circle. In the power struggle following the abrupt execution of the Grand Vezir in office, he, having learned how to survive, came out near the top of the heap, ready to fight to win.

This arrogant and unscrupulous man disposed of immense private means, some of his wealth inherited from his mother, the Imperial Princess Selchuk Sultan, but more from his first wife. The Lady Kansu Gavri was the heiress of the next to the last Mameluke Sultan of Syria and Egypt. She must have died conveniently before he was given in marriage to Selim the Sot's grand-daughter the Imperial Princess Hüma after the death of her great-grandfather, Sultan Süleyman Khan; for otherwise, forced to set aside the Egyptian Imperial Princess in order to marry the Ottoman Imperial Princess, Lala Mustafa Pasha would have had to return her regal dowry.

Over the years, Sinan built for him a number of lordly pious foundations and public works, the most important near Damascus, another with a caravan-sary at Ilgin near Konya. When Lala Mustafa Pasha was governor of Erzerum, on his way to victory in the Caucasus in 1578, he ordered the Royal Chief Architect to provide his provincial capital with a suitable prayer hall. Recognizably built by local workmen and adapted to the conditions of the harsh climate, the mosque in Erzerum has proved powerful enough to withstand the earthquakes of that high eastern city on the plateau above the Anatolian rift. Sinan built the prayer hall without windows so as not to weaken the massive walls, and in eliminating light, he also protected it from the fierce winter cold and the scorching summer heat.

The most notable of the mosque's positive architectural features is a door opening into the rear of the prayer hall from a (now vanished) flight of outside steps at the eastern corner of the kibla wall. This private rear entrance in Lala Mustafa Pasha's day opened inward on to a tribune that, in the Imperial Friday Mosques, is called the *Hünkâr Mafhili,* the Sultan's loge. Lala Mustafa Pasha either had assumed the remote majesty of his imperial descent or had assumed the better part of brutal valor, which was not to turn his back on the common men in his command even to worship God in his own mosque at Erzerum.

In action he was courageous, but he feared and envied the total power in the hands of his imperial cousins in the male line. He despised the *damat* pig drover and Croatian slave, the Grand Vezir Rüstem Pasha. In 1529, Rüstem Pasha knew that Lala Mustafa Pasha strongly favored Prince Bayazid, the younger brother, to succeed his father Süleyman the Magnificent. Therefore, in a twist of double subtlety, the Grand Vezir assigned the former tutor to his other erstwhile pupil, Prince Selim the Sot. In Manisa as governor of the Shehzadé's miniature court, Lala Mustafa Pasha received orders to curb the Prince Imperial's extravagances.

The solitary Prince Imperial had at least one virtue: he was not a silent drinker. Evliya Chelibi says of him: "He was an amiable monarch, who took much delight in the conversation of poets and learned men, and indulged in pleasure and gaiety." And again, "he was a sweet-natured sovereign, but given to pleasure and wine." He surrounded himself with twenty boon companions, all of them poets, wits, and tipplers.

Selim loved his First Lady Nûrûbanû. She was always to him the "Holder of Light," gloriously beautiful. She illuminated his life. She is taken to have been (no one is sure of it) a daughter of the noble Venetian family of governors and merchants, Venier-Baffo. The virgin girl was captured on her way to or from Crete or Negroponte and handed over to Hürrem's Black Eunuchs. After Selim the Sot's death she, as the Validé Sultan, began the rule of the harem ladies when, in 1574, her eldest, and epileptic, son Murad III acceded.

Sinan built a very large pious foundation for her in 1583, the year of her death. It stands in the folds of the highlands behind Üsküdar on the Asian shore. Irregular in plan, its disposition shaped by the lie of the land, the complex is most excellently adapted to its terrain and its purpose. On a hilltop, descending on three slopes into a valley, the mosque and its dependencies still function. The hospital served as an insane asylum until recently; a caravansary is still a military prison; a college has been restored as a clinic.

The brilliantly successful series of compromises in Sinan's various buildings surely accord with his reading of the life and the character of the Lady Nûrûbanû. There is no lovelier, no more peaceful, and no more practical, courtyard — low walled, enclosed by arcades, but open on the leveled, terraced hilltop in front of the mosque, in which the tiles are beautiful – in any of the mosques along the Bosphorus. In summer contentment, old men sit there on benches by the fountain in the speckled shade under trees to take the air. There is always a gentle breeze blowing. The imam's wife hangs out the family washing to dry on lines strung along the pillars of the loggia to the northwest. Could the Lady Nûrûbanû have had a cast in one eye? On the terraced shelf below the courtyard, Sinan built a squinting set of arcades and domical cubicles, part of an open square, less than half, cut across on the oblique, askance. (Three roads on the edges of the property, cobblestoned lanes intersecting at a transverse, dictate the arrangement; the high, tunnel-arched foundation of the lecture hall bridges one of them, with a public fountain set inside against the wall.)

Busbecq described Selim as totally unlike Süleyman, in gait pompous, in person corpulent (apparently he waddled). In his view Selim resembled his mother. He lived a lazy life, and was at the same time a sluggard and a sot. "In the small courtesies of life, he was singularly ungracious; he never did a kindness and he never gained a friend. He did not wish, he said, to win the favour of the people at the expense of his father's feelings. The only one that loved him was his father. Everyone else hated him and none so much as those whose prospects depended upon the accession of a generous and warlike Sultan."

He was meat for a butcher like Lala Mustafa Pasha, who had a light hand and, according to Hammer, "a rare genius for intrigue." Lala Mustafa Pasha set one of his student princes against the other. He sold out his favorite, Bayazid, and backed the elder, his father's choice, to win. The lala and Selim worked out a snare in triple subtlety in which to entice Bayazid to trap himself. They baited the jaws with the younger brother's own grinning death's head. "Secretly" (of course Selim was in the know), Lala Mustafa Pasha wrote off to Bayazid, then in Konya, to suggest that he provoke Selim to take direct, treacherous, and lethal action. (Ali, the Lala's secretary, made a copy of the correspondence for his own private files.)

The Janissaries called Bayazid the *Softâ,* the "Student Prince." He thought up a sophomoric practical joke. He wrote an insulting letter to Prince Selim, pinned the letter to one of his own ladies' discarded petticoats, and wrapped it all around a distaff. He capped the bundle with another lady's bonnet. And he sent it off.

When the parcel arrived at Manisa, Lala Mustafa Pasha and Selim the Sot, the one wholly pleased, the other not so happy, promptly forwarded Prince Bayazid's letter and what Hammer called "these objects" through official channels to the Grand Vezir Rüstem Pasha in the Divan of the palace in Istanbul. He had to bring them to the attention of the Sultan Süleyman Khan.

The father reacted according to calculated expectations. He dictated and dispatched a stern reprimand to his younger son in Konya. Bayazid never got it. Lala Mustafa Pasha had the imperial courier waylaid and murdered, and the Sultan's epistle burnt. Carefully, but apparently carelessly, he left evidence strewn about the scene of the crime to indicate but not to implicate or to demonstrate the identity of the perpetrator: himself. Death was the punishment of the crime of lèse majesté; and torture before death the punishment for the outrageously high-handed act of tampering with the imperial postal service. Lala Mustafa Pasha knew what he was doing.

Prince Selim and his tutor sat tight in Manisa. Prince Bayazid, burning to take action, quit his post in Konya without his father's knowledge or permission, and incognito went secretly into Istanbul. There he tried to bribe one or two men of the Sultan's Own Life Guard. He failed. He crossed the straits to rejoin his small band of adventurers, and went down to skirmish in Sarukhan around Prince Selim's court of Manisa.

Süleyman, informed by his faithful chosen guardsmen, stayed his hand. Then Selim sent off a letter dictated by Lala Mustafa Pasha to his secretary Ali, tattling, telling all to his father – and placing the blame squarely upon Lala Mustafa Pasha's head! The gist of it was that their tutor preferred Prince Bayazid, always had, always would; and Rüstem Pasha had known so all along; it was the Grand Vezir's own fault!

The Sultan then took action. Thinking to shake up the two fatuous and terrified brothers, so that they might settle down to read the Will of God written on one another's foreheads, Süleyman ordered Bayazid to transfer from Konya to Amasya. But Bayazid defied his father and refused to go.

Behind Konya he had an escape route into Persia to the east. Konya, ancient Iconium, is a prehistoric natural human habitation, today a provincial city on a high, dry plain. The remaining Seljuk stone monuments, solidly built, elaborately tiled and decorated, deeply arabesqued, stand up in the luminous air above the winter snowfields and the summer-scorched plain, in the sunlight, to make evident the extremes of the Turkish character. The stonemasonry is sober, built in the disciplines of steadfast mysticism and virtuous obedience. The interlocking, knotted, twisted arabesques, carved deep in the frames of the portals, writhe like intrigues across the surfaces. The human brain, excised and pickled for study, sliced, is no more complex a sight. Konya is an open city on a high plateau of wide horizons. A minaret makes a good watch tower. In Konya, Prince Bayazid could protect himself in depth of space.

Amasya, built for vertical defense, lies at the bottom of a deep and rocky defile. The descending currents in the Large Green River turn watermills among green and flame-like poplar trees growing along the banks. At peace, Amasya is the more beautiful; but at war, the city is a trap. High up in the sheer faces of the rock cliffs there are centuries of tombs and stone coffins to be seen. Bayazid would not take his ladies and his sons and daughters and go there.

Süleyman sent off his most trusted Slave of the Gate, Sokollu Mehmet Pasha, second vezir of the Divan, to reason with the disobedient Prince Bayazid. When his outposted spies brought him reports of his father's emissary's approach on the march with enough Janissaries and Sipahis to man an expeditionary force, Bayazid assembled an army of twenty thousand Kurds, Turcomans, and Syrians, a riffraff of wild desperate men, led by trained officers from among the strangled Prince Mustafa's bodyguardsmen, who had turned against the Sultan. According to Busbecq, the Janissaries respected Bayazid's courage and admired his conduct. " 'Why had the father,' they murmured, 'disowned a son who was the living image of himself?' " They made him their chosen candidate for the throne.

But before Sokollu Mehmet Pasha crossed the horizon, Prince Bayazid wrote his father to request permission to fight for the succession according to the law of fratricide, then and there, on the high plateau of the Domain of Peace, in pitched battle with his brother Selim, and within his father the Sultan's lifetime. It was a reasonable request; no other Sultan had lived so long to reign and rule. Süleyman refused to tamper with the ancestral sovereign law, by then entwined with the *urf* and the *Shar,* and thus sacrosanct. However, he had already ordered Prince Selim to join forces with Sokollu Mehmet Pasha. From the watch tower, the highest minaret in Konya, the lookout saw the cloud of dust rising above the encircling hills of the horizon. Prince Bayazid rode out to do battle. Busbecq reports that the younger son would have won had not "a great blast come from the shrine" of the Mevlâna, the tomb and *tekké* of the most powerful, most mystical Ottoman saint, Jelalettin-i-Rumî. There, in a hall built for them by Sinan, the Whirling Dervishes invoke God in ecstasy. Above the tomb a truncated octagonal tower, peaked with a faceted cone, is surfaced with blue-green tiles.

The "blast" from the tomb of the Master, Jelalettin-i-Rumî, who died and was buried there A.H. 672 (A.D. 1230-31), stirred up a thousand whirling dust devils. They blew dust into the eyes of Prince Bayazid's superstitious soldiers; or, as Busbecq cautiously remarks, they did so "if one can believe the Turkish story" of this "supernatural assistance," God-given out of the Mevlâna to Prince Selim. The wind blew from the west. The sandstorm "darkening the atmosphere and blinding the eyes" caused Bayazid to turn tail and gallop off at the head of his remaining men in the direction of Amasya, to the northeast (perhaps the sandstorm was, then, a sirocco?). He got there safely, and his popularity increased, but it was an ill wind for him.

From Amasya, he sent off one more letter to his father in Istanbul, again to beg to be forgiven for what he called his "youthful indiscretions," although he was no longer eighteen but thirty-four. A man in Turkey is thought to be wholly mature, at the peak of his masculine human nature, at the age of thirty. This time, once again, or so it seemed, the Sultan forgave Hürrem's favorite son.

"But in reality the crafty old man," Busbecq surmised – and he had listened to Rüstem Pasha as well as to the future Grand Vezir Sokollu Mehmet Pasha – planned to capture Bayazid alive: "For if driven, he would try to escape to Persia."

And that is what he did. Prince Bayazid took his four oldest sons, Abdullah Sultan, Mahmud Sultan, Mehmet Sultan, and Orhan Sultan, seventeen, sixteen, fifteen, and about thirteen, and fled with an escort of his remaining faithful and able-bodied retainers.

On June 6, 1559, Sultan Süleyman Khan crossed the Bosphorus to plant his standard of seven horsetails, and his colors of seven banners on the heights above Usküdar, in declaration of total Holy War against the Shah of Persia, who had received his son as his own son. Busbecq watched Süleyman go forth riding alone among his golden pages and his white-plumed Color Guardsmen in their red and blue uniforms, glittering in full panoply and weaponry. "His years are beginning to tell on him, but his majestic bearing and indeed his whole demeanor are such as beseem the lord of so vast an empire." The Prince's flight "came upon Solyman as a very heavy blow." In a rage of grief and fury, he had impaled in public one of Bayazid's captured spies. Bayazid and his four sons with their able-bodied retainers got through the mountain passes and into Persia before the snow fell which blocked Sokollu Mehmet Pasha's pursuit. The punitive expeditionary force went into winter quarters at Aleppo.

On November 24, 1559, Prince Bayazid was received on Persian carpets by Shah Tahmasp, who had thirty silver bowls, full of gold and silver coins mixed with pearls, emeralds, rubies, and diamonds poured over the Son of Osman's head, and he promised him to regard him as his own son. Süleyman sent off ambassadors to cross the scorched earth of the Persian frontier with protests and imperial communications that described Bayazid as a rebel, a haughty devil, a pillager of provincial treasuries and merchant caravans, a common thief, and an unworthy man. He quoted the Persian poet Saadi to the effect, "To do good to the evil is to do evil to the good."

Süleyman had instructed his ambassadors orally to request the immediate execution of Prince Bayazid. One of the young man's retainers, foreseeing grief to come, snatched off his own turban, threw it down to unwind as it rolled across the silken carpets, and then threw himself down to roll upon the ground. Bayazid put out his arms to gather his four sons together, to kill them himself. The Shah persuaded him not to abandon hope.

Then, on February 12, 1560, in what appears to be a recurrent disregard for the code of Oriental hospitality, the Shah gave a banquet for Prince Bayazid at which on his orders a detachment of the Imperial Bodyguard fell upon his guests, slaughtered the remaining retainers, and led off the four young imperial princes. Bayazid was thrown into prison.

The Persian Shah then began to negotiate in secret with Prince Selim while at the same time he openly negotiated with Sultan Süleyman. The bickering and bargaining went on until the Grand Turk lost his temper. He declared Holy War against the Shiite heretics, so to capture and execute his son.

The Janissaries refused to march. The Turkish raiders began to desert. "They shrank," Busbecq wrote, "from an unnatural contest." But the show of force brought results. The next Ottoman ambassadors to arrive in Tabriz were conducted into the presence of Prince Bayazid. They found this Son of Osman "so disfigured by the dust and filth of prison, and with his hair and beard so long that they could not recognize him. They were obliged to have him shaved." The Shah sent hand-me-down garments to the prison. Belted with a rope, Bayazid confronted his father's muted Slaves of the Gate. He asked to be allowed to embrace and to kiss his four sons. The executioner, after all, had not been muted. He said, "There is other business that requires your immediate attention." Bayazid died on September 25, 1561, as did his sons Abdullah, Mahmud, Mehmet, and Orhan.

CHAPTER

13

With the Süleymaniyé completed, with Haseki Hürrem buried in her tomb of flowers, in 1558, Sinan and the Sultan got on with the building of the third of Süleyman's "heart's desires," and the last of the three goals, the aqueducts.

In those years at the end of his life, Süleyman the Magnificent — or as the Turks prefer to call him, the Lawgiver — must have seen ahead of him the end of the Ottoman Golden Age. After Hürrem's death and the many deaths of all his eight sons but one, the Sot, the great Sultan put aside his own life as a man. He was never again known to smile, not even when, as the Son of the Slave, his mother, he walked among his fellow Janissary Slaves of the Gate of the Sultan's Slave Household, in the celebrations of triumph in victory when all wars were holy.

Leaden of skin, made up with powderings and rouges, made up in the public image in the public eye, dressed somberly in fine stuffs woven from the belly wool of Angora goats, spun and dyed in the Prophet's chosen color, a dull green, in robes of honor and of state, in winter lined with Russian imperial crown sables, his head erect under the weight of an immaculate and precise turban as big as the world, plumed with black heron aigrettes pinned on with invaluable gross emeralds and great dull diamonds — straight and spare Süleyman walked his way alone. But at what cost! Each stride of his long legs, each step of his gouty feet sent pain shooting up the length of his body above the earth.

He walked alone in company, surrounded by his Slaves of the Gate, into his own memorial, the Süleymaniyé, which means "of Süleyman," to prostrate himself before his God. Even the vast spaces that Sinan designed for him are not big enough to contain the eighty thousand Slaves of his Household upholding the canopy of state in the Ruling Institution. Nor could the walls contain the free men, at least as many more, in the Religious Institution of the Ulema, with the Grand Mufti standing at the apex of the pyramid to administer justice and to define religion in the armies, the cities, the colleges, the courts, the houses and highways, and the mosques of the land.

As a patient, unlike the poorest of his subjects, the ailing Sultan could not enter the hospital that Sinan built for him at the west corner of his own *küllîyé*, the pious foundation "of the whole," the universe. To have done so would have sent out rippling waves of fear, the rumors of his approaching death. But he may have gone in to visit and to cheer the sick. At the time of his death this hospital was the finest in the world. Osmanlija is rich in names for such places: *Mâristan, Darülafiyé, Dârüttip, Bimartisan, Darüshshifa,* and two that usually mean insane asylum, *Birmarhané* and *Timarhané.*

Sinan chose to build the hospital and insane asylum of the Süleymaniyé on steep ground. The walled enclosure fronts on the Vefa, the main street of the quarter of the same name that means Fidelity, Loyalty, Faithfulness. The ill and the insane walked or were brought into the first courtyard. They were diagnosed in the surrounding domical rooms opening onto an arcade. Those with the ordinary maladies or fractures were put to bed in high and spacious rooms full of light and air, where they were tended by physicians and surgeons, who were for the most part fair and blue-eyed Sephardic Jews.

Those found to be insane were led on into the second courtyard. For them, it was specially designed. Sinan built it into the high foundations raised upon the precipitous slopes. This courtyard, rectangular and arcaded like the other, with splendid rooms opening from it, is open to the sky. But the central space is not a garden surrounding a fountain. Instead it is sunken; a modern eye might see it as a dry swimming pool. It might have struck the eyes of our ancestors as a bear pit.

In the cells opening from this deep and rectified space, the worst of the insane were locked up – the powerful men, young or middle-aged or old, slaves or free men deranged by Holy War or by the conditions of peace; and likewise for their own safety, the women, too, all of them either slaves or ladies of the harem, to be married, already married, or widowed. Sinan understood the diseases that we call paranoia and schizophrenia, and their complexes, vertigo, claustrophobia, delusions of grandeur and of persecution, as well as the illusions and the realities of enclosures, deserts, and establishments.

But make no mistake, Sinan did not design a Bedlam or a snakepit. Nor were the ill and the insane scanted in treatment and care by the best qualified and best trained medical practitioners and nurses in Europe, Asia, and Africa, which was the extent of the civilized world of those days. The patients were kept clean; they lunched and dined and supped off pheasant, partridge, woodcock, doves, wild duck and geese, table and game birds out of the Sultan's and the Slaves of the Gate's hunting bags, as well as the delicate fresh fish of the Bosphorus, and the meat of the flocks and herds on the estates assigned to the pious foundation. The white bread of Istanbul was famous, as were the fruits and vegetables, the olive oil, and the produce of the dairies.

The ill had flowers from the imperial gardens. The insane, in their sunken courtyard, heard the gentle splashing of the fountains and listened to the soothing music played by the court orchestra. In his palace, Süleyman enjoyed the sound of lutes and violins.

Next to the hospital and the insane asylum (still occupied in 1965 by the Turkish army's printing presses installed by the Germans after 1914), Sinan built the charitable kitchen and refectory where the poor of the parish, the students of the schools and colleges, and the distinguished visitors from the neighboring guest house were fed — perhaps not so well as the ill and the insane, but very well, indeed, a balanced diet of good and plentiful food. Charity is one of the cardinal virtues of Islam. The Sultan's sons had failed him; it is agreeable to imagine that Süleyman visited the refectory, perhaps even to take a meal with the students at the high table, who might have been his own sons and grandsons.

The rooms of the *imaret*, some of them rectangular and vaulted, some of them square and domical, all of them generous in proportion, now house the displays of the Islamic Museum's collections. In one room are the carpets, some of them ' Holbeins;" others from Konya, fragmented but woven in the thirteenth and fourteenth centuries, dyed with indigo and madder, might have been seen and praised by Marco Polo. The Metropolitan Museum in New York owns one of the great Persian carpets, taken as the loot of victory from Tabriz in 1535 by Süleyman and Ibrahim, and left behind in the rout at the last siege of Vienna in 1683.

In another room of the *imaret* are the manuscripts and the samples of the calligraphists' "beautiful writing," along with the tools of the scribes, pens, inkpots, penknives, eggs of rock crystal to smooth and polish the parchment and the paper roughened by erasures. In another, in a glass case, stands a reliquary. Made by goldsmiths in the Tulip Era of the eighteenth century, it is a small tube hollowed from rock crystal, about four inches tall. It stands upright in a round gold base studded with rubies. It is covered by a gold dome topped by an open rose, multifoliate, full blown, a larger ruby at its heart. Inside, there is a tulip of gold on a curving but upright stem, its leaves dewed with diamonds, holding on its petals a small square velvet cushion, now more gray than blue, into which a single hair of the beard of the Prophet has been pricked. The coarse hair is red-brown; under the henna, the beard was gray.

Sinan planned the arcaded courtyard as a garden, with walks and flower-beds and borders, and with marble benches for the poor to sit upon. They contemplated the rippling and jetting water of a fountain. It is a white marble basin surrounding a delightful square confection, part wedding cake, part palace of marzipan. In the corners, the plane trees, much worked upon by tree surgeons, might well be the saplings that Sinan planted; they have gone past their great days of thick shade. Here the "burning" students and the dervishes, the august and distinguished visiting savants, the cameleers of the caravans, the imams and the muezzins and the professors, along with the poor of the parish, came to eat and to sit for a while in the pleasant democracy of the courtyard. There is no humiliation in the charity of Islam, but instead, comfort and peace.

In the north corner, next to the refectory for the students, all of them scholarship prizewinners, Sinan built the guest house. From the *imaret*, the Sultan went out into the street and through the portal into the *tabhané* to welcome his distinguished visitors to the university. Sinan put an *ayvan*, a deep alcove like a stage, into the northwestern side of the noble courtyard. Here the pillars are all monoliths of porphyry, verd antique, pink Egyptian granite, and rare colored marbles. Here the Sultan took part in conferences and listened to the discourse of men, like himself, who were educated, learned, and cultivated. Here the most famous men of the pen and of the learned professions came to stay in cupolaed apartments of several chambers. They came from Morocco and North Africa, from Egypt, from Damascus, from Persia, from Central Asia – Bokhara and Samarkand – and from the Grand Moghul's Lahore, Delhi, and Agra. One of Akbar's ladies was an Ottoman Turkish princess; she lived in a pavilion at Fatihpur-Sikri.

In front of each apartment in Sinan's and Süleyman's *tabhané*, the distinguished visitor, sitting cross-legged on carpets and cushions spread on a raised platform under the arcade, received his visitors, the students, the Architect, the Sultan. This is a civilized place. There is no fault to find in the urban arrangement outside the resounding empty spaces of the Imperial Friday Mosque.

In the last year of his life, the Sultan, with his Royal Chief Architect, who had twenty-two years of life ahead of him, saw the water of the aqueducts pour in from the Belgrade Forest to the Forty Fountains in abundance, clear, fresh, pure water, sparkling in the sunlight. It has never since ceased to flow (except today in the hours of the night when the supply now has to be rationed in the expanding city).

Süleyman was seventy-two in 1566. One day in the midst of the seven years of work on the aqueducts, and in the legend of Sinan and Süleyman, the Sultan rode out of his walled city into the green hills and valleys; he went on a tour of inspection of the work in progress. As in all legendary, and in the good sense, mythical stories, the actual date is hard to fix. But it must have been a good day, a summer's day, clear and dry. The Sultan's ailment has been described as gout. It may have been just that, a painful disease for which a man has to inherit a predisposition in his body chemistry. It may have been phlebitis; more probably it was one form or another of arthritis. Whatever it was, the disease was incurable, and painful. The climate of the Bosphorus is heavy, humid, in itself depressing, and bad for arthritics.

On one of his good days, probably before 1564, Süleyman rode out to get away, to take a breath of air, and to savor his only remaining pleasure –

watching his Royal Chief Architect at work. Sinan, seventy-five that spring, was five years older than the Sultan, but he was flexible and quick in all his muscles and joints. The Sultan rode along, ambling, following the line of the aqueducts that Sinan had surveyed and drawn on the maps. The water from the springs and reservoirs in the Belgrade Forest flows by gravity seeking its own level, a matter of fifteen or twenty miles to the fountains in the city. The forest watershed took its name from Süleyman's and Sinan's first victory, the one as a young Sultan in the first year of his reign, the other as the Janissary engineering cadet out in 1521 on campaign, in action for the first time. As the phrase goes, Belgrade was the baptism of fire for both men; and it had taken place forty-two or forty-three years earlier in their lives.

Süleyman searched the piers and arches of the masonry aqueduct, some of them complete, others rising from the centering and scaffoldings, with the stone-cutters and masons at work on the ground and on the platforms in the air, shouting down for mortar. Süleyman reined in to looked for Sinan, and, not finding him, to watch the men pulling at the end of the system of ropes and pulleys to haul up the required load.

He looked at the arches and the piers striding across the rolling landscape of hills and valleys, green and sunlit on that good day, the skies blue and high above the white clouds scudding from the north and casting moving shadows on the fields of wheat and the groves and orchards of apples and peaches with Lombardy poplars standing guard. Here and there the finger of a minaret pointed above a village dome to call attention to God and to man in his nature.

From the imperial walled city on its seven hills to the Belgrade Forest on the Black Sea, the landscape is old and gentle. There at the end of winter first wild cyclamen and snowdrops bloom, and later in spring pink tree peonies. Above the Bosphorus there is no violence to be seen in the fertile country-side. But at the mouth of the strait craggy little mountains pile up, one topped by the frowning ramparts of a Genoese castle above rock cliffs along the wild shore. The upended strata there bear witness to the cataclysm that raised the Alps and the Himalayas, sunk the basin of the Mediterranean, and split open the channel that lets the waters of the Danube and the Russian rivers flow out of the Black Sea past Byzantium-Constantinople-Istanbul into the deep Sea of Marmara. Turkey is a country of earthquakes.

In 1564, before the mortar of the finished aqueducts had had the time to harden, an earthquake threw down the greatest of the spans, the largest of them built up in two and three tiers of arches to carry the water across ravines, the longest 170 meters (560 feet) and 265 meters (875 feet) in length. In those days before geologists charted the faults and the rifts in the earth's unfinished surfaces, earthquakes were accepted as mysterious acts of God.

Pipes, however, were man-made. Sinan had found the proper clay pit, built the kilns, trained the men; and he had seen to it that the conduits were made to his specifications. The substance is as hard as rock. He got to work to put the arches up again. Süleyman opened his privy purse to the builder. By then the Sultan's annual revenues from Egypt, his private estate, brought in one million two hundred thousand gold pieces.

On the day of the unannounced, casual imperial tour of inspection – it must have been before the earthquake – once outside the land walls in the highlands, the Sultan in the legend looking for his Royal Chief Architect, followed along the trench dug into the rolling hilltops. He came upon Sinan down at the bottom of a muddy ditch showing the workmen, who were a third his age, how to lay the pipes according to his system. Perhaps the shadow of the Shadow of God on Earth fell upon him. Sinan looked up; Süleyman looked down. He had no need to paint his face to please his old friend and fellow worker. It was a pleasure. Each man got on with it. When the Padishah rode off into his Domain of War in Europe on his last campaign at the head of his armies, Sultan Süleyman Khan pitched camp under the arches of his aqueduct on his first night in the field. He left Sinan behind.

In 1561 the Grand Vezir Rüstem Pasha died of dropsy. He left his widow, the Imperial Princess Mihrimah, whom he had married when she was seventeen, the wealthiest woman in history. She inherited eight hundred and fifteen farms in both the Domains of War and of Peace; four hundred and sixty-six water mills; one thousand seven hundred domestic slaves and field hands; two thousand nine hundred war-horses; one thousand one hundred six camels; unnumbered flocks of sheep and heads of cattle; five thousand kaftans and robes of honor, richly embroidered, those for winter richly furred; eight thousand turbans (some if not most of them for his private troops); one thousand one hundred bonnets or berets of cloth of gold – worn by the pages of the palace schools assigned to his grand veziral retinue; two thousand nine hundred shirts of chain mail; two thousand cuirasses; six hundred saddles garnished with silver; five hundred saddles encrusted with gold and jewels; one thousand five hundred steel helmets, some plated with silver, others plated with gold; one hundred thirty pairs of gold stirrups; seven hundred sixty sabers, the hafts and the sheathes ornamented with semiprecious and with precious stones; one thousand lances decked out with silver; eight hundred copies of the Koran, of which one hundred thirty, bound in fine leathers, had clasps and cornerings of gold and decorative bosses of gold set with diamonds; and for a man who was the sworn enemy of poets, and who was impatient with belles-lettres, Rüstem Pasha left his widow a great library of five thousand illuminated and illustrated manuscript volumes of the Islamic classics.

And he left Mihrimah Sultan seventy eight thousand goldpieces; thirty-two gem stones worth one hundred twelve donkey loads of silver coins, to the value of eleven million two hundred thousand *akchés* in ready money. The other liquid assets discovered in the vaults and strong rooms in the palaces that Sinan had built for him amounted to another thousand donkey loads, or another hundred million *akchés*.

In his own lifetime, Rüstem Pasha had already spent the greater part of his fortune to build and to endow pious and commercial foundations — banks to the Holy Spirit and Business — in all parts of the European, Asian, and African Ottoman Empire. He was, then, by far the wealthiest self-made man in history. He did not live to see his own memorial built for him by Sinan.

Besides the precious objects and the gold and silver hoards of liquid assets, the remaining estates and commercial properties that his widow inherited were worth — how much? As much again as the coins and the jewels and the robes and the weaponry and the books and the divers objects? Say one hundred fifteen million one hundred thousand in those astronomical eagles of one more obsolete monetary system. Mihrimah Sultan was richer than anybody else alive.

Rüstem Pasha had always been liberal with his wife. After all, she was a collector's item in her own right. But free of her mother's strings, free of the inconveniences of her marriage, free of her miserly husband, the Lousy Ikbal, the Abominable, in the first year of his death, she set about spending a great deal of his wealth.

First, if not to speed his souls's progress through limbo, then at least to see to the comfort of the long long journey, she prevailed upon her father to let the Royal Chief Architect take time off from the building of the aqueducts, then in the third year of construction. She asked Sinan to design and build her husband an appropriate memorial. Probably the Grand Vezir had talked things over with the architect in the year of his slow death; and surely, he had set aside a property to build upon. Sinan, I think, went about the job with a certain good humor.

The Rüstem Pasha Jami, called the Tile Mosque, has no chronogram carved above the portal. That is to say, no man of letters worked out a literary conceit in which the letters of the wording in the epitaph, or the acronym of the versified eulogy, cut in stone, were given numerical values to add up to the date of the memorial. *De mortuis nil nisi bonum*, in effect, left nothing for the despised poets to say of Rüstem Pasha, deceased. Therefore, the construction cannot be precisely dated. But the charter for the pious foundation was granted in 1561, which was the year of his death.

Once again, the penny-pinching Grand Vezir had set aside a difficult parcel to build upon. It is a corner lot at a right-angled intersection of narrow

cobblestoned streets in Tahtakalé. For five centuries, tinsmiths, woodwork-
ers, rope walkers, ironmongers, potters; wholesalers in nuts, raisins, dried figs,
and apricot paste; retailers and brokers in grains, the staples, dried beans and
peas, seeds, olives, and spices, the oils and the cheeses, all the less perishable
produce, have worked and traded in the noisy bustling quarter. It smells
strong; it smells good. The market lies on the steep slopes of the Third Hill
and along the littoral of the Golden Horn from the spice bazaar at Eminönü
almost to the valley of the Lykos. The streets are too narrow for two carts or
a single truck to pass between the stalls of merchandise offered for sale in
front of the open shops.

In the good season, here and there, grapevines thicker than a man's wrist
and forearm grow up the side of a shop and cross the streets from rooftop to
rooftop to shade the people at work or passing by under the arbor. In
summer the dust rises from the cobblestones, which hurt the feet; in winter,
the slimes of all sorts make the footing slippery. The smell of fish frying in
pans of oil on charcoal braziers standing on the quay, a good, strong smell in
the old days, has disappeared with the Balik Pazar, the fish market, on the
shore. There the Bosphorus fishermen moored their orange and blue and red
and green boats to sell their catches equally colorful. The fish market was a
fine place, but most of it had to go when the town planner of the 1950's put
through the four-lane highway along the Golden Horn. Before then, Tahtakalé around the Mosque of Rüstem Pasha was a slippery and a slimy and a
smelly stretch of twisting narrow streets full of men and women going about
their business, full of life that was at once recognizable as reality. Even
opened up, Tahtakalé is still worth the trip to Istanbul.

The north corner of the Rüstem Pasha Jami now stands free, revealed
upon a bank of bare earth that is human detritus. The minaret has fallen, and
although the blocks of Sinan's dressed limestone have been carted away for
eventual restoration, the chips and the dust of mortar, and perhaps some
spilled blood, remain in the cobbled street to add the current stratum.
sixteen and a half feet. The minaret has fallen, and although the blocks of
Sinan's dressed limestone have been carted away for eventual restoration, the
chips and the dust of mortar, and perhaps some spilled blood, remain in the
cobbled street to add the current stratum.

Rüstem had acquired another bargain, a ruinous Byzantine business
premise. On the given vaulted substructure made of narrow, hard-baked
Byzantine bricks set in rock-hard mortar, Sinan built a row of shops with
storerooms behind them. He planned the pious foundation as a mosque
surrounded and supported by a complex of workshops, ateliers, offices for
wholesalers and retailers, and warehouses. Such a commercial building in
Turkish is called a *han*, which also means "inn" or "caravansary." Usually the
han is rectangular and has two floor of massive brick masonry built around an

open courtyard, arcaded, with shops below and factories or offices above. Istanbul is full of these great business premises, some of them covering whole city blocks with their many interconnecting courtyards. Sinan's palaces have all gone, but the *hans* show us his secular architecture. Those surrounding and supporting the Mosque of Rüstem Pasha are still in use — I found stacks of stiff and bloody fleeces for sale in one. The large, plain bathhouse, privately owned, has been converted into a cold-storage plant.

At Rüstem Pasha's corner in Tahtakalé, above the shops at street level, Sinan built the platform for the mosque. Three twisting and enclosed stone staircases, each occupying a minimum of valuable commercial space, lead up from the streets to the high *sahn*. This platform stands at six meters, twenty-one feet nine inches, above the cobblestones. There is no other courtyard. The edges of the level, stone-paved *sahn* are walled in and railed with pierced stone slabs.

To compensate for the loss of the suppressed courtyard arcades, Sinan more than doubled the covered space by building an outer porch around the inner porch, a sloping penthouse roof supported by right-angled arcades of slim pillars that rises to the row of five domes of the inner porch, held up by the usual monoliths and arches.

Inside, the mosque itself, again as usual, is built on the floor plan of the circle in the square, which Sinan extended on either side by an aisle roofed by three cradle vaults in a row; and, again as usual, he brought in the buttresses from the façade to widen the space behind the northwestern wall. But in the circle, Sinan drew an octagon, and built a pier at each of the eight angles. Two of the piers are engaged, as pilasters, in the kibla wall; two join the buttresses on either side of the portal. Each of the two pairs on either side, freestanding, is octagonal in section.

Sinan chose the octagon for both the Rüstem Pasha *medresé,* built ten years earlier in 1550, and for the mosque in the memorial, finished in 1561. The college and the mosque stand in different quarters of the city. Perhaps, therefore, Sinan used the octagonal plan to link the two foundations. But my belief is that Sinan saw Rüstem Pasha as a complex and complicated man of many-sided character, neither as simple as a circle nor as forthright as a square. Eight is one of the Bektashi mystical numerals. Perhaps Sinan, himself a member of the Bektashi order of dervishes, chose to stress Rüstem's liberality in religion. As Busbecq noted, the Grand Vezir, in Islam, was liberal and catholic to the point of heresy and, indeed, misbelief. In private conversation, he allowed that Christians, Jews, and even Shiite Muslims, as such, were not excluded in life or in death from God the One's salvation.

Apparently he worshiped Mammon. It may be that Sinan chose the octagon to point out Rüstem Pasha's many sides, both good and evil. Or again, Sinan may have seen the unhappy man fixed and transfixed at the top of the heap of the slave hierarchy, caught in Hürrem's spiderweb, pulled this way and that by the network of power spinning together his wife, his mother-in-law, his father-in-law, his brothers-in-law. Pinned, he spun like a Catherine wheel. But he did not burn out, he died of water unnaturally hoarded in the cavities and tissues of his body.

On the other hand, Sinan may have been experimenting with a newly discovered architectural form. He owned a country property on the south coast of Asia Minor in what were Greek, Hellenistic, Roman, and Byzantine landscapes. While there he may well have measured the ruins of the Martyrion of St. Philip near Ladik. The chapel in the necropolis was built by early Christians in the fourth century; it is domical, octagonal, and cruciform inside square walls. Sinan almost certainly would have visited Ladik to order carpets made to his specifications, rows of lilies woven against cerulean or brick red ground. Perhaps Sinan took his fellow slave Rüstem to be a sort of martyr. Such men and women, after death to be sanctified, must have been difficult and distorted in their lives. Rüstem, whatever else he was, was a dedicated man.

The choice of an octagonal plan for his memorial raised both technical and architectural problems, all of which Sinan solved admirably in the construction. He built in the proportions, roughly, of 1:1.5 — a scanted golden section. From floor to crown the dome rises, again roughly, 26.5 meters (80 feet). Sinan had no trouble with the eight small pendentives upon the eight piers that carry the ring and the dome. He filled the high arches in the four corners with small semidomes, but reduced the screen walls in all the others to clear glass, half-moons of elephant's-eyes. Wherever else he could, he opened windows. The mosque is full of light. But despite the elevation above the marketplace, and despite the transparent curtain and screen walls, the interior seems heavy, dark, oppressive — because of what ought to be its glory, the load of Iznik tiles covering every square inch of the flat surfaces of its walls and piers and buttresses.

Rüstem Pasha bequeathed Sinan a miser's collection of hundreds and thousands of Iznik tiles, each one today worth about what each one cost to make, between two hundred fifty and one thousand paper-gold American dollars. They overwhelm the space with their impersonally perfect patterns of dark blue, light blue, leaf green, and sealing-wax red, the colors enameled upon a dead-level snow-white ground, and covered with a glaze as clear as distilled water. What is wrong with this millionaire-billionaire interior?

That, precisely, is what is wrong with it. Rüstem Pasha knew the monetary value of things. The mosque smells less of the museum than of the dealer's showroom. The Grand Vezir purchased — or, as museum curators now put it, acquired — samples of the various master potters' art from the most successful of the many kilns in Iznik. This man was famous for his floral patterns; Rüstem Pasha bought enough from him to cover half a wall with red tulips on green-leafed stems planted in rows in a vertical bed and nodding their heads this way and that. The next master was best at geometrical arrangements of mandala rosettes in dark and light blue; their interconnecting petals and crisscrossing lines, in Rüstem Pasha's mosque, surface half of another wall with a great many regimented spots. Another kiln had a more fanciful designer. He produced a field of swirling feathers blowing this way and that way in a high, obliging wind. The Grand Vezir bought up half-a-wall's worth. And so on. Only the prayer niche and its surrounds in the center of the kibla wall and the panels made to fit the spandrels of the gallery arcades reveal Sinan's sure hand at working out the appropriate patterns.

Curiously, the effect of all these disparate elements is at once static, incoherent, repetitive, and monotonous. Sadly, the individual tiles, some nine inches square, are not as good as they might be — and in another decade were to be. They look almost machine-made, mass-produced; and they have faults.

As it happened, the Grand Vezir's collector's collection does not represent the purely Ottoman art of faience at the great period. He died too soon to realize that his investment would not appreciate but instead would decline to second best.

By 1561, the potters of the third generation born in Iznik after their Persian grandfathers' and grandmothers' enforced immigration from Tabriz had just begun to find their own native and purely Ottoman art and craft. Their fathers, the elder enamelers of Iznik in the middle period, 1555-1570, had not discovered how to master the troublesome bolus clay, the "Armenian bole" of the sealing-wax red pigment. Laid on too flat in a thin and liquid state, the enamel in the firing often burnt brown. Only *circa* 1570 did the younger potters learn the trick, which was to pile up a thick impasto inside the outlines of the tulip or the apple so to guarantee an unburnt and true tomato red. The potters then had to invent a new glaze, gin-clear but viscous, thick enough to stick and not to flow down from the heaped-up piles of fired red enamel, so not to expose the top and the flanks. (The two secrets of the bolus red and the clear thick glaze have since been lost.)

In Rüstem Pasha's mosque everything else about the individual tile is perfect, save for the uncertain red and the lack of freedom in the design, a hard constraint as of the work of slaves. The white background, however, is immaculate. The turquoise and the dark blues are true; the tree trunks and the branches of the fruit blossom are dark purplish brown (a pigment of manganese?). The green of the foliage is right. But the disparity of pattern, the several kinds arbitrarily brought into juxtaposition, work against Sinan. Only his sobriety and the strong order of his disciplined architectural plan keep the Mosque of Rüstem Pasha from quantitative gaudiness. I refer to the interior. The exterior, because of the limestone and the lead-sheathing, is, as it should be, discretion itself.

The present-day workmen of Tahtakalé are proud of their mosque. Washed clean at the big fountain of the ablutions they climb the stairs as they roll down their sleeves, the clean wooden clogs on their bare feet clattering on the worn stone steps. Reverent and serene in the characteristic self-respect of the Turkish artisan and peasant, they fill the mosque five times a day. They pray on a brand-new hand-loomed wall-to-wall carpet, red to match the bolus pigment of the tiles, and marked across from side to side with white lines to space the ranks of men, standing broad shoulder to broad shoulder, bowing from the waist, genuflecting, sitting back on the heels, leaning forward, upended, to place the forehead on the red carpet, and sitting back to listen, then to stand to follow the leader in prayer, the imam in responses. Their worship is ceremonial, a courtly drill, each courteous act meaningful at the moment in the prayer, which is not a semi-divine bargaining, not a confession, but a declaration and an affirmation of faith in God, a sort of loyalty oath.

It becomes apparent that the current fashion in tight Italian pants and Edwardian trousers and blue jeans does not suit devout Muslims. Islam is a religion best clothed in the loose trousers of the latter-day Janissaries and our own later Zouaves, and the long, flowing, comfortable robes of honor and of state awarded the admirable Slaves of the Gate.

The imam of the Mosque of Rüstem Pasha, a friendly, smiling, elderly man, delights in showing his mosque to visitors. He is pleased to have us stay, to stand quietly at the back, throughout the prayer service. It is correct for the man to keep his hat on – the woman also should cover her head – but because it is my habit as a Christian to uncover in a house of God, I do so. The Turks take off their felt hats in the Western style, some of the best of them Borsalino; they take an embroidered white skullcap out of their pocket and put it on. The men with peaked caps turn them front to back, so to be able to place the forehead on the carpeted ground. The imam wears a red felt fez, wound at the base with a length of white muslin.

Down in the street, I look up at the mosque; but it is hard to get a good perspective. It seems probable that such has always been the case. The uncompromising solid brick and stone masonry of the bulky *hans* crowds close. Therefore, Sinan could not rely upon the bared structural elements – the thrusting piers and buttresses, the springing arches – to give vitality and dynamics to the building. Only the superstructure of the mosque is visible, and only from a distance. On high, rising from the crest of the Third Hill, the mighty Süleymaniyé dominates the skyline. It commands attention.

I think that in the Rüstem Pasha Jami, Sinan chose to expose the lead-sheathed shell of the conchs at the four corners, between the octagon and the square, and not to hide them in cornerings of masonry, in order to accelerate the transition from the square walls to the round dome. Above them, on top of the octagon, Sinan placed the crown, or the drum, of alternating vertical buttresses and round-arched windows, cut through the base of the dome. As usual, it is excellent, a mixture of hard-edged verticals and graceful curves. But even so, to give the always bland form and soft shapes of the dome some nervous energy, Sinan rippled the bottom edge of it (it was a Byzantine device).

By rippling the base of the dome, he raised the circular line in a second dimension. Both vertical and horizontal, the rippling circular band almost flutters — it would do so without the absolute discipline imposed upon the exactly spaced and controlled but fast rising and falling and rising and fast falling interlocking arcs. Rüstem Pasha appears to have been a man who used nervous energy to dominate the Divan. He was an irascible man, Busbecq tells us so, foul-mouthed and readily irritable. The waves on the surface of the Golden Horn ripple similarly in the wake of the fast commercial vessels. Even so, elevated in the air, the Mosque of Rüstem Pasha is squat and heavy, in effect, both inside and out.

As a man and as a Grand Vezir, Rüstem Pasha was honest in his dishonesty. Having established the system of bribery, he drew up a sort of scheduled and graduated price list. He understood the cash value of everything. He refused to bargain. Busbecq paid him a price (carefully unspecified in his letters written home) to obtain favorable terms in a peace treaty being drawn up between the Sublime Porte and the Holy Roman Emperor. When the Grand Vezir could not fulfill the contract, the Sultan or the (by then) six lesser vezirs of the Divan, the two Judges of the Armies, the Defterdar, the Keeper of the Privy Seal, and the Grand Mufti having outvoted him. Rüstem Pasha voluntarily returned to the Austrian ambassador the amount paid in gold coin of the realm in advance for the services impossible to render.

When a beylerbey of Erzerum sent the Grand Vezir — eight hundred and fifty-four miles (by nonexistent road) away in Istanbul — a thoroughbred horse worth five thousand gold pieces, and also a gift of five thousand gold pieces in cash, along with the request for special preference in some quasi-illegal, underhand double-dealing, Rüstem Pasha did the work, kept the horse and three thousand of the gold coins, but, judging himself to have been overpaid, returned two thousand to the distant beylerbey in Erzerum.

Perhaps his curious discretion gives evidence of the man's devious honesty; but perhaps it gives proof of the terror inspired in him by his father-in-law, the Sultan. To pay the mounting expenses of his mighty, and fixed, establishment, Süleyman had need of the additional revenues, no matter how the Grand Vezir raised the cash. By the middle decades of the sixteenth century, costs had gone up in the spiraling inflation brought on by the Peruvian gold and the Mexican silver brought into Europe across the Spanish main. Therefore, Süleyman turned his leaden countenance away, but he controlled his son-in-law's excesses by means of salutary fear. After both men died, total corruption set in — to keep the Ottoman Empire mysteriously going throughout the long, slow, gentle decline down the three hundred and fifty-seven years of its course.

But once Sinan had finished the Tile Mosque as the memorial for the dead Grand Vezir, who rose from Croatian pig drover to leave his widow all that wealth, Mihrimah Sultan hadn't a care in the world. She had no need for a memorial. In 1547 Sinan had built in her name a mosque and pious foundation in Üsküdar (restored, it is still there, and handsome it is if clumsy on the interior) near her summer palace (likewise for her and Rüstem Pasha by Sinan; it has been destroyed) on the Asian shore. In 1562, the widow Mihrimah, the Moon of the Suns, free of her mothers's and her husband's reflected phases, chose to shine in her own right. She commissioned the Royal Chief Architect to build for her a great mosque on the highest point of land in the imperial city. The Mihrimah Jami stands just within the land walls next to the Edirné Gate on top of the Sixth Hill. It serves as landmark for the Ottoman armies marching off to Holy War and returning from victory, or defeat, in Turkey in Europe.

The legend is that she paid the enormous costs out of her "slipper money" or, as we say, pin money. But ignorant foreign chroniclers, both European and Asian, wishing to call attention either to the Grand Vezir's excessive wealth or her own excessive frivolity, read slipper money to mean that she sold a pair of shoes to build her house of God. In bad weather the Ottoman ladies wore pattens of inlaid and jewel-studded wood, six or eight inches high — how deep the mud must have been. They wore velvet slippers embellished with pearls and precious stones. Mihrimah Sultan was tiny; she could have worn no more than size three or four in shoes — apparently weighted with diamons as big as a "mountain of light," the Koh-i-Noor.

Sinan built her a mosque as full of light. She must have been a merry widow at the age of forty — she did not choose to remarry. She certainly was liberal, as neither her father nor husband had been in giving Sinan a free hand to do as he saw fit for her. She had known him all her married life, and all his, since 1538. Sinan at the age of seventy-three turned revolutionary, and he began to experiment. Her mosque marks the turning point in his career from journeyman to master builder, the final period in which the architect dominates the patron.

In building the Süleymaniyé, he had stripped off all the superficial ornamentation that distracts the eye in the Shehzadé Jami from his architecture and his engineering. Even as a journeyman he had begun to rely upon the structural elements of the mosque to dictate the architectonics. But as a Slave of the Gate, he was, of course, constrained to carry out the Sultan's orders for the building of the imperial monument. He did what he was told to do. The Süleymaniyé succeeds not only as a memorial to Sultan Süleyman Khan, the Son of Osman, the Shadow of God on Earth, but also as an apologia, in grandeur and glory, for the life of the magnificent man, his master.

To build the mosque for the Imperial Princess Mihrimah, Sinan was under no constraint save, of course, to design and build upon the requisite formula of the circle inscribed within the square, the irreducible, insoluble equation, tense in its conditions that cannot be otherwise restated, and cannot be got around, the most vital, the most dynamic known to man. He and she understood one another, both as a powerful man and a fragile woman, the one a tall and muscular, white-bearded slave, wholly achieved; the other a Daughter of Osman, privileged, delightful, and prized; and as architect and patroness, each coming into his and her own freedoms.

In her mosque, Sinan's architecture is inseparable from his engineering, the theory from the practice, the purpose from the function, the idea from the reality, the one from the other. The Mihrimah Jami is the most architectonic of Sinan's mosques. In sculpture, outside Islam or Judaism, it would be called heroic, and it would be seen to be nude – the Apollo of Olympia or the Aphrodite of Cyrene or both of them.

But as Islamic religious architecture, there is, I feel, some nagging lack in it. Certainly there is something disturbingly experimental and therefore transitional about this building; and there is more of the witty tour de force, a feat of strength, an extravagant display. Mihrimah, like other *belles laides,* must have been a woman of elegance, high style, and great chic. And she was the wealthiest of women in the world in an empire ruled by men and poised in the moment of its fullest growth and greatest power. No, as a study in the nude, Sinan's mosque is comparable rather to his contemporary Michelangelo's marbles before he went into his tormented and tumultuous world of the frescoes. There are all the elements of the Mannerists and the Baroque ahead of both Michelangelo and Sinan in the David and in the Mihrimah Jami.

The Imperial Princess Mihrimah remains a veiled figure. Certain women can stand still and make us smile, they can make us jump through hoops. Athletes, in their exercised and concentrated strength, vault, and bring us to our feet cheering. Sinan built something of these qualities into the Mihrimah Jami. This mosque is his exercise in virtuosity.

By 1562 Sinan knew what he could do; he apparently was dissatisfied with what he had done. His mosque for Mihrimah Sultan shines like a seashell cast up on the shore of a warm sea. It has in it the aspect of a Renaissance conceit. In its controlled exuberance, there is something of the palindrome. "Madam, I'm Adam," Sinan might have said as he escorted the delicate imperial princess into and out of her completed memorial. The exterior is a statement in mass, the interior in space. Each is what the other is not. The two play variations on the same theme. A hall of prayer, a house of God, is not a divertissement. Perhaps Sinan's mosque for Mihrimah Sultan lacks only religion. After all, in Christendom, a woman received God and bore God; in Islam, Jesus is a being only less human than Mohammed. And Mary, in both religions, bore him miraculously. She is the realist in the concept, essentially so.

The building stands high on a stone platform leveled on the top of the Sixth Hill. Sinan may have planned it on the drawing board in the perfected geometrical proportions of one to two, the globe upon the cube, and then in the construction upon the highest point of land in the imperial city, found that it would not do. He lowered the dome ten feet. It rises 37 meters, 122 feet, in height from floor to crown. In diameter, the circle measures 20 meters, 66 feet, within the square, which is 20 meters, 66 feet, to a side.

It seems to me that in this mosque Sinan put most of the intellectual symbolisms to one side. The nature of God, the nature of man; the life eternal, the life on earth; the celestial dome, the desert floor; the meaning of victory, and of failure; the inseparable and yet distinct elements, human and divine, in the sacred jurisprudence; the two aspects of power – Sinan silenced these perpetual dialogues upon the circle in the square for the time being; and he got down to facts. Let us see, he might have said to himself: what in truth does a man have to go on? He then threw away the modular.

It might as well be said that the mosque of Mihrimah Sultan is a product of Sinan's passionate mind. From the outside, there they are – the essential male and the essential female principles. The single minaret is most elegant: slim, piercing, penetrating, erect, at once a finger pointing and also unmistakably the male virile member. It also has a single gallery, which fits the image only in the greatest of sophistication; and although all this is everything that is erotic, nothing can be called pornographic, not even in the abstract. The minaret towers higher than the dome and it goes up into the sky. The single great dome, and all the many, many, many smaller domes are breasts, breast-shaped, the finial *alem* is the nipple; they are young breasts.

Startled by the evidence of the senses, the mind gets to work, humorously, to notice the fact of singularity among a multiplicity of ladies lying on their backs. Where is the free choice hereabouts? Or are these all remembrances? Artemis of the Ephesians! Alma Mater is the courtyard. Euclid! Come on down to earth. I find myself standing on top of the crumbling land walls. I scrambled up to get a better view. It is a matchless view.

I look across the rows of domes – yes, domes, small, twinned cupolas, the ones on the arcades and the cells of the courtyard, and the larger, but by no means matronly, domes of the porch. They are the color of the breasts of doves. Above them rises the stonemasonry of the superstructure of the mosque. There are no semidomes at all, but what a quantity of glass! Each curtain wall – it is the outline, the silhouette, of a breast – is a screen of nineteen windows in three rows, all but four of them topped by pointed arches; the four are rounds, great elephant's-eyes.

The four piers rise as the four corners, each a many-sided tower, a bastion, each one topped by a cupola, a pointed cap lead-sheathed. Between each pair springs the single leaping arch; its intrados a smooth rising and falling curve, its extrados jagged with the horizontal and the verticals of zigzagging right angles, stepping to a level on the top. Behind the caps of each corner tower, Sinan revealed the outer surface of the spherical triangle. The four pendentives, seen from the outside, uncovered and identified, do their work. Sheathed with lead, rising and curving inward from each masonry tower, above the cornering abutments the spherical triangles join to form the circle upon which Sinan put a simple but a bold ring cornice, a sort of flange.

Upon this ring, he set the bezel, the crown, a gallery of round-arched windows and their alternating, slanting vertical (and yet in breadth horizontal) buttresses, lead-sheathed. He marked the dentation of their summits with a severe plain cornice. Upon this crown, he set the dome, hemispherical but not a hemisphere, not the half of a globe, lead-sheathed. Here again the wedge-shaped sheets of lead ridged at the joins in a pattern of latitudinal and longitudinal lines, shadowed in the sunshine, gather together at the pole of the dome. The finial of gilt-bronze, the *alem,* ends in the horned moon, the crescent of Artemis, of the Virgin, and of Islam.

Behind the mosque of the Lady as Beautiful as the Moon, which rises on the top of the Sixth Hill, the triangular city of streets, of roofs, of domes, and of minarets falls away within the sea walls and the land walls. The blue water of the Sea of Marmara rises like another wall to receive the dome of the blue sky. It is a matchless sight, an urban landscape, a view of civilization, man-made. The vision sets the imagination off on the old familiar round in nostalgia to find perfection. Then, out of the corner of the eye, a jagged diagonal line cuts across the nebulous emotion. Sinan once again puts reality to work.

I see that in the rear elevation of the mosque Sinan saw fit to build a triangular wall to fill the empty space of a corner, an abrupt right angle, between the vertical mass of the east tower pier and the horizontal coping line of the extended kibla wall. He cut a flight of steps in the hypotenuse to make a puzzlingly useless staircase. The towerlike pier has a vice inside it to give access to the roof, and it has a turret chamber on top of it. The lead sheathing of steps, in this diagonal wall, shows the indentation made by the feet of workmen climbing up to enter the door of the turret chamber. But even so, there was no real need for Sinan to build this outside staircase; it must be vertiginous to climb. And in the triangle of the wall itself, no more than a stone wide, he cut a high-arched opening to no practical purpose, except to reduce the dead weight.

And he chose to emphasize the uselessness by cutting jagged steps into its rising diagonal edge. The thing is not a buttress. It seems to be an after-thought, an addition.

Puzzled by the apparently extraneous detail, I decided to go around behind the mosque to see if I could make sense of the abrupt and arbitrary line joining, and yet emphasizing the differences between, the vertical and the horizontal masses. I took one more look. The jagged steps hacksaw across the eye-filling curves of the many small paired domes covering the arcaded courtyard.

Then, from my high place on top of the crumbling land walls, I slid and slipped down and jumped onto the cobble stones of the narrow sunken street. I wonder if Sinan, having climbed up to take a similar look at the mosque nearing completion, had not done much the same thing as I exactly four hundred years before me? It seems to me that he had found fault with the rear view of the mosque. Oriented, perforce the building presents its back to the city.

I walked around behind the mosque to stand in an empty lot, a waste space covered with weeds and turds among the rubble of Mihrimah Sultan's ruined caravansary and *hamam*. I looked up. From the rear, the masonry towers rise like the corner bastions of a fortress, a donjon keep. But the beetling effect of such a stronghold is negated by the curtain walls — they are reduced to screens of glass — hanging from the four massive arches.

Once again, it seems clear, Sinan chose to stress the power not of stone but of faith — faith in the balanced and calculated structure of the . . . of the Sacred Law as well as of the scientific "laws" of engineering within the law of gravity and according to the nature of stone masonry. According to his understanding, and thus his control, of the dynamics implicit in the architec-ture, he reduced his fortress to a house of glass. There was no further need, in the golden age of the Ottoman Empire, to defend the city, the civilization, and the faith. Mihrimah Sultan, the wealthiest of women, and every other woman alive at that supreme moment of Islam, lived and had her being in perfect security. That was the fact, re-observable in this mosque as the truth. Once again, there it is, the obverse and the reverse of human nature, perfectly stated in the insoluble formula of the circle in the square.

So much for the act of faith and for the virtuosity of statement of it in terms of architectonics. That jagged and rectified line connecting the hori-zontal and the vertical outlines of the kibla wall . . . what does it say? It is arbitrary. It cuts across the corner as it rises to fill the space. There is violence in it. It roughens the powerful rising and falling arcs between the tower-piers.

In the urgency of its short, hard-bitten rhythm, the stepped diagonal offsets the bland culmination of the dome. It puts teeth into the transition between the supine horizontal and the erect vertical bastion, and speeds up the mounting copulating rhythms. Whoever does not see and feel the evidences of his senses has led a dull life.

Certainly, the steps likewise brief the eye to look for the invisible pyramid in which the domical, four-square building rises. But to me those jagged edges against the sky yell; they shout. This is a most passionate sexual piece of erotic architecture. They knew what it was all about, those two; the diminutive witty widow, richly free to be herself at the center of her privileged power, and the hardpacked, white-bearded, tough old man, wholly done with ignorance and innocence, a man experienced and alive.

It is after all good to be a civilized and a cultivated human being, male or female; and as such, men and women grow in age and in experience. It is even better to put imagination and invention to work. The violence of those jagged steps, rough against the sky, recall the fact of the mammalian animal out of which man, classified as *Homo sapiens,* hatched his human wisdom. They remind the eye that soft is soft and hard is hard. I wonder if such architectonics, which is to say, balanced and symmetrical design and construction united in harmony and function, and achieved by hard work out of a strong preference for order, do not underlie all the other sorts of man-made order: aesthetic and political and legal and . . . my God! – moral?

The mosque is crystalline. The eye, from inside or from out, sees clear through the building. In the four screen walls that fill the four high arches, barely pointed, Sinan made bold patterns of the fenestration. There are three levels of windows: the first of seven not quite identical rectangles, the largest in the center, pointed-arched on top; the second of five such windows with a round elephant's-eye at either end; the third, high up under the closing springers of the arch, of three pointed oblongs and two rounds.

In the exterior walls of the prayer hall, which are in fact curtain walls filling the spaces of the engaged but not "blind" rectangular arcade, three arches to a side, five each in the façade and the kibla wall, Sinan opened great windows. They are rectangular, not arched. He glazed those at floor level with clear glass and grilled with the Ottoman rectilinear iron bars; and provided with simply paneled wooden shutters that open and close. The lower windows can be said to be straightforward and masculine in design. But high up, Sinan cut those banks of arched and pointed windows in the screen walls. A lancet arch is tense as a round arch appears not to be. There is no need for iron grilles or wooden shutters at that height.

Today the windows are glazed with a mixture of clear and ruby glass leaded in patterns of the nineteenth century Ottoman baroque style (in the reconstruction after the fierce winter earthquake of 1894, the interior walls of the mosque were stenciled with a bad all-over chintz design). Perhaps Sinan left the walls white and filled the windows with glass as clear as air to let in the light of the sun and the moon of the Lady Mihrimah's name. Their light compounds the space in her mosque. But if he had Drunken Ibrahim design screens of stained glass to fill the high windows with the patterns and the colors of flower beds and rainbows, then the interior must have been glorious. On a sunny day, on entering, a man might have put out his hand to find it filled with God's first gift. Let there be light! So God sent the Angel Gabriel to give the Sacred Law to a man, the Prophet Mohammed, standing benighted in the desert.

The mosque is an illumination. It is a statement in architectural terms as clear as logical thought based upon an act of faith expressed in civilized and cultivated language. In the Ottoman idiom, Sinan worked to suit himself. He began with the circle inscribed within the square. He made the liturgical extensions. He raised the four corner piers to carry the calculated weight of the dome. He sprung the four high arches and closed the corner pendentives to make the circle. He built the exterior walls as rectangular engaged arcades. Then he opened all the windows.

To carry the window-filled curtain walls of the two sides, he set up four smooth monoliths of granite, freestanding, two to a side, on the line of the sides of the central space and the piers. From their immense capitals of Proconnesus marble, which he cut in most crystalline stalactites, he sprung three arches in a row between the corner piers. Each pillar, once again, is masculine, complete in itself, if need be, but here functional. Standing in place in the plan, the four do not impede but instead direct the flow of space. Above them, upon the four piers, upon the ring cornice of the four joined pendentives, Sinan raised the dome.

Behind the columns in the lateral spaces of the aisles, Sinan built galleries upon the arches of the interior colonnade of slim marble monoliths. He alternated the voussoirs, the rippled edges cut to fit into one another's concavities and convexities, of blocks of verd antique (or rosso antico, I forget, at this distance in space and time, I forget the color of the dark stone) and white marble. In the polished spandrels of Proconnesus marble, he fixed plain discs of red marble.

This exquisite gallery continues in a series of tribunes between the buttresses of the northwestern wall (joined by tunnellike arched openings cut through the heavy masonry). The portal of this mosque is both unusually and perfectly successful. Outside, under the porch, the very wide doorway is set not in a niche but, instead, flush with the façade. It is framed in a moulding of diamonded lozenges, "Turkish triangles," which are cut and fitted together in a zigzag band of marble.

In the portals of all Ottoman mosques, two niches, facing one another, are cut into the thickness of the walls. They are raised some three feet above floor level, and, in this instance, topped by ribbed conchs set on stalactites. It may have been that guardsmen stood in these niches, like secret-service men, to survey the crowds and so to guard the life of the imperial personage entering, and once inside, worshiping. Inside the portal of the Mihrimah Jami, the portal is equally wide and simple.

Along the parapet of the northeastern gallery, and in the east corner where ordinarily Sinan placed the Sultan's loge, he raised a gilt screen for the convenience of the Imperial Princess Mihrimah and her secluded and veiled ladies-in-waiting come in answer to the call to prayer. The women who did not stay at home to pray were specifically segregated in the mosques because, even in the act of worship, the sight of one bowing, kneeling, sitting, leaning forward upended would otherwise distract a man's attention even from God.

Sinan's diamond-clear, diamond-cut mosque for Mihrimah Sultan is pure — no, it is not. Nothing here is unnatural. It is the work of a supreme artificer. It is faulty. Just possibly Sinan pushed the techniques of building in stone, brick, mortar, lead, and glass too far. The five-day earthquake in the winter of the heavy snowfall of 1894 opened fissures in the high arches and the pendentives. Enough masonry fell to bring down some of the delicate pillars and the wide arches of the arcades supporting the ladies' gallery. They have been restored, but without the ripple-edged voussoirs of alternating dark and light marble. Sinan's rough stonemasonry can be reproduced, but not his fine carving. *Sui generis?* Each virtue, each genius casts its shadow, which is its flaw, the defect of the virtue. In 1965, the fissures high up in the arches and the restored pendentives reopened; the mosque will be difficult to repair without the use of steel.

Sinan never again permitted himself to build in such extravagant exuberance. After the Mihrimah's bravura display of virtuosity, he put his genius to the service of his architectonics.

14

With the building of her mosque, the Imperial Princess Mihrimah Sultan retired from the scene. She may have had nothing at all to do with the crisis that she, or her mosque, or the Lady Gülruh's wisdom may have precipitated in Sinan's private life. His first and his second ladies of the harem, the one his full-blown rose, the other his winter's sun, got on together in harmony within his great house. The crisis passed with the completion of the mosque, God's house of glass, His fortress built upon the rock of the Sixth Hill inside the land walls by the Edirné Gate.

Widowed, bereft of the Lousy Ikbal's power in the Divan, broken free of her mother's fine-spun intrigues, alone the Imperial Princess tried to take Hürrem's place behind the throne as her father's companion. Dabbling in power can be a sign of something or other, a lack, in the lives of women of a certain age. Freed and idle, she began to meddle in the man's world, where, very often, women admirably succeed. She did not.

In the forty-fifth year of Süleyman's reign, Mihrimah Sultan pushed her very old father, the Sword of Islam, into the disastrous amphibious campaign of 1565. He sent his Janissary marines against the re-established Knights Hospitalers, formerly of Rhodes, then of Malta. In those years, the Ottoman fleet controlled the Mediterranean Sea, under the command of the famous scourge of Christendom, the Grand Admiral Turgut Pasha, called Dragut by the Spaniards. Malta should have fallen, but the Knights of the Maltese Cross drove off the Turks.

But neither Dragut, nor Süleyman, nor Mihrimah Sultan took the blame. The Slaves of the Gate and the people of the imperial city knew that the Grand Vezir Fat Ali Pasha had put the evil eye on the expeditionary force as the ships sailed out of the arsenal on the Golden Horn. He had made a joke about the admiral's flying off on a trip to the isles of bliss, the holds of his cargo vessels packed full of the dangerously stimulating coffee beans from Arabia — and not the hashish of the Old Man of the Mountain's Assassins but a new mind-expanding drug called *jusquiamo*, which was the juice of the deadly nightshade, *Atropa belladonna*.

The Grand Vezir Ali Pasha was too fat to march in ceremonial parades; with the Sultan's permission, he rode a white mule. Busbecq describes him in considerable surprise as a thorough gentleman, a considerate man of delicate sensibilities and a kind heart. During the summer's epidemic of the Black Plague that year, the Grand Vezir had thoughtfully warned the Austrian ambassador to leave the city. Busbecq got away in time to take up residence nearby in the Princes' Islands of the Sea of Marmara.

Fat Ali Pasha was a jocund and a witty man. In high office, wit is out of place; but in the instance of the defeat at Malta, his ill-timed laughter did not prove fatal. He died a natural death in 1565. For his memorial Sinan designed a mosque that is elegant and plain in balanced construction, the interior given over to light and space. It stands in the country town of Babaeski, near Edirné on the Istanbul highway. Perhaps the Grand Vezir owned a country estate nearby.

Like Rüstem Pasha's, Fat Ali's mosque is octagonal in plan, and it can be seen as a small-scale full-dress rehearsal for the third of Sinan's Imperial Friday Mosques, the memorial to Selim the Sot. Süleyman's approaching death, then, must have been apparent. Certainly the miniaturist of the secret account recording his son's accession the next year painted, from memory, the Angelic Countenance gray-green — a living corpse seated upon the golden, jewel-studded throne.

After the gentleman from Dalmatia died in office, Süleyman, who had but a few months to live and who lived by act of his own will power, prepared his empire for the succession of his only living son, the Stalled Ox in Manisa. As his last Grand Vezir, the Sultan appointed Sokollu Mehmet Pasha, a Slave of the Gate, a *damat*, a man of sixty-two, whom he had trained, tested, tried, and watched for thirty years. In 1535 Süleyman had received the man as part of the sequestered and then confiscated properties of the humiliated and hanged Defterdar Iskender Chelebi. Ironically the strangled favorite, Grand Vezir-Serasker Ibrahim Pasha, who totally destroyed himself in the exercise of his shared power, bequeathed the Sultan a successor who inherited the absolute power and responsibility that he lacked, and with it did his best to rule the Ottoman Empire according to Süleyman's impossibly high standards.

The new Grand Vezir was born the son of a village priest in Bosnia. He entered Ottoman captivity either as a prisoner of war, in which case the Sultan's *penjik* appraiser found him second rate, or as an independent slave-raider's prize, in which case Iskender Chelebi, a connoisseur, chose to purchase him in the slave market. Converted, he was named Mehmet and, to distinguish him from all the other namesakes of the Prophet, he was called Sokollu, the One from the Falcon's Eyrie, which was the name of the castle in the Balkan hill town of his birth and capture.

He got his training and his education in the excellent private schools maintained for his young slaves by the Defterdar in his great estates. As one of the disgraced and hanged man's five or six thousand slaves, he reverted to the possession of the Sultan when he was thirty-three or thirty-four, in the year that Süleyman was forty-two. He replaced his former owner as the Sultan's Defterdar. Ten years later, in 1546, Sokollu Mehmet Pasha was appointed to the Divan as Kapudan Pasha, the Captain Admiral of the Fleet. Either of these high offices would have come as the culmination in the careers of any other admirable Slave of the Gate in the hierarchy of the Ruling Institution. But Süleyman gave them to Sokollu Mehmet Pasha as part of his long-range strategic planning to prepare this greatest of the grand vezirs to maintain the standards of the Ottoman Empire in its Golden Age after his death.

In 1562, when Sokollu Mehmet Pasha was fifty-nine years old, Süleyman's granddaughter, Esmahan Gevher Sultan, aged seventeen, demanded him in marriage. Named All the Sovereign Names of God, and called Jewel because of her witty sayings, the Imperial Princess was short of stature and very plain of face. Sokollu Mehmet Pasha, who was tall and thin, and by that time gray-bearded, had to put aside two wives of his own choice and all his sons and daughters to obey his master and to marry the Daughter of Osman, one of the daughters of Selim the Sot. The Sultan dowered her generously. Sokollu Mehmet Pasha, by then, was himself a very wealthy Slave of the Gate.

Upon the ruins of the Byzantine emperors' great palace, Sinan built them a great house of many pavilions in a high walled garden. It stood on the southeastern side of the Hippodrome on the gentle slope of the First Hill down to the Sea of Marmara, opposite the Palace of Ibrahim. (In 1609, Sultan Ahmet had it demolished to erect the Blue Mosque.) From there the view is splendid and the sea air was famous for its health-giving purity. Sinan built them a summer palace on the Asian shore of the Bosphorus, another at Eyüp at the head of the Golden Horn by the Sweet Waters of Europe, and also many country estates. In 1565, Sokollu Mehmet Pasha was well prepared; he was ready "to bear the burden."

On May Day of that year, the Sultan and the Grand Vezir set out from the imperial city on the road to Hungary. It was Süleyman's thirteenth and last campaign. They took with them, as usual, all the lesser vezirs of the Divan, and the two Judges of the Armies of the Domains of War and of Peace.

In the army's first camp on the line of march, they pitched the imperial tent under the arches of the aqueduct that Sinan had just completed. Hammer reports that Süleyman contemplated this feat of engineering with pride and joyful admiration. Crippled by gout, the old man could not sit a horse. He rode in a carriage less comfortable than our trailers. The Sultan did

not get out even for the meetings of the Divan. On horseback, the Grand
Vezir, the Grand Mufti, the lesser vezirs, and the two Judges gathered round
the carriage drawn up in a field at the edge of the road. The military highway
from Istanbul to Edirné is still rough going. Sokollu Mehmet Pasha rode
ahead with a crew of roadbuilders to smooth the worst of the ruts and
potholes.

At Büyükchekmejé, a village in the neck of an inlet from the Sea of
Marmara, he found Sinan at work building the new bridge. It is one of the
great bridges of the world. Begun two years earlier, the masonry piers and
arches and the approaches may have been complete, but not the roadbed.
Sinan had a day or two to fit timber cradles into the new masonry spans to
shore them up; he laid down planks upon them and, it seems probable, spread
a thick layer of sawdust to cushion the passage of the Sultan's carriage. Sinan
finished the bridge in 1567, a year after Süleyman's death.

In September 1563, the Sultan had gone hunting for migratory water birds
at Halkaderé, the Ringed Valley, inland from Büyükchekmejé, the "Great
Coming and Going" of Waters," which is about what the name of the inlet
means. Streams from the deforested hills run down into the shallow, marshy,
and almost landlocked cove. Ten years earlier, Busbecq, in the last stage of his
first journey from Vienna, had crossed the existing stone bridges built by the
Romans and the Byzantines, restored and rebuilt again and again. He camped
by the "two lovely bays" and "feasted on most delicious fish, caught before
our eyes." The country gentleman from Flanders remarked that "if these
places were cultivated, and nature were to receive the slightest assistance from
art, I doubt whether in the whole world anything could be found to surpass
them. But the very ground seems to mourn its fate," and in pathetic fallacy,
"to complain of the neglect of its barbarous master." The observant young
man was ignorant. Too many centuries of barbarian invaders had passed by
that mournful ground on their way to lay siege to the walled city on the
Golden Horn. It was the Ottoman policy to cut down the forests and to lay
waste the approaches so as not to encourage the Christian enemies. The
ever-present threat of an united European last crusade determined Ottoman
foreign policy for a century after the Fall of Constantinople.

The hanged Defterdar Iskender Chelebi had owned a country estate at
Büyükchekmejé. Süleyman kept the confiscated hunting box for his own use.
He was in residence on September 20, 1563, when the equinoctial storms
began with a cloud burst that lasted twenty-four hours. Lightning struck
sixty-eight buildings in the capital, fifteen miles away. (Since Ben Franklin's
practical discovery, grounded lightning rods have been fixed to all the *alems*
of the high domes and the minarets of Sinan's and the other architects'
mosques.) The streams of the Ringed Valley turned into torrents. Flood
waters brought down uprooted bushes and trees, the timbers of demolished

sheds and houses, and the drowned bodies of sheep, goats, cattle, horses, and, as it is usual, of men and their families. The detritus clogged the arches of the existing stone bridge; a great weight of flood water rose behind the barrier.

The water rose inside Iskender Chelebi's hunting box. Süleyman would have drowned had not one of his powerful slave soldiers picked him up, slung the gouty old man across his shoulder, and climbed up into the rafters. Perched on a tiebeam, Süleyman waited until the bridge gave and the flood subsided. Back in the city, the Sultan allocated the equivalent of twenty-five million gold dollars to restore the disaster caused by the cloud burst. Selim the Sot gave Sinan another sum of money equal in purchasing power to twenty million more of those obsolete American gold dollars to complete the bridges. Today they are bypassed and a causeway carries the heavy traffic of the modern military highway that goes through Edirné to the Balkan frontiers.

Sinan designed a stone bridge to withstand any subsequent flood. It is in fact not one but four linked bridges in a row. The first (from Istanbul) is 519 feet long, with seven pointed arches, the highest 23 feet from mean water level to the keystone. The bridge rises from the masonry approaches on the bank to a peak, and then the roadbed descends to an artificial island, irregular in shape, grass-grown within thick and solid stone embankments. The next bridge, likewise camel-backed, has seven arches and is 448 feet long; the third, of five arches, is 335 feet long; and the fourth and largest, of nine arches, the highest rising forty feet above the water, carries the road the remaining 606 feet to the further bank. In all, the masonry bridge of dressed and carved limestone blocks is 20 feet wide between the yard-high parapets, and 2,097 feet long.

When floods bring down trees and timbers to clog the spans between the piers, the water rises above the level of the artificial islands. Then the currents pull the detritus clear of the arches of the four linked bridges and wash the flood-borne waste out to sea. The water level sinks; the pressure on the masonry piers subsides. Automatically swept clear of the logjam, the bridges stand and the waiting traffic moves from shore to shore. Sinan put the flood to work to counteract its own destructive forces.

Today only men on foot, a local farmer with his horse and cart, and I cross the bridge. One sunny day in June 1965, four centuries after Süleyman crossed the unfinished bridge, I saw a tethered cow grazing on one of Sinan's green and level islands in the current. I found, when I went down to get a close look at the stonemasonry of the spans, that he had carved a birdhouse in a stone block built into one of the piers (it was empty). Lichens and mosses, gray, yellow, and green, cover the weathered surfaces; snapdragons, valerians, and seeding wild grasses had rooted in the crumbling mortar; but the structure is sound, and all the detail is as Sinan would have it.

A bridge may be a matter of engineering rather than of architecture, but nothing man-made is more beautiful or more moving than a bridge across flowing water. Sinan was pleased with his work. On a stone post at the farther end of it, he signed his name to it: Joseph Son of the Slave of God. It is not the official Islamic name given to the enslaved and converted tribute youth; it is not his Janissary name. He clearly did not give a hoot about his confused biographers. Who knows? It may have been that with the death of Süleyman, he felt himself released from a contract, from a bondage, and as a free man chose to sign himself Yusuf Abdullah, and not Sinan abdür-Mennan.

It must have been a sight to see, the miles and miles of Janissaries, red, blue, white, plumed, and glittering, marching in close formation, eight men abreast, to the sound of the big drums and the little drums, the cymbals, the triangles, and the hautbois, in wave after wave, rising and falling as they marched across the bridge. The Sultan's matched horses, a dozen teamed, harnessed in tandem, strained at the harness as they pulled the heavy gilt carriage up the ascent, and then leaned back to brake the descent. The carriage was surrounded by gold-clad and shining pages of the palace school, and by gentlemen-in-waiting, the Sword-Bearer, the Standard-Bearer with his thrice-crossed gold staff of seven horsetails; and by the crescent-plumed veterans of the Color Guard, the Honor Guard, the Sultan's Own Life Guard, all of them reflected in the slow and placid water as they marched up and then marched down again and again and again under the blue cloud-driven sky. In the middle of the bridge, on a peak, Süleyman called a halt (or so I say).

From his coach, he looked out, gray of countenance, if not to smile, then to show his pleasure. Sinan, work-stained – it can be very hot in May and June – would then have stepped up to the carriage to salute, to kiss the hand, and then to talk things over with the Sultan. Today fishermen hang their nets on poles along the beaches of the inlet to dry in the sunshine. Sinan built a caravansary at the end of the bridge on the near shore, and with it a small mosque. In 1565, the limestone, fresh from the quarries, was yellow; the hills are still green. The Sultan and Sinan came to the end of their talk; Süleyman ordered his coachmen to drive on across the unfinished bridge. On his signet, which is now in the Topkapi Museum, the Royal Chief Architect had engraved, "Sinan the poor and humble."

It took Süleyman's carriage forty-nine days to get to Belgrade, the fortress in the fork of the Danube and the Sava, the site of his first victory in his first campaign forty-six years earlier. Brigands, bands of Christian outlaws and highwaymen, klephts, attacked the train of pack animals. Those who did not get away were hanged and left hanging in gibbets along the line of march. It rained hard that summer. Above Belgrade, the pontoon bridge across the swollen river broke apart; the camels carrying the imperial silken tent were swept downstream and lost. From then on Süleyman made do with the Grand Vezir's less sumptuous tent.

When the army reached the Drava, it was found that floods had washed out a span of the timber bridge built by Sinan forty years earlier. It took seventeen days to build a floating bridge of one hundred and eighteen pontoons. The Sultan, jolted out of temper, left the carriage to board an imperial barge awaiting him. A fragment of the carved and gilt prow of the white yacht is now on display in the Naval Museum at Beshiktash. Escorted by three war galleys, the barge had sailed out of the arsenal in the Golden Horn, up the Bosphorus, across the Black Sea, up the Danube, and into the Drava. Süleyman on board watched his armies cross the pontoon bridge; he noted the date in his journal: 16 July 1566.

As they began their final march, the Janissaries took to breaking ranks and, as in huntsmen's battues, set fire to Christian villages to smoke out and capture whole families of slaves. The Sultan ordered his Grand Vezir to hang the offending slave soldiers in the embers at the scene of the crime. The aging, aching, and in fact dying Sultan impatiently gave way again and again to bouts of imperious bad temper. He ordered a tightening of discipline. The Grand Vezir Sokollu Mehmet Pasha humored him and took over the command.

Letters arrived from John Sigismund Zápolya, the tributary Prince of Translyvania and the Sultan's choice as puppet King of Hungary for some future date. Süleyman despatched the imperial barge to bring "his son" to kiss the hand of the Padishah. The Prince, strong in his claim to the disputed iron crown of Saint Stephen and indeed equal in his armorial quarterings to any Hapsburg, was the Lutheran protégé of the Grand Turk in the dispute for the nonexistent throne with the Roman Catholic Holy Roman Emperor. Uncertain of his own majesty, the twenty-six-year-old Prince and putative King refused to salaam in the Divan to the Grand Vezir. Sokollu Mehmet Pasha was but a slave not to be recognized as the equal, let alone the superior, of the young man in whose veins ran Polish, Hungarian, French, Swedish, Bohemian, and gouts of other European royal bloods.

To get the business over he agreed to an interview with the Grand Vezir to be conducted on horseback in the open field. He got down from his high horse in front of the Grand Vezir's tent, in which Süleyman received "his son" ceremoniously, heaped upon him gorgeous presents, and promised him the Hungarian throne. The Sultan then requested the Grand Vezir to arrange a state banquet. Sokollu Mehmet Pasha demurred. He argued that the pallid weakling Prince, a stranger to the luxuries and the delicacies of the Ottoman imperial kitchen, would suffer stomach upsets. The rumor then would spread among the Hungarians that the Grand Turk had fed poison to King John II of Hungary, his guest at table. Thus he would destroy the sobering effect upon the Holy Roman Emperor of the Sultan's diplomatic gesture. The young man did not get the iron crown.

On August 5, 1566, the Sultan and the Grand Vezir, by then wholly acknowledged in absolute power, arrived at Szigetvár. It had taken them ninety-seven days to bring the full force of Ottoman power to bear on this pinpoint, a castle and a fortified town built on piles in marshy islands in the Hungarian swamplands of the Almas River. Süleyman left his barge for the tents of the Grand Vezir which were pitched on a mound in the water meadows beyond the reach of arrows and cannon balls. He watched the yoked water buffaloes drag the big bronze guns through the green fields to their emplacements. The greatest of the cannons was called the Penetrator.

Szigetvár is not far from Mohács, where, forty years earlier on his third campaign, Süleyman had won the clearest and the greatest victory of his reign. The castle and town were being defended by Count Nicholas Zrinyi (1508-66), Ban of Croatia in the Holy Roman Empire and one of the successful defenders of Vienna. He opposed the Sultan's choice of John II Sigismund Zápolya as the rightful king of the nonexistent kingdom of Hungary. He was a Roman Catholic Croatian nobleman in the highest of high style of the late Renaissance. He chose a flamboyant death for himself, and so he merits a brief mention in the encyclopedias. But as a threat to the power and the glory of the Ottoman Empire of Sultan Süleyman the Magnificent, surely he was no more dangerous than a thorn in the flesh, his castle in the marshes no more than a flyspeck on the map.

In the library of the Topkapi Museum there is a most beautiful book, a delicately bound calligraphic manuscript illustrated with classic Ottoman miniatures: *Nuzheti-Esrar el-Ehba der Seferi Sigetvar,* "Account of Secret Events during the Campaign of Szigetvár." Dated 1568, it was written by Ahmet Feridun Pasha, an eyewitness. At the time of the campaign, he was the confidential secretary of the Grand Vezir Sokollu Mehmet Pasha, to whom he dedicated his history. One of the miniature paintings gives a bird's-eye view of the castle and the upper and lower villages, each one walled in on three irregularly oblong, man-made islands in the waterways among the marches. Time has darkened the rippling water in the miniature, which was once polished silver but is now oxidized and it is sooty black. But all the other mineral colors are still bright – the flames rising from the burning houses, for instance, are yellow, orange, and flame-red.

On one of the islands, Zrinyi's castle of Szigetvár is seen to have been a donjon-keep inside a pentagon of five bastions, surrounded by three concentric moats inside outer ramparts. This fortress island was connected with the other two by means of narrow stone bridges crossing the once burnished, now blackened silver water. On August 5, Count Zrinyi began his destructive defense of the castle by setting fire to the evacuated houses of the villages on the other two islands, so as to give the Janissary bowmen, fire-hurlers, and riflemen no shelter. He then put out red banners flying from his tower, which he had plated with polished bronze. By August 19 the Janissaries had penetrated the outer ramparts of the castle, but Zrinyi held out inside his pentagon and his bronze donjon.

The Sultan, hoping to stop the slaughter, offered to cede Croatia to the Hungarian count if he would capitulate. Zrinyi refused. Süleyman and the Grand Vezir then ordered Feridun the scribe to write out proclamations in German, in Hungarian, and in Croat. The archers shot the messages bound around arrows over the battlements. If any of Zrinyi's few remaining men knew how to read, they read, it may have been, between the lines and understood the polylingual offering of honorable terms of surrender to be propaganda. None deserted to the terrible Turk.

On September 5 the Janissary engineers successfully exploded a mine under the main bastion of the pentagon. Sultan Süleyman in his tent saw the flash; he heard the blast; he felt the shock. The soft ground quivered, but Count Zrinyi would not yield the donjon.

Süleyman died that night "of decrepitude, of dysentery, of apoplexy, of a heart attack" — of furious, impotent old age. Gutted, stuffed, stitched together, and embalmed, he was dressed in his Ottoman imperial robes of state. His leaden face was painted; his imperial turban, jeweled and plumed, was set on his head (held upright by some means or other). Behind thin silken curtains in the innermost pavilion of his Grand Vezir's tents, he was seated, to stiffen into place, upright upon the golden throne, the one like a square chair, high-backed, enameled in pentagonal repetitive patterns and jeweled with cushion-cut rubies and emeralds. It had accompanied him from the palace. Upon his throne, Süleyman the Magnificent ruled for forty-six years alive; and for forty-six days more, he reigned dead.

Four men were in on the secret: the Sultan's anonymous physician; Jafer Agha, the Sword-Bearer to the Sultan and First Gentleman of the Bedchamber; Ahmet Feridun, the Grand Vezir's private secretary; and the Grand Vezir himself, Sokollu Mehmet Pasha. They did the necessary work. They buried the Sultan's viscera under the floor of the tent and spread the great Persian carpet (such as the one, and it may well have been that one, known as the Anhalt carpet now hanging in the Metropolitan Museum of Art in New York) over the disturbed earth. Perhaps someone thought to burn jasmine wax in a jade incense burner, or to sprinkle rose-scented water from one of the long-necked, jeweled, and enameled golden perfume casters now on display in the Treasury of the Topkapi Museum.

Then, still quietly by night, the four men washed themselves and dressed in robes and kaftans. They would not be black (according to Busbecq), which was considered to be a mean and an unlucky color, ominous of disaster and evil; nor would they be purple, highly esteemed except in times of war when it was believed to be ominous of bloody death; nor green, the sacred color of the Prophet, preferred by Süleyman. Probably they wore state robes in one or another of the fortunate colors, light blue, dark blue, violet, or what Busbecq calls "mouse-color." The Grand Vezir put on his usual white, as did the Grand Mufti Ebüsuud, who surely had to be taken into the secret before long. Who carried in the trays? Who ate the Sultan's food?

In the morning while it was still dark, Sokollu Mehmet Pasha despatched his secretary to inform Prince Selim in Kutahya that he was, as from September 7, 1566, the Sultan Khan, the Padishah, and to advise him to make haste to Istanbul, and to gird himself with the Sword of the Prophet, and with the Sword of Osman at the shrine of the saint at Eyüp. Surely not alone, but with an Honor Guardsman or two, Feridun set off on the finest of the horses from the imperial stables, carrying letters written in the Grand Vezir's hand, known to Prince Selim, and probably with some sort of positive proof such as Süleyman's own imperial seal. It would not be the Sultan's ring which had to stay in place on the little finger of the right hand of Süleyman regnant, to be kissed in audiences of fealty and during these forty-six days, to sparkle or to glow through the silken curtains from a distance. Selim the Survivor knew better than to trust any man. He had to have positive proof.

In the morning, outside Szigetvár, the Grand Vezir allowed it to be known that the Padishah had suffered an indisposition in the night. The physician in attendance upon him had ordered the cancellation of all the imperial engagements. The Sultan would receive no visitors for the next few days. Sokollu Mehmet Pasha, Serasker and Grand Vezir, took over the command of the siege.

On September 8, in his bronze tower, Count Nicholas Zrinyi heard the sound of the Janissary woodwinds and drums, and they came closer. He looked out from his high donjon and saw a column of men in the familiar red and blue uniforms, white-capped, marching across a narrow stone bridge that ended at the portcullis of castle. Six hundred of his three thousand two hundred men remained alive with him. One of them survived. According to his account, Zrinyi, with admirable tranquility of spirit and unbroken dignity, calmly and quietly prepared for his last hours as master of his own house. He dressed himself in silken garments of the puffed and slashed high style, a doublet cinched in at the waist above knee breeches, all of black velvet beribboned in black satin, cuffed and collared with white lace. He hung a chain of massive gold around his neck. To his wide-brimmed black velvet hat, he pinned a white plume with a diamond of the finest water and of great price. He pocketed a hundred Hungarian gold sequins so that the man who robbed his corpse could have no cause to complain of him. He chose the most ancient of his four swords, all of them awards for valor on past battlefields of honor, this one encrusted with gold. It was, he remarked, the sword he wished to carry when he appeared before the Prince of Peace on Judgment Day. Come to think of it, because he died in bed, Süleyman had not been translated, as a hero and a martyr, a true Gazi, to Paradise. He had already begun his long, slow journey into Islamic limbo.

Then, fully dressed according to his own ideas of order, Count Zrinyi, preceded by his standard-bearer, and followed by a squire carrying his shield, went down the spiraling staircase, unarmored, unhelmed, at the head of his six hundred men to open his own portcullis. He had one of his men throw a bomb, a kind of hand grenade, to clear the opposite bank of the castle moat. Then he ordered the drawbridge lowered.

Like lightning, or like a shooting star, he threw himself upon the sea of red and blue and white-capped Janissaries. Zrinyi fell among them with two bullets in him. An arrow pinned his plumed and diamonded black velvet cap to his head. At the sight of such courage, the Janissaries cried out "Allah! " and "Allah! " and "Allah! "

On their red shoulders, they carried the Hungarian, who still had life in him, to their *agha*. He ordered Zrinyi to be stretched out face down upon the gun carriage of the great bronze Penetrator, and struck off his head.

In the vaults of the donjon the Janissaries forced the locks of the iron-bound coffers of the count's treasure of gold plate and gold coins. Zrinyi had set a booby trap for them. The looters, in forcing the treasure chests, had fired a spark that lit a fuse that led to the powder magazine next to the strong room. Three thousand of the Janissaries were blown to bits. Those outside, who survived, dismembered the huddle of women, girls, and boys; the men were already dead. The Grand Vezir Sokollu Mehmet Pasha strode among the enraged slave soldiers to beat them off with a bull whip. Never in his thirteen years as the ruler of the Ottoman Empire did the Janissaries make further trouble for him.

In the Sultan's name, the Grand Vezir sent off to the Hapsburg Holy Roman Emperor in Vienna Count Nicholas Zrinyi's pickled head, his arrow-pierced black velvet hat, his white plume intact, the diamond still in place. The chain of massive gold had fallen from his severed neck. It had to be sent separately, with letters to announce the victory of Szigetvár.

Sokollu Mehmet Pasha put the engineers and all the able-bodied Janissaries to work on the rebuilding of the castle and the walls. But on the ninth day after Süleyman's death, the eighth after the victory, the Slaves of the Gate in all the ranks of the hierarchy began to speculate aloud. Why did their Padishah sulk in his tent? Had they not brought him triumph over his enemies?

In full Divan, the Grand Vezir explained that their Padishah, suffering the humiliations of a bad attack of gout, knew himself to be too short of temper to risk spoiling this time of joy. However, he promised to lead the faithful in prayers at the Friday midday services to thank God for the victory given them — as soon as his good men had finished building the mosque inside the restored fortress.

On September 24, the new Sultan Selim II Khan, son of Sultan Süleyman Khan, crossed the Bosphorus in another imperial barge. He had to borrow fifty thousand gold pieces from his sister Mihrimah Sultan to buy from the veteran Janissaries and the ten thousand cadets in Istanbul the right to enter his New Palace. He also had to distribute charitable largesse at the shrines of Eyüp, the Prophet's Standard-Bearer, after the ceremony of the girding on of the two swords; and at the tombs of his great-great-grandfather, Mehmet the Conqueror; of his great-grandfather, Bayazid the Sainted; and his grandfather, Selim the Grim. Then he set out on the road to Edirné and on up into the Balkans.

Before the mosque in Szigetvár had been completed, Sokollu Mehmet Pasha struck camp. I take it that by then all the grandees of the ruling and the religious hierarchies, and all the officers of the Janissaries and the Sipahis suspected that much more than gout ailed the Padishah. However, it was done, the Grand Vezir, the physician, the sword-bearer, and, surely, Süleyman's body servants, got the dead but reigning Sultan into a canopied, latticed, and curtained litter. Surely the chosen men – they must all have been wrestling champions, young Janissaries of the Sultan's Own Life Guard – shouldering the palanquin must have been taken into the secret; for otherwise they would soon have learned the difference between a dying and a long-dead man. The Sultan did not shift his weight; he did not groan when one of the men in the relays of eight misstepped or stumbled on the march through the green and forested hills and valleys; or when they crossed the rivers. Surrounding them the army of one hundred fifty thousand silently marched home.

Sokollu Mehmet Pasha pitched camp on the edge of a forest in a high pasture on a hill four days march from Belgrade. On October 24, Feridun brought word that Sultan Selim Khan awaited him in Belgrade. On the edge of the forest in the night, the Grand Vezir had the dead body, laid out straight, wrapped in a shroud, put into its imperial coffin and set on – what? Sawhorses, spread with a pall? He had the catafalque placed under a silken canopy out in the open field, and at the head, he planted a post in the earth to carry the weight of the jeweled imperial turban.

Four hours before dawn, the cantors began to chant in strophe and antistrophe, two hundred to the right of the silken pavilion, two hundred to the left of it: "All dominion perishes, and the last hour awaits each one and all mankind." And "The everlasting God alone lives on untouched by time and death."

The Janissaries, pulling up their blue trousers, buttoning their red tunics, capping their shaven heads, spilled out of their tents in the field below. Illuminated by lamps inside it, the funeral canopy glowed in the night against the dark forest. The Janissaries silently closed in around the bier of their magnificent Sultan. They joined the muezzins in chanting "The Opening," the Islamic act of faith: "Praise belongs to God, the Lord of all Being, the All-Merciful, the All-Compassionate, the Master of the Day of Doom. Thee only we serve; to Thee alone we pray for succour. Guide us in the straight path, the path of those whom Thou hast blessed, not of those against whom Thou art wrathful, nor of those who are astray."

To them at daybreak came the eleventh Son of Osman chatting with his court of boon companions. He wore black. By the catafalque, watching the imperial progress, the Grand Vezir stood with his secretary, Feridun Bey, who remarked (I paraphrase): "He has not paid the Janissaries their perquisite donative. Had you not better step forward to suggest to him that he do so, and at once? He runs the risk of trouble. The men are wild with grief and anger."

"No, we shall stay out of it," Sokollu Mehmet Pasha replied. "I do not know for a fact whether or not I still hold office. He may have already fulfilled his part of the secret bargain. I may have already been replaced by his tutor, Lala Mustafa Pasha." This man had accompanied Selim.

The new Sultan waddled across the meadow grass among the Janissaries and the Sipahis, sullen with mourning bands cutting across their foreheads on the cuffs of their sleeve-like white felt caps, or wound into the folds of their plumeless turbans. He made his way unsteadily among soldiers weeping silently, their eyes wide open upon him. The line of mourners filing past the bier wound up the hill and down again, serpentine, from the edge of the forest.

The new Sultan, puffing and blowing, stopped to catch his breath at the foot of his dead father's coffin. Then he stretched out his plump arms, and raised his hands, open, palms uppermost, in the gesture to bring down God's mercy upon his father's soul already forty-seven days gone on the journey. Then Selim II went away again to change his robes for the ceremony of the kissing of the hand in fealty.

In Feridun's manuscript the anonymous miniature court painter has recorded the scene. He was an artist, and he was an ironic man. Of it he made a formal pattern built up of squares and rounds out in the open under high pale blue hills as denuded and as wrinkled as the skins of any of the great pachyderms, tufted with regimented blades of grass. For the throne, the high-backed, square golden armchair, patterned in pentagons, studded with cabochons, the Grand Vezir had raised a stiff backdrop of crimson silk, worked at the top with patterns of dark blue and violet, all embroidered in gold. Over the Sultan's head, he had opened the upright Central Asian parasol of majesty, a domical canopy of violet brocaded around in lozenges of gold, the lower edge gold braided and bordered with powder blue and crimson tasseled; and on top, with black and gold, crimson and gold, and a round of black topped by a solid gold ball.

In front of the throne, over the Persian carpet spread on the grass, the Grand Vezir set up the two taut rectangular awnings, one of blue silk centered by a solid gold medallion, the edge of the flat oblong fringed with alternating scarlet and green stripes. The dark sky of this one is embroidered with a flight of symbolic royal birds of good omen, peacock-like, phoenix-like, clearly Chinese birds. The second rectangle — both of them tilt perilously, although there is no wind apparent — held up on the thinnest of exactly vertical crimson corner staves, is mauve, centered by gold in a classic Islamic medallion, cornered in dark blue, fringed in crimson and light blue, and embroidered with a circling flight of what appear to be geese, alarmed, hurtling into the air.

In the miniature, Sultan Selim II Khan sits off-center on the right-hand page. He is plump, no longer rubicund but pale of face, fair of beard, blue-eyed, dressed in sleeves of crimson, a robe of white and gold brocade, and a long, open, collarless, sleeveless kaftan, floor-length, tailored of heavy blue silk brocaded with patterns of floating Chinese clouds. On his head he wears the round imperial turban, a blue enameled gold phoenix feather, the emblem of immortality, thrust upright in the folds at the peak, and a cascade of limp black heron's feathers falling as a sign of mourning. He sits, arms akimbo, the knuckles of his fists planted on his fat thighs; he pays no attention to the veteran Janissary officer of the Honor Guard caught in the act of kneeling to kiss the hem of the kaftan. He stares into space — somewhere off into the lower left-hand corner. The stiff white tuft of plumes of another bowing officer points out the line of the abstracted gaze. The Sultan and all the Slaves of the Gate standing in rigidly hierarchical court etiquette and rank are listening in almost intolerable tension to the noise of grief and fury of the mourning Janissaries outside the scope of the miniaturist.

The round Sultan on the square throne sits disconsolate, the stigmata of dismay upon his face. Selim the Sot was a thoughtful man; he was an honest man; he was a humble man, well aware of his unworthiness. And he was frivolous; he knew himself to be unfit to rule, a most miserable man alive to the contempt of the hierarchy and of the Janissaries.

When the imperial body riding in the Sultan's coach, relaxed in death and coffined, arrived at the bridge five months after Süleyman had crossed the inlet of Büyükchekmejé on his last campaign, Sinan stood waiting. The Royal Chief Architect accompanied his master on the last stage of the journey. There was no need to spread sawdust on the unfinished roadbed of the bridge.

At the Edirné Gate in the land walls on the Sixth Hill, Sinan rode ahead of the coach in order to prepare the waiting mausoleum on the Third Hill. He had built the tomb to receive not the man but the idea of Sultan Süleyman the Great, the Lawgiver, the last of the Sons of Osman in the Golden Age.

There the Royal Chief Architect rolled back the carpets and lifted the stones of the pavement. He saw the grave dug in the earth beneath the floor. Sultan Selim II Khan, son of Sultan Süleyman Khan, scanted the ceremonies to bury his dead father, so as not again to have to watch the people of the imperial city measure him against the memory of the magnificent old man. Then he hurried back to Edirné and the palace on the island in the river. Sinan, Mihrimah Sultan, and the Grand Vezir Sokollu Mehmet Pasha closed the grave.

Before her death in 1578, Süleyman's only daughter, the moon to his sun, chose not to be entombed beside her husband, the Grand Vezir Rüstem Pasha in his tiled mausoleum behind the Shehzadé's Mosque; nor with her honored brothers, the Princes Mehmet and Jehangir, in the monument like a bower in Paradise that Sinan had built for the dead Shehzadé; nor, of course, in the far-distant *türbés* of her dishonored brothers, the Princes Mustafa and Bayazid, the one in Bursa, the other beside a dusty road in the wilds of eastern Asia Minor; nor in the tomb of the three boys, Süleyman's sons, the Princes Mahmud, Murad, and Abdullah, buried beside their grandfather Selim the Grim; nor in Selim the Sot's most sumptuous mausoleum that stands next to Haghia Sophia (by then it was already crowded with dead nephews and nieces); nor in her mother Haseki Hürrem's solitary arbor of spring blossoms; nor in a *türbé* of her own behind the Mosque of Mihrimah Sultan. She lies beside her father, eclipsed in somber majesty behind the Süleymaniyé.

Selim the Sot reconfirmed his father's Grand Vezir in office. Sokollu Mehmet Pasha ruled while the Sultan reigned. The stern and august Slave of the Gate upheld the standards set by Süleyman the Magnificent throughout the eight years of the reign of the Stalled Ox, and he survived in office to rule the empire for the first five years of the succeeding reign of the epileptic Murad III.

Selim the Fair, as his court of boon companions called him, was intelligent. The plump, red-golden-bearded, blue-eyed, and melancholy man of forty-two knew himself to be incapable of wielding either the Sword of Osman or the Sword of the Prophet in battle. He did not dare to lead the Janissaries into Holy War. In his way, Sultan Selim II Khan is to be seen as a modern man, helplessly spindled upon his reality. He was begotten in love by a monument upon a joyous witch. He was, if Freud has the truth in him, cradled in a case history, and launched, like the infant Moses, upon the course of current events. But unlike Moses, his God of all the ninety-nine beautiful names was the God of the Beggars. He drank perhaps to keep up his courage. But he knew his faults and his failings; humorously he drank from the shell of a coco-de-mer, not a phallic but (say) a bollock symbol; it held quarts and quarts; he had it set in jeweled gold.

Back from his father's burial, fortified by a double gobletful of his favorite Cyprian wine, he rejoined the Lady Nûrûbanû in Edirné where she had gone part way to meet him on his return from the frightening enthronement in the fields by the forests outside Belgrade. Then Selim II petulantly refused to bribe the Janissaries. To get into the palace in Istanbul, he had borrowed money from his sister Mihrimah Sultan to pay off the cadets and the old slave soldiers; but once safe, as he thought, in the palace in Edirné, he put down his foot — if he did not stamp it — and refused their bakshish to the fighting men. Rightly, he knew their perquisite donative to be no better than blackmail; and logically he reasoned that their bought-and-paid-for loyalty had no value. After the ringleaders of his father's Janissaries, now in revolt, had battered down the gates of the Hunting Palace on the island in the Tunja river, and had nearly flushed the Lady Nûrûbanû out of her bath in the inner courtyard, Selim II, terrified and trembling, gave in to them; and he paid the price.

Then, having thought about it, Selim went further. If bribery could buy the loyalty of the Slaves of the Gate in the Ruling Institution, he might as well ensure the good will of the Ulema in the Religious Institution. He gave splendid gifts to the Grand Mufti Ebüsuud, and raised his emoluments by one hundred *akchés* to seven hundred a day. He gave robes of honor of gold brocade to the two Judges of the Armies of the Domains of War and of Peace; and each man got a gift of thirty thousand *akchés*. The Judge of Istanbul got a robe of honor of angora mohair, and ten thousand *akchés*. The Judge of Baghdad got a similar kaftan and eight thousand *akchés*. The chancellors of the colleges of sacred jurisprudence in the three great universities of Istanbul — at Ayasofya, at Fatih, and at the Süleymaniyé — hithertofore paid ten *akchés* a day, were given purses of seven thousand. The professors got six thousand each.

Thus Selim began the systematic corruption of the Ulema, the high and the low courts of justice, and the faculties of the universities. At the end of the empire, there had grown up among the families of the pashas a ruling aristocracy of inheritance, with power and privilege handed down from father to son. The men of the learned professions likewise had formed themselves into an intelligentsia that was not necessarily intellectually honest but was very rich. The professors in their academic circles passed their chairs down through the generations along with the sins of the fathers. Their salaries from sacred funds of the Religious Institution were exempt from taxation. They speculated with the properties of the pious foundations; and being custodians of the law of God and of man, they allowed no change to be made.

Selim the Sot interfered in the Grand Vezir's government no more than once or twice. On January 8, 1569, when he was out hunting with his court — he could bring down a skylark with his bow and arrow — he trotted up to Sokollu Mehmet Pasha, blurted out that he had appointed Lala Mustafa Pasha to the Divan, and galloped off. He was afraid of both men, and he knew they were enemies. But earlier, when he had thought his chances of survival were slim, he had followed his tutor's advice and promised to reward him when he became Sultan.

Selim the Sot got drunk. He rode under the twisted serpent column, which now stands beheaded in the Hippodrome but which then stood intact in the forecourt of Haghia Sophia. He stood up in his stirrups, raised his ceremonial mace of jade and rock crystal, took a swing, and knocked off one of the Delphic oracle's snakes' heads. That year an invasion of serpents plagued the city.

The Sultan organized a summer festival in the Hippodrome. He had the usual invitations sent out to all but one of his neighboring sovereigns. The uninvited Prince of Muscovy, Czar Ivan the Terrible, turned his enmity against the Ottoman Empire. Otherwise the festival proved to be a great success. Selim was especially delighted with a Turkish acrobat, an agile man of mature years who danced the tightrope strung between the two obelisks, the one Egyptian, the other Byzantine. To reward the man, the Sultan called him over to the imperial tribune, and in the expansive gesture of a caliph in the *Arabian Nights' Entertainments,* granted him the fulfillment of any single wish. The Turkish acrobat asked that his adolescent son, like him a tightrope walker and a freeborn Muslim, be enrolled as a cadet in the Janissary corps. He was the first Turk to be so privileged. Within two generations most of the Janissaries were neither slaves nor servicemen. They chose and they deposed the Sultans. In 1683, for the second time at the gates of Vienna, they broke and ran. But as early as the third year of Selim the Sot's reign, the Janissaries were both drunk and corrupt. A fire broke out in the city under the Second Hill on the shore of the Golden Horn. The Janissary policemen and firemen fed the flames, which conveniently spread to the ancient Jewish quarter. There the Janissaries looted the houses of the wealthy Sephardim; and then the Janissaries crucified a Christian youth. The pious Muslims of the city blamed the Jews and blamed the incompetent Sultan — or rather, his dead mother, the witch Hürrem.

They revived and spread the old story that Selim the Sot was not a Son of Osman, but instead either a bastard or a changeling. The Sephardim, a much persecuted tribe of the Diaspora, wanderers among the migratory Visigoths and Vandals into Spain and Portugal, were very often blond and blue-eyed men and women. Expelled by the Inquisition, the wise and learned Jews were invited by the Sultans of the Golden Age to settle in Istanbul. There they became physicians to the court and to the ladies of the imperial harem.

According to the gossip, the cowardly and drunken Selim II was not the son of Süleyman, who was the son of Selim the Grim, but he was either the child of Hürrem by a Sephardic physician or a Sephardic baby boy introduced into the harem by the doctor and the wet nurse. They had allowed the Sultan's son to die. Perhaps he had permitted the real Selim Sultan to fall on his head; perhaps her milk had poisoned the imperial prince . . . and so on in endless elaboration of the fantastic changeling story. Selim the Sot was born with his mother's Russian coloring; the rest of Haseki Hürrem's sons, like their father the Sultan, were dark. The myth of his Sephardic origin grew out of a scene in a drunken party at Manisa. Selim, then Prince Imperial, had thrown his arms about his banker Joseph Nassy and been heard to babble, "Really and truly, if my ship comes in, you'll be King of Cyprus."

Despite the sobering enthronement at Belgrade, Selim the Sot got drunk again when he got back to Istanbul. There Joseph Nassy threw himself on his knees before his sovereign, who raised him up, named him Duke of Naxos, and gave him a monopoly of the wine trade. He made an annual profit (in gold dollars) of one million eight hundred seventy-five thousand dollars before taxes. For the monopoly, he paid the Defterdar one hundred thousand a year, and another seven hundred thousand in duties. The treasurer protested to the Sultan. He pointed out the anomaly as well as the loss of revenue, and suggested that the Grand Vezir and the Grand Mufti restudy and revise the law of prohibition. From the permissive state monopoly in the illegal wine trade, the Sephardic favorite cleared one million seventy-five thousand dollars in gold a year.

Selim the Sot refused. Perhaps he smiled as he explained that his hands were tied by his father's sumptuary laws prohibiting the sale of wine within the empire. Everyone knew that the Greek tavern keepers undermined morale by openly encouraging the Janissaries on leave from the barracks and on liberty from the arsenal to drink to get drunk.

But to admit of flaw and error in the sovereign edict of the Sultan the Lawgiver's codified sacred jurisprudence would shake the foundations of both the Ruling and the Religious Institutions, as well as of the House of Osman. Therefore, nothing could be done. The new Duke of Naxos seems to have been the first official bootlegger in history.

The Grand Vezir agreed with Selim the Sot in principle. In fact, he dictated a memorandum to the Sultan gravely to point out that his own extravagant example encouraged the Janissaries and all the citizens of Istanbul as scofflaws to carouse and to endanger the public weal. He urged the Sultan to abstain from "the exquisite wine of Cyprus" so that the police force in the exercise of impartial justice in the eyes of God might crack down to enforce the law. His secretary Feridun looked up from his notebook (the Arabic script used for Osmanlija was a kind of shorthand). He remarked that it might do more harm than good. If Sokollu Mehmet Pasha rigorously enforced the law, the people might revolt. The Janissaries especially needed a safety valve. The little harm that they did when drunk — mayhem, assault and battery, breaking and entering, an occasional rape — resulted from their pent-up high spirits. Soured and repressed, the men might well revolt in flaming mutiny. In any event, there was no use in appealing to the Sultan. Whatever he did, he did because his pattern of life had been written by God on his forehead at the instant of his conception.

The Grand Vezir listened. Feridun suggested that he get around the Sultan by ordering the generals and the admirals to tighten discipline in all branches of the service. Was there no way to keep the slave soldiers occupied other than in active warfare? It was not then politic to organize a major campaign. The Grand Vezir was negotiating peace treaties. The Sultan refused himself to take to the field at the head of his armies in any sort of Holy War.

Then the Grand Vezir suffered a reverse. He mounted an expedition into southern Russia north of the Crimean khanate, but more in the interests of stimulating the flagging economy, beset by inflation because of the influx of Aztec and Inca gold, than in true militant religious conquest. On August 4, 1569, Sokollu Mehmet Pasha sent off three thousand Janissaries and twenty thousand Sipahi and Turkish cavalrymen by land along the Black Sea shore, and five thousand Janissary engineers with three thousand skilled laborers by sea, into the Don Basin. It was his idea to open a canal between the Volga and the Don.

There is no way to know whether or not the Grand Vezir had consulted his old friend and co-worker the Royal Chief Architect, who was then living in Edirné and working on the Selimiyé. To have done so would have been reasonable. To accompany the Janissary engineers, almost certainly Sinan supplied a contingent of his trained foremen and skilled laborers to do the work under the command of one of his assistant architects and builders in the Office of Public Works.

On the maps in Istanbul there were many blank spaces. To show the Grand Vezir, the engineers had drawn the line of the projected canal between the Russian rivers through unexplored territory that seemed flat and feasible to the success of the enterprise. The line lay to the north of the Khan of the Crimean Tartar's flexible borders. This ally and cousin of the Ottoman Sultans, preserved and protected by them as their heirs to the throne in case the Sons of Osman died out, was to have sent thirty thousand Cossacks to reinforce the Janissaries, and to protect the men at work digging the canal; but he held back. The ditch seems to have been begun north of the narrowest point between the rivers where Hitler met defeat at Stalingrad, now called Volgograd.

From Moscow, Ivan the Terrible sent down fifteen thousand Russians led by Prince Serebinoff. The Janissaries fought listlessly for lack of sleep. They were defeated by time as told by the clocks of the Christians. In Islam the days and nights are equal. Accordingly, each is twelve hours long. In northern summers, where the nights are dark for but three hours, each Islamic daylight hour, according to the Christian clock, lasts for one hundred and five minutes. Each short hour of the night following such a day would be but fifteen minutes long.

In such latitudes the Janissary Muslim was called to prayer two hours — which is to say by modern clocks, thirty minutes — after sunset. He was roused at dawn ten Islamic, or two and a half Swiss, hours later. A Muslim peacefully living there would get at most but a hundred and fifty minutes of sleep on midsummer night. In Islam, no man can live in the land of the midnight sun.

As it happened, the Grand Vezir Sokollu Mehmet Pasha's canal was to have been dug in the steppes between the Russian rivers lying beyond the limits of the Prophet's faith. God may have damned the benighted Russians, as the Janissaries believed, to hell for all time, which is to say to live and to die in Russia. But on their own ground, Ivan the Terrible's Muscovites defeated Sokollu Mehmet Pasha's earth movers and the Janissary expeditionary forces. As the survivors crossed the shallow and treacherous Black Sea, a violent storm blew up. All but seven thousand of the original thirty-one thousand workmen and soldiers were drowned.

From Istanbul the Grand Vezir then sent off Lala Mustafa Pasha in command of another force of Janissaries and engineers. They sailed across the Mediterranean to dig a Suez canal. But Lala Mustafa Pasha had made other plans, so this canal lying well within Islamic time had to wait exactly three hundred years to be dug.

Hammer believes that the impèrial tutor and his ally Joseph Nassy sent off secret agents to sabotage the arsenal at Venice, then at peace with the Sons of Osman. If the Austrian historian, who spent thirty years examining the archives in Vienna, in the Vatican, in Venice, and reading the Ottoman historians' manuscript books in his own collection to write his labor of love, is right, then Lala Mustafa Pasha and Joseph Nassy chose September 13, 1569, to activate, as the military say, their project.

Their plans were ripe. On that date, in historical fact, an explosion in Venice set fire to the shipyards and the arsenal at the naval base of the commercial republic. Wars have been fought over Jenkins' ear. The French in 1830 took Algiers and then Algeria because the Bey, with a horsetail fly whisk, flicked a fly that wasn't there from a Frenchman's face. The Ottoman conquest of foam-borne Aphrodite's island was fought not for love or for money but for wine. Selim the Sot drank it; Joseph Nassy purveyed it; Lala Mustafa used the vineyard island as a base for his assault on the Grand Vezir Sokollu Mehmet Pasha. The Grand Admiral Piyalé went along because a man of action enjoys action and a sailor loves the sea.

But first Lala Mustafa Pasha and the other *Damat*, Admiral Piyalé Pasha, both married to granddaughters of Selim the Sot, had to get around the Grand Vezir, who was against any war with the Venetians, and who had signed articles of peace with the Doge of Venice. Things were further complicated by the two first ladies of the imperial harems. Sultan Selim's favorite wife, the Lady Nûrûbanû, and her son Shehzadé Murad's only wife, the Lady Sâfiyé, were both Venetian, captured as virgin girls of good family by Corsairs at sea, and as prizes of great worth and beauty given or purchased or procured for the Sons of Osman.

Such difficulties only whetted Lala Mustafa Pasha's appetite for subtle intrigue. He and the Croatian Slave of the Gate Piyalé Pasha, both men lesser vezirs only less powerful than Sokollu Mehmet Pasha, turned from the Divan to the Ulema. They convinced, or conned, the aging and formidable Grand Mufti Ebüsuud, who had codified Süleyman the Lawgiver's canonical sovereign laws, that God was on their side in this Holy War to be waged for wine, vainglory, and personal ambition. The Grand Mufti's standing was equal if not superior to the authority of the Grand Vezir Sokollu Mehmet Pasha.

In the name of the Ulema of the Religious Institution, Ebüsuud handed down a judgment abrogating the peace treaty signed by the Doge of Venice and in the Sultan's name, by the Grand Vezir of the Sublime Porte. No Son of Osman need regard the terms of any contract with an infidel as binding – it was but a bit of paper. The Sword of Osman, sheathed, could at any time be drawn to cut the bonds of the waiting world – the Cypriots in this instance – from ties of ignorance and sin and Venetian red tape.

Confronted by the fait accompli, Sokollu Mehmet Pasha named Lala Mustafa Pasha to be Serasker of the amphibious campaign to take Cyprus for the glory of Islam. The Grand Mufti pointed out that the Sultan's share of the booty, and the conquered island's annual revenues, would pay the costs of the construction of the Imperial Friday Mosque of Sultan Selim II Khan in Edirné and endow the pious foundation that Sinan was building as the memorial to the Sot's powerful thirst.

On August 1, 1570, the Ottoman fleet anchored off Limassol. Inside the walled harbor, the Cypriot women killed their daughters, their young sons, and themselves. Or so the Christian chroniclers have it; they retell the same old story, which, in fact, may also have been a true one. As in Süleyman's and Ibrahim's conquest of Rhodes, so in Lala Mustafa Pasha's and Piyalé Pasha's conquest of Cyprus, one Greek heroine, screaming "No!" stabbed her boy, and cried out, "Never will you satisfy the infamous lusts of the Janissaries!" She then jumped from the roof of her house to her death. When Nicosia fell, two thousand boys and girls were captured alive. In the harbor, two Ottoman galleys, which were tied up at the dock, laden with gold and treasure, and ready to set sail for Istanbul with a thousand captive young virgins of the best Greek and Venetian families bound for the harems, exploded when one of them set fire to the powder magazine. Only a few Janissary sailors managed to swim to shore.

In April of 1571, Lala Mustafa Pasha began the siege of Famagusta. Marco-Antonio Bragadino, the Venetian commander in chief of the island, held the walled city. Before he began the siege, Lala Mustafa Pasha allowed safe passage through the Ottoman lines for eight thousand Cypriot civilians, the old men, the cripples, the women, the children. They scattered among the farms and the villages of the hinterland. Bragadino's garrison numbered seven thousand, half of them Venetians, half of them Greek.

They held out until they had eaten all the donkeys, the dogs, and the cats of Famagusta. On August 1, Bragadino hoisted the white flag. On August 5, three hours before sunset, the Venetian commander with his officers and an escort of forty men rode their emaciated horses to Lala Mustafa Pasha's tent. Bragadino had put on his robes of purple silk; he rode under the crimson parasol of a Venetian magistrate. In the pure Greek sunlight, he addressed Lala Mustafa Pasha, and he spoke as a free man, a Christian, a Venetian aristocrat speaking to a slave, a heathen.

Imperial son-in-law, grandson of a Son of Osman, tutor to imperial princes, vezir of the Divan, commander in chief of the Sultan's armies of the Cyprus campaign, Gazi-victor in Holy War, Lala Mustafa Pasha nodded. The Janissaries ran forward. All but a likely youth named Enrique Martinengo and his uncle Marco-Antonio Bragadino were executed on the spot. The nephew was castrated and sent off to the Imperial Palace as a White Eunuch.

The mutes then cut off Bragadino's nose and ears. Ten days later — it was a Friday — Bragadino was tied to a chair like a throne with a crown fixed to his feet. While Lala Mustafa Pasha watched, the Venetian was hoisted to a yardarm and plunged time and again into the harbor — just as he had treated his distinguished Ottoman captives. Next, untied, Bragadino had two baskets of earth hung on a yoke around his neck. He was put to work as a common laborer on the rebuilding of the bastions of Famagusta. Each time he passed Lala Mustafa Pasha, he was made to prostrate himself.

Next, Bragadino was tied to a stake and flogged, as he had ordered his Ottoman prisoners flogged. Then, still tied to the stake, uprooted, he was laid flat on the ground and skinned alive. "Now where is your Christ?" Lala Mustafa Pasha mocked him. "Why does Lord Jesus not come to save your skin?"

All the historians of the Ottoman Empire, so far, from first to last, have been enemies. According to the Christians, Bragadino, uttering no protest, neither begging for mercy nor crying out in pain, recited the *Miserere* while he was being flayed: "Behold. Thou desirest truth in the inward being; therefore, teach me wisdom in my secret heart. Purge me with hyssop, and I shall be clean; wash me, and I shall be whiter than snow. Fill me with joy and gladness; let the bones which Thou has broken rejoice. Hide thy face from my sins, and blot out all my iniquities. . . . The sacrifice acceptable to God is a broken spirit; a broken and a contrite heart, O God, Thou wilt not despise . . . then bulls will be offered on Thy altar. . . ."

I cannot believe that he got to the end of it; they say that he did, and that after the last verse, he prayed in a loud firm voice to God: "Grant me, O Lord, a pure heart!" Then he died.

Lala Mustafa Pasha continued. He had the flayed body quartered and exposed on the four batteries of Ottoman artillery. He had the skin stuffed with hay, tied in a seated position on a cow's back, and, sheltered from the

33. The canopied fountain of ritual ablutions in the courtyard of the Mosque of the Grand Vezir Sokollu Mehmet Pasha, in Istanbul, with the curious pairs of twinned domes flanking the vertical mass that leads the eye up to the high dome — variations on a theme.

34. The Mosque of Sokollu Mehmet Pasha, from the southeast.

35. The modest, classic tomb at Eÿup of Sokollu Mehmet Pasha, the greatest and most powerful of all the Ottoman "Bearers of the Burden," assassinated in the Divan in 1579.

36. The Ottoman grille of wrought iron in the wall of the *sahn*, Mosque of Sokollu Mehmet Pasha.

37. BELOW: The east corner of the courtyard, Mosque of Sokollu Mehmet Pasha, showing the "baroque" arch of the arcade and the gate keeper's lodge.

38. Interior, Mosque of Sokollu Mehmet Pasha; the twinned domes on hexagonal drums on either side of the portal (for exterior view, see Figure 33), and the clumsy monolithic beam, which were perhaps afterthoughts. Or, if "God is in the details," as Mies van der Rohe believed, perhaps these puzzling small domes were Sinan's built-in flaw by which he avoided the impiety of competing with Allah, who alone achieved perfection — in creating Adam, *Homo sapiens.*

39. Sokollu Mehmet Pasha Jami, the mandala of the dome in the snowflake hexagonal, within the square; and the tiled kibla wall of the prayer niche.

40. Lüleburgaz, the country complex in Thrace built by Sinan for Sokollu Mehmet Pasha as a rural center of Islamic civilization. This domical archway covers the crossroads where the path from the mosque and medrese courtyard to the caravansary meets at right angles the street of shops and factories. A stork in its nest in June hides the finial.

41. The view from the southeast of the Mosque and tomb of witty and corrupt Shemsi Ahmet Pasha, built when Sinan was ninety-one, in 1580, on the Asian shore of the Bosphorus, at Üsküdar.

42. Ramazan Efendi, the oratory for the "whirling Dervishes," Sinan's last work built in 1586, two years before he died aged ninety-nine — and very well restored since this photograph was taken in 1937 or 1938.

43. The interior, Ramazan Efendi.

44. The prayer niche, Ramazan Efendi.

45. Ramazan Efendi, four tiles in a panel from Iznik of the great period, 1570 to 1620. The secret of the four enamels, dark blue, "bolus" sealing wax red, turquoise blue, and emerald green, all on a snow white ground, has been lost, as has the formula for the spring-water-clear glaze.

46. Sinan's tomb with the white marble fountain house for thirsty passersby in the sharp corner of the steep cobbled streets below the Süleymaniyé on the third hill above the Golden Horn.

sun by the Venetian commander's crimson parasol, paraded through the camp of the Janissaries, and through the streets of Famagusta. He then had the stuffed skin hung from a yardarm of an Ottoman galley — perhaps to cure in the salt wind and the hot sun of August while the mutilated and severed head pickled in a vat of brine. He then sent off the emptied and folded skin along with the pickled head, packed in a coffer, back to Sultan Selim the Sot, whose wife, the First Lady, Haseki Nûrûbanû, was a Venetian. Bragadino's skin finally got back to Venice; it was placed in an urn and put in the Church of Santi Giovanni e Paolo, behind the equestrian statue of the condottiere Bartolomeo Colleoni.

On the night Famagusta fell to them, the Janissary marines and sailors of the fleet got drunk on Cyprian wine. In later years, back in Istanbul, increasingly refined of palate, they got into serious oenological discussions about the merits of the cellars of the many new taverns opened along the shores of the Bosphorus and the Golden Horn. They soon found out which of the proprietors, wise men and connoisseurs, but not Greeks, instead the justices of the Ulema, had bought up and laid down the finest vintages.

The Sultan's share of the spoils did, indeed, go to pay the cost of Sinan's masterwork, the Selimiyé in Edirné; but within a century, in the epoch of the rule of the Ladies of the Harem, the revenues of Cyprus were reallocated from the pious foundation to finance the expanded Household of the Validé Sultan's administration.

More important as an immediate consequence of Lala Mustafa Pasha's victory of Cyprus, as the Grand Vezir Sokollu Mehmet Pasha had foreseen, was the union of the European Christian enemies in a sort of league of nations. The naval Battle of Lepanto began a little before noon on October 7, 1571. Led by Don Juan of Austria, the allies destroyed or captured two hundred twenty-eight vessels of the Ottoman Mediterranean fleet. Ninety-four burnt and sank in the Gulf of Corinth below Delphi and Parnassus; one hundred thirty-four, taken intact, were shared out among the victors — the Spaniards, the various Italians including the Pope, the French, and the Knights of Malta. They freed fifteen thousand Christian galley slaves, chained by the Ottoman to their oars; and took three thousand four hundred sixty-eight Ottoman Turkish prisoners. Thirty thousand Janissary marines, gunners, and sailors, with their officers, perished. The allies lost eight thousand men and fifteen ships. Cervantes lost his left arm.

Only the Ottoman Admiral Kilich Ali Pasha escaped with any sort of honor, to figure in *Don Quixote* and, by order of the Grand Vezir, to bring his forty ships, all that remained of the flotilla, into their berths at the arsenal in the Golden Horn in the dead of night, so as not to reveal the extent of the disaster to the people of the imperial city.

The Sultan honored Kilich Ali. The portrait in profile in the Naval

Museum at Beshiktash shows a big man, blond and blue-eyed, strong-featured and good-humored. He was a Norman of Calabria. He had been captured as a young mariner and, as a recalcitrant Christian, was chained to an oar. After a year as a Turkish galley slave – the whip convinced him – he saw fit to volunteer as a renegade to join Islam. He remained faithful to the sea. After the Battle of Lepanto Sinan at once began to enlarge the arsenal. The Grand Vezir ordered Piyalé Pasha to bring back one hundred twenty galleys and thirteen transports and cargo ships from North Africa and Egypt. He collected thirty-seven more battleships from among the Greek islands. To these were added the forty galleys saved from Lepanto and now repaired and refitted. By the spring of 1572, the arsenal had sent down the ways one hundred and fifty new galleys and eight new transports.

To outfit them was more difficult. On a tour of inspection, Kilich Ali Pasha remarked to the Grand Vezir that he wondered where the masts and rigging were to come from. What of cotton canvas for the sails? What of the five hundred anchors of forged iron and the miles of anchor chain?

"Lord Pasha," the Grand Vezir replied, "we are rich. If need be, we can cast the anchors in silver, twist the ropes of silk, and cut the sails from satin." It was not hyperbole. The precious metal, the silk fibers and fabrics lay piled up in the imperial treasury. But it was not necessary. Outfitted in the ordinary, two hundred and fifty warships were ready by June 1572. But the Ottomans never again risked or invited a major naval engagement in the Mediterranean. Lepanto appears in all the lists of battles that have changed the course of history. It serves historians to date the beginning of the Ottoman decline. The allies could not hold together long enough to follow up their victory.

Winner take nothing. Having restored the Ottoman fleet to its full strength before the disaster at Lepanto, the Grand Vezir turned his attention to the desert island of Cyprus. Evacuated by the Venetians, stripped of the valuable young women, girls, and boys by the Janissaries and the raiders, almost all the able-bodied Greek males slaughtered, the island had to be repopulated. The Grand Vezir's problem was to find a good breeding stock of field hands to tend the vineyards now owned by the Duke of Naxos, Joseph Nassy, in order to make the delicate wine pleasing to the palate of Selim the Sot.

For years the inhabitants of the Ottoman province of Karaman in south central Asia Minor had made trouble. This province, once the ancient Greek kingdom of Cappadocia, then the heartland of the Byzantines and later of the Seljuk Turks, then the independent emirate of the warlike Karamanlis, bred a sturdy race of people, ethnically resistant to assimilation by any of the many conquerors. It was Sinan's homeland. After his collection as a tribute youth, the other young men of his stock, left behind in the highlands, having only their lives to lose, took to rebellion. They fought off the Sultan's tax collectors. In patriotic Christian or heretical bands of outlaws, or as just plain highwaymen, they harassed the beylerbeylik government of the neglected Domain of Peace.

In 1573, two years after the momentous Battle of Lepanto and the trivial conquest of Cyprus, the Grand Vezir issued a directive to the beylerbey of Karaman. He was to round up all the delinquents, the klephts, the brigands, the known criminals and the scofflaws, and all the nonbelievers — Greek Orthodox in the majority — with their families living in the province. I take it that in the usual way, the men, women, and children were put into stockades. Properly sorted out, registered, and ticketed, this riffraff (or these heroes and heroines), the ancestors of the present day Cypriots, were then marched down to the coast, herded into cattle ships, and sent off to Cyprus, some forty miles off the south coast of Turkey.

But before the Beylerbey of Karaman could begin to carry out his unprecedented orders to enforce this mass emigration, Sinan got word of it. By 1573 the Royal Chief Architect had moved his household to Edirné for his comfort and convenience during the short reign of Selim II. He spent eight years building his third Imperial Friday Mosque, the Selimiyé, his master-work. However, he visited Istanbul from time to time. In 1571, he built the Grand Vezir's own Mosque of Sokollu Mehmet Pasha, to my mind the greatest of them all. It stands on the slopes of the First and Second Hills above the Sea of Marmara; and it took his close attention. In these years he also built the Grand Vezir's most beautiful country complex at Lülebürgaz, more than halfway on the road from Istanbul to Edirné, and the restored bath house in the rich market city, and several country residences for Sokollu Mehmet Pasha, his divorced ladies, and his Imperial Princess wife.

In 1573 while Sinan was living in the capital of the Domain of War, he buried his young granddaughter Fatma, the daughter of his son Mehmet, who had been killed in battle, perhaps at Cyprus, perhaps at Lepanto. For the dead child, he carved a tombstone, that, in Islamic art, is as a kouros by Phidias.

This was the year of the edict expelling, among other Greek Christians, Sinan's cousins from his home town of Aghirnas, near Kayseri, and from two other towns in the province of Karaman, to repopulate Cyprus. He was the Royal Chief Architect; he was an admirable Slave of the Gate; he had served Sultan Süleyman Khan as a Janissary and a general and a favorite of the chosen Guard of Honor. Sinan was a family man. He got to work to save his Greek Christian relatives from enforced expulsion from their ancestral lands.

He mounted his horse and rode to Istanbul. Perhaps he sought audience with Selim the Fair, who received him. Perhaps the Royal Chief Architect, in his robe of office, an honored man of eighty-four, appeared at dawn at the

Divan to appeal to his old friend and patron, his fellow grandee among the admirable Slaves of the Gate, Sokollu Mehmet Pasha; and he knew all the lesser vezirs as well as the Judges of the Armies and the Grand Mufti Ebüsuud. Officially, he wrote out a petition addressed to the Sultan Selim II Khan, which he presented to the Grand Vezir, who took action. In the Sultan's name, he wrote hand-carried directives exempting all the inhabitants of the town of Aghirnas from the enforced emigration to Cyprus. The berlerbey of Karaman was nonplussed. He sent back to the Divan a post-haste dispatch asking for confirmation and clarification of the firman of exemption. He got it; and he was told to see to it that Sinan's relatives were neither menaced, nor harassed, nor intimidated, but left in peace. By the time their descendants were expelled from Aghirnas in Atatürk's exchange of populations in and after 1924, these Greeks of Central Asia Minor for generations had called themselves by the family name of Stonemasonson. In his last will and charter, Sinan endowed and built a fountain for them. It still flows in "The Village of the Royal Chief Architect Sinan," not far from the leaf- and rubble-filled ruins of a grotto church called locally Sinan's Chapel. Long before his day, it had been hollowed out of a cliff below the hill town, and painted with tall Byzantine saints, who are now eyeless. Sinan, in 1573, was powerful enough to confound Ottoman bureaucracy. Having accomplished his purpose, he went back to work.

The Venetians, whose business was business, profited from the loss of Cyprus. They agreed to pay the cost of the Ottoman conquest (eighteen million dollars gold), and the increased annual tribute in exchange for their peaceful occupation of the Greek island of Zante, which was raised from five hundred to one thousand five hundred gold ducats (they had paid eight thousand a year on Cyprus). In return, the Grand Vezir agreed to sign "capitulations" guaranteeing the Venetian merchants settled in Istanbul and the Levantine cities the extra-legal and extra-territorial right to do business.

The Slaves of the Gate of the Sultan's Household of Slaves thereby sold not their birthrights but their business futures in a viable economy. And not for a mess of pottage, but for the tedium of parasitical aristocracy. The Ottomans' refusal to soil their hands in trade in fact marks the beginning of the decline. And their change of attitude, a result of the refusal to alter their perfected system, led to the conspicuous lack of gumption that economic determinists delight in spotting.

The citizens of Istanbul — artisans, craftsmen, hard-working Muslims — blamed the favorable trade agreements with the Venetians upon the influence of the two Venetian first ladies of the imperial harems, Nûrûbanû, Selim the Sot's belovèd, and the Shehzadé Murad's adored Lady Sâfiyé. As Ottoman great ladies, the Venetian mother-in-law and daughter-in-law came to terms when Murad ascended the throne. The younger woman, who had held

Murad's love for twenty years, had given birth to only one healthy son. The others had been stillborn. To safeguard the future of the House of Osman, Nûrûbanû the mother, and Sâfiyé the first lady, with the help of the new Sultan's sister, who was the Grand Vezir's Imperial Princess wife, supplied Murad III, who proved to be hyper-potent, if indolent on the throne, with the first of the enormous harems that have made of the Grand Turk a byword and a joke in cartoons down to this day.

But in 1572, the year after the defeat at Lepanto, Selim the Sot took a turn for the worse. Saddened by the sudden death of his second son and favorite, Mehmet Sultan, he drank heavily for two years. A comet crossed the night sky. A flood in the deserts damaged the shrine of the Kaaba in Mecca. An earthquake threw down four hundred houses in Istanbul. The Grand Mufti Ebüsuud died in September. Badly frightened, the Sultan was terror-stricken when a fire broke out in the kitchens of the palace and destroyed his cellars of vintage Cyprian wines. He was a superstitious man and he feared God. A similar fiery ill omen had foretold the death by cancer of his grandfather and grim namesake, "the Man without Flaw."

Selim the Sot resigned himself by sending off his wine steward to recoup the losses from the coarser vintages of Egypt. He drank the last of the wine of Cyprus and plunged into the deepest melancholy. When his Royal Chief Architect, at the age of eighty-five, returned from Mecca where he had restored the damaged Kaaba and rebuilt the desert aqueducts, the Sultan, to cheer himself up at the age of fifty, commanded Sinan to build him a new bathhouse within the Gate of Felicity.

On December 10, 1574, Selim took pleasure in a tour of inspection. Sinan warned the Sultan that the plaster in the domes had not yet dried. Selim fortified himself against the cold and damp with a bumper of his favorite wine and waddled into the cold room. A step behind him, Sinan followed. He turned on the fountain. The Sultan walked across the floor arabesqued in inlays of precious marbles. Sinan went ahead to open the door into the narrow tepidarium, and then into the hot room, which for lack of fire in the furnaces was cold. Perhaps the Sultan bent back his head to look up into the dome pierced by lights in the shapes of moons and stars. He slipped on the polished inlaid floor. Perhaps he struck his head on the raised belly stone of marble and *opus sectile*. He cracked his skull. He lived five days and died, apparently of pneumonia, on December 15, 1574. His heir, the eldest son, the Sultan Murad III Khan, came placidly from Manisa and had his five younger living brothers strangled on December 21.

16

The road from Istanbul to Edirné is Sinan's highway. It begins with the Mosque of Mihrimah Sultan, which is an exclamation of the joy of life within Islam, inside the Edirné Gate of the land walls on the high point of the Sixth Hill. This is the old road, once a Roman and a Byzantine road, the way up into Europe from the East. Heavy traffic today goes along a new avenue a mile or so away and out through a cut — not a gate — opened neatly through the tumbled walls, thrown down not by man but by earthquakes. The road goes on to the airport at Yeshilköy, Greentown, and beyond.

Twenty-five years ago when I first walked through the Edirné Gate and out of the city to see what I could see, it seems to me, the land walls on top of the Sixth Hill were not so ruinous. Things were much more peaceful then, and greener. The walls are still tremendous, five miles of square towers and round towers and octagonal towers joined by massive ramparts rising straight up; except, of course, where earthquakes have thrown down solid blocks of stone and brick and concrete masonry as big as houses. How high are they? Five or six or seven times man height; under them he is dwarfed. The land walls of Constantinople, now spelled Istanbul, contained and maintained civilization from the fifth to the seventeenth centuries, a good long time. They go down hill and up hill into the distance. Outside them the cemeteries begin, acres of graves, their tombstones leaning or fallen among old black cypress trees.

Beyond the dry moat on the glacis, green in spring, camels, a dozen or two, Bactrians and dromedaries, nibbled the grass, shabby aristocrats, expendable but once essential. In their great days the Grand Vezir Sokollu Mehmet Pasha once refused the gift of a giraffe to the Holy Roman Emperor for the very good reason that it was the only giraffe he had. He needed it to strike terror among the horses of the Holy Roman Emperor's hussars.

Beyond the cemeteries and the airport on the shores of the Sea of Marmara, the old road and the modern highway come together. At Büyük-chekmejé they split momentarily, the new one to bypass Sinan's four-humped bridge of twenty-nine masonry arches, which still leaps across the water from stepping-stone island to island. The fishermen still hang out their nets to dry in the sunshine, but along the sand beaches summer bungalows, motels, and commercial bathing establishments have grown up – not, I think, in the sort of artifice to aid the natural beauty of the inlet that Busbecq had in mind in 1555.

At Silivri, a town farther along on the old shore road – it once was important enough to give its name to a gate in the land walls, and it is still famous for its Silivri yoghurt, thick enough almost to be fresh cheese – Sinan built another long, masonry-arched bridge across the neck of a marshy inlet. Here there were – and are – no flood waters. The bridge is straightforward; it rises imperceptibly to a crown in order to drain the rainwater from the roadbed still in use. The mosque of Silivri is said to be one of Sinan's one hundred and one, but the claim is dubious.

Further along the Edirné highway, which bends inland to run almost due northwest, at the roadside country village of Chorlu, there is one more small mosque said to be Sinan's work. Perhaps it is, for at Chorlu both Selim the Grim and eight years earlier his violently deposed and exiled father, Sultan Bayazid the Sainted, died beside the road, the one of cancer, the other if not of a broken heart, then of poison that his patricidal younger son gave him to help him on his way.

Where the road crosses a small river on another of Sinan's bridges stands Lülebürgaz, which has the best of Sinan's country as opposed to urban complexes. The name of the market town describes its nature. Lülebürgaz lies at the bottom of a shallow bowl in the rolling hills of Thrace on "a little twisting bend" of the stream, or "fold" in the well-worn face of the land. The car or the bus speeds along the road in the pleasantly monotonous bucolic landscape, toward the town, unseen below the horizon.

The Grand Vezir Sokollu Mehmet Pasha owned a farming and a hunting estate nearby. Sinan built him a town house which has now gone, and this pious foundation, a center of religion, law, commerce, learning, cleanliness, and coherence – civilized order made practicable and visible. The town has grown up to surround the complex that he built on a level space in the fields. He walled in a rectangular space and built the small and classic mosque in the center of it. He put order, man-made, upon nature.

Circle in square – the dome of the mosque rests on four pendentives. In the interior, the kibla wall is flush with the engaged arch and the two engaged piers. Sinan deepened the soffits of the three other arches to make room for galleries. Those of the sides are supported by arcades of four arches and three pillars – thin, smooth monoliths of Proconnesus marble from the Marmara, topped by stalactite capitals. How did Sinan bring the white monoliths and the blocks of marble from the sea? Packed on camels, or dragged by oxen along the road? Perhaps, when the river was full in the time of winter rains, in barges.

Opposite the kibla wall, right and left of the portal, which is a great success, Sinan put shallow *ayvans*, now glassed in to make rooms for the imam and the muezzin. The enclosed spaces are small enough to heat in winter by means of charcoal braziers. There the senior leader in prayer teaches students how to chant the Koran, teaches what to some of us is Sunday school, and gives advice or consolation to men and women who have come to him in their several needs.

Outside, along the rectified edges of the mosque garden, planted to trees, with purple larkspur, scarlet poppies, yellow mustard, the blue anchusas and the borages, and daisies, such wild flowers blooming along with weeds, and in the summer the tall grasses, Sinan built the typical Ottoman stone wall. Taller than a man, regularly pierced with rectangular openings, into the wall Sinan fitted the significant Ottoman grilles of upright and vertical iron bars. The dome and its gilt-bronze finial rises from an octagonal drum built up above the top of the square mosque walls. Sinan set a free standing octagonal turret in each corner and topped each chamber with a pointed cupola. There are no graves or *türbés* behind the kibla wall. Instead, with its back to the mosque, in the line of the rear wall of the enclosure, he built a library. It is a square of masonry, a hollow cube, the courses alternating: three shallow bricks laid in mortar on top of one another, and the other course of limestone blocks. The library opens into the dusty country square behind the enclosure. Stone staircases lead up from the ground level to the porch, a domical canopy, and the door in the southeast wall. Again Sinan set this dome on a high and strongly marked octagonal drum. Storks nest where the gilt-bronze finial used to rise. The storks of Lülebürgaz have made this *külliyé* their own with six or seven of their untidy nests of twigs upon the domes.

The single minaret stands against the southwest wall at the west corner. The porch extends beyond the façade of the mosque on either side. Above the portal Sinan placed a rectangular cradle vault and flanked it with four domes in a row — the porch arcade has nine equal, barely pointed arches. The vault and the shallow cupolas rise from sharp-edged drums, the one rectangular, the others octagonal. Behind and above the porch, Sinan stepped the extrados of the arch between the piers with his usual hard-edged, saw-toothed vertical and horizontals to work against the rise and fall of the dome.

It rains a lot in Lülebürgaz. Sinan added an exonarthex to the porch, a penthouse roof supported by a colonnade. The almost square open courtyard is much bigger than the covered floor space of the prayer hall. At the corners of the outer porch to north and west of the courtyard arcades, Sinan chose to avoid the clumsy truncated pillar and the bastard corbel-capitals that elsewhere receive the springers of the arches at two levels. Instead, he built a square gatehouse, its massive masonry foundations at ground level tunneled for a passage and topped by a loge. It is a square domical room in the apartments of, it may have been, the resident professors in the college of sacred jurisprudence.

In shape the dome on each of these two handsome gatehouses is getting on for Oriental like the follies of the nineteenth century gazeboes, or, indeed, like the dome of the Taj Mahal. Sinan raised each one in a baroque silhouette — a tulip bulb, an onion. On the point he set an elegantly decorative gilt-bronze finial. From the loges, the lower pointed arches of the courtyard arcades begin, seven spans in line, and seven cupolas; they end with a slightly bigger dome set in the corner. Behind the arcades, Sinan built the domical cubicles for the students.

This utilitarian plan for a small mosque, in which the courtyard doubles as the atrium of the *medresé*, was Sinan's invention. It is logical and reasonable, as well as functional and efficient, and also economical and beautiful.

In Lüleburgaz, Sinan placed the lecture hall, which ordinarily stands at the center of the wall opposite the mosque, against the gatehouse over the southwest entrance, at the beginning of the arcade along that side. He did so because a market street runs along the outside wall to the northwest, and beyond the street of shops, Sinan built a caravansary. It is (or was, for it has been razed) a huge commercial center of two open courtyards and covered markets. The country buses now park and start up on their runs from the dusty open square where the caravansary once stood.

To cover the passage from the caravansary across the street into the courtyard of the mosque and college, Sinan built a sort of utilitarian triumphal arch. It is a rectangular building of dressed limestone, cut open on all four sides. The arches of the longer sides spanning the market street are almost round; the arches of the smaller sides covering the way from business to prayer and back again are smaller and sharply pointed. Sinan stressed the masonry and the engineering of the spans by bringing out the blocky limestone voussoirs. He stressed the horizontal roofline with a cornice moulding — it breaks and rises a step exactly its own width above the top of the arch. On the rectangle, he placed an equally strongly marked octagonal drum of stone, from which the lead-sheathed dome rises. Storks have taken over the finial to anchor their tall nest of interwoven twigs. There is no other structure like this one in the world.

Along the market street, grapevine arbors shade the barrel-vaulted open shops. I suppose Sinan designed them to serve the agricultural community. Today the shops are given over to greased-blotched garages and store rooms of spare parts for the mechanics who overhaul the tractors and harvesters.

Surely the fountain of the ablutions in the center of the mosque-*medresé* courtyard cannot be Sinan's original. But maybe so. It has a flaring, fluttering canopy like a whirling skirt, as baroque as can be, but it serves to cover the men seated at the taps to wash themselves. Inside this crazy shell is a pearl, an arcade like a crown around a basin of water; it supports a dome. Sinan's original may have been pointed like those of the two gatehouses. If so, he is to be held responsible for the frivolous and delightful excesses of his followers. He knew, as they did not, *jusqu'où on peut aller trop loin* [just how far he could go].

Across the country street to the northeast, Sinan built a double *hamam*, sold, stripped and ruined in the bad old days of the nineteenth century. The men and women of Lülebürgaz can no longer bathe in it, but they have carved themselves commercial premises to house various enterprises in the solid ruins. Grass grows where it should not on all the high level places, as does valerian and snapdragon; and acanthus weed-tree seedlings and saplings have rooted on top of the walls and drums, stripped of lead sheathing. The fringed bald domes need haircuts.

Originally the two, and twinned, frigidaria — cold rooms for the dressing and undressing of the segregated men and women — were square, octagonal, and domical. One of the domes has fallen; the other, a wall cut open under it, now roofs a depot and a salesroom. Sinan himself built a row of shops on the street. They still operate. I ate lunch in a restaurant cut into and out of one of the tepidaria; other enterprises have taken over the caldaria. The lunch, as usual in Turkish country towns, was palatable, but the strong fragrance of the madonna lilies — *Lilium candidum* is native to Thrace — jammed into a jar on the table is not to everybody's taste. Nor was the original content of the jar, which was *ayran*, and that is something like buttermilk but is yoghurt thinned with water. Pink cabbage roses bloom among the madonna lilies in the dooryards of Lülebürgaz in June.

On the way out of town the road crosses Sinan's bridge and then runs in a straight line, up hill and down dale, to the northwest across the rich and fertile rolling green landscape. Ten or a dozen kilometers this side of Edirné, the road dips, crosses a bridged stream, rises — and there it is! The Selimiyé's single great dome rising between two startlingly tall thin towers on a hilltop, rising above the trees and the pantiled roofs of the town. But soon the pair of minarets separate; the eye takes in the fact that there are four of them, two and two in exact alignment standing at the four corners of the greatest of Sinan's mosques. He built them to be seen from the Istanbul road running along the straight line from Mecca to the southeast.

Edirné used to be a great city. In the eighteenth century Lady Mary Wortley Montagu, writing from Venice, remembered the rich array of jewels, the brocades and the velvets, the silver plate and the gold luxuries sold in the long covered market street that Sinan built for Fat Ali Pasha. As late as 1907, when earthquakes threw down the many small synagogues, the community of two hundred and fifty thousand Shepardim, with contributions from their connections in the Americas and the help of the Rothschilds' *Alliance Israélite*, built a single spacious new synagogue. The actual flock of about two hundred and fifty hold services in an outbuilding, not in the vast and empty basilica-temple, dubious in architectural worth. The rest of the Sephardim have moved to Istanbul, or migrated to Israel, to California, to São Paulo, or elsewhere. None, or at most no more than a few chance travelers, went into the gas chambers across the shrunken frontiers of the old Domain of War.

From 1566 to 1574 Sinan lived with his family in Edirné. Once the second capital, called Adrianople by foreigners, it was the second city of the empire, the great Ottoman rear base in the Domain of War. Cairo, Damascus, Baghdad were more populous, even greater as centers of Islamic culture and civilization, but they were distant capitals of caliphates and sultanates reduced to provinces. Bursa in the Domain of Peace, the first capital of the Sons of Osman with its shrines to the eponymous progenitor and the first six khans and sultans, flourished as a kind of mystical if not holy place.

For whatever reason, Selim the Sot chose to build his memorial in Hadrian's city. The Caesar of the second Roman Golden Age was a great builder and a patron of the arts. When the Turks dug the foundations for the power plant in Bergama (Pergamum), the workmen uncovered a larger-than-life-size nude marble of the man, who was heroic in his proportions. He and Selim II can be seen as "modern" men, plagued by what we choose to call neuroses (and thereby to pride ourselves on our scientific progress). Each man was well aware of his defects; the earlier of the two emperors used his to virtuous effect. It is to be said of the Sot that he gave Sinan a free hand: he gave him his freedom to build at liberty as he saw fit. Selim surely took great delight in the most noble mosque that Sinan built for him.

The legend is that once Sinan and, of course, the plump Sultan had chosen the site, the old lady owner refused to sell the hilltop rose garden, where her tulips blossomed in the early spring. Her refusal stubbornly held back the work of construction. In fact, there may be truth in the myth. Selim the Sot prized tulips. Shortly before he died, he wrote the kadi of El-Aziz, a town in eastern Anatolia, to send him fifty thousand assorted bulbs to plant in the imperial gardens landscaped by Sinan. It is unlikely, however, that His Imperial Majesty did not send the old lady of Edirné a purse of gold and a requisition for her property. But as the story goes, she finally consented to have her rose and tulip garden transplanted with the proviso that both she and her flowers be remembered in the mosque.

There is an upside-down rose (or tulip, I forget which) badly carved in low relief at the base of one of the square marble pillars that support the muezzin's tribune inside the mosque. It is pointed to as proof of the historic truth. But surely some bored young cantor or student imam, in less pious days of lax supervision, carved the tulip (or the rose) upside-down upon the surface of the square column. Such is the way in which the Gothic choir stalls came to be enriched. It does not matter. Yet such a mild and charming myth could not have grown up in the memorial mosque around any earlier Son of Osman, not even in the legend of the Golden Orhan Khan, certainly not around the three greatest sultans, Süleyman, Selim the Grim, and Mehmet the Conqueror. In style, the flower belongs to the carvings of the Tulip Period, and at the end of that.

The tribune of the muezzins is otherwise extraordinary, as well as beautiful. Square, with four square and slim marble pillars to each side, the three "Louis XV" arches cut in the broken flowing line of the delicate baroque, a carved spiraling marble staircase protruding from the west corner like a work of art, and a low railing set around the top. The tribune stands as tall as a tall man. Sinan placed this very high dais, big enough for a choir of muezzins, most unusually at the exact center of the square floor plan, directly under the crown of the single dome. And he put a fountaining jet of water in a basin under it. It might have been the fountain in a rose arbor in the old lady of Edirné's hilltop garden.

The tribune itself, even to the arches and spandrels upon the marble pillars, is made of wood. Someday some skilled artisans will scrape off the accumulated coats of paint, the last one blue-gray. They have cleared an exploratory patch or two, to reveal Sinan's original work. It is an all-over decoration of formal floral patterns painted in the colors of a spring garden on a rose-red background, all enhanced with burnished gold. The work is delicate; it is classical; the hand that painted it was sure.

Having centered the attention, the tribune allows the eye to go free to follow Sinan's directions. The single dome rises 44 meters, some 145 feet, from the fountain to the crown. Free of semidomes, it rises from the cornice ring upon the stalactite pendentives of eight arches springing from eight piers. Thr four arches: one on either side, one over the portal, the other of the kibla wall, are filled with many-windowed screens. The four arches at the corners (they are to be called squinches) carry conchs. The dome is 31.28 meters in diameter — (103 feet 3 or 4 inches). Evliya Chelebi and Hammer, and perhaps Sinan himself, believed the dome to be two aunes (i.e. the old French system, which is to say, according to that platinum alloy meter rule in Paris), 2 meters and 23 centimeters and 6 millimeters, or 7 feet 3 or 4 inches wider than the dome of Haghia Sophia. In fact it is as much and more the smaller in diameter. Sinan never did surpass the irregular old celestial dome.

Inexact in any system of relativity, the height and the diameter of the dome of the Selimiyé are not to be classified and called mathematical or geometrical. Nor did Sinan calculate them in the dimensions of the classic man of Humanism, nor in the natural way that vines spiral upward and leaves grow on a stem in the golden section. Perhaps he let the building have its own way as it took shape, which is, I am told, the modern way in "brutal" architecture to build in freedom. It seems to me that in the wisdom of his extreme old age, he trusted his eye to determine the true proportions as his hands built this mosque. The dome rising from the octagon of the eight piers standing equidistant upon the circle within the square takes shape in the proportions more or less of one to one and a half.

To extend the central square into the liturgical rectangle, Sinan widened the soffits of the side arches almost to make pointed barrel vaults of them, which he repeated to make the aisles. Similarly he deepened the space behind the façade. Then for the prayer niche, he built out an apse or *ayvan* between the pair of piers engaged in the kibla wall. It is a raised squared space, a kind of stage, the arch (as of the proscenium) between the piers filled by the covering semidome. This quarter segment of a hollow sphere he set on bold and exact stalactites carved into the rear corners of the apse. Curiously, as with the high altar behind the iconostasis in the apse of Haghia Sophia, the prayer niche in the *ayvan* of this mosque is thereby removed from the celestial shelter of the dome. Perhaps thus both Anthemius of Tralles and Sinan the Great placed the focus of the worshipers' prayers outside the tensions of the power structures, that of man on earth, that of God in heaven.

As I understand it, when they worship God, men and women in Greek Orthodox Christianity, by means of ecstasy and enthusiasm, enter into a purely spiritual experience which is contained and confined within the space within a space within the church. Refreshed from the encounter with neither God the Father nor God the Son – nor, for He is consubstantial, with the Son of God distinct from the Son of Man – but with the Holy Spirit, they go outside to re-enter reality, in which it is necessary to sin all over again in order to stay alive as man or woman, on earth.

But in the greatest and simplest, yet subtlest and most complex, of all Sinan's classic Ottoman European mosques, in Islam, the architectonics inform me that the Muslims in orthodoxy have come to terms with themselves as men, and with God as God the One. He is in heaven; they are on earth below. The law alone unites them in the one true faith. In Islam, God and man are separate, by no means equal, but inseparable in their relativity.

So in the Selimiyé are the volumes and the voids. In its architecture, Sinan achieved clarity and simplicity. The mosque is coherent and serene. In the engineering of this effect of infinite unity, Sinan is at his most complex. He dovetails mass and space.

The outer walls, as usual, are engaged arcades meeting to form a rectangle. The arches spring from buttressed piers of stonemasonry. Engaged, the arcades are not blind; nor are they filled with straight screen walls. At the sides of the mosque, to right and left, Sinan built a solid stone wall between the pairs of piers, and the piers and the corners. The wall begins as though it were going to continue to the springing line of the arcade engaged in the side wall; but it does no such thing. Sinan cut three windows in it, at regular intervals a step up from floor level; rectangular, each one about eight feet tall. Sinan put clear glass in them, and the usual Ottoman iron grilles. He raised the wall above the windows about another seven feet, and stopped.

Along the top edge, he set a cornice of corbels. Upon this bold dentation of projecting brackets, he placed a marble railing, a row of many squared uprights topped by a long horizontal stone line. He filled each rectangle at the top of the railing with cornering "draperies" of stone cut to make arches.

Behind this parapet, he set two slim smooth marble monoliths. Properly spaced, they stand on top of the stone walls between the windows in the wall below; and they carry the springers of three arches that span the space between the massive piers (this arcade continues on either side between the piers and the corners of the mosque). The spandrels and the extradoses, rectified, carry the base of the screen wall of fourteen windows in two rows that rise to fill the arch at the top of the arcade engaged in the side walls.

Behind the pillars of the colonnade opens a gallery; it is the gynaeceum of the mosque, roofed by flat vaults. Under the floor of this gallery, and behind the stone wall below the railing and the pillars, there is a loggia, arcaded, that opens to the outside. The arches and pillars of the loggia carry the fenestrated wall behind the gallery that opens upon the interior space of the mosque. By means of the gallery superimposed upon the loggia, back to front, Sinan brought the outside space in, and let the inside space out of the prayer hall.

Subtle in intention and in design, complex in construction, complicated; hell in detail to describe, and impossible to translate from volume and void into black on white, from stone to words, the loggia and the gallery, the one below the other above – it all sounds as though Sinan were playing in space, juggling with reality and illusion, and with the nature of the Sacred Law. Henry Moore today makes a similar statement in terms of volume and void, but in a different idiom and with a much freer use of mass and space. A man walks up and down, into and out, and around and about a building.

The eight piers of the octagonal plan, at first sight, appear to be freestanding, which they are not. In section, each is dodecagonal, each of the twelve sides strongly paneled in rising lines to the first of two string courses. From this height spring the deepened soffits of the arches of the engaged arcades – those of the exterior rectangular walls. They spring from brackets built out behind the side piers; the brackets then turn into arches tying the freestanding lower sections of the piers to the buttresses of the outside walls.

Above this string course, the piers continue, but now they are engaged; the half that emerges from the walls is still dodecagonal in section, but the visible sides are no longer paneled. Sinan did not put capitals upon the piers; instead, he built out stalactite corbels to receive the springers of the eight high arches, those of the stalactite pendentives that join to make the ring cornice for the dome. The corbels are not identical; their function prescribes their shape and place.

Four arches, four squinches, eight piers, each of twelve sides — four, eight, and twelve are the mystical numbers of the Bektashi order of dervishes. There is no end to their significance and (right here) no beginning. Four, eight, and twelve mean whatever symbols mean. In all the high arches on two levels, twelve in the lower rectangle of the walls, eight in the octagon, the voussoirs are strongly accentuated. Cut from red marble and golden limestone, those of the twelve are smooth truncated wedges; those of the eight are not dovetailed but rippled at the edges to fit into one another.

The caretaker of the mosque — he is an old man, one of the imams — told me that there are nine hundred ninety-nine upright rising lines in the mosque, the verticals that lift the eye into the dome. He told me that there are nine hundred ninety-nine windows to let in the light. He must mean — that is to say, if the numbers are not mystical — all the elephant's-eyes in the high windows, as well as the clear and the stained glass panes in the windows of the lower walls, which number, according to my tally, three hundred seventy-five in all. The imam smiled when I asked and remarked that he himself had not counted them against the names of God multiplied . . . how? Raised to infinity from ninety-nine to nine hundred ninety-nine. The dervishes, sitting in a circle under the dome, recited their prayers on a single rosary of nine hundred ninety-nine carved wooden beads. They chanted the ninety-nine beautiful names as they fingered the polished and darkened beads passing on the cord from hand to hand; and the ninety-nine beautiful names soared up into the dome. By night as many as twenty-five thousand flames flickered from their floating wicks in the clear glass bell-shaped hanging lamps. In their starred mandalas of wrought iron overhead, just out of the reach of a tall man, they made a ceiling of light.

Sinan brought in all the Islamic arts to adorn, carefully, this quiet place. He set rectangular plaques of *opus sectile,* sober geometrical arabesques inlaid in rich and somber marbles, in a line along the base of the kibla wall. Above them on the kibla wall and in the *ayvan* of the prayer niche, he made sparing use of the most brilliant Iznik tiles. Enameled perfectly in clear patterns, all of them arabesqued, some of them calligraphic, he set them in the pointed demilunes above the rectangular windows at floor level. The windows, framed in marble, are about eight feet high inside the embrasure; they give the eye a human, if heroic, standard of measurement.

Sinan covered the spandrels in the arcades of the galleries with more tiles made to his order in Iznik and enameled with branches of fruit blossom, tulips, and hyacinths on green stems with green leaves. He set a band of calligraphy running along all three walls of the apse-*ayvan* on either side of the prayer niche. Below the calligraphic band he set panels in patterns of medallions surrounded by floral arabesques in arched frames. Against the immaculate white background, the colors under the clear glaze are sealing-wax red, dark blue, turquoise blue, and the green as rare and as translucent as emerald.

In the Sultan's loge, built into the east corner of the gallery, there is the portrait of an apple tree in the tile panel on the wall. Round red fruit grow among green leaves from strong limbs branching from a stout tree trunk rooted in green fields. To look at Sinan's and Selim's apple tree makes me smile. I take it that they enjoyed both the apples, famous in the orchards of Edirné, and the Iznik potters' tree. (There was a second tree until January 20, 1878, when Russian soldiers pried out the tiles, and after the peace treaty, carted them off to Russia. There the apple tree tiles may still serve a peasant to stand a samovar upon a table. The Russians left behind them a rusty iron cannon ball lodged high up in the northeast wall, outside, in a tight limestone cavity of its own making.)

Inside the mosque, the *minber*, which is the high pulpit of the imam's sermon at the midday service on Friday, stands at right angles to the kibla wall. It is not in the raised apse-*ayvan* but outside and below on the floor to the right of the prayer niche. Triangular in shape, the flight of steps cut in the hypotenuse are guarded by pierced marble railings. Under the tiled canopy at the head of the steps, the Prophet, in spirit, looks down upon the faithful. From his place in this mosque, he smiles. The imam does not intrude upon him; instead, he stops his ascent on the third step from the top and turns to address the congregation. In the Selimiyé, the *minber* is a work of abstract sculpture. Sinan reduced the solid marble sides to annul the heavy substance of the stone. He pierced the slabs with daylight carvings to make a series of triangles, one within the other, centered upon a wheel. He used the traditional patterns of both Rumî and geometric arabesques. The first is pagan and Christian in origin and is taken from nature. The name Rumî comes from Rome, which Shakespeare tells us was pronounced "Room"; it came to mean first Byzantine and then Seljuk. The Rumî arabesque is cursive, flowing; the line comes from the silhouettes of water birds, long-legged, curving of neck and breast, long-beaked, wide-winged, standing among vines and water plants. The geometrical arabesque likewise is interlocking, without beginning or end, but the straight lines join and intersect in many angles and in man-drawn patterns as logical and as abstract as intellection.

Sinan covered the wide floors with Ushak carpets designed in similar arabesques but in formal, stylized flower beds, woven to his order in glossy woolen yarns that were dyed with natural dyes such as indigo and madder. They have long since been worn out. His original paintings in the dome likewise have been replaced clumsily. The dome leaks, such is the vulnerability of lead-sheathed, brick-and-mortar, hemispherical domes; however, no engineer or roofer has yet thought out and put to work a better drainage system of gutters and vents than Sinan's, and none so beautiful to watch. The plaster has fallen here and there from the painted inner surface of the dome. The architects of the Vakiflar have thus found and traced Sinan's own designs, which are classical. He painted them in the blue of the sky and the yellow of the sun.

The mosque of Selim the Sot is a noble building, flooded with a kindly light. The man could not have been so bad a man as he was a poor ruler. The imam told me that after Sinan had finished his memorial, visitors from Rome – they seem to have been the very same Frankish architects whom Evliya Chelebi got to know in the early seventeenth century at the Süleymaniyé – walked into the Selimiyé. This time they did not bite their fingers, throw their hats in the air, and cry out *"Mama mia!"* Instead, they told the imam of their own day that Sinan's dome was nobler than his contemporary Michelangelo's Saint Peter's. It is serene and it is joyous. Here Sinan is triumphant, as in the triumph achieved by man at peace on earth in Islam.

Sinan called this mosque the work of a master builder. It is built of the knowledge of experience, of wisdom. The single dome soars in the shape of human understanding, of freedom. There is no beginning, there is no end to it. It is as fresh as ever-returning spring.

Outside the mosque the paved courtyard duplicates the covered floor space. Arcaded, centered upon a fountain, a monumental portal rising in the northwest side opposite the equally splendid entrance to the prayer hall, the court is traditional in the disposition of all its elements. In plan, it is similar to those of its predecessors, the Süleymaniyé, the Shehzadé Jami, and the Mosque of Selim the Grim. At first glance, the eye takes in the familiar essentials, and only then sees the revealing details. At Edirné, for the second Selim whom the Janissaries, the Slaves of the Gate, and the people of Istanbul called variously descriptive ugly names, Sinan, apparently, chose to remember him not as the Sultan, but as the man, a human being like himself.

On the way to prayer in the Mosque of Selim the Fair, a man walks through a shapely open space that is more than serene and harmonious; it is a matter of freedom and of choice, various in repose, welcoming and joyfully at peace. Herein, the religious discipline comes about as an act of quiet faith, not as in arbitrary obedience to the fixed system of a rigid law locked in by a closed gate; and certainly not out of desperation and despair. Here there are no dialectics. There is nothing of the circumscribed enclosure, nothing of the cage.

On all sides, Siann broke the military rhythm of the arcades. He gave the colonnade of the high porch five arches. But of these, three are round, and they are higher and wider than the two that stand among them. These are sharp-pointed lancet arches, narrower and necessarily lower. Four of the six pillars in the row are smooth monoliths of pink Egyptian granite, as usual taken from some Byzantine or Roman ruin. But the four pillars separate into two pairs of the same height but of different girth. The two thicker columns flank the entrance and support the central one of the three high, round arches. Next, close by on either side stand the thinner monoliths. They receive both springers of each of the lower, pointed arches. The next arches on either side again rise high and round. Their far springers rise from the two corner pillars.

And these corner pillars are composites, half pink granite monoliths, the upper half made of piled up drums of smooth white marble in the (to me) markedly clumsy makeshift solution of the corner pillars in the courtyard of the Süleymaniyé. Half corbel, half capital brackets, set on top of the dense pink granite truncated monolith, receive the end springers of the side arcades that come in at right angles. On top of the assembled voussoir-and-haunch-engaged drums of white marble, the more-than-half stalactite capital, likewise engaged in the haunch of the side arch, receives, as in a flanking attack, the high round arch at the end of the porch. Once again these complex corner piers propose the problem of engineering, and demonstrate the architectural solution (as well, it may be, as the imperfectibility of mankind. I find them no longer troublesome, but instead thoroughly interesting. They demonstrate and prove their own efficiency). Sinan was expert.

All the voussoirs alternate in red and white marble blocks. Above the two low-pointed arches, in their spandrels, Sinan placed a pair of white marble discs carved in calligraphic wheels, literally meaningful today only to the highly educated Orientalist, but beautiful to any eye.

Sinan convered the square spaces at the ends of the porch with appropriate domes, as well as the three round arches, that of the high round arch in the center, over the doorway, raised and grooved. Flanking it, the narrow rectangular spaces above the low and pointed arches are roofed with cradle vaults.

The rhythm of this uneven colonnade does not falter. Major and minor? How to say it? There appears to be less effort, greater ease, in the forces exerted to uphold the dome: a kinetic freedom? Again the complexity — it is an irregularity — results in an effect of light-hearted freedom. The broken rhythm lifts the sense of strain from the tensions implicit in the thrust and the resistant counterweight. Sinan knew what he was doing.

I walk out through the monumental portal (it is one that Sinan took complete from an earlier mosque, and it is classic). I turn — and find it impossible not to look up, and equally impossible not to smile. True, the jaw tends to fall open as the head upon the neck bends back; but the smile is not mechanical, it comes from delight. The four minarets, each of three galleries, are (I am told) 86 meters high (283 feet 9 or 10 inches). It does not matter, ells, aunes, inches, feet, meters; in whatever scale, the minarets are astonishingly tall. Such was Sinan's intention.

He placed them at the four corners of the rectangular walls of the mosque. They stand guard over the dome. In section, these four masonry towers are decahexagonal. All their tapering lines ascend, broken, as in rhythms of penetration, by the ringing galleries on circular stalactite corbels.

The four minarets lift the dome. Without them, the dome, as soft as a breast, as heavy as a pregnant belly, and as vulnerable, as smooth and as gentle in coloring as a dove's breast in the patina of its lead sheathing, would press down heavily upon the round hilltop. The four upright minarets lift and hold up the dome in space above the rolling landscape, feminine in its fertility, of groves of trees and orchards, ploughed and planted fields, and slow-moving streams. Once again, there they are, the masculine and the feminine principles. In balance, they underly the architectonics of any ethos. I do not understand the significance of four to one. The dome is dominant. Can it be that the female principle is unique in the realities? And that the male is free to create and to multiply his ideas of order?

When a Muslim, a man in the climax of love, ejaculates his sperm, he cries out *"Bismillah!"* "O gracious and compassionate God!" For, if it please God, *Inshallah!* The woman conceives the child, who then begins the journey. When she brings forth, it is a recurrent miracle. *"Mashallah!"* "What (wonders) God hath willed!"

And I, about to enter the low doorway at the base of the north minaret, hear myself say *Bismillah!* — inordinately pleased with myself for knowing enough to say the word uttered, in Islam, when a man enters upon any undertaking. I have put my foot on the first step into the unknown, to go spiraling up into the dark and towering space. Sinan built three separate helices, one above the other, around the central pillar which the steps themselves construct inside the minaret. The first staircase ends at the lowest gallery, the second at the next, the third at the topmost. In such virtuosity, designed to reduce the crushing weight of the tapering mass of stonemasonry, I climb the minaret. If they were not hollow, they could not rise so high.

The substance of this minaret is limestone, coarse and weathered but fresh-cut from the quarry, once golden. It is a sedimentary rock, not a magma; it is a slow growth, a piling up at the bottom of a prehistoric ocean, a bed of the calcareous remains of infinitesimal organism that lived higher up in the fathoms below the surface, died, and drifted down. Then the earth shook; and in the upheaval the dry land emerged. In it Sinan found the quarry he chose. There are whole spiral shells in the limestone of this minaret.

The door at the base opens through massive walls as thick as an out-stretched man. Then, rising in the calculations of Sinan's long experience, the minaret tapers as it takes place. He knew what he was doing from the start; but the three spiraling staircases rise from the level in a virtuosity of technique, each wedge-shaped step at the wide end built into its place in the rising shell, its pointed end blunted in the shape of a round. The minaret is as solid in its economy as a molecule.

Each stone step is worn hollow with the mounting footsteps of four centuries of muezzins. They were young men, God knows. Each one had a head for heights. On the Night of Power at the end of Ramazan, seventy-five of them, or sixty-six, or forty-five, or at least thirty-six, divided into thirds, spun the spiraling staircases, the men soundest in wind and limb went all the way to the top, the others raveled off in strands below. None could have been six feet tall; for otherwise he would have had to bend his head or bloodied it, or been scalped by the stones above, abrasive with snail shells. Coughing loud-speakers of a public address system have supplanted the young muezzins.

It is a long, and to the halt, an increasingly difficult ascent, this dark and spiraling crescendo, punctuated by flashes of light coming in through narrow vertical openings like arrow slits. Through them, the eye measures the width of the walls that taper as the tower rises. There seems to be no end to it. Perhaps so it feels to be born. Panting, the heart pounding, ejaculating (if I remember rightly) *Mashallah! Bismillah! Inshallah!* I come out at the top of the spiral through the small portal onto the high gallery, my eyes dazzled by the glory of the world.

From on high, the dome in its crown of eight prongs, which are the pointed turrets on top of the eight piers — and below them all the descending squared levels, the four conchs of the cornered squinch arches; and all the buttresses, some of them flying — whirls, as though not the law of gravity but the laws of aerodynamics lift the mosque from the ground. Earth, air, fire, water — Sinan's construction is elemental.

Wit is penetration; it is wisdom, serious joy. The minarets of the Selimiyé in Edirné may be tours de force; but they are strong towers. The dome may be soft; there is nothing more enduring. Sinan built in the effortless perfec-tion of a flower, of a crystal. Style is substance put to its own shape. The volume designates the void; the space gives mass its meaning. Obverse and reverse — from any point of view, inside or out, the mind behind the eye can see and know the shape of the other side: interior and exterior.

Whatever a dome is, this is a dome. Whatever a minaret may be, these are four minarets. In perfect mastery of his craft, call it the science of engineer-ing, Sinan used his experienced hands to make whatever architecture is — it is an art. Whoever God may be, in all the ninety-nine beautiful names, God is God. So man is man. Stone is stone, each in its own nature; or otherwise Sinan's Imperial Friday Mosque of Sultan Selim the Sot is a powerful great lot of nonsense. It fits him like a shell.

17

When, early in December of 1574, the fat little monarch, bored and out of work at the age of fifty, choosing to go on a tour of inspection against Sinan's advice, tossed off his bumper of Cyprian wine, and, waddling into the new *hamam,* looked up, saw stars, slipped and fell, cracked his skull, and caught his death of cold in the chill of the hot room, the Royal Chief Architect, a powerful old man of eighty-five, bent, picked him up, and shouted for the palace pages and the Janissary guardsmen. Selim the Sot's memorial in Edirné was ready, but his mausoleum in Istanbul was not. Sinan got to work to build the tomb. He finished it in 1577.

The Royal Chief Architect did his finest work over the dozen years in which he completed the Friday Imperial Mosque of Sultan Selim II Khan, in Edirné; the mosque and college for the Grand Vezir Sokollu Mehmet Pasha, in Istanbul, in 1571; the mausoleum for the Sot, ready to receive the embalmed body two years and more after the death; and the witty and wry complex for Shemsi Ahmet Pasha, on the Asian shore of the Bosphorus, in 1580. These four buildings alone give the full measure of Sinan as a man, a Slave of the Gate, and an architect.

The Sultan's tomb is a fine but not a typical example of Ottoman funeral architecture. It stands in the enclosure of the Church-Mosque of the Divine Wisdom. Two years before his death, Selim had ordered his Royal Chief Architect to restore the fabric of Haghia Sophia, then nine hundred thirty-five years old. Sinan built the buttresses at the four corners which still shore up the weight of the celestial dome, and erected the limestone minarets at the north and the west corners (the other two, of brick, were built in earlier reigns). He thereby gave to the ancient building of Anthemius of Tralles its final aspect. Sinan did not change, he preserved, the space within a space of the Byzantine Christian interior, but he gave the present museum its Ottoman Islamic exterior.

Such may well describe Sinan's own character in his green old age. Into the Shehzadé he had built the ornamented splendor of a disciplined soldier. The first of his "cathedral" mosques is as handsome and as powerful as the general of the Janissary engineers and the *Haseki* of the Sultan's Own Guard of Honor must have been when he built it to stand and to serve, a mighty bulwark of the Lord.

Into the Süleymaniyé, Sinan built the enormous and intolerable power of the magnificent Sultan, which is the unavoidable weakness in the architectonics of this tremendous place of prostration. Too vast, too big, the absolutes confound the man at prayer, who is inescapably lost in the overwhelming volumes and their consequent voids within the prayer hall under the power of its strength.

Selim the Sot, a sultan who refused to rule his inheritance, was the first Son of Osman to be despised by both the Janissaries and the vezirs and pashas of his Slave Family and by his people; worse, even by himself. For him Sinan built his masterwork, the Selimiyé in Edirné. The complex simplicity of this noble building houses the mysterious dualism of Selim the Second, the Sot, the Fair, and, it may be, of all men and all man's works. As a sultan, he was worthless; although forced by birth to live beyond his capacities and, perhaps in consequence, driven to acts of fearful duplicity and to drink, as a private person, when left alone, he was a good man. As a patron of the arts, in particular of architecture, Selim II has no superior. He knew Sinan's worth, Sinan knew his. Together they got on well to do their particular work.

The mausoleum is a quiet place, full of light, and adorned with the finest of Iznik tiles. There is nothing in it of gloomy, stately, funereal pomp. Sheathed on the exterior with Proconnesus marble, which is white streaked with gray, and here flushed with pink, the tomb is square and domical. Inside, Sinan erected an octagonal colonnade to carry the interior dome. These two domes, it may be, once again stand for the life on earth and the life eternal; man and God; the body and the soul; or for any man's public and private lives. One within the other, the domes may well symbolize the illusion and the reality.

At the head of the empty coffin, the dead Sultan's imperial turban was placed on its post; but there is no canopy of state above the body in the grave beneath the floor. Sinan — or more probably, the Grand Vezir Sokollu Mehmet Pasha, who was Selim the Sot's imperial son-in-law and who had ruled the empire while his father-in-law reigned — decided against erecting a baldachin over this failure.

But in the generosity of the interior space, Sinan gave Selim II plenty of room. He lies surrounded by his family. The tomb has filled up with history; as usual, there is too much of it. Selim the Sot's coffin, like his empire, was much too big for the man; he lies surrounded by thirty-four lesser coffins. They once were spread with palls of velvet in dark colors embroidered with bright gold and seed pearls in texts from the Koran. Over the past four centuries the palls have fallen apart. Today the empty wooden coffins, four of them very big indeed, some of them very small, have been re-covered with green baize in the usual color of the stuff on conference and pool tables. Selim's widow, the Lady Nûrûbanû, who survived him as the Validé Sultan; their favorite son, a prince who died young; and their daughter, Esmahan Gevher Sultan, the widow of the assassinated Grand Vezir Sokollu Mehmet Pasha, once occupied the major coffins. Five of the lesser coffins contained the embalmed bodies of the younger sons who had been strangled shortly after their father's death by their elder brother's mutes when Sultan Murad III Khan ascended the throne.

Other small coffins served Selim the Sot's minor grandsons, the imperial princes who had to be strangled along with their fathers by their uncle, the reigning Sultan, all according to their ancestor Mehmet the Conqueror's law of fratricide. The rest of the small coffins were used for imperial princesses, who died ordinary deaths.

The new Sultan Murad III was twenty-eight in 1574. He was as tall as his grandfather Süleyman, but an epileptic like the Prophet; the Sultan, unlike Mohammed, retired from public life into the remote Byzantine majesty of the court. He reappointed the Grand Vezir Sokollu Mehmet Pasha, his sister Esmaham Gevher Sultan's husband, to administer and to rule the empire. To see what Sinan built into the mosque that Esmahan Gevher Sultan commissioned him to build as a memorial foundation for her husband, it is essential first to understand the personalities of the men and women, and then the history either that made them what they were, or that they made.

Sinan knew Esmahan Gevher Sultan as well as he knew her husband, the Grand Vezir. She was intelligent; she showed both good sense and good taste in providing Sinan with the means to build his masterpiece. An imperious Daughter of Osman, she was a short and a very plain woman, but, as her given name Gevher implies, she was known for the jewels of wit that fell from her lips. Certainly, like her grandmother Haseki Hürrem and like her aunt the Imperial Princess Mihrimah, Esmahan Gevher Sultan enjoyed meddling in politics. Equally certainly, her choice of Sokollu Mehmet Pasha for a husband when she was seventeen years old gives a measure of her intelligence. It is true that after his death, when she was thirty-three, she failed miserably in her attempt to maintain her power. In her indecorous search for a second husband, one man, Osman Pasha, her first choice among the Slaves of the Gate, turned her down. Her second choice, Ali Pasha, the governor of Buda, a vezir of the Divan, and a beylerbey, divested himself in such unseemly haste of his wives and children that nothing but ridicule came of the marriage of convenience. Both the Imperial Princess Esmahan Gevher and Ali Pasha, "The Joker," drop out of history.

The Grand Vezir was an austere man, tall, thin, and powerful. In his great days, he was gray of beard and hair, high-nosed, beaked like the falcon of the eyrie of his name. In his younger days in power, he had enjoyed a display of masculine grandeur when he went forth in state to carry out the Sultan's orders. Then he surrounded himself with a suite of glittering Janissary guardsmen and a retinue of pages of the palace clad in uniforms of cloth of gold. He rode under banners striped red and white on a war-horse dyed red and white.

In his sober old age, he carried himself erect under the burden of not quite total power, which was the heavier for being less than absolute. The Grand Vezir may have intimidated both the short, stout, and rubicund Selim the Sot and the tall, dark, and remote Murad III, but he could control neither the person nor the whim of the Son of Osman on the throne surrounded by a court of boon companions. They chafed under the restrictions imposed, willy-nilly, by the model Grand Vezir upon their frivolous and costly and idle and extravagant pleasures.

The Grand Vezir knew what all of us know, that change is essential to the continuity of strength and health in any viable social and political and religious order. He tried and he failed to make the changes possible within the established system of the Ruling Institution. When denied the force of growth, first stagnation and then corruption set into any human being or any body politic. In part it is to be said that Sokollu Mehmet Pasha's moderate reforms were arrested by the dead hand of Süleyman the Magnificent, which would not admit of change.

Prevented from revolutionizing the basis of Ottoman economy from the loot and booty of constant victory in Holy Wars to the peaceful revenues brought into the Golden Horn by means of trade and commerce, the Grand Vezir fought a losing battle against inflation and extravagance. The state revenues declined as Mexican and Incan gold poured into Spain, and the wealth of the Indies and of Brazil poured into Portugal and Holland. As Selim the Sot found Joseph Nassy and gave him the monopoly in the wine trade, so Murad III found his own man and his own means to supply him with private means.

Shemsi Ahmet Pasha takes the credit for bringing on the decline and fall of the Ottoman Empire. This scion of a most ancient family, the Isfendi-yaroghlus, that was nobler than the Sons of Osman, was a direct descendant of the once-independent Emirs of Kastamonu and Sinope and a collateral descendant of the early sultan-khans' formerly hereditary Grand Vezirs, the Jandarlis. These good men had established the Janissary corps and had worked out both systems of recruiting the slave soldiers from the *penjik* prisoners of war, of whom the Grand Vezir Sokollu Mehmet Pasha was one, and the *devishirmé* Christian tribute youths, of whom Sinan was one.

Sinan knew Shemsi Ahmet Pasha, and knew him to be a delightfully corrupt man. In 1580 the Royal Chief Architect, then ninety-one years old, built for him a witty and a wry complex that is shaped like a boomerang – a mausoleum, a mosque, and a college which (restored) is still the ornament of the Asian shore of the Bosphorus. Into this "sweet little mosque," as Evliya Chelebi described it in the seventeenth century, Sinan built a portrait of the man.

Shemsi Ahmet Pasha, one of the boon companions and favorites of Sultan Murad III, came to be known as the "Hawk of the Petitioners" for justice, or redress, or special treatment in the Divan. He feathered his nest as a lobbyist. In the interests of one of his clients, he brought off his greatest coup by persuading his remote cousin on the distaff side, the then Shehzadé Murad, to accept a bribe of forty thousand Venetian gold ducats – a fortune that was the equivalent in purchasing power of some two million American gold dollars, pre-World War I. In return, the Prince Imperial, apparently in the year before he ascended the throne, was asked to use his influence to go over the head of the Grand Vezir, who, it seems, had found against Shemsi Ahmet Pasha's client.

His own success appears to have astonished him. Bubbling over with laughter, Shemsi Ahmet Pasha retired to his own rooms in the palace, where the Ottoman historian Ali was awaiting him. "At last," he said (or words to this effect), "I have avenged my ancestors for what the Sons of Osman did to us. Bayazid the Thunderbolt annexed our emirate and our estates. Mehmet the Conqueror disgraced and executed the Jandarli Halil Pasha, the Grand Vezir, on trumped-up charges of corruption in accepting bribes from the defeated Byzantines. Today I have arranged to bring down the House of Osman."

"How so? " asked the venerable historian Ali, who had begun his career as an usher in the court of Süleyman the Magnificent.

"By catching the Prince on a hook. True, I offered him a powerful bait – forty thousand Venetian gold ducats. From now on the Sultan himself will set the example of corruption, and corruption will dissolve the empire."

Ali ironically remarked that Shemsi Ahmet Pasha's act was in all ways worthy of the descendant of the Companion of the Prophet named Khalid ben Walid, who, to gain special treatment, had introduced corruption into Islam by bribing the chamberlain of the third Caliph, Osman, a son-in-law of the Prophet, whose powerful family later usurped the succession, to establish the hereditary dynasty of the Omayyad Caliphs of Damascus.

Shemsi Ahmet Pasha, chuckling, said, "What a lot you know, Ali." And he set to work to compose the mock epic in which he celebrated his revenge by means of the flagrant corruption of Murad III. About 1800 the Austrian historian of the Ottomans, Graf Josef von Hammer-Purgstall bought from a *hamam*-bathman in Istanbul the manuscript copy of the poem annotated in the margins by the Grand Mufti Ebüsuud, who died in 1574, the year of Murad III's accession to the throne.

Sinan belongs to all time. But while the Grand Vezir Sokollu Mehmet Pasha did his best to maintain the standards of the great days, Shemsi Ahmet Pasha rode the wave of the future. In the first years of Murad III's reign, the spreading corruption took the form of frivolity in the abuse of power in acts of gross buffoonery. For instance, when the Austrian emissaries of the Holy Roman Emperor, on their way from Vienna to sign peace treaties with the Grand Vezir in Istanbul, crossed the frontier at Buda, they were captured by ruffians, stripped, and publicly humiliated – some of them were mutilated in impious mock ceremonies of actual circumcision. Then, after such border incidents, the captured Christians were decapitated and their heads on pikes were carried in grisly parades that, intended as shows of strength, revealed the weakness implicit in the breakdown of Janissary discipline.

The Sultan's favorites, encouraged and emboldened, moved in closer to rid themselves of the Grand Vezir. Too much of a man for them to attack outright, he was a monument which they chipped away at through his friends, his associates, his protégés, and finally through members of his family.

The Grand Vezir's old enemy, Lala Mustafa Pasha, the conqueror of Cyprus, and, by that time, as the husband of Murad III's daughter, Hüma Sultan, a demi-imperial *damat*, joined the favorites to make a great self-righteous display of bringing to justice one of the Grand Vezir's appointees. Perhaps because he could not find an Ottoman Turk willing to soil his hands in business and commerce, the Grand Vezir – mistakenly, as things turned out – had awarded the monopoly in salt to his Greek friend of noble Byzantine family, Michael Cantacuzene. The Greek Patriarch Metrophanes, who had made the highest bid, objected. Lala Mustafa Pasha saw to it that the Grand Vezir's reputation for probity suffered in the ensuing scandal, and saw to it that Michael Cantacuzene was lynched – hanged in the arch of his own portal.

Then, on Cyprus, the Janissaries were encouraged to revolt against the governor of the island, an Arabian Negro, a Muslim slave from Mecca, whom Sokollu Mehmet Pasha had purchased, freed, and adopted as a son. Hacked to death, his bloody clothes were delivered to the Grand Vezir along with the news of the mutiny.

The favorites came in closer. They got the Sultan to dismiss from high office the Nishanji Pasha, the Keeper of the Privy Seal, a sort of secretary of state. This man, Feridun Pasha, had been the Grand Vezir's secretary at Szigetvár at the time of Sultan Süleyman's death; and he had carried the news of his succession to Selim the Sot in Manisa. An honest man and an able administrator, Feridun Pasha could not be put to death, but the favorites had the Sultan demote him and banish him from the Grand Vezir's administration to govern the minor district of Belgrade, all this to humiliate the Grand Vezir.

They next accused of malversion and malfeasance Mustafa Sokollozadé Pasha, the Grand Vezir's nephew, a Slave of the Gate, and Süleyman the Magnificent's last appointed governor of Buda. This time the favorites struck quickly. They removed Mustafa Sokollozadé from office and had him strangled on the same day, October 10, 1578.

Two days later, in Istanbul, a Bosnian petitioner, dressed as a dervish, entered the Divan in the grand vezirate; as he presented his plea, he drew a knife and stabbed the Grand Vezir in the breast. Sokollu Mehmet Pasha had the strength to draw his own jeweled dagger and jump to his feet before he fell dead.

The assassin was a petty nobleman thought to be deranged but known to be from Bosnia, as were his victim and Sokollu Mehmet Pasha's mortal enemy, Lala Mustafa Pasha. They were born in the same town, the one the son of the village priest, the other the heir to the castle on the crag known as the Falcon's Eyrie. The one was the Grand Vezir; the other had been promised the grand vezirate as a reward for his part in the fratricidal struggles between the sons of his first cousin, Süleyman the Magnificent, that ended with Selim the Sot's survival to accede to the throne.

Lala Mustafa Pasha survived Sokollu Mehmet for only two years. Although he was successful in the wholly unnecessary Caucasian campaign to capture Tiflis, he was not appointed Grand Vezir upon his return. In 1580, he died conveniently "of chagrin," or of an undiagnosed disease, or of poison, perhaps self-administered. If so, then like his elder brother, Hüsrev Pasha, Sinan's earliest patron, he died a suicide. Or so the gossip of the Favorites at court, and in the harems, and in the bazaars had it. Lala Mustafa Pasha, who successfully schemed to bring about the death of Prince Bayazid, who succeeded in skinning alive Bragadino on Cyprus, and who had a hand in the assassination of the greatest of the Ottoman grand vezirs but who failed to reach his own goal, was buried in Bursa in the same year that the successful corruptor, Shemsi Ahmet Pasha, was entombed in the complex that Sinan had built for him on the Asian shore of the Bosphorus.

As usual, the small mosque and mausoleum, although clearly the work of Sinan's own hands and eyes, is unlike any other. The tomb is a sort of annex to the prayer hall. Against the northeast wall of the mosque, Sinan built the tomb as a rectangular lean-to and roofed it with a kind of oblong dome. Before he died, Shemsi Ahmet Pasha, out of his ill-gotten gains, had thoughtfully paid for an eternity of prayers to speed his soul's journey on the long road through limbo into Paradise. To help the humorous man to sample the only remaining joys left untasted, those of Paradise, Sinan opened a high and wide arch in the masonry wall separating the tomb from the mosque. He filled the archway with a splendid grille of bronze that does not hinder the speed of sound that the hired mourners make in the adjoining prayer hall as they raise their voices loud and clear to beg God's forgiveness of Shemsi Ahmet Pasha's ancient sins.

The imam in the spring of 1965 was blind; he sat sunning himself in the evening on the porch that Sinan built along both the northwestern and the southwestern sides of the little mosque. It has no courtyard but instead a kind of lawn. From across the greensward of the open space between the buildings, the blind old leader in prayer, at ease, could smell the fragrance of the blossoming white rose vine that climbed a monolith of green porphyry and spread along the springers and the spandrels in the boomerang-shaped arcade of the college. Then as today, young men, no longer burning theological students but fishermen, dive from the stone embankment on the far side of the low stone wall of the mosque enclosure to swim in the Bosphorus.

On the evening of the Grand Vezir's death by assassination, or perhaps, for it was late in the day, the next morning, October 13, 1578, Sinan and his workmen opened the floor in the modest tomb and dug the grave to bury his old friend Sokollu Mehmet Pasha. He lies alone in his mausoleum, which is octagonal and domical. It is severe and simple in its classic Ottoman plan.

The Grand Vezir chose to be buried at Eyüp by the shrine of the Prophet's Standard-Bearer in sacred ground that, after Mecca, Medina, and Jerusalem, is the most holy place in orthodox Islam. Sinan adorned the tomb of the most powerful of grand vezirs only with glass stained almost as pure a blue as the blue of Chartres. He set the glass in screens of arabesques to fill the lancet windows placed high in the walls of the mausoleum that stands outside the joining of the land walls and the sea walls at the top of the Golden Horn. Blue is the color of fidelity.

He had prepared for his death. As was the custom, Sokollu Mehmet Pasha and Sinan worked together on the design for the memorial mosque, the minaret, the courtyard, and the college that the Royal Chief Architect had completed seven years earlier, in 1571. At the end of that summer when Sinan and the Grand Vezir walked into the new mosque, Sokollu Mehmet Pasha saw that he was not alone. The Royal Chief Architect understood the dimensions of the task that he had seen fit to shoulder. The fact that both men proved to be irreplaceable proves that the Golden Age had come to its own end. Both men must have known that there were no more Slaves of the Gate like them to carry the empire to new heights.

First in the courtyard and then inside the mosque, the gray-bearded, high-turbaned "Bearer of the Burden," as I imagine it, looked about him and then turned to look at Sinan, a white-bearded, white-turbaned man, his companion in the service no longer of the Son of Osman on the throne, but of the Ottoman idea of order. The one man was as tall, as straight, and as powerful as the other, although Sinan was the elder by some fourteen years. I think that they said very little to one another. Whatever there was, and still is, to say is all there in the architecture. The courtyard and the mosque are still silent places.

Portraits exist of Sokollu Mehmet Pasha; they are not necessarily apocryphal. The gossip leading up to his death by violence whispered that he had a secret cabinet in the palace that Sinan built for him, and on the walls impiously he hung paintings, such as those portraits by the Bellinis, and who knows? by Carpaccio, by Titian, or indeed by Giorgione (if so, these paintings may well have been the lost landscapes). After his assassination, some of the paintings were destroyed, and some were sold in the bazaar to Byzantine Greeks, Armenians, the Sephardic bankers — or perhaps the Venetian bailiff brought them back. Sokollu Mehmet Pasha was a connoisseur.

For his mosque he and Sinan chose a site behind the Hippodrome, within easy walking distance of the Grand Vezir's palace. It stands on the steep western slope where the First Hill joins the southwestern slopes of the Second Hill that go down to the sea walls along the crescent shore of the Marmara. The mosque is not far from where Anthemius of Tralles a thousand years earlier built the Church of Saints Sergius and Bacchus, which the Turks today call Küchük Ayasofya, Little Haghia Sophia, and which he may well have designed as a sort of dress rehearsal for the Church of the Divine Wisdom. The church is the earliest example of Byzantine architecture left standing in the City of God.

Oriented to point to Mecca, which lies due southeast, the kibla wall of Sinan's masterpiece faces the retaining wall of a deep excavation. To level the platform for the foundations, Sinan cut into the Devonian rock of the hillside, and with the fill built out a terrace to support the courtyard and the college that therefore rise above the narrow floor of the valley to the northwest.

From the now-vanished Palace of Sokollu Mehmet Pasha on the water side of the Byzantine Hippodrome, I cross to the opposite side and walk under the walls of the existing palace of the Grand Vezir, the strangled favorite Ibrahim, which Sinan helped to enlarge, and where he was trained as a Janissary cadet in engineering. Just before I come to the curved end of terraced Hippodrome, I turn right to take the same steep and cobblestoned road that Sokollu Mehmet Pasha took. It is now grass-grown, but it still leads down to the east corner of the rectangular walled enclosure. Here I stop to look. The eye of the beholder is on a level with the gilt-bronze finial *alem* on top of the lead-sheathed dome that is ridged like the latitude and longitude of a globe.

I look beyond the finial and the cone of the minaret that rise out of treetops and I see an amphitheater of streets and houses, of squares, of other domes and minarets and other trees. It is an old section of the city. Many of the houses are built of unpainted wood that has weathered. Having escaped the fires, these houses are all that remain of Ottoman domestic architecture. Many-windowed, with pots of carnations and sweet basil growing on the ledges, the houses look good to live in; they are roofed with handmade red-brown pantiles. Dove-gray and sunny orange-colored lichens grow on the ridges, with green moss in the grooves. Below the houses and across the sea walls, the Marmara rises flat and steep and blue to the horizon in the afternoon of an autumn day. Beyond the land walls on the crest of the far hills, the sun begins to set.

Watching my footing on the worn cobblestones, I descend the straight street that follows the long northeastern wall of the mosque enclosure. Part way down, at a rectangular opening out in the slanting wall, I stop to look through the grid of the iron Ottoman grille into the thin treetops and down on the graves and marble tombstones in the garden at the side of the mosque.

From the dark floor of the garden, trees — walnuts, terebinths, sycamores, trees of heaven, a pine or a cypress or two — have grown up tall and thin as they reach for the sunlight. To enter the mosque I turn left through the arched gate halfway down the hillside. I cross the open space, walk through a tunnellike passage under the gatekeeper's lodge, and step into the courtyard. I walk along the raised platform of the high-pillared porch and go through the portal. It is monumental, set in a classic niche, the conical section at the top filled with most elegantly carved, white marble, geometrical stalactities, most of them engaged, but some hanging free in the round overhead. Sometimes a pigeon takes advantage of the lifted heavy leather curtain and the opened carved and inlaid door to fly in after the man who has come to look, or come to prayer.

Stone, mortar, and lead are sober, weighty substances. Inside the mosque, the square walls and the hemispherical dome define the limitations of the mass-enclosed space. But were no other of Sinan's buildings to remain, the Ottoman Islamic Mosque of the Grand Vezir Sokollu Mehmet Pasha would alone give sufficient evidence of his supremacy among the world's architects.

For his friend, a perfect Slave of the Gate, Sinan chose to build upon the hexagonal plan. To uphold the dome, he set six pillars of masonry on the circumference of the circle inscribed within the square, which he extended to right and to left in order to accommodate the Islamic liturgy. If from each pillar a line in the radius of the circle is drawn to the center, it becomes evident that six equal isosceles triangles have been joined at their apices, with their joined bases forming the hexagonal, as of a snowflake.

Such is the pattern of the droplet of water frozen as it falls through the air. The molecule H_2O prescribes its own and its inevitable crystalline pattern. The snowflakes, like Sinan's hexagonal mosques, take their shapes as forms of the mandala, which Sinan took to carving into the surfaces of his building as his signature, his sign manual. They are all similar but infinitely various, no two alike.

In our current passion to explain everything, it has been said that this hexagonal and triangular pattern, which implies the circle and the square, and which is built upon six frozen water molecules, satisfies the mind, the spirit, the soul, and the instinctive body of mankind as no other shape in nature can. It is perfect in that it contains all forms, as white, which is the color of the snowflake, contains all colors in the sunlight.

In the plan of the mosque of Sokollu Mehmet Pasha, Sinan did not draw a perfect crystalline hexagonal. He spaced the pair of piers engaged in the kibla wall, and the corresponding pair of piers opposite that are attached to the buttresses flanking the portal, just a bit wider apart than the others. That is to say, in his floor plan, each of the two remaining piers at either side of the mosque stands equidistant from the adjoining pier engaged in the kibla wall and from the buttressed pier beside the portal. Therefore, they carry four equal arches that are not so wide as the other two.

I think that Sinan arrived at this barely altered, slightly distorted hexagonal plan because, in its subtle logic, it gave him a central space like the nave of a basilica, thereby to lead the man from the portal to the prayer niche in the kibla wall. He was by then wholly at ease within his Islamic faith as well as in his mastery of Islamic architectonics; yet he remembered the advantage of Anthemius's axis that cuts through the space within a space of Christian liturgy to take the worshiper directly from the door to the mystery in the apse behind the iconostasis.

This almost but not quite perfect hexagonal plan also enabled him to lead into the lateral extensions – the aisles and above them the side galleries – without doing violence to the flow of space, or to the eye. The six piers carry six pendentives, which join to form the circle from which springs the dome.

The two side piers are freestanding, with the aisles and the galleries behind them. Sinan opened the corners of the square that he had extended into a rectangle. He covered these corner spaces by springing twinned semidomes from the pier standing free at the center of either side of the extended square.

A sound of wings fills the space under the celestial dome. The eye catches sight of an abstract angel like a headless, armless, and indeed bodiless, but not wingless, victory. Quickly the man looks up to see that these twinned semidomes rising into the arches from the freestanding pier are supported by corbels, pendentives, and cornices that are carved with rows of crystalline stalactites. They fit together like the pinions and feathers growing in half unfurled, arching curving wings.

He smiles, particularly if he has had the presence of mind, and the good fortune, to dodge the splattered droppings let fall by the actual pigeon that, having filled the quiet space with the sound of winged flight, has come to perch on the iron tiebar overhead. In Arabic, such as that of the calligraphy, pigeons do not coo; they murmur, "God is one with nature." Even so, the mosque has in it the serenity of peaceful angels — or of the dove of peace. In wingless victory, even in the ultimate defeat that ends the life of any man, such stalwarts as Sokollu Mehmet Pasha and Sinan carry the weight of any system, or any canopy of state in the architectonics of order.

Color is the glory of this mosque. Upon entering from the sunlit court-yard through the deep and dark portal that resembles the mouth of a cave, in the quiet light within the prayer hall, Sinan focuses the eye directly upon the prayer niche. This classic *mihrab* takes the shape of the monumental portal exactly opposite, of which it is the man-sized miniature. Surely, Sinan enjoyed the illusion of great distances that this juxtaposition gives the space across the floor, which he spread with carpets woven in the colors of vegetable and mineral dyes, natural substances, and in the patterns of formal gardens. Entranced, the mind behind the eye sees that Sinan once again has taken liberties, as in the optics that we call surrealism, with the laws of perspective.

Sinan framed the prayer niche in the kibla wall with a screen — it is the finest array in the world — of glowing Iznik tiles. They rise from floor level to fill the high arch between the engaged piers of the blind arcade.

In the four colors, dark blue, emerald green, light blue, and the piled-up pigment of true bolus red, enameled on a white surface like a field of snow, and glowing through the glaze that is as clear as water running in a mountain brook, Sinan drew patterns of geometrical and floral abstractions. On either side and above the prayer niche, he placed texts from the Koran in lozenges and calligraphic wheels of "beautiful writing." High up in the demilune that fills the "blind" arch — twelve meters above the ground, forty feet, five times the height of a tall man's reach — he planted a garden of spring flowers, ever-blooming red-petaled tulips on nodding stalks with bladelike green leaves, carnations, roses, peonies, blue hyacinths, and sprays of fruit blossom. They are recognizable flowers but much more than ordinary everyday imita-tions of nature. In all ways these flowers are larger than life.

Here they are functional. In Ottoman Islam, a man who wishes to soothe the troubled mind and clear the spirit looks at a tulip or a rose so that he may stand face to face with God and with God's handiwork, himself, to pray. The flowers that Sinan designed and that the Iznik potters fired for this wall grow large on high because they do not recede into the distance, but instead grow in the gardens of Paradise, which, in Islam, is an oasis blossoming in the desert wilderness at the end of the road.

Sokollu Mehmet Pasha and Sinan could read the calligraphic verses from the Koran as most of the worshipers even in their day could not. The Grand Vezir, surely, chose them himself. In the oblong plaques above the rectangular windows at floor level and in the galleries, the enamelers wrote the ninety-nine beautiful names of God. In the discs and the lozenges of the kibla wall, the scriptural arabesques give the *Hadis*, which is the call to prayer and the declaration of faith, and which, in translation, reads, "There is no god but God, and I bear witness that Mohammed is His slave and His Prophet."

Then comes the First Sura of the Koran, an early one revealed to Mohammed in the desert mountains surrounding Mecca. It is called "The Opening," and it is the Islamic Paternoster:

> In the name of God, the Merciful, the Compassionate.
> Praise belongs to God, the Lord of all Being,
> The All-Merciful, the All-Compassionate,
> the Master of the Day of Doom.
> Thee only we serve; to Thee alone we pray for succour.
> Guide us in the straight path,
> the path of those whom Thou hast blessed,
> not of those against whom Thou art wrathful,
> nor of those who are astray.

In the medallion surrounding the crown of the high dome, Kara Hisari, the illuminator, painted verses from Sura XXXV, "The Angels," that in part read, "God holds the heavens and the earth, lest they remove. . . . Surely He is All-Clement, All-Forgiving." Under a heavy weight of snow, the dome fell in the winter earthquake that shook the city for five days in 1894. It has gone up again upon its firm foundations.

Facing the *mihrab* under the celestial dome, Sinan and Sokollu Mehmet Pasha uttered their prayers. They got down on their knees; they touched their foreheads to the thick carpets on the floor; they stood upright. One of them – or as I imagine it, both of them, one after the other – put out a hand to run the flat of it over the smooth marble colonnettes that Sinan had set in sockets (they are like goblets, the one at the top set bottom up) at either corner of the prayer niche. As the palm rubs over the precious marble, the little pillars swivel.

I smile when I do what I imagine Sinan and the Grand Vezir did four hundred years ago. It is satisfactory; it is a pleasure to touch the revolving shafts which, it was explained to me, Sinan put there to inform us that he had built on solid rock that has neither settled nor shifted out of the true.

When he looked around him, Sokollu Mehmet Pasha did not have to try to figure out such things as the module, which is the unit that gave Sinan the proportions for this mosque. By then he built as easily as a tree grows, if not instinctively, then according to the pattern imprinted upon his mind. He let his seasoned hands and eye do the work that they knew how to do. He had the calculations and the techniques at his fingertips.

The dome measures a bit more than 12 meters in diameter; say that it is 40 feet across. From floor to crown the height is 22½ meters, or 74 feet 3 inches. Thus, in proportions roughly 1:1.856 the module is taller than Le Corbusier's London constable, and taller than the classic shape of humanism's ideal man in the golden section that is one to one point six one eight. If Sinan's proportions are, to the Western eye, imperfect then perhaps even these two august and admirable Slaves of the Gate, the Royal Chief Architect and the Grand Vezir, found their almost ideal form of slavery to be distorting. Certainly to carry the weight of both the canopy of state and the celestial dome upon the shoulders forces a man to stand "unnaturally" straight, and to grow in strength larger and taller than life.

Imperfection — the saving flaw? Sinan stretched the width of the central space between the piers of the hexagon (perhaps below the level of the consciousness) in order to form a nave. He counteracted the heaviness implicit in all domical buildings by stretching the height a bit beyond the "natural" relations of how things grow in the golden section. But the built-in flaw that saves this man-made place of prostration from impiety in Islam meets the eye when the man turns on his way to go out. On either side of the portal, high up, to roof the deepened space between the side of the square and the inner surface of the façade, he sees that each of the two narrow oblongs seems logically and reasonably to call for a cradle vault to cover it.

My hunch is that Sinan put the cradle vaults up in place and as an afterthought at the last moment broke them out. If so, he replaced the long and low canopy of masonry with a covering that nags at the eye like pimples on an otherwise flawless skin. Across the narrow width of the oblong he put up a heavy monolith, a clumsy beam of stone that cuts the length in two. Upon the two square openings he raised high octagonal drums which carry two small domes. Humorously, they echo the shape of the floor plan and the great central dome; but they are bothersome, as wit can be, or as sharps instead of flats, out of harmony. So he appears to call attention to the fault. It is only a detail, but for such an expert builder and designer, whose great achievement was to marry the techniques of construction with the architecture, it is curiously makeshift, a ponderous flaw.

Outside the mosque, by the canopied fountain of ritual ablutions at the center of the arcaded courtyard, I turn to look up behind the symmetrical row of cupolas rising above the high arcade of the porch. There I find the other aspect of these puzzling little twinned domes, a pair on either side of the central cupola that covers the space in the porch above the monumental portal. I see that on the exterior they are exactly right in shape and in dimension and in function, shrewdly placed to make the transition from the arches of the colonnades up to the rising, curving mass of the lead-sheathed central dome. Sinan sacrificed the harmony of the interior for the symmetry of the exterior.

Can these small twinned domes on their very high octagonal drums mean that Sinan knew very well that the inside of things has a life of its own which is distinct and separate from external appearances? The interior is not only the negative of the exterior. Space is not void. The outside is less, and at the same time more, than the shell of what it contains. Are we again confronted by the irreducible ancient formula of the circle within the square? If so, then these little domes that seem to me to be afterthoughts are as important as the celestial dome that, reduced and multipled by four, they chucklingly echo. Whatever the built-in flaw may mean, it tells me, for one, that Sinan knew that the question is more important than any answer; and that as a man and as a builder, he went on making his mistakes and his discoveries right up to the very end of his long life.

I like to think that Sinan and Sokollu Mehmet Pasha looked at the little domes and then looked at one another. Not having the need to say a word, they smiled in their recognition of a fact — call it a flaw — in their lives, and in the life of any purposeful responsible man, which is to be seen as something like this. A public man must sacrifice the perfect harmony and symmetry of his private life, in order to maintain the established order in which he has faith; but this faith, being man-made and arbitrarily applied to nature, must be artificial, and thus "unnatural," even though it obey the law of gravity. In order to live the life of a man, a man must be willing to die in his faith.

Once again, Sinan made the quiet, sunlit courtyard serve both the men come to prayer in the mosque and the college of "burning" theological students (their cells, their study hall and lecture room, their iron ground, and their water closets efficiently open off the arcade). There I find and I think Sinan and the Grand Vezir found peace.

Sinan herein avoided the overloaded and momentous corner pillars that, in the courtyards of the Imperial Friday Mosques, stand at the south and the east corners where the high arcade of the porch joins the lower arcades of the sides. Here the two functional gatehouses, which are cubical and domical pavilions, serve logically to make the difficult transition. What is more, Sinan broke the militant marching rhythm of the monoliths and the arches of the arcades in this courtyard as in no other of his mosques.

The arches are not round but pointed. Sinan drew each springer in the broken line of the Baroque: the springer rises from the stalactite capital in the slightly concave arc; at the center, it jogs, and then continues in the slightly convex arc to the point of the lancet. This most delicate S-curve, as natural as a tendril, evokes the elegancies of the eighteenth century, the Age of Reason.

I like to think that Sinan, like Michelangelo his contemporary, both of them universal men, foresaw the Baroque experiments, or discoveries in line and in space that naturally followed after each classic architect, the one of the Ottoman Golden Age, the other of the Italian High Renaissance.

Sinan was more fortunate than Michelangelo in that he finished all his work before he died; in that he saw his world to be not terrible, not tormented, not tumultuous, but serene and joyous in the triumph of man's life on earth at peace, or at Holy War, in Islam. He was also fortunate in his patrons, and especially in working with the Grand Vezir Sokollu Mehmet Pasha, the Bosnian youth enslaved as a prisoner of war; the son of a priest in the Falcon's Eyrie; the *damat* husband of a demanding, imperious, trivial, and Imperial Princess wife; the supreme Slave of the Gate, who chose to carry on the traditions of the Golden Age, and who shouldered the burden of a form of government that, having come to the logical end of its perfected scope, proved to be intolerable.

In 1571, in the sunlit courtyard of his mosque and his memorial, the Grand Vezir and the Royal Chief Architect saw the end. It was in sight; it was inevitable, although, perhaps, neither man could know the shape that it would take – the dagger in the hand of a possibly deranged petitioner for justice, a country squire with a grievance, disguised as a dervish, spurred on by the frivolous favorites of the Sultan who were lethal men. Whether or not they actually encouraged the assassin, or otherwise knew what they were doing when they brought down the one remaining monolith that upheld the canopy of state, they put an end to the Ottoman Golden Age. Sinan's mosque that he built for the Grand Vezir Sokollu Mehmet Pasha makes clear that as times go it was an exceedingly good time of life for those men fortunate enough to be called Slaves of the Gate and Slaves of God to live on earth.

Some hand, in the years after Sokollu Mehmet Pasha's death – I think it may have been Sinan's; if so, then it was in the year and a half before his own death – brought back from a pilgrimage to Mecca three bits chipped from the black Kaaba stone and set them in the mosque of the Grand Vezir. One was set in the frame at the peak of the prayer niche, one in the canopy at the top of the stairs of the *minber*, the third above the door on the way out. There is mystery embedded in the heart of every man.

18

When he was ninety-four, Sinan made his second trip to Mecca; it was his first pilgrimage. In the last years of the reign of Selim the Sot, he had gone there on business to restore the arcaded enclosure surrounding the Kaaba stone. He built one more minaret, the sixth. In the desert hills and wadis, Sinan restored the existing aqueducts thrown down by the flash flood and built another that Mihrimah Sultan paid for, to bring water into the holy market city.

In 1583 Sinan made up his mind to go back, this time as a pilgrim, to purge himself of sin. To do so is to fulfill the least of the five demands that the Prophet made upon the faithful: To bear witness that there is no god but God, and that Mohammed is the Slave, the Messenger, the Prophet (as the Arabic word is variously translated) of God; to pray five times a day; to give alms to the poor; to fast throughout the month of Ramazan; and to make the pilgrimage to Mecca at least once in the lifetime of every pious Muslim, provided, of course, that he has the means (no Son of Osman on the throne found the time). To make the pilgrimage is a hardship and a sacrifice even for the strong and wealthy. It would have taken Sinan six months or more. It seems probable that he left the Golden Horn by ship bound not for Beirut and Damascus but for a port on the Nile and then for Cairo. From there it took the armed and organized camel caravan thirty-seven days to get from Cairo to Mecca, following Moses across the Red Sea, or the isthmus, into the Sinai Desert . . . no, probably, the pilgrimage took ship, and landed at Djidda. From the port, Sinan rode his camel across the desert mountain coastal ridge in a landscape as barren as a skull, and as satisfactory.

He traveled in luxury, it is true, but not in comfort, which is a modern invention. Travelers across Egypt and the three Arabias took hardship for granted and knew the pilgrimage to be hazardous. Sinan took with him a company of his own slave men, and he hired an escort of armed guardsmen — perhaps they were retired veteran Janissaries, the youngest of his former command. Perhaps he rode in a camel litter, like the Sultan's own, now in the Topkapi Museum, curtained in silk embroidered with gold set with corals and turquoises. When he was weary of the undulant motion, he got down to ride astride an Arabian horse. By night he and his men stayed in caravansaries along the march, or pitched tents by wells and cisterns in the desert — as he had done throughout those eighteen years on active duty as a Janissary. But two generations earlier he had been a young man.

Perhaps from Mecca he returned with the caravan that had come down from Damascus. If so, he may have visited Medina, Jerusalem, Bethlehem, and Nazareth. I think he did. He was a man of strong curiosity as well as piety. As a Janissary engineer and the Royal Chief Architect, he had rebuilt the walls of Jerusalem and saved — by conversion — many a church, most notably the Haghia Sophia of Nicaea-Iznik, which was full of golden and figurative mosaics of the thirteenth century (destroyed in 1922-23).

However he made the pilgrimage, and however long a time it took him, when he got back to Istanbul in the spring of 1584, he wound a strip of green in his turban, and he was called Haji Sinan, "Pilgrim." In that year he got to work on building an oratory for a monastery of dervishes. The site was on a wide plain in what is now a poor man's section of the city, near the Silivri Gate in the land walls, between the low Seventh Hill and the Sea of Marmara.

The donor of this pious foundation was called Haji Hüsrev Agha. I think he was Sinan's fellow pilgrim, and I know that he was a well-to-do merchant of the city, a respected man who had earned the right to be called by the Ottoman honorific "lord, master, gentleman."

The small mosque, not a *jami* but a *mesjid,* is called Ramazan Efendi after the first abbot (or sheikh, which means "wise man" or "ancient" of Islam, or "venerable") of the order, which may have been Bektashi but more probably was Mevlevi — the Whirling Dervishes. According to the charter, the mosque should rightfully be called Bezirgân Mesjid, Oratory of the Merchant.

Sinan built half a hundred such oratories. They are rectangular buildings, some of them brought into the square by means of an enclosed porch along the length of the northwest wall, the whole covered by a low-pitched roof of pantiles. Built of rubble and of clapboards at a modest expenditure of money, Ramazan Efendi is plain on the exterior, although the minaret of dressed limestone is fine and elegant. Inside, the walls are faced with the best of floral Iznik tiles. The adorned rectangular space is full of light streaming in through two levels of many clear glass windows.

The beams of the sun at morning and at evening shine on floral patterns that are like latticed hanging gardens planted in the four colors and growing in the clear air of snowy mountains. The light obliterates the walls. Volume and void, space and mass merge in eternity. Such is spring time. This is an oratory built by a man known to be close to death; it is as full of life as a young man at a time when his flesh can do no major wrong.

There is no room for imperfection here. God, Who, like all other gods and Gods, is at times a jealous God, could not let loose His wrath upon so modest and so humble a prayer hall; nor upon the men who built it to His purpose. For one thing, Ramazan Efendi could not withstand the blast; the mosque is fragile, and thus precarious. In the city of earthquakes, such oratories that escape the fires take constant work to keep up.

Sinan finished the last of his works known to have been built by his own hands in 1586. He asked his old friend the poet Mustafa Saï Chelebi to carve that date in the inscription over the portal. That was the year of Sinan's last will and testament of the charter in which he made over the rest of his property to the Religious Institution. Sinan, at the age of ninety-seven, made ready to die.

I do not know what sins weighed upon him or what crimes he knew himself to have been guilty of, in the Sacred Law Islam, in its assumption of impossible perfection, absorbed the idea of original sin from the Christians and the Jews. Sinan's second trip, his first pilgrimage to Mecca, gives it to be supposed that he went to purge himself of what he took to be his own wrongdoings.

Perhaps they were the early and ordinary sins of the flesh, such as a military man, in whose life everything that he does is either black or white or bloody, lives through. Perhaps he felt himself to be guilty of the sin of pride in his own achievements. By 1580 he had delegated most of the work coming into the office of the Royal Chief Architect to his assistants. He may have done so because of a period of illness; perhaps he had fallen, say, from a scaffolding. Perhaps, even, he had suffered a small heart attack or a stroke as the result of an excess, and in the dismay of a man who had never known physical disability, he had heard himself blaspheme to try to shift the blame.

Or his invention may have flagged as a result of overwork, and in an attempt to keep it from both himself and his patrons, he had lied. Such might explain the curious mosque of Kilich Ali Pasha, built in 1580, or the odd throwback to the Bursa style in the mosque of the Admiral Piyalé Pasha, of 1577. It may explain the unsatisfactory Azap Kapi Jami, also built in 1577, for the Grand Vezir Sokollu Mehmet Pasha. Perhaps he had been guilty of taking credit for buildings designed by his school of assistants.

Whatever their nature, whether of commission or omission, his sins in private were and remain his own business. In his building he was virtuous. Therefore, when he saw himself beginning to fail – out of evil cometh good. He took stock. He may have made an example of himself in order to force his dozen assistant architects, the oldest by then elderly men, to strike out for themselves. They had lived and worked for a generation in his protective shadow. In this light, the faulty plan of the Azap Kapi Mosque begins to take on meaning outside its structural limitations. As an illustration of one more way to vary the prescribed circle in the square, it succeeds – but as a bad example (often copied, as in the new Mosque of Eyüp). By his eighty-eighth year, Sinan may well have momentarily exhausted himself. Yet to build this mosque, if he sinned, he did so in generosity.

In it he sinned not so much against God as against the Shadow of God on Earth, Süleyman the Magnificent. Sinan had learned the lesson from the long reign and absolute rule of the Sultan, who had, if the man, the husband, and the father had not, killed his own sons, the Princes Mustafa and Bayazid, when their lives had threatened the structure of the Ottoman Ruling Institution. In consequence, his dead hand had ruled the empire of his son Selim the Sot and his grandson Murad the Epileptic for thirteen years in the person of the Grand Vezir Sokollu Mehmet Pasha — whom he had likewise condemned to death in consequence. What Sinan thought of these monstrous imperial dynastic acts is not known.

Whatever his sins may have been, they were great enough to have sent him off in the winter months of 1583 and 1584 to cross the seas and the deserts of his extreme old age, and, having been lifted from his shoulders, to bring him back again for another three years of life. He made his will; he was ready for death.

Sinan died. It took him six months to get it over with. The last order issued from the Divan addressed to the Royal Chief Architect Sinan is dated January 26, 1588, a Saturday. It had to do with the repairing of a pavement (as I recall). In January snow falls on the Seven Hills of Istanbul. Perhaps on one such day, walking the slippery cobblestones, he slipped and fell. Or if he rode, perhaps his old horse stumbled, and Sinan fell. Old bones break easily.

The hospital that he had built for Sultan Süleyman stands near at hand at the end of the Vefa. A book of miniatures from the time of Mehmet the Conqueror illustrates the surgical instruments and shows how the Ottoman physicians set fractures and cauterized wounds. They knew the uses of opium. The faces of the patients depicted reveal no pain; instead, eyes wide open, in the middle of the operation they look out from the pages, interested in what was being done to them, wholly absorbed in the recorded moment that may have been their next to last.

However death overtook him, it seems likely that Sinan chose to die in his own house. If so, the interns and the medical students, or, better, the masons and the carpenters, who were strong men of his own work force, carried Sinan in a litter the short distance from the hospital past the courtyard of the kitchens and the refectory, and in front of the guest house for distinguished visitors to the university. Carrying the old man on his stretcher, slowly they walked out of step along the northwestern wall of the monumental portal to the mosque enclosure and through the gate of his own walled garden. They carried him into his great house and up the staircase. With such passages in mind, he had built it wide enough.

His ladies in three generations had made ready. In his rooms on the top floor, his wife the Lady Gülruh had prepared his bed, a comfortable pallet unrolled on Persian carpets, covered with quilts and banked with cushions of brocade and velvets. She had embroidered some of them with gold thread, worked in patterns of seed pearls — he may have drawn her the designs to please her eye.

After he realized that he would never recover to walk again, I imagine that he called in his carpenters and blacksmiths. Together they designed and built a bed on rollers and a wheelchair. Thus, as morning changed to midday and then to evening, he could follow the sun from window to window of the spacious room built out on brackets above the garden on the hillside. He had provided himself with many wide views. In winter, the snow falls as in a Chinese painting on the City of the Seven Hills above the Bosphorus and the Golden Horn. From the white ground, the cypresses flicker like black flames. In the stillness few people move about, and they are small. The cold puts a sharp edge to everything. In the early morning on the window panes frost crystals take shape in the patterns that Sinan remembered from his childhood; he had built them into his mosques. Sometimes in the winter a blue and gold day dawns clear, as sparkling as the first morning of creation.

In February his daughters, granddaughters, and perhaps his great-granddaughters gathered the first wild cyclamen and snowdrops. Spring came. They brought him hyacinths and narcissus. Then came the branches of fruit blossom and bunches of tulips, the wild ones like pointed radishes, pink and white, those from the garden, the huge, feathered "Rembrandt" tulips. Below his windows the Judas trees covered their smooth brown branches with deep pink blossoms as dense as fur. Then the nightingales began to sing. The wisteria had climbed up to frame his view with pale green leaves and hanging clusters of green buds and lavender and lilac flowers that fade to gray as they fall. The bushes of Persian lilac bloomed, and the salt breeze carried their fragrance up to him.

He watched the days lengthen and the light change. When he lay back, as he chose, he looked up at the high ceiling that he had carved in arabesques and painted in gold and polychrome, orderly interlocking patterns without beginning or end, as flashing and yet as logical as thought. He mulled things over in his mind. What did he think about? He thought Old man's thoughts. He remembered.

For the sunset, he moved his wheelchair to the western windows, to look out toward Eyüp, the most holy ground beyond the walls at the top of the Golden Horn. There his friend the Grand Vezir Sokollu Mehmet Pasha had chosen to be buried. He lay alone in the earth that he and Sinan had designed and built well before the assassination in 1578. It is a modest tomb for so powerful a man. His death put an end to the classic order of the Ottoman

Golden Age. In the ten years that had passed since then, Sinan had watched corruption set in. The Sultan, surrounded by his favorites, the witty, meddlesome boon companions, never once led his armies onto the battlefields of Holy War. The Janissaries, now a Praetorian Guard of married men, for the most part no longer tribute youths or *penjik* slaves but freeborn Muslim volunteers, no longer respected the Son of Osman whom they no longer obeyed.

In the hot weather Sinan wheeled himself over to the northern windows that were open to the breeze from the Balkan Mountains and the Russian steppes across the Black Sea. He looked out and down the hill over the dome and minaret of the mosque of Rüstem Pasha and across the Golden Horn to the arsenal. He had last enlarged the shipyards for the Grand Vezir Sokollu Mehmet Pasha in order to rebuild the fleet destroyed at Lepanto sixteen years earlier. Since then, the admirals had risked neither defeat nor victory.

To the east he could look out over the terraced college courtyards on the hillside beyond his garden to hear and to see the students in the beginning of their lives. They washed in the fountain; they wrestled on the iron ground; they laughed or they went soberly into the lecture halls. From there through the open windows Sinan heard the droning of the professors' commentaries upon the readings of the Sacred Law, the Hanafite, the Shafiite, the Hanbalite, and the Malikite. The Path to the Oasis was closed to new interpretation. At dusk Sinan watched the wood smoke rising from the chimneys of the students' cells. He observed that, indeed, he had known how to build the flues of the hooded fireplaces to warm the impatient young men. In the mornings when the wind was right, he could hear the young ones of the school for muezzins chanting the suras of the Koran from the belvedere that he had built for them high on the wall. He smiled — or so I say — as he listened to the voices of the sopranos and altos crack and descend to baritone and bass. He remembered the voices of his own two sons and of his adopted nephews speaking to him. The sons of old men who have outlived their sons speak not from the tomb but from the long road, or, when they are killed on the battlefield, from the oasis at the end of the road. Sinan reflected that of his living grandsons, Dervish Chelebi, soon to take on his work as head of the family, had things well in hand.

When Sinan turned further to the southeast, he looked up at the four minarets and the great dome that he had built — how long ago? Thirty years ago, no, thirty-one — for Sultan Süleyman the Magnificent. Perhaps then he wheeled himself over to his drawing board, and took up his compasses to finger the engraved steel. It was smooth and familiar. Perhaps he took up a string of thirty-three prayer beads of amber or of black coral, the one light and fragrant, the other heavy and lustrous in his hands. Then he arrived at his own critical estimate of one man's life work: the period as an apprentice, followed by his work as a journeyman, and then the freedom of the master builder. He glanced through the windows to the east and saw the dome of Haghia Sophia that still appears to float mysteriously upon the golden light of its own creation. No, he had not surpassed Anthemius of Tralles in divine inspiration; nor had he intended to do so. He himself had never deceived the eye. He knew that his own contribution to architecture had been not technical trickery but transparent honesty.

He had no fault to find with his Islamic faith. God is God. All prophets are the Prophet. Into the mosque of Selim the Sot, whose God was the Lord of Beggars, Sinan had built the mystic numbers of the most generous Bektashi order, four, eight, and twelve, of all-embracing charity, compassion, and wisdom. Sinan smiled (or if he did not, I do) remembering the four minarets that he set up at the cardinal points surrounding the single great dome. He had enjoyed building them; he had enjoyed himself as a man on earth working in submission to the law of gravity and the will of God. But he wished that God would get on with it.

He was ready. By this time, what God had written on his forehead held little mystery for him. Perhaps he reached out to take up a hand mirror to read – not between the lines, but to read backward from the end to the beginning.

One of his assistants came in to interrupt his solitude and to report at the end of the day on the work in hand. The office of the Royal Chief Architect finished the mosque of the Nishanji Mehmet Pasha in the year of Sinan's death. Murad III's vezir, the Keeper of the Privy Seal, was a colored man, perhaps the son or the grandson of a Nubian slavegirl in the harem of a Slave of the Gate. Perhaps he came to visit Sinan with the assistant architect. As usual, there is no record of the builder's name.

The Lady Gülruh, a sane woman, took over the management of Sinan's household during his last illness. When he was on his feet, if his ladies fell to bickering in the confines of the harem, he might have got up and walked out, leaving them alone to enjoy themselves. They led dull lives; he knew that their words and their scenes did nobody any harm in the barely tolerable conditions of their segregation.

But alone, the Lady Gülruh came into her own; she knew how to make Sinan's new helplessness bearable for him. Perhaps, then, after he had had a good night and a good day for several nights and days, she arranged a family party, perhaps in April on his ninety-ninth birthday, if, indeed, he was born in the middle of that month of spring. The children of two and three generations filled the great high room with their laughter.

To keep them amused if not to keep them quiet, the Lady Gülruh, if she were intelligent and wise as I think she must have been, provided them with some sort of entertainment, a magician, an acrobat, some dancing dogs – no, come to think of it, not animals or acrobats in the living room of a dying man. A puppet show, that would have done the trick. She brought in the best of the itinerant shadow theaters.

Sinan would have enjoyed Karagöz as much as his great-grandchildren. Together old and young heard the latest jokes and comments on the imperial scene, the talk of the town, the gossip of the bazaars, the voice of the people – all the passing show. Yes, the Karagöz shadow theater was the very thing. The puppeteer would give the old man something to think about in the long nights when pain kept him awake. We are all puppets, life is but a shadow theater – that sort of thing, not tragic but, in the end, comical indeed.

All the types and the characters of the empire passed before his eyes, not the Sultan reduced and shrunk in two dimensions, but from the Grand Vezir to the drunken Janissary, a lethal and a farcical slave soldier, terrible and funny in his red and blue uniform, his white sleeve-like cap askew on his shaven head, his fierce eye rolling, his bull's-horned moustache ferocious above his scowling cruel mouth, a carafe of red wine, half empty, clutched by the neck in one fist, his naked curved scimitar at the ready in his fighting hand. One of the horror-comic plays shows the shadow of a naked and bleeding girl just raped off stage.

The cast of characters of this Turkish commedia dell'arte includes the prostitute, smiling but shrewd of eye above her transparent face veil and skeptical of speech in her gown painted in the colors of the flowers of the season; the Greek dancer from Trebizond in her flowered "harem" pants, castanets held ready in either upraised hand; her partner, the smiling Greek, with his fiddle; the Armenian housewife with a red parasol and a red and blue striped gown, her naked face in profile – she obviously is bargaining in the market; the Persian opium smoker, twisted, clearly addicted; the yokel from Thrace; the backwoodsman from Kayseri; the Black Eunuch; the "nervous" dwarf Beberuhi in his tall dunce cap; the elegant young rake of Istanbul; the foreigner, a Frank, clutching a pair of gloves; the cringing Jewish ragpicker; Sheytan, who is Satan, a recognizable international type, not red but clearly a devil of cloven hoof, horned, tailed, and grinning with delight in what he saw going on as he walked up and down the earth; and, of course, the principal figures, the antagonists, Karagöz and Hajivat.

Each puppet, about twelve inches tall, is as flat as a paper doll but cut in profile from camel's skin, which is stiff and translucent. Articulated, as needs be according to the character, at the knees, hips, waist, elbows, shoulders, and throat, the puppets do not dangle from strings but are manipulated at the end of a stick. Each is colored like stained glass. In profile Karagöz has a wide-open "black eye," which is the meaning of his name; the white of his eye cut out, the outlines of his costume pierced, his brilliant shadow cast on the taut white screen gives an effect of indomitable vitality.

He is dressed in women's clothing for the play in which he gets into, and safely out of, a pasha's harem. His close black beard shows through his veil, as does his rolling, lecherous black eye. Ordinarily, he wears a splendid red hat which is fixed to his shaved head by a knotted thong of rawhide so that, in the excitement of the inevitable chase, he can almost, but not quite, lose it.

Karagöz is a wily and an attractive man of thirty, witty, quick, irreverent, and obscene; always he gets into trouble of his own making, and out of it by the skin of his teeth; and he runs off stage laughing. According to the Turkish legend, Karagöz and his foil Hajivat were real men, a mason and a foreman who worked to build the mosque of Murad II at Bursa, shortly before the fall of Constantinople. Karagöz, the man alive, protested some high-handed act of Hajivat's authority, and in rebellion, perhaps, organized a sort of strike, or at least provoked laughter among his fellow workmen. The ribald sally cost him his life. Hajivat had the man arrested and executed. His fellow workmen immortalized him as the voice of the people.

But in fact the shadow theater came from *les ombres chinoises* either in caravans from China along with such things as Süleyman's celadon and Ming blue and white porcelain; or by sea from his remotest cousin Kublai Khan's port of Xanadu in the holds of Arab merchantmen sailing past Java across the Indian Ocean and up into the Red Sea. In Istanbul, Hajivat spoke in the voice of authority, most elegantly in flowery Osmanlija. Karagöz mocked and parodied him in plays on words, puns, and gross obscenities. The plays are topical, full of sly allusions to current events, and full of protest.

Süleyman and Ibrahim looked and listened when the puppeteer was a poet and a philosopher. The Sultan laughed; the Grand Vezir kept his temper; but they paid attention to public opinion. Selim the Sot thoroughly enjoyed himself at the shadow theater where he saw himself burlesqued in the subtlest of lèse majesté as a piece of folklore. He saw himself in reality to be but a caricature of a Son of Osman, but apparently he did not mind. He was a tolerant and a permissive man. He laughed at the thinly veiled attacks upon the stern Grand Vezir's government; and he guffawed at the broad allusions to the scandalous, insufficiently private lives of his pashas and the boon companions of the court.

Sinan, who was lenient and very old, sitting in his wheelchair, watched his grandchildren, the smallest of them rolling on the floor, howling with laughter at the witty dirty words and the lewd acts of the colorful shadows of the puppets. Projected two at a time from behind the screen by the puppeteer, who kept himself out of sight behind his lantern, the puppets filled the room with life; each spoke in characteristic voice and accent. Sinan watched the antics of the illusion, and he laughed as hard as the youngest of the children. But I do not think that he indulged himself in two-dimensional, shrunken philosophizings on the theme of all the world's a stage and all men on earth dangle from the hand of God.

Whatever else he was, Sinan was not a shadow projected by God the Puppeteer upon a set-up screen.

But after Karagöz had left the screen blank and after the children weary with laughter had gone home, a different cast of shadows stayed on to keep Sinan company. His was a crowded stage. In the twilit evening, he may have rolled his wheelchair over to the western windows to look out at the blazing horizon of the ancient city of Byzantium-Constantinople-Istanbul. His mina-rets still clamp together the jagged edges of the earth and the sky. Today about two million people live within the walls and beyond them on both shores of the Golden Horn, the Bosphorus, and the Sea of Marmara. He looked out at a greener urban landscape of perhaps a tenth as many inhabit-ants. He and the sultans had made it the greatest city in the West, although it was the capital of the Near and the Middle East. Today no longer the capital of any country, the indomitable city is still imperial, and it still lives a life of its own.

As the fire of the sky died down, in the quiet light of evening, Sinan's eyes fell upon his own white tomb. He had seen to the building — he had built it for himself. In the sharp angle of the garden, he put up a *sebil*, a public fountain house, its wide grilled window opening upon the streets which join at the top of the hill. He had provided for wages to be paid an attendant and money to buy ice to cool the spring water offered in the hot months of summer. Then the thirsty passers-by stopped for a drink. The servant in the fountain house passed through an opening in the grille a tin-plated copper cup full of good water. It was chained to a ring in the underside of the marble sill. The chains have worn grooves in the smooth stone. The Turks savor water as the French delight in wines. The august visitors who stopped for a drink at Sinan's fountain house drank from a hammered silver cup in which a fish made of links was fixed to a pin at the bottom of the bowl. The wriggling fish appeared to swim in the clear fresh water as the drinker lifted the cup to his lips.

Behind the *sebil*, Sinan built his tomb. Perhaps humorously, he thought that the drinkers at his fountain house would praise his name and keep his memory fresh. He put up a marble canopy, a dome; it is a small one, on four pillars, the sides left open to the winds. Under it, at the head of the grave, he set up his marble tomb post. On top of it, as was the custom, he carved a turban; it was the ensign of his rank, like a cardinal's hat or an earl's coronet. I am sure that he carved the gravestone himself.

He did not select the turban that he had worn for fifty years as the Royal Chief Architect; nor the Janissary *ketch*; nor the headgear of the uniform of the general of the Janissary engineers. Upon this tomb post, he chose to carve the turban of the *Haseki,* the "chosen" man honored by appointment to the Sultan's Own Guard of Honor, in which he had served as commanding officer from 1534 to 1536. It may have been that this distinction, like the Garter or the Golden Fleece elsewhere, was not to be surpassed in the Ottoman hierarchy. It was the highest award for any Slave of the Gate to earn in his lifetime. If it were not mandatory, Sinan's choice is puzzling. He had no need to remind any passer-by of his achievement. As Saint Paul's is Sir Christopher Wren's, so the Süleymaniyé is Sinan's monument.

But that *Haseki* turban brings back the memory of another Greek slave. The favorite Ibrahim had brought the great honor to Sinan. In the ceremonies at the Divan following the victory of Tabriz, and after the joining of the Sultan's and the Grand Vezir-Serasker's armies on the march to Baghdad, Ibrahim had proposed the general of the Janissary engineers for the Sultan's choice. Then, after Sinan had restored the walls and the gates of Baghdad, with the high-plumed turban of the *Haseki* on his head, Sinan had marched along with his fellow chosen in a hollow square surrounding Ibrahim and Süleyman on horseback, as they rode in triumph into the city of the caliphs. An old man remembers clearly the past.

Sinan remembered that two years later, in 1536, back in Istanbul, as dusk closed in, Ibrahim, as was his custom, had walked alone through the little gate opened for him in the palace walls. He had thought to join the Sultan for the night, and he went smiling, thinking of the entertainment of the day that he would offer for Süleyman's smile; instead, he went to his death. If Sinan, wearing the white-feathered Haseki turban was standing guard duty that night of Ramazan, which fell in the Ides of March that year, he knew, as Ibrahim did not, that the Sultan's mutes awaited the favorite, while Süleyman slept the sleep of a dead man in the imperial harem. From the deserted bed chamber in the men's quarters, Sinan heard the cries for help, and he heard them cease. He may have been (he probably was; he knew as I never shall) the man — the loyal, faithful, trustworthy friend — who picked up the favorite's dead body, washed the blood from the wounds, closed the eyes, wrapped the corpse in a shroud, and gave Ibrahim burial in an unmarked grave across the Golden Horn in the gardens of a Bektashi dervish *tekké.* A century later, Evliya Chelebi knew where it was; a tree had grown up out of it, a weeping willow. There is no sign of it today. Sinan had then petitioned the Sultan for permission to volunteer for action. It may have saved his life; it certainly changed the course of it. In no other remembered monument the turban of the *Haseki* on Sinan's tomb post recalls the story of the rise and fall — "like a comet in the night sky," as Hammer phrased it — of Sinan's fellow Greek slave, and patron, Ibrahim.

Sinan learned from him (or so it seems to me) not to put his life, as most men do, into the lives of others, but instead to invest it in the solider substances of stonemasonry. He worked with his hands to give concrete shape to his own ideas of order. Thereafter, for fifty years, free of competition, outside the struggle for place and power but in the confidence of Sultan Süleyman, he worked. No other architect has been so well served, and so fortunate, as he in his chosen profession. He used his head; he may have smiled ironically as he carved the folds of his old turban into white marble on top of his gravestone. He had outlived them all.

Had Süleyman been alive, surely, he would have come incognito and probably by night to visit Sinan; perhaps he might have stopped off for an hour or two on one of his wanderings through the streets of his city. Together they would have talked over the imperial plans, say, to open thoroughfares for the increasingly congested traffic; or to enlarge the capacity of the reservoirs and the aqueducts in the water system (something that needs doing today). They would have sorted out the gossip of the bazaars to find the meaning of public opinion. After the death of Ibrahim, no other man spoke familiarly to Süleyman, except his architect on the job.

Haseki Hürrem, had she been alive, would have sent gifts of fruit and flowers, and perhaps for Sinan's wife, the Lady Gülruh, a jewel – earrings, a pair of gold enameled birds, each with a pink pearl held in its beak. She might well have dressed herself once again in servant's dark clothing and, veiled, gone with her husband, incognita, to visit the old man. She might have asked him to sketch for her something like a new pavilion for the summer harem at the bottom of the palace gardens on the water front of Seraglio Point, a request that she knew would give him pleasure.

Sinan's Lady Gülruh, having sent up slave men – no, slave women – with a screen to put in place around her husband's bed or wheelchair, would have kept herself out of the Sultan's sight in her own women's quarters. Then, having seen to the saving of the conventions, Sinan on his side of the screen and Hürrem on her side would have burst into roars of laughter. She surely would have regaled him with the latest gossip all about herself, the redheaded sorceress, the Russian witch, the enchantress. They could laugh together while the Sultan said nothing; but, I think, he looked on and smiled. All of Sinan's sons, and all but one of theirs were dead. So, in fact, was she, lying buried in the bower of springtime that Sinan had built for her. So was Süleyman. Perhaps indeed, as the later Turkish chroniclers are pleased to place the blame, Hürrem may have brought "bad blood" into the House of Osman. Whatever the causes of the later Sons of Osman's inadequacies, and whatever her effects upon the Ottoman Empire, Sinan remembered Hürrem as that most dangerous of women, a fascinator.

The Sot's widow, the Validé Sultan Nûrûbanû, would not have paid a visit to Sinan, but she might have sent a Black or a White Eunuch to wait upon the dying Royal Chief Architect, to leave gifts, cherries and roses from the imperial gardens that he had designed. The Sot himself would have stayed away; the sight of death was not to him supportable. But he would have sent wine from Cyprus in a crystal flacon; or a box of enameled gold set with rubies and emeralds and filled with comfits, or, more likely, with opium. He was a thoughtful and a generous man. Of all his father's inherited Slaves of the Gate, Sinan was the one with whom he could talk on terms of equality. He had a connoisseur's eye for the Islamic arts, of which architecture is the major one.

Selim might have lent the old man a book of erotic miniatures from his private library, one such entitled *Forbidden Sins* and catalogued as precepts and examples for the protection of the morals of the young, to chuckle over. Like his mother the Sot had a joyous sense of the ridiculous. Sinan had built him a spacious, a splendid mausoleum, full of color and light, almost a cheerful place, where he does not lie alone.

His eldest son Murad III, an epileptic, a shy man who withdrew to protect himself from, among other things, hard work in remote majesty would by no means have broken the, by then rigid, court etiquette to condescend to honor a Slave of the Gate with his presence. To him, the Royal Chief Architect was merely one more old man inherited from his grand-father's and his great-grandfather's great days, of whom and of which he had already heard far too much. However, his majordomo of the palace, in the course of routine business to make up the calendar, having noticed the report of the Royal Chief Architect's accident or illness, would have seen to it that one of the lesser gentlemen-in-waiting, a recent graduate of the palace school of pages, an usher, went to convey the Sultan's respects and perhaps to leave a handsomely bound copy of the Koran.

They came to visit him, the imams, from all his mosques and oratories. The chaplain of the Janissaries, the Grand Mufti, and the Judges of the Armies and of the city came to call. Sinan told one of them (or so I imagine), the Kazasker Mehmet Efendi, whom he called Molla Chelebi and for whom he had most extraordinarily built the most excellent small mosque in the hazel grove beside the Bosphorus, that he had better hurry up and die. For if he did not get it over with soon, his well-wishers would eat and drink him out of house and home, and kill off his wife, his daughters, his granddaughters, and his old slaves in attendance — these last before they could enjoy their free-dom granted as of forty days before the hour of his death. They ran up and down the steps all day long and on far into the night, carrying trays of dishes of rose-petal jam, glasses of fresh spring water, and cups of freshly brewed, hot, sweet, thick, black coffee.

The vezirs and the pashas came; their ladies spent the time of the visits with the Lady Gülruh in the harem. They stayed on and on — waiting, remarked Sinan, for something to happen, namely, for him to die, the vultures! Perhaps he laughed a last belly laugh. He was willing, but his flesh was strong.

What finally killed him? Pneumonia in midsummer? Heart failure? On July 17, 1588, he heard death rattle in his throat, he felt the cold in his extremities, and he died. His ladies and the old slave women knew what to do. They washed the body, combed and brushed the white beard, and composed the limbs. They cried out in grief; but in decorum, they mourned according to the custom. Islam does not make of death and burial a long ordeal for the living.

His men knew what to do. They came with the coffin that they had made to Sinan's remembered measurements. They lifted the body, wrapped from head to foot in a shroud (green, I think it was, for green is the pilgrim's as well as the Prophet's color), and put it in the wooden coffin. They closed but did not hammer down the peaked lid. They carried it down the wide staircase and out through the garden into the street. The Lady Gülruh, and all the beneficiaries of his will, remained indoors.

In front of the house, a crowd of mourners, all of them men, had gathered, the neighbors, the merchants, the veteran Janissaries of his old command, the Slaves of the Gate old enough to know him, but not too old to walk, the youngest of his patrons, the pashas, the citizens of Istanbul from the Chief Architect's Quarter and from all seven of the hills. The young men and the strong workmen shouldered his coffin.

The others fell in line behind him on the way to the mosque. Silently, in a continuous ebb and flow, a few men at a time walked forward from among the river of mourners to take the load and to carry the coffin for a pace or two, or for longer stages of the march. The sins of the living rolled from the shoulders of the pallbearer with each step that he took under the burden. So he shortened his own future road through limbo.

Perhaps the mourners carried the coffin all the way from the great house on the Third Hill down the Vefa, past the workshop of the Royal Chief Architect, along the highroad of the Fourth Hill, and down to the plain of the New Garden where Sinan had built his own small mosque in the Chief Architect's Quarter. But I think not. Ordinarily, a man's body is carried to the mosque in the parish where he lived at the time of his death.

Sinan was extraordinary. The Grand Mufti with the chief imam of the Süleymaniyé, the lesser vizirs, and the Grand Vezir of the Divan, in the Sultan's name, surely, would have seen the need for a public funeral. Such ceremonies are for the living. If so, then it was no distance at all for the mourners to carry the body from Sinan's house across the street and through the monumental entrance into the walled enclosure of the Imperial Friday Mosque that he had built for Sultan Süleyman the Magnificent. The pallbearers set the coffin down on a marble table outside the portal of the dead.

Through one or another of the other portals, each according to his rank and office, the mourners filed into the mosque. The Sultan may or may not have entered by his own staircase built into the east corner and gone into his loge at the end of the kibla wall. Down on the floor, the vast spaces of the prayer hall reduced the crowd of Sinan's friends — all those who were still alive — to order. The muezzins chanted; their voices soared up into the dome. All dominions perish save God's and His is glory.

Then silently the men filed out. The imam and the pallbearers picked up the coffined body from the table at the door and brought it back to the tomb in the garden. By then the gravediggers of the guild had opened the grave in the summer-dry earth. There is not space enough for more than the family to stand in the narrow angle of the walled garden. From his coffin, his workmen lifted Sinan's shrouded body and lowered it into the grave. Dervish Chelebi, the new head of Sinan's household, and the Lady Gülruh, who was veiled, watched as the workmen's shovels filled in the earth upon "the Eyes of the Engineers; the Capital on the Column of Builders; the Master of the Masters of his Epoch; the Foremost of the most dextrous Artisans of his Era; the Euclid of Time and the Ages; the Royal Chief Architect, the Royal Teacher, Sinan Agha, Son of the Slave of God the All-giving."

Born *circa* 1489, he died *circa* 1588. In all, he lived for ninety-nine years. If I have mislaid a year or two of his long life, I have done so in ignorance. Had I been one of his workmen, and had he caught me writing this biography, he might have laughed, and he might not, as he took up his ivory- and coral-handled steel penknife to sharpen the triangular reed, to set me right on every page. At the end of his long life he himself could not have recalled accurately the sequence of the major and the minor days of his experience.

He was collected in the Village of Sinan the Builder by the Janissaries' Keeper of the Cranes in the summer of 1512 after the spring of his twenty-third birthday. He served in the campaigns of Belgrade, Rhodes, Mohács, Buda, Vienna, Lake Van, Tabriz, Baghdad, Corfu, Apulia, and Moldavia. He built his first mosque when he was the general of the Janissary engineers in winter quarters at Aleppo. As Royal Chief Architect, he built his first mosque in Istanbul for Haseki Hürrem in 1538. He was forty-nine that year, in which he chose to marry the Lady Gülruh and begin his private life. In the next fifty years, he built more buildings than any other known architect. The best of his body of work survives, crowded with the great men and women of his lifetime. He served four Sultans: Selim the Grim, Süleyman the Magnificent, Selim the Sot, and Murad III.

On his signet, a bloodstone set in pure gold, Sinan the Great had carved "Sinan the poor and humble." He knew better! He knew the truth. Four hundred years later, in May, the purple irises still bloom in the sweet soil among the marble tombstones under the limestone walls of the terraced hillside above the Golden Horn.

GLOSSARY

BIBLIOGRAPHY

INDEX

⤝ GLOSSARY ⤞

Abutment: A structure that receives or resists the lateral thrust of an arch or a vault or a dome, such as a buttress.

Agha: The *gh* is silent. It means "headman, chief, superior officer." The *agha* of the Janissaries was the commanding officer.

Ahiler: In the singular *Ahi;* the Brotherhood of "the Generous," the Islamic Society of Chivalry and Virtue that grew up in Asia Minor in the thirteenth century to maintain law and order as the Seljuk Sultanate broke up under the pressure of Mongol invaders. Ankara was the *Ahiler* stronghold. Gradually the trade and craft guilds absorbed the secret brotherhood only remotely to be compared with the Freemasons. The Janissaries inherited the *Ahiler* cap and other aspects of the secret and mystical confraternity.

Aisle, side aisle: The lateral sections of a basilica, or in this book, a mosque, separated from the nave or the central part of the building by colonnades or arcades and roofed by vaults or cupolas lower in height than the central dome.

Alem: "Sign, mark, flag, peak of a minaret, the crescent and star on top of a mosque"; the finial. Also the color guard made up of *Hasekis,* the "Chosen" men, Janissaries of the Sultan's Own Life guard of honor.

Allah: God, the "Supreme Being" of the ninety-nine beautiful names. I have yet to see a complete list in English. At first abstract and impersonal, the names gradually reveal a recognizable male being: The Almighty, the All-Powerful, the All-Giving — more like God the Father than God the Ineffable.

Apse: The eastern end, usually semicircular, of the nave in an oriented church.

Arabesque: An intricate, abstract, and intellectual linear pattern without beginning or end, either geometric, or, in outline, reduced from the silhouettes of birds, foliated vines, their tendrils and flowers. Calligraphy, the "beautiful writing" of the various Islamic scripts, is to be called an arabesque.

Arcade: A range or a row of arches carried on piers or pillars, usually freestanding but sometimes engaged in or against a wall, and then called "blind." The arcade usually supports a roof, or in Islamic architecture, a row of cupolas, which are small domes.

Ashlar: Masonry of rectified dressed stone blocks, their courses set in true horizontal and vertical joins.

Atlas: In the plural, atlantes; a male caryatid; the carved representation of a male being, or part thereof, used as a bracket, a supporting column, or in the abstract, I say, as a buttress for the kibla wall of the Süleymaniyé.

Ayvan: A stagelike alcove, usually oblong, enclosed on four sides, opening upon a court or the central space of a covered building. The *ayvan* can be as small as a niche, a bed alcove, an apse, or as large as a transept; it can be deep or shallow, raised a step above the floor, or raised as high as a stage.

Bailiff: In this instance, the title of the representative of the doge of Venice in Istanbul; the Venetian ambassador to the Sublime Porte.

Barrel vault: The simplest of vaults, semicircular in section, semicylindrical in shape, rising from walls, covering a corridor or an aisle.

Basilica: An oblong covered building, Roman in origin, with a double colonnade inside it marking off the aisles from the nave; usually ending in an apse.

Bastion: A tower usually engaged at the corners of a castle.

Bektashi: A dervish of the Bektashi Islamic confraternity of mystics, associated with the Janissaries; the followers of Haji Bektash, the patron "saint" who lived in the thirteenth century. This most liberal and catholic of Islamic orders believed in a trinity: God; the Prophet; and Ali, the martyred Fourth Caliph, Mohammed's uncle's son, the husband of his daughter Fatma. They made symbols of the numbers 4 and 12; believed in the transmigration of souls; took wine, bread, and cheese in a kind of Holy Communion; confessed their sins. (According to orthodox Muslims, the Bektashis sinned a great deal; they drank, they smoked, they accepted the various monotheistic deities and messiahs.) The Bektashis were notoriously liberal in politics; they believed in the brotherhood of man; they permitted women to join as dervishes, and to unveil their faces at the secret conclaves. The Bektashi emblem is a twelve-pointed star or a twelve-fluted disc of onyx worn on a cord around the neck.

Bey: A courtesy title that once meant "prince" but came to mean "sir" or "lord" — inferior to pasha, superior to *agha.*

Beylerbey: "Lord of lords," the governor-general of a major Ottoman province or domain, a kind of viceroy or proconsul; *beylerbeyler* is the plural.

Buttress: A rectangular pier of masonry usually engaged in, or attached to, the wall which it reinforces and supports.

Caliph, caliphate: "Successor" to or "substitute" for the Prophet Mohammed, but more as chief of state and less as Prophet of the Faith. The first four caliphs — Abu Bakir, Osman, Ümer, and Ali — were true successors and substitutes, but the hereditary Omayyad and Abbasid Caliphs of Damascus and Baghdad were really emperors who assumed a divine right to inherit the caliphate from father to son. Caliphate means empire. The word caliph is not to be translated as pope. There is no actual caliph in Islam today.

Capital: The head or crowning feature of a pillar or column. On monoliths, the capital is a separate stone variously carved according to the various orders and the style of architecture. The capital rises from the round of the pillar and, in the Ottoman order of Islam, by means of carved stalactites or the lozenges of "Turkish triangles," makes the transition to the square top, the better to receive the springers of the arches which the pillar and the capital support.

Caravansary: A lockup, a stronghold, a fortified stopping place at the end of a day's march for caravans on the trade routes, usually with two courtyards: one for the stables, the cameleers and hostlers, the other a sort of hotel and shopping center for the merchants and travelers. The Seljuk caravansaries of Asia Minor are particularly splendid, with mosques, baths, and strong rooms.

Centering, centers: The removable falsework of wood, often called a cradle because of its shape, that of the masonry arch to be built upon it. The outer edge, the extrados, of the centering cradle supports the voussoirs of the intrados, or inner, lower edge, the soffit of the arch, until they are locked in place by the keystone.

Chelebi: "Well-mannered, courteous," the word in Turkish is an honorific translated as "gentleman." It was once a royal title; the Chelebi Sultan was the prince acting as royal governor of a province, such as Trebizond. The title "gentleman" was reserved for freeborn Muslim Turks as distinct from converted Christian Slaves of the Gate.

Colonnade: A row of pillars or columns usually, but not necessarily, equidistant and freestanding, and usually supporting an entablature, a beam, a roof, or a row of arches (which changes the colonnade into an arcade).

Column: The pillar, pier, or upright member, a structural element that supports a load in compression. The column may be a monolith, a single stone; it may be constructed of drums, which are solid drum-shaped stones cut to fit upon one another. It may be round, square, or polygonal in section, smooth or fluted or twisted. A pier usually is a massive column of masonry.

Conch: "Shell," the semidome like a scallop or a clam shell that fills a squinch arch; which is to say, the conch fills the upper corner of a square walled building that, by means of squinches, is prepared to receive the base of a dome.

Coping, coping stone: The uppermost course of a wall, usually made sloping so to carry off water; the last and top stone put in place.

Corbel, corbeling: A bracket; a stone projecting from the face of a wall or a column into which it is built. The corbel or bracket receives and supports the weight of some structural element, such as the springer of an arch. Corbeling is a technique of reducing the span of a vault, arch, dome, or roof by shelving out successive rising courses beyond the face of the one below.

Cornice: A projecting band or coping or ornamental moulding along the top of a building, a wall, or an arch, primarily decorative in nature, to finish or to crown the building, the wall, or the arch.

Course: A continuous horizontal range of stones or bricks, usually all of the same size, usually set in mortar, as in the building of a wall.

Cradle, cradling: Falsework, the timber structure in the convex shape of the arch to be built upon it. See Centering, centers; Voussoir; Keystone.

Crown of arch, vault, or dome: The keystone, a stone shaped like a wedge at the top of an arch, or for a dome, shaped like a truncated cone, that, by means of its lateral trusts, locks the voussoirs in place or closes a dome.

Cuerdo seco: "Dry cord" used, as are ribbons of metal cloisons in cloisonné enamel, to separate the dry or thick pigments of the polychrome enamels being laid on tiles in patterns stenciled upon them before they are fired in the kilns. Then the enamels fuse and the dry cord goes up in smoke. This technique was used only in the first period of the Iznik potters in their great days, circa 1515-50.

Curtain wall, screen wall: A wall that carries its own weight but no other load. It can fill an arch or an arcade. Usually the screen or curtain walls of Sinan's buildings are largely fenestrated, which means that they have a great many windows cut through them.

Damat: An imperial "son-in-law," the husband of an aunt, a sister, a daughter, or granddaughter of a reigning Sultan; the implication is that the damat is a member of the Sultan's Household of Slaves, usually a Slave of the Gate high in the hierarchy. An imperial princess of the House of Osman would not be given in marriage to a Christian king; the Shah of Persia or the Moghul Akbar the Great married to the sister or the daughter of the Ottoman Sultan would not be called damat.

Dead load, dead weight: The weight of the structure itself, as against the live weight of a workman upon the roof, or of the wind, or of a snowfall that temporarily is brought to bear upon a building.

Defterdar: The Sultan's "treasurer"; the minister of finance in the Divan.

Dervish: A member of an Islamic religious confraternity, a mystic, an ascetic, a "poor man," a "humble man." A Mevlevî was a dervish of the Mevlâna (Mevlâ means "the Lord God") order of Whirling Dervishes. A Janissary was also a Bektashi dervish.

Devshirmé: Literally, "collection" − of the tribute youths levied in a blood tax upon the Christian communities living in hill towns within the Ottoman Empire.

Divan: The Ottoman Council of State made up of members of both the

Ruling and the Religious Institutions. Originally the nomadic chieftain's council of elders, by the reign of Süleyman, although the Sultan nominally presided, for the most part the Grand Vezir, as prime minister, was the presiding officer. The Divan met at dawn on Saturday, Sunday, Monday, and Tuesday in the Chamber of the Cupola in the Middle Courtyard of the New Palace (Topkapi Saray); the sessions lasted until midafternoon. Sometimes as many as five thousand petitioners and their retainers filled the Middle Court; they were fed a midday meal by the palace kitchens: *pilâv,* a bit of meat or fish, a vegetable, a piece of fruit, bread, and water.

Neither a cabinet nor a legislative body, but in fact a council with something of both, the Divan was the highest tribunal to right the wrongs of the people, to dispense justice in the empire, and to advise the Sultan. In Süleyman's reign, the Slaves of the Gate in the Ruling Institution in the Divan, the highest ranking members of the hierarchy, were: the Grand Vezir, six lesser vezirs, including the Kapudan Pasha, the "Lord High Admiral of the Fleet"; and, as need be, the Defterdar, the "Treasurer"; the Nishanji Pasha, a kind of Secretary of State, the "Keeper of the Privy Seal." However, the duties of each of these officials in the Divan varied according to the individual Slave of the Gate's character, influence, and ability. The Defterdar Iskender Chelebi was also quartermaster general of the army; two of the lesser vezirs were also *beylerbeyler* of Rumelia and Anatolia, the Domains of War and of Peace.

Beside these members of the Sultan's Household of Slaves in the Divan, there were the two *Kazaskers,* the "Judges of the Armies of the Domains of War and of Peace" and, in Süleyman's reign, the Grand Mufti of the Ulema representing the Religious Institution.

Domain of Peace: The province of Anatolia, which means the "Eastern Province" in Asia Minor of the Byzantine Empire, and is *Anadolu* in Turkish; in the Ottoman Empire specifically meant western Asia Minor from Sinope and Samsun on the Black Sea through Amasya and Ankara southwest to the island of Rhodes in the Mediterranean.

Domain of War: *"Rumelia,"* "Turkey in Europe"; the Balkans and Hungary.

Dome: A hollow hemispherical structure of masonry, a vaulted construction spanning and roofing a circular, polygonal, or square space, wherein all sides curve upward and inward toward a single high point. A true dome is stable at the completion of any horizontal ring, or course, of brick or stone, usually set in mortar. Therefore, the dome need not be closed — see the oculus, the "eye," of the Pantheon in Rome. See Vault.

Drum (of a dome): The ring, usually a section of a tube, but the drum can be polygonal, from which a dome rises.

Drum (of a pillar): One of the cylindrical blocks of solid stone, each shaped like a drum, that make up the shaft of a column.

Efendi: A courtesy title, "Master, Mister, Monsieur."

Elephant's-eye: Our bull's-eye window, usually a single small pane, but pointed or oval, not round.

Elephant's foot: One of the four freestanding, massive piers upholding the dome in an Ottoman Imperial Friday Mosque.

Elevation: A drawing, a blueprint, a geometrical projection on a plane perpendicular to the horizon, usually of the façade, but of any side of a building, as though seen at eye level.

Emir: In Turkish *emîr;* emirate: "chief, commander"; in Ottoman days, the independent prince of a *Gazi* Turkish principality.

Extrados: The upper or convex surface of an arch or a vault.

Falsework: Any of the temporary structures used in the erection of a building: scaffolding, platform, centering, cradle, formwork, shoring.

Fikh: The body of Muslim sacred jurisprudence. The Arabic word, in Turkish spelled *fikih,* literally means the "path" to the watering place in the desert.

Fluting, fluted: The channeling or grooving, usually concave, cut vertically in the round of a pillar; the two flutes or channels are separated by a ridge. In melon domes, the fluted segments are convex, broad at the base, narrowing as they rise to a point at the crown, and separated by narrow grooves.

Flying buttress: A masonry strut, usually a segment of an arch spanning the distance from a wall to a freestanding vertical buttress-pier; the flying buttress is not engaged in the wall that it supports against the lateral thrust, but joins it in the perpendicular (a T with a bent upright); a kind of permanent shoring.

Formwork: Centering, cradle, part of the scaffolding and falsework upon which arches and domes are erected.

Gazi: "One who fights for Islam," the Conquering Hero; a distinction earned by a victorious general (Atatürk is The *Gazi*). The *Gazi* Turks were nomadic clans, like the Dulkadirli and the Osmanli, who invaded Asia Minor when it was the heartland of the Christian Byzantine Empire.

Glacis: The ground sloping from the top of the rampart of a fortress to the level of the countryside: earthworks.

The "Golden Section" of Humanism: The proportions of 1 : 1.618 in which a line is divided so that the smaller part is to the larger as the larger is to the whole, roughly 5 : 8; a unit of measurement taken to be magical in Pythagorian aesthetics; a modulor.

Grand Mufti: The chief official of the Religious Institution; the chief wise man *(müfti)* in sacred jurisprudence of the Ulema, in effect comparable to the Chief Justice of the U.S. Supreme Court and the Pope in the College of Cardinals combined. Not an active judge in the Ottoman courts of law, and not a priest (in the Christian sense of the word), he was appointed by the Sultan for life as his adviser and consultant on affairs spiritual and legal. He could not be deposed; he could restrain and overrule the

Emperor, as the Grand Mufti Jemali Ali did Selim the Grim on interpretation of moot points of Sacred Law, such as Yavuz Selim's proposed
final solution (massacre) of the Christian problem. As in English usage
mufti means civilian dress, so the Grand Mufti was never a Slave of the
Gate and therefore not a soldier – a man of the pen, not a man of the
sword. The Grand Mufti later came to be entitled the Sheikh-ül-Islam.

Grand Vezir: The "Chief Bearer of the Burden" of government, a Slave of
the Gate, the Prime Minister in the Divan, the Sultan's deputy, his
administrative and executive assistant, his lieutenant; the head of the
Ruling Institution.

Gynaeceum: The equivalent of the harem in the Byzantine Empire, the
women's quarters. In Haghia Sophia, the galleries are reserved for women
and called the gynaeceum.

Haghia Sophia: The Church of the "Divine Wisdom," Saint or Sancta
Sophia.

Haj, Haji: The "pilgrimage" to Mecca; "pilgrim." To make the Pilgrimage
once in a lifetime is one of the five Islamic duties. The others are: (1) to
bear witness that there is but one God; (2) to pray five times a day: at
sunrise, just after midday, in mid-afternoon, at sunset, and two hours
later. The midday Friday prayer service is obligatory in the mosque;
otherwise a man can pray wherever he happens to be at the hour (women
pray at home); (3) charity – the giving of alms; (4) to fast throughout the
daylight hours of the month of Ramazan.

Hamam: Public bathhouse, a "Turkish bath"; a building of three rooms,
cold, warm, and hot.

Han: A caravansary, but usually one in a city: business premises for wholesalers, retailers, factories, and workshops; in Istanbul, a masonry building
of two stories and of one or several courtyards.

Harem: The Turkish spelling of the "forbidden, defended" women's quarters in any Islamic house. After Haseki Hürrem moved the Imperial
Harem into the inner courtyard of the New Palace (Topkapi Saray), the
imperial residence and administration center, the *saray,* came to be confused with the Italian misspelling, *seraglio;* in the foreign imagination, the
women took over.

Haseki: "Chosen," the title of the Sultan's "Favorite" Lady of the Harem,
one of several who had borne a Son of Osman. The "Chosen" Janissary
Haseki was honored by appointment to the Sultan's Own Color Guard,
Honor Guard, and Imperial Body and Life Guards.

Iconostasis: The screen of carved stone or wood, often covered with gold
leaf and hung with icons, separating the nave from the sanctuary in the
apse.

Imam: "Leader in prayer" – not priest or pastor; Islam is not sacerdotal.
"The Twelve Imams," who were not hereditary caliphs, were "of the
blood of the Prophet," *sharif* and *saiyid,* which words mean descendants

of the martyred Fourth Caliph Ali through his and Fatma's sons Hasan and Hüsseyin; and thus they alone were the Supreme Leaders of Islam — to the Shiite "sectarians," but *not* to the "traditional" Sunnite Orthodox Muslims, the Ottomans.

Imperial Friday Mosque: Memorials to the sultans, the equivalent of Christian cathedrals in size and importance, large enough to hold the entire congregation — the parish, the imperial entourage — for the obligatory Friday midday prayer service in which the chief imam delivers a sermon.

Impost, impost block: The level at and from which an arch, a pendentive, a vault, or a dome rises from a wall, a pier, or a column. The impost is usually marked by a string course, a moulding projecting from the surface of the wall, or a cornice; or in arcades by an impost block on top of the capital of the column. The impost block, usually with splayed sides, serves to concentrate the complex and multiple thrusts of an arch or pendentive, and to redirect them down upon the capital, and thus through the pier or pillar to ground them.

Intrados: The concave or inner surface of a vault or an arch, a soffit.

Islam: "Submission" to, "Resignation" to the will of God. As Christianity and Christendom are to Christians, so Islam is to Muslims. A Muslim (or Moslem) is a man who "submits" or "resigns himself" to carry out God's will. The word Mohammedanism is a Christian's ignorant misconception of Islam.

Jamb: The vertical side of a door or a window opening.

Jami: Mosque.

Janissary: *Yeni Cheri* mispronounced in the Germanic languages; a slave soldier of the "New Troops," which standing army, the handsomest and finest body of military elite in history, was founded, according to the legend, early in the fourteenth century by Orhan Khan; his brother and vezir, Alaettin Ali Bey; their general and cousin, the Jandarli Kara Halil Pasha; and blessed by Haji Bektash. In history, the Janissaries were organized (probably) by Murad I (1359-1389) and by the then Grand Vezir Jandarli Kara Halil Pasha. *Allahüekber!* "God is Most Great!" was the Janissary battle cry.

Kapudan Pasha: The "Lord High Admiral" of the Ottoman fleet. Spelled *kaptan* in modern Turkish, it means "captain of a ship."

Kazasker: A "Judge of the Army," one of two, of the armies of the Domains of War and of Peace, each with a seat in the Divan. These men of the Religious Institution were the supreme judges of the Ottoman Empire.

Keystone, key, keying: The keystone or key is the wedge-shaped central or top voussoir in an arch. Keying is the placing of this specially cut block of stone in place.

Khan: *Han* in modern Turkish; as a royal title it means the sovereign, the hereditary tribal chieftain of the peoples in the Manchu-Mongol-Tartar-Turkish language group.

Kibla: *Kible* in Turkish, *qibla* in transliterated Arabic, literally means "south," because, in Jerusalem, the Prophet borrowed from the Jews their custom of facing the shrine when they prayed. Kibla then means the direction of the Kaaba in Mecca, the axis of Islamic prayer.

Kismet: "Destiny, lot, fate, luck." In Islam, a man is predestined, but not necessarily doomed so to obliterate the exercise of free choice and free will within the law. It came to be said that his course of life in detail was written on his forehead by God at the instant of his conception.

Külliyé: The "complex" of a pious foundation surrounding a mosque.

Mandala: The magic "circle" in Sanskrit, a graphic symbol of the universe most typically taking the form of a circle inscribed in a (magic) square, but seen variously in the many forms of the cross, the multifoliate rose, the Tudor rose, the rosette patera, the sun disc, the halo, the glory, the medallion, the wheel of Buddha, the wheel of the Zodiac, Shiva's wheel of fire, yang and yin, the two swastikas, the lotus. Jung, having found the mandala in the dreams of his friends and his patients, and in the art of all the cultures of the world, makes of it the symbol of human aspiration, our hankering and yearning for perfection. As such, in the presence of a mandala like the mosque and especially the courtyard, a man finds harmony and serenity. A mandala brings the order of peace to the spirit.

Masonry: Anything constructed of stones, either dressed or rubble, or of bricks, or of tile, and usually set in mortar. Specifically, a construction – wall, arch, vault – made of stones each one of which has been shaped or dressed to fit its exact place to the purpose of the structure.

Medresé: "College," a combined theological seminary and law school in Islam. The large *medresés,* such as those of the Süleymaniyé, made up universities of many colleges and schools.

Mesjid: A small mosque, a chapel, an oratory.

Minaret: The tower attached to a mosque from which the müezzin calls the faithful to prayer five times a day.

Minber: The elevated pulpit, a triangular structure of wood or of marble, with a staircase in the hypotenuse, topped by a dais and a canopy, usually conical. It was the Prophet's throne when he presided at his courts of justice held in the early community hall which also served as the place of prostration. The *minber,* always a handsome work of Islamic art, stands back to the kibla wall and to the right (stage left) of the prayer niche.

Mihrab: The "sanctuary," the prayer niche centering the kibla wall, in which the imam stands, sits, and kneels to lead the congregation in prayer.

Mimar Bashi: "Chief Builder" retranslated for Sinan as "Royal Chief Architect," a Slave of the Gate, the director of the Sultan's office of public works.

Modulor: Le Corbusier's term, a system of proportions based on the measurements of an ideal (French) male human being. He later raised the height to equal the measurement of an ideal London constable.

Monolith: A pillar cut from a single stone usually round in section and smooth of surface; or any other structural element, usually large and essential, cut from a single stone.

Mortar: Consists primarily of lime, water, and sand. Used while it is soft and plastic to join the stones or bricks of masonry, mortar sets, hardens, and finally crystallizes.

Mosaic: A medium in which small cubes of stone, porcelain, or glass are set in a mortar or a mastic cement applied to the surface of a wall, a dome, a vault, a soffit, a spandrel, a pendentive, or a floor, a plaque or a panel, to produce either a work of art or of decoration.

Mosque: A "place of prostration," the Islamic equivalent of temple or church.

Müezzin: A cantor, he who calls the faithful to prayer.

Muslim, Moslem: The man or woman who "submits," who "resigns him- or herself" to God's will. See Islam.

Mu'tik: A purely Arabic word only to be exactly translated as "emancipator, manumitter." Mutik (without the Arabic ain) in Osmanlija meant "backer, supporter, patron."

Narthex: The antechamber of a Byzantine church, a covered and enclosed porch.

Nave: The central lengthwise space of a church. The main axis, the long "upright" of a cruciform plan crossed by the transept.

Nedim: "Boon Companion," courtier, even court jester, one of several gentlemen who may have been slaves, and after Selim the Sot, often were also Slaves of the Gate, but who were not officials in the Ruling Institution: poets, musicians, wrestlers, wits, gossips, they occupied the Sultan's leisure hours.

Nishanji: "Lord Privy Seal," the keeper of the Sultan's seal affixed to all documents issued from the Divan (the Grand Vezir had a duplicate); a sort of Secretary of State. The four pillars supporting the canopy of Mehmet the Conqueror's reorganized government were the Grand Vezir, the Nishanji Pasha, the Defterdar, and the Kazasker.

Oda: "Room" in the Janissary barracks, later regiment, still later division.

Opus sectile: "Cut work" of stone, a geometric pattern of varicolored marbles, basalts, porphyries, and granites inlaid upon white marble. Sinan used opus sectile on the belly stone — the raised, usually round platform in the center of the hot room of the hamam — and in the floors of the embrasures of the Süleymaniyé, and in rectangular plaques set in a row at the base of the kibla wall in the Selimiyé of Edirné, and the mosque of Sokollu Mehmet Pasha in Istanbul.

Ottoman: The Germanic mispronunciation of the eponymous ancestor's name spelled Othman in Arabic, and Osman in Turkish.

Padishah: Like Sultan, it means "Sovereign" or "Emperor," but is used alone in direct address without the Sultan's name: "The Emperor"; or in the United Kingdom, "The Queen."

Pasha: "Lord," the only official title of the Ottoman Empire, awarded only by the Sultan for excellence and merit to individual Slaves of the Gate; it is a military title in a life-time peerage, never inherited (until the end of the empire, when *pashalik* came to apply to a ruling aristocracy). The word today means "general" in the Turkish army.

Pendentive: An equilateral spherical triangle, a segment of a hollow sphere: four pendentives are used to effect the transition from the corners of a square building, or from the four freestanding piers rising from the corners of a square floor plan, to the ring from which the dome arises. The four "apices" of these spherical triangles point down into the corners, or onto the four piers. The arcs of their equilateral sides rise as springers to join in four side arches. The upended "bases" of the triangles, each an arc, the quarter of a circle, join overhead to form the ring of the dome. The pendentive is a concave spandrel.

Penjik: "Fifth part" as the tithe is a tenth part; specifically, the *penjik* was set aside from the total loot and booty collected as spoils of the holy war by the Prophet to pay the costs of government in the state religion. A *penjik* youth was a prisoner of war, a Christian enslaved, chosen for his high quality and entered in the palace school as a page, or in the Janissary cadet schools in the Sultan's Household of Slaves.

Pent-house, or pent, or lean-to roof: a roof usually of a single slope, but possibly of three sides, whose upper edge abuts a wall, as in a porch.

Peribolos, enceinte, counterscarp, etcetera: Technical words describing the land walls of Constantinople-Istanbul, handsome, and now useless, to be seen and experienced.

Pier: The principal supporting member, usually built of solid masonry, usually square or compound in section, usually freestanding, from which spring the arches and the pendentives essential to Byzantine and Ottoman domes; an elephant's-foot.

Plan, as in floor plan: The horizontal cross section of a building viewed from above.

Pious Foundation: The *külliyé;* in the Religious Institution, an endowed urban or country complex of buildings surrounding a mosque: a minaret (or more, from two to six in Imperial Friday Mosques); a *medresé* (college — as many as eight in the memorial foundation of Mehmet the Conqueror); a grammar school, a school for *müezzins* (cantors); an *imaret* (charity soup kitchen and refectory); a hospital; an insane asylum; a hostel for distinguished guests; a bathhouse; a fountain for ablutions; a fountain house to dispense free drinking water; a mausoleum of the founder; a library; a *tekké* ("monastery" for dervishes); shops; perhaps a caravansary. Some pious foundations are large, some small. The moneys and properties donated for upkeep could not be taxed by the Sultan or by any man in the Ruling Institution.

Porphyry: A very hard, dense rock, purple from the quarries of Egypt, dark green from Mount Taegetus in the Peloponnesus, both rare and precious, used for monoliths and decorations.

Proconnesus marble: A white marble streaked and veined with gray and sometimes suffused with pink, still quarried on the island once of that name, now called Marmara, in the Sea of Marmara, the Propontis.

Rayah: In Turkish *râya,* once a head of cattle in a herd, then any subject of the Sultan who was not a Muslim.

Religious Institution: In Albert H. Lybyer's division of the Ottoman government into the Ruling and the Religious Institutions, that department of the Sultan's administration outside the Household of Slaves and concerned with all matters of justice and the law, religion, health, education, and welfare.

In theory, the Ruling and the Religious Institutions were separate; their duties in principle did not overlap. In practice, they did. The Ottoman system grew like a mushroom out of roots in the family, the clan, and the nomadic tribal customs. It was never wholly able to adapt to the conditions of a stable and a settled empire. Until Süleyman's death in 1566, the Sultan had his hand in everything because none of his absolute and total power could be delegated. In his reign and rule, the Grand Vezir bore the brunt of the actual work, and the Grand Mufti, the guardian of the Sacred Law, counseled and advised the Sultan on all matters of justice — when called upon to do so. He also administered an enormous bureaucracy, that of all the courts of law within the empire.

However, from the beginning, the Ruling and the Religious Institutions were not clear-cut. The family of Jandarli Kara Halil Pasha, Orhan Khan's general of the armies, the organizer of the Janissary New Troops of slave soldiers, and the first of the hereditary Grand Vezirs, belonged also by inheritance to the Ulema, the Council of Wise Men learned in sacred jurisprudence, the supreme tribunal of the Religious Institution. The Jandarlis, which family name in Persian means "Of the Bodyguard," moreover, were the cadet branch of the Isfendiyaroghlullari Emirs of Kastamonu and Sinope; as such, they were descendants of a Companion of the Prophet, not Turks of the Osmanli clan.

In Süleyman's reign, the Grand Vezir, a Slave of the Gate, a *Damat,* and the head of the Ruling Institution, dispensed justice in the Divan aided by the two Judges of the Armies, and thus members of the Religious Institution ranking just below the Grand Mufti. They accompanied the Sultan on campaigns of Holy War.

Later, the Grand Mufti Ebüsuud, who codified the canon laws, the imperial edicts resulting from the Sultan's exercise of the *wilaya,* the sovereign law and royal will, took his seat in the Divan of the Ruling Institution. He was never a Slave of the Gate.

The very rich educational institutions with the chancellors, the professors, the teachers, the students, and the staffs were administered by the Religious Institution, as were the imams, the muezzins, the employees and the caretakers of all the mosques. So were the religious confraternities and the many orders of dervishes. The Vakiflar (or as it was then, the *Evkaf*), the holding corporation of all the tax-free pious foundations in the Religious Institution, soon owned more than half the real estate of the empire.

Revetments: Panels, usually of precious marbles, covering a masonry wall.

Rib: A salient engaged arch, as those in the dome of Haghia Sophia. The ribs, intersecting at the crown, divide the dome into compartments.

Rolling scaffolding: A tower of timbers and planks upholding a platform, and built upon a chassis set on wheels or rollers so that it can be moved across a floor for the use of plasterers, marble cutters, painters, or men making repairs.

Rubble, rubble masonry: Generally taken to mean solid masonry built of rough or irregular blocks of stone sometimes veneered with ashlar or bricks, or covered with revetments.

Ruling Institution: The active arm of the government, the Sultan's Household of Slaves, the *Kapi Kullari*, "Slaves of the Gate," all of whom were military men, ninety percent of them converted Christian *penjik, devshirmé*, purchased or presented youths trained for the purpose and encouraged, in the systematic competition of merits and rewards, to rise through the ranks of the hierarchy. Ten percent were volunteers who reduced themselves to the conditions of this exalted servitude; these were the freeborn Muslims of the many tribes and clans; or the descendants of renegades such as the Byzantine nobles, or the Dukaginzadés, sons of "Duke John" or "Jean," a Frankish crusader who had stopped off to carve out a dukedom for himself in Albania; or the Hersekzadés, descendants of the Christian Duke of Herzegovina, who, overrun, opted to join the winning side.

The vezirs of the Divan were the ministers of the Ruling Institution; each had a staff and an entourage. The Defterdar with his huge staff of tax collectors and accountants; the Nishanji Pasha and his bureaucracy; the postal service; all the governors-general, the governors, and the officers and employees of the provincial governments; the Janissaries on active duty, including the guards of the various palaces, the detachment that policed the city, and the men of the frontier guards; as well as all other soldiers in the various branches of the army were members of the Ruling Institution.

Sinan, as chief of the office of imperial public works, and as custodian of all the immense imperial properties and estates, directed a relatively small department in the Ruling Institution.

The palace kitchen ordinarily fed five thousand men and the very few

Ladies of the Harem with their domestic female slaves; on the days of the Divan, the palace fed as many as ten thousand. At its peak, the Sultan's Household of Slaves numbered eighty thousand.

The old joke has it that when the Turk got down from his horse, he sat down at a desk.

Rum: "Rome" of the Eastern Roman Empire, later the Byzantine Empire; or, as in the Seljuk Sultanate of Rum, Asia Minor. A *Rumî* is a citizen of Rum; Rumî is the possessive adjective.

Rumelia: "Europe" to the Ottomans; "Turkey in Europe"; the Balkans and Hungary; the Domain of War.

Sahn: The oblong stage or platform, sometimes excavated or built up on terraces, usually surrounded by a wall, in which the mosque, its court-yard, and its garden with the mausoleum stand, surrounded by the dependencies of the pious foundation complex.

Scaffolding: A temporary structure, part of the falsework, usually built of timbers and planks, used for the construction of walls and the rest of the superstructure of a building.

Sebil: A fountain house attached to pious foundations for the distribution of free drinking water to passers-by.

Section, cross section: A plan drawn or projected on a plane, horizontal, vertical, or otherwise, to give the silhouette or the outline of a building, a pier, a moulding, and so on. The cross section of a smooth pillar is round.

Seghmen: Or *sekban* — a slave-soldier of a division or *oda* incorporated in the Janissary corps; in the early days, a "kennelman," in charge of the hunting dogs or the hounds of war.

Selâmlik: The Turkish spelling of the men's quarters of an Islamic house. *Selâm* means "greetings; salutations; salute." The suffix *-lik* adds the sense of place.

Seljuk: A Turk of the first tribe to take power in Islam. Brought into the Abbasid Caliphate as slave-soldiers, the captain of the Seljuk Turkish palace guards reduced the caliph to a figurehead, and, by 1090, ruled the Great Seljuk Sultanate from Baghdad. By then Egypt had been taken over by the Mameluke, the "White Slave," sultans, who were Turks, Circassians, and renegade Europeans. With the Battle of Manzikert, in 1071, the lesser Seljuks entered Asia Minor, eventually to rule from Iconium, which they pronounced Konya, in the Seljuk Sultanate of Rum. By the end of the thirteenth and the beginning of the fourteenth centuries, the Mongols had broken the Seljuk power. The late-coming minor clan of *Gazi* Turks, to be called the Osmanli, the Ottomans, rose and took the power of Islam.

Serasker: "Commander in chief" of the armies or the campaign, named by the Sultan; one of the Slaves of the Gate.

Shadirvan: The fountain for ritual ablutions usually centering the courtyard of a mosque.

Shar, Shari'a: The body of the Sacred Law; but specifically, that part firmly based upon the text of the Koran and the accepted Traditions, which are the recorded descriptions of the Prophet's acts, and his reported words and deeds in decisions and judgments as remembered (and "authenticated") by his companions and later commentators.

Shehzadé: In Persian, "Son of the Shah"; in Ottoman usage, "Royal Prince." I make it mean "Prince Imperial, Crown Prince, Heir Presumptive"; the son of the Sultan installed in Manisa.

Sheikh: In Turkish spelled phonetically *s*-cedilla *e y h* ("Shayh," the final *h* aspirated); in modern Arabic transliteration *shaikh*, the word is a title. It means "old man, elder, head of a family or a tribe, head of a religious order." The Sheikh-ül-Islam, literally, the "Ancient of Islam," was, in effect, Chief Justice and Pope, but not a temporal power.

Shi'a, Shiite, "Sectarian": the first off-shoot of the monolithic religion and state, followers of Ali, the martyred Fourth Caliph, the husband of the Prophet's daughter Fatma, or Fatima; and the son of the Prophet's father's brother — Mohammed's first cousin in the male descent — which makes Ali and his descendants the Twelve Imams "of the blood of the Prophet," who was sanctified if not quasi-deified (against his own contentions of mortal humanity), all according to the genetics and the biology of Islam. This split between the Shiite "Sectarians" and the Sunnite "Traditionalists," like that between the Greek Orthodox and the Roman Catholic Christians, was less a matter of theological dispute and more a result of political and social differences in current events. Therefore, passionate convictions override common cause and common sense to keep the sects apart.

Sipahi: A cavalryman of the Sultan's cavalry of slave soldiers.

Soffit: The finished underside of an architectural element such as an entablature, a cornice, a lintel, a window frame, and an arch (as such it is the intrados).

Sons of Osman, the Osmanli, the Ottoman Sultan Khans: The first twelve of whom were:

Ertughrul, the progenitor, d. *c.* 1281, at about the age of 90

Osman I Khan, the eponymous, b. 1258?; acceeded in 1281 or 1300; abdicated, 1320; died 1324

Orhan Khan, b. 1288? ac. 1324; d. 1360

Murad I Khan, b. ? ac. 1360; d. 1389

Bayazid I Sultan Khan, called Yildirim, "The Thunderbolt," b. 1360; ac. 1389; defeated by Tamerlane at the Battle of Ankara on July 28, 1402; d. October 3, 1403

Interregnum, 1402-1413

Mehmet I Sultan Khan, b. 1389; ac. July 5, 1413; d. May 26, 1421

Murad II Sultan Khan, b. 1404; ac. May 26, 1421; abdicated December 1, 1444; recalled September, 1446; d. February 8, 1451

Mehmet II the Conqueror, b. March 30, 1432; ac. December 1, 1444; deposed September, 1446; ac. February 3, 1451; conquered Constantinople May 29, 1453; d. May 3, 1481

Bayazid II the Pious, b. January, 1448; ac. May 3, 1481; deposed April 24, 1512; d. May 26, 1512

Selim I the Grim, b. 1470; ac. April 24, 1512; d. September 22, 1520

Süleyman I the Magnificent, b. November 6, 1494; ac. September 22, 1520; d. September 7, 1566

Selim II the Sot, b. May 28, 1524; ac. September 7, 1566; d. December 15, 1574

Murad III, b. July 4, 1546; ac. December 12, 1574; d. January 16, 1595

Span: The distance between the supports of an arch, a vault; or the diameter of a dome.

Spandrel: In an arcade, the flat wall space above the pillar and between the springers of the arches, rising to the horizontal line between the tops of the keystones, is called the spandrel. It takes the shape of an upended equilateral triangle with the two sides concave. In a single arch, the spandrel is the space on the far side of each springer, a triangle this time with its base (the arc of the extrados) concave, one side horizontal, in line with the top of the keystone, the other side vertical rising from the impost or springing line. These spandrels are the haunches of the arch.

Spring, springing, springing line: The point on the level from which the springers of the arches or a vault rise and curve to join at the keystone or the crown. The spring usually begins at the center of the impost block, or the capital, on a column or a pier. In a vaulted corridor, the springing line is the top of the side wall.

Springer: In an arch, the two arcs that rise to meet at the keystone.

Squinch, squinch arch: The arch thrown across the corner of a square building in the transition from the square to the octagon from which the dome arises. The squinch arch is usually filled with a conch, a shell-like semidome, but it can be filled with stalactites. The pendentive is a development from the squinch arch.

String course: A continuous horizontal band, either plain or carved in a moulding, set into the face of a wall. In Sinan's buildings, he used a string course to stress the springing line of the arches and pendentives.

Sublime Porte: A high-flown translation of the *Bab-i-Âli*, or "High Gate" of the Palace. As we imprecisely say White House and Washington; the Kremlin and Moscow, the Court of St. James and London, the Sublime Porte came to mean the center of power and Constantinople-Istanbul. In effect, Sublime Porte was the Ministry of Foreign Affairs — Whitehall, Foggy Bottom, the Quai d'Orsay.

Sultan: "Emperor" when used as a title before the name of a Son of Osman on the throne; but Sultan means "Imperial" otherwise; and when used after a man's or woman's name, translates as "Prince" or "Imperial Princess," the son, grandson, great-grandson, daughter, granddaughter, great-granddaughter of a reigning Sultan. Validé Sultan means "Imperial Mother."

Sunni, Sunnite: The "Traditional," orthodox, and major sect in Islam.

Tekké: Inexactly translated as "convent" or "monastery," a *tekké* is a complex housing the dervishes and the activities of a religious confraternity.

Tessera, tesserae, tessellatus, tessellata: The units in mosaic, the one in the singular and the plural for floors, the other, ditto, on walls, in domes, on icons. Some are cubes of marble or colored stones; some are porcelain; a few are semiprecious gems or mother-of-pearl; the Byzantine gold tessellatus was indeed beaten gold leaf fixed to a cube of dark red glass and covered with a thin square of clear glass, so to keep the gold from dissolving in the acid exhalations of prayer and chant, flickering lamps, candle flames, and body heat rising in the humidity into the dome.

Thrust: Usually lateral, a force out of the vertical that, following the curves of an arch or a dome, tends to spread them, flatten them, and collapse them. Tiebeams and tiebars spanning the arch at the springing line, contain the lateral thrusts until the mortar hardens, or until the next arch in line in an arcade sets the two thrusts in opposition, the one to counteract the other. The vertical thrust of the dead weight, once the superstructure has been completed, tends to overpower the lateral thrusts. However, these thrusts, however checked, balanced, buttressed, or overcome, are dynamic, not inert. An earthquake sets them in action.

Tiebeam, tiebar: The horizontal timber, or the similar iron bar that, fixed into the impost, the capital, or the corbel, spans the arch or the vault.

Transept: In a cruciform plan, the lateral arms at right angles to the nave.

Trompe dome: Shaped like a trumpet, a cone.

Tugh: The horsetail, the standard, the sign and symbol of the Ottoman Sultan Khan; in time, he came to have seven horsetails.

Tughra: The imperial device of the Ottoman Sultan, a stylized print of his hand outlined in calligraphy, the thumb a series of whorls, the little finger outstretched, the three middle fingers vertical strokes of the pen (or brush), the name of the Sultan written in the lines of the palm. Murad I (1359-1389) signed the first Ottoman treaty with a Christian (vassal) state, Ragusa, now Dubrovnik. Illiterate, he inked his hand to make his mark.

Türbé: Mausoleum, tomb.

Ulema: In the Religious Institution, the council of wise men, *müftis,* learned in sacred jurisprudence, in very rough comparison, a Supreme Court combined with the College of Cardinals, presided over by the Grand Mufti. He took his seat in the Divan; but no member of the Ruling Institution ex officio sat in the Ulema; nor did the Sultan.

Urf: The customary law, recorded in a code or not; the customs of the country conquered, overrun, and absorbed by the expanding state of Islam. The *urf* of the Hebrews; of the Syrian and Egyptian Byzantine Christians; and of the Magian, the Zoroastrian, or Manichaen Persians thus entered the caliphates and sultanates, and in time were incorporated in the body of the Sacred Law of the Ottomans. The Hebraic prohibition against graven images, to cite one instance, thus was absorbed by Islam. Sometimes the laws of conquered provinces were neither changed nor absorbed; for instance, the laws of taxation and land tenure varied from place to place within the Ottoman Empire.

Vakiflar: The ministry for religious properties in the present government of the Republic of Turkey. Formerly called the *Evkaf,* the plural of the Arabic word *vakf,* which means "pious foundation," it was the Ottoman department of the Religious Institution in charge of these religious estates held in mortmain.

Validé Sultan: "Imperial Mother," the widow of a sultan, which is to say, one of his surviving Haseki Ladies of the Harem, the mother of his son the Sultan; the sole title for the only woman in her own right an official member of the Sultan's Household in the Ottoman Empire. The Validé Sultan directed the Imperial Harem. At one time, her estates included Cyprus and Mount Pelion with its chestnut forests.

Vault: A curving masonry ceiling, if hemispherical called a dome, is semi-cylindrical, a barrel vault, if oblong with rounded bottom, ends, and sides, a cradle vault; all vaults are based on the principle of the arch in which the stones or bricks are laid in courses mutually to sustain themselves. The vault usually rises from solid parallel walls. The dome, being circular in section, can rise from round walls (as in the Pantheon in Rome); or from a crownlike arcade; or from a drum; or from the ring of four or more joined pendentives; or from the octagon formed by four squinch arches and the four walls of a square building; or, like a beehive, from the ground; or, as with the sail vault, which looks like a square sail tied at each corner and bellying out, taut, full of a following wind, from four points.

Verd antique: "Ancient green"; in Byzantine and Ottoman buildings, a conglomerate marble from a single quarry, still in operation in northern Greece, mottled, varying from dark green to pale gray green, prized for monoliths, not to be confused with other green marbles or serpentines.

Vice: A spiral or circular staircase, as in the threading of a screw, usually built into buttresses or piers for the convenience of the laborers building the superstructure.

Voussoir: (through Middle English and French from Latin, *volvere* "turn"), the individual wedge-shaped block of stone, in tranverse section a truncated cone, one of many that rise from the springing line in an arch to be locked together on top by the keystone. Sinan frequently rippled the edges, and puzzled them together, as in dovetailing. He used alternating voussoirs of, say, red and white marble to call attention to the arch as a structural element of his engineering, and to stress the dynamic tensions in his architecture.

Wilaya: "Sovereign law," the "royal will," a canon law issued as an imperial edict, and gradually absorbed in the body of sacred jurisprudence. The

Law of Fratricide is the most notable example. Süleyman, called *Kanunî*, "the Lawgiver," had his Grand Mufti Ebüsuud codify not the *Shar* or the *urf*, but these acts of *wilaya*, the canon laws of his ancestors and his own edicts.

Zemberekji: "Longbowmen, crossbowmen; fire-hurlers; handlers of high explosives"; the pioneers, miners, sappers, makers of war machinery, bridge builders — the *oda* of the Janissary engineers.

Ziggurat: The spiral Tower of Babel, the origin of the minaret; upside-down, Frank Lloyd Wright's Guggenheim Museum in New York.

BIBLIOGRAPHY

The archives of the Ottoman Empire are intact in Istanbul. The documents date from the beginning, *circa* 1300, to the end in 1922. They have yet to be catalogued.

History is always modern history. The historian, who is a man, is, as Benedetto Croce remarked, caged in his own lifetime. There is no modern history of the Ottomans. All those of the past were written either by foreigners, or by enemies, men who usually were both. The historian, whether he is a scientist or a philosopher, if he is any good, is also an artist, a writer; and the artist is the work of art.

An adequate bibliography for *Sinan* would have to include a bibliography for the life, and the biography of the writer, from *Alice* to *Zuleika*. Therefore, the following list of books is inadequate. There is no point in setting down the titles and the authors of all the books that I have read to write about Sinan; nor even for those that I have quoted or echoed consciously or otherwise. Few of the books that I do list are sufficient, and one or two are downright bad as books. All the encyclopedias are useful; but Alderson, Eyice, Hammer, Konyali, Levy, and Lybyer are essential.

Alderson, Anthony D. *The Structure of the Ottoman Dynasty.* Oxford: Clarendon Press, 1956.

Arberry, Arthur J. *The Koran Interpreted.* London: Oxford University Press, 1964.

Arseven, Celal Esad. *Les Arts Décoratifs Turcs.* Istanbul: Milli Egitim Basimevi, n. d.

——. *L'Art Turc.* Istanbul: Devlet Basimevi, 1939.

Baynes, Norman H., and Moss, H. St. L. B. *Byzantium; An Introduction to East Roman Civilization.* Oxford: Clarendon Press, 1962.

Birge, John Kingsley. *The Bektashi Order of Dervishes.* Hartford, Connecticut: Hartford Seminary Press, 1937.

Bozkurt, Orhon. *Koca Sinan'in Köprüleri.* Istanbul: Pulhan Matbassi, 1952.

Brockelmann, Carl. *History of the Islamic Peoples.* London: Routledge and Kegan Paul, 1949.

Creasy, Edward S. *History of the Ottoman Turks.* Beirut: Khayats, 1961.

Djevad Bey, A. *État Militaire Ottoman depuis la fondation de l'empire jusqu'a nos jours.* Paris: Leroux, 1882.

Egli, Ernst. *Sinan der Baumeister Osmanischer Glanzzeit.* Zürich: Verlag für Architektur, 1954.

Eliot, Sir Charles. *Turkey in Europe.* London: Frank Case, 1965.

Esin Emel. *Turkish Miniature Painting.* Rutland, Vermont, and Tokyo: Charles E. Tuttle, 1960.

Ettinghausen, Richard, Eyuboğlu, S., and İpş iroğlu, M. S. *Turkey: Ancient Miniatures.* United Nations Education, Scientific and Cultural Organization. Greenwich, Connecticut: New York Graphic Society, 1961.

——. *Turkish Miniatures from the Thirteenth to the Eighteenth Century.* A Mentor-UNESCO Art Book. New York: The New American Library, Inc., by arrangement with UNESCO, 1965.

——, Akurgal, Ekrem, and Mango, Cyril A. *Treasures of Turkey.* Geneva: Skira, 1966.

——. "The Islamic Period." In *Catalogue of the Art Treasures of Turkey.* Washington, D.C.: The Smithsonian Institution, 1966.

Evliya Efendi. *Narrative of Travels in Europe, Asia, and Africa, in the Seventeenth Century.* London: Oriental Translation Fund, 1834, 1846.

Eyice, Semavi. *Istanbul, petit guide à travers les mmonuments byzantins et turcs.* Istanbul: Istanbul Matbaasi, 1955.

Fitchen, John. *The Construction of Gothic Cathedrals: A Study of Medieval Vault Erection.* Oxford: Clarendon Press, 1961.

Forster, C. T., and Blackburne Daniell, F. H. *The Life and Letters of Ogier Ghislin de Busbecq.* London: Kegan Paul, 1881.

Freeman-Grenville, G. S. P. *The Muslim and Christian Calendars.* London: Oxford University Press, 1963.

Gabriel, Albert. *Les Mosquées de Constantinople.* Paris: Geunther, 1926.

Gibb, Hamilton A. R., and Bowen, Harold. *Islamic Society and the West.* Volume One, Part I and Part II. London: Oxford University Press, 1963, 1965.

Grunebaum, Gustave E. von. *Medieval Islam.* Chicago: University of Chicago Press, 1963.

Guillaume, Alfred. *Islam.* Baltimore: Penguin, 1962.

Gurlitt, Cornelius von. *Die Baukunst Konstantinopels.* Berlin: Wasmuth, 1912.

Hammer-Purgstall, Joseph von. *Histoire de l'Empire Ottoman depuis son origine jusqu'a nos jours.* Translated by J.-J. Hellert. 18 volumes. Paris: Bellizard, Barthès, DuFour & Lowell, 1835-43.

Hony, H. C., with the advice of Fahir Iz. *A Turkish-English Dictionary.* Oxford: Clarendon Press, 1957.

Kocainan, Ziya. *Mimar Sinan.* Istanbul: Kenan Basimevi, 1939.

Konyali, Ibrahim Hakki. *Mimar Koca Sinan.* Istanbul: Nihat Topçubaşi, 1948.
——. *Mimar Koca Sinan'in Eserleri.* Istanbul: Ülkü Basimevi, 1950.
Kritzeck, James, ed. *Anthology of Islamic Literature.* New York: Holt, Rinehart and Winston, 1964.
Lane, Arthur. *A Guide to the Collection of Tiles.* Victoria and Albert Museum. London: Her Majesty's Stationery Office, 1960.
Levy, Reuben. *The Social Structure of Islam.* Cambridge: Cambridge University Press, 1965.
——. *A Mirror for Princes: the Qābūs Nāma of Kai Kā'ūs Ibn Iskandar.* New York: E. P. Dutton, 1951.
Lewis, Geoffrey. *Turkey.* London: Ernest Benn, 1965.
Lybyer, Albert Howe. *The Government of the Ottoman Empire in the Time of Suleiman the Magnificent.* Cambridge, Massachusetts: Harvard University Press, 1913.
Mamboury, Ernest. *Istanbul Touristique.* Istanbul: Çituri Biraderler Basimevi, ayer, L. A. Islamic Architects and Their Works.
Mayer, L. A. *Islamic Architects and Their Works.* Geneva: Albert Kundig, 1956.
Meredith-Owens, G. M. *Turkish Miniatures.* London: The British Museum, 1963.
Meriç, Rifki Melûl, ed. *Mimar Sinan, Hayati, Eseri, the Tezkeretül Bunyan and the Tezkeretül Ebniye.* Ankara: Türk Tarih Kuruku Basimevi, 1965.
Miller, Barnette. *Beyond the Sublime Porte.* New Haven, Connecticut: Yale University Press, 1931.
——. *The Palace School of Muhammad the Conqueror.* Cambridge, Massachusetts: Harvard University Press, 1941.
Penzer, Norman Mosley. *The Harem: An Account of the Institution As It Existed in the Palace of the Turkish Sultans.* London: Harrop, 1936.
Refik, Ahmet. *Mimar Sinan.* Istanbul: Kanaat Kütüphanesi, 1931.
Siyavuşgil, Sabri Esat. *Karagöz.* Istanbul: Publication de la Direction Générale de la Presse, de la Radiodiffusion, et du Tourisme, 1961.
Smith, E. Baldwin. *The Dome; A Study in the History of Ideas.* Princeton, New Jersey: Princeton University Press, 1950.
Vogt-Göknil, Ulya. *Les Mosquées Turques.* Zürich: Éditions Origo, 1953.
——. *Living Architecture: Ottoman.* New York: Grosset and Dunlop, 1966.
Watt, W. Montgomery. *Muhammad, Prophet and Statesman.* London: Oxford University Press, 1964.
Wittek, Paul. *Devshirme and Shari'a.* University of London, *Bulletin of the School of Oriental and African Studies,* 1955, vol. 17, no. 2.

⫸ INDEX ⫷